BENJAMIN RUSH

ALSO BY ALYN BRODSKY

The Great Mayor
Grover Cleveland
Imperial Charade
Madame Lynch & Friend
The Kings Depart

BENJAMIN RUSH

Patriot and Physician

ALYN BRODSKY

Truman Talley Books

St. Martin's Press ✺ *New York*

www.stmartins.com

Library of Congress Cataloging-in-Publication Data
Brodsky, Alyn.
    Benjamin Rush : patriot and physician / Alyn Brodsky.—1st ed.
      p. cm.
    Includes bibliographical references (p. 385) and index (p. 389).
    ISBN 0-312-30911-2
    EAN 978-0312-30911-4
    1. Rush, Benjamin, 1746–1813. 2. Statesmen—United States—Biography.
3. Revolutionaries—United States—Biography. 4. United States. Declaration of Independence—Signers—Biography. United States—Politics and government—1775–1783. 6. Physicians—United States—Biography. 7. Social reformers—United States—Biography. I. Title.
E302.6.R85B76   2004
973.3'0922—dc22
[B]   2003069770

First Edition: June 2004

10 9 8 7 6 5 4 3 2 1

For Addie and Lowell—
On their fiftieth

CONTENTS

When Dr. Benjamin Rush died in 1813, Thomas Jefferson wrote to John Adams that "a better man than Rush could not have left us, more benevolent, more learned, of finer genius, or more honest," to which Adams replied that he knew "of no Character living or dead, who has done more real good in America."

BENJAMIN RUSH

Prologue

In the morning of Friday, August 29, 1774, word spread through Philadelphia that the Massachusetts delegation to the First Continental Congress had arrived in the suburban township of Frankfort. The Congress was the first intercolonial convocation intended to confront the situation that had become exacerbated over the previous decade by an obtuse British Parliament's determination to ignore the wisdom of treating fairly, let alone logically, with its North American citizens.

Calls for independence had been commingling with calls for compromise throughout the colonies. It seemed as if the Americans could never achieve a consensus on which side of the fence they belonged in what Thomas Paine defined as "the times that try men's souls. The summer soldier and the sunshine patriot," he predicted, "will, in this crisis, shrink from the service of their country; but he that stands it *now*, deserves the love and thanks of men and women."[1]

Though delegates had been arriving over the preceding days from all the other colonies except Georgia, which declined to attend, attention was focused on the Massachusetts delegation. For it was in Boston, as a result of the citizens' overt hostility to Parliament's oppressive measures, that the idea of the Congress originated. The delegation included forty-three-year-old Robert Treat Paine, jurist and revolutionary agitator who had prosecuted the British soldiers tried for murder for their part in the Boston Massacre of 5 March 1770, when popular hatred of the city's British garrison troops precipitated a public brawl in which several citizens were killed or wounded; the thirty-nine-year-old former schoolteacher turned lawyer and future president, John Adams; and John's fifty-two-year-old cousin Samuel, who had influenced every important aspect of the prerevolutionary struggle against King George III's various governments: an irremediable advocate of the natural rights of man, and first among equals of those colonials who challenged the authority of the British Crown and championed the cause of rebellion against and separation from the empire that crown symbolized.

It was Samuel Adams who had orchestrated the Boston Tea Party of the previous December, when a band of patriots disguised as Native Americans boarded three British ships under cover of night and dumped their cargos of 342 chests of tea into Boston Harbor. This was not the first overt act of defiance to various British policies that the colonists found insupportable. Ironically, the "party" (replicated in some of the other colonial ports) need never have been held, had Parliament repealed the duty on tea when, in a rare moment of transient sanity, it repealed most other provisions of the hated Townshend Acts taxing imports to the colonies. But the tea tax remained, and catalyzed a dynamic for independence that was as unstoppable as it was doubtless historically inevitable.

In March 1774, Parliament retaliated by passing a series of punitive measures against the Bay Colony that were intended to make it an example to the other colonies. These so-called Coercive Acts—known among the colonials as the Intolerable Acts—included the Boston Port Act; the Massachusetts Government Act, which enlarged the colonial governor's powers while depriving the people of most of their chartered rights; and the Quartering Act, which mandated the billeting of British troops in private residences. All were intended to force the people into total submission to British authority. Of the lot, by far the most draconian was the Port Act, which closed the port of Boston after June 1 to overseas trade (with tightly controlled exceptions for food and fuel). This was tantamount to forcing this most troublesome of Great Britain's American possessions into submission.

When word of the Port Act reached America, Boston circularized all colonies with a call for suspension of trade with England. By the end of July, all the colonies except, as already noted, Georgia had selected delegates to convene at Philadelphia, the most centrally located city on the coast, on September 5 in Carpenter's Hall.

Its purpose: to arrive at a consensus on how to deal with England.

A *consensus*, it must be noted. Not a call for *separation*. At least, not

yet. Many of the merchant class, for example, hoped that a mutually satisfying accommodation could be arrived at with London. And while
there were many forceful and compelling vocal agitators for independence, such as Virginia's Patrick Henry, who achieved immortality with
those seven haunting words—"Give me Liberty, or give me Death"—
there were other considerations militating against a precipitate break.

The total population in the thirteen colonies had grown tenfold
since the beginning of the century, to 2.5 million—of whom more than
20 percent were of African ancestry, predominantly slaves.* There
were many intracolonial differences and antagonisms, little if any
industry, and no standing army—not even the semblance of one. Of
perhaps greatest consequence, not only was Britain the major market
for American exports, its navy could easily cut off exports to or necessary imports from all world markets.

Besides those tepid to the idea of separation were those openly
opposed. Throughout the colonies were large and influential concen-
trations of American Tories, more often referred to as Loyalists. In
Philadelphia, the British Empire's second-largest city in area and
North America's most prosperous, the dominant faction was the
Quakers, who put pacifism above pragmatism, and conciliation above
confrontation. Even a large number of delegates to the forthcoming
Congress were determined reconciliationists.

Immediately upon learning of the New Englanders' arrival at
Frankfort, a small group of independence-minded Philadelphians rode
out to deliver a welcome—and a warning. Among them was the subject of this book: Benjamin Rush, a popular and highly respected
twenty-nine-year-old physician as dedicated to hating kings as to alleviating the ill and infirm.

In the seclusion of a private room of a tavern where they had
stopped to refresh themselves prior to entering the city, the New Englanders were warned by their welcoming committee that they were
"suspected of having independence in view" and thus perceived by
many of the other delegates already in the city of being "too zealous"
in resolving the conflict with Great Britain through revolutionary

---

*Most worked the tobacco and rice plantations in the Southern colonies; some slaves,
along with free blacks, were also to be found in the Middle and Northern Colonies as
farm laborers and, in the cities, mostly as servants but some in various trades.

means, should it come to that. Additionally, they would be well advised not to assume leadership of the Congress they had conceived. The "very proud" Virginians, they were reminded, comprising the largest, most populous, and richest of the colonies, believed that the right to lead was incontestably theirs. Adams would later admit that Rush's advice figured prominently in the selection of George Washington to head the Continental Army.[2]

After discussing strategy—specifically, how to bring around the reconciliationists to their belief that separation from the mother country was the colonies' only viable option—the group made ready for their entrance into the city. The Philadelphians dispersed themselves among the New Englanders' carriages. Rush rode with John Adams, of whom he recalled, "This gentleman's dress and manners were at that time plain, and his conversation cold and reserved." Adams, for his part, would recall that he initially found Rush to be "too much of a Talker to be a deep Thinker. Elegant not great."[3]

But these recollections date from before the two became the closest of friends, a friendship strengthened by the flood of correspondence between them that ended only with Rush's death three decades after they met. The Adams cousins were Rush's houseguests ("domesticated themselves in my family") until they found lodgings. Like a number of the pro-separation delegates from the other colonies, they spent many an evening after Congress had risen for the day enjoying Rush's hospitality, which included "the very best of Claret, Madeira, and Burgundy. Melons fine beyond description."[4]

Rush's recollection of Samuel Adams is worth recording, as it is perhaps our best clue to this firebrand who was over fifty when he took his seat in Congress, "but possessed all the vigor of mind of a young man of five and twenty." Being "a republican in principle and manners," he would later tell Rush that "if it were revealed to him that 999 Americans out of 1000 would perish in a war for liberty, he would vote for that war, rather than see his country enslaved. The survivors in such a war, though few (he said), would propagate a nation of freemen."[5] Harsh though the words may be, they were words with which Benjamin Rush was incapable of finding fault.

The two Adamses' places in history are secure to the degree that they are as celebrated as Washington and Jefferson—in whose public careers, by no small coincidence, Rush would figure conspicuously.

But though he appears so often, and so meaningfully, in the biographies of these titans, he remains by comparison little more than a historical footnote.

He was more. Much more.

One of the most accomplished American physicians and medical teachers of his generation, he trained more than twenty-five hundred students; it is said that every outstanding American physician down to the Civil War was either a pupil of Rush or of a Rush pupil.

Insisting on humane treatment for the mentally ill—he was one of the first to argue that mental disorders should be treated as are organic ones, instead of locking those afflicted away in asylums—he is recognized as the father of American psychiatry.

Among the work for which he achieved international recognition, Rush was the first to proclaim, during the horrendous yellow fever epidemic of 1793—one of Philadelphia's many but by far the worst—that the disease, like so many others, such as malaria, was indigenous, and not endemic like, say, the plague, and was therefore avertable through proper hygiene and maintenance of salubrious environmental conditions.

He was the first to reduce the chaotic disorder in the treatment of illness by repudiating current nosology, that branch of medicine concerned with classifying and describing known diseases.

He purged the materia medica of its many accretions and nostrums that had led to their repudiation and abandonment by even respected physicians who had long, however innocently, prescribed medications we usually associate with the "miracle cures" that comprised the pharmacopoeia of snake-oil salesman of the Old West.

He was a pioneer in America in experimental physiology, the system of biology that deals with the internal mechanisms of living things—such functions as respiration, metabolism, and reproduction—rather than merely with their structure or shape.

But Dr. Rush's accomplishments were not confined to the field of medicine.

It was he who encouraged Thomas Paine to write *Common Sense,* for which Rush not only supplied the title but many of its ideas. He worked (and wrote prodigiously) to abolish slavery and capital punishment, establish public schools, new colleges, and better education for women, attacked the evils of strong drink and the use of tobacco, founded the first free dispensary in the United States, introduced veterinary medicine, and was one of the earliest advocates of the modern penitentiary system. He was one of the first ardent public agitators for independence from England.

Rush served with distinction in the Revolutionary War.

And he was one of the signers of the Declaration of Independence.

Physician, Founding Father, reformer: let us not ponder why Benjamin Rush is not as remembered today as he should be. Rather, let us examine why he deserves to be so.

Part One

1745–1776

I

Ancestry and Early Years

Benjamin Rush carried on a voluminous correspondence with just about all his contemporary major figures, in which all parties ruminated at times willy-nilly on a variety of subjects that were, by turn, political, philosophical, social, critical, horticultural, medical, historical, and biographical. To Thomas Jefferson on the eve of his election as the new nation's third chief magistrate, Rush wrote (6 October 1800) of a particular ancestor, "To the sight of his sword I owe much of the spirit which animated me in 1774, and to the respect and admiration which I was early taught to cherish for his virtues and exploits I owe a large portion of my republican temper and principles. Similar circumstances I believe produced a great deal of the spirit and exertions of all those Americans who are descended from ancestors that emigrated from England between the years 1645 and 1700."

To his wife, Julia, he wrote, three days before the promulgation of the Declaration of Independence, that "the spirit of my great ancestor, who more than once dyed the sword which hangs up in our bedchamber [over the Rush bed] with the blood of the minions of arbitrary power, *now* moves me to declare—the spirit of my ancestor did I say?—nay, I trust the spirit of God himself moves me to declare that I will never desert the cause I am embarked in [*sic*], till I see the monster tyranny gnash [his] impotent teeth in the dust in the Province of Pennsylvania."

The ancestor in question was his great-great-grandfather John, the first Rush to relocate to America. Referred to by his famous descendant as "the Old Trooper," John commanded a horse troop in Cromwell's army during England's Civil War. The Lord Protector's high opinion of Captain Rush is evident in a story passed down in the family that one day, on seeing his mare come into camp riderless and assuming Rush had perished in battle, Cromwell exclaimed, "He has not left a better officer behind him." Benjamin knew nothing of "the Old Trooper"'s antecedents. It was "a sufficient gratification to me to know that he fought for liberty, and migrated into a remote wilderness in the evening of his life in order to enjoy the privilege of worshipping of God according to the dictates of his own conscience."[1]

After the Stuarts were restored to the throne in the person of Charles I, John and his seventeen-year-old wife, Susanna—his "pretty little maiden," by whom he fathered a daughter and six sons—settled down to farming in Oxfordshire. Despite the dangers it posed for an ex-Roundhead, he refused to conform to the Church of England. In 1683, twenty years after Quaker William Penn began his "holy experiment" for settlement in America, John, age sixty-three, sold all his holdings and took his entire family, including his children's families, off to the American colony settled by Penn, of which he was the proprietor and son of the eponym.

(The British had established three types of colonies in America: proprietary, corporate, and royal provinces. Descendants of their founders, who chose the governors and councils, ruled the proprietary colonies: Pennsylvania, Maryland, and Delaware. The corporate colonies, Rhode Island and Connecticut, were founded under charters granted by English monarchs, in which corporate rights were vested in property owners who elected the royal governor and council as well as the assembly. The royal provinces of Georgia, the two Carolinas, Virginia, New Jersey, New York, Massachusetts, and New Hampshire were ruled by governors appointed by the king on the advice of the Board of Trade, the British administrative agency that supervised colonial affairs. In Massachusetts, however, the ruling councils were nominated by the governor and approved by the Board of Trade.)

John Rush, in Benjamin's words, "had been persecuted for his religious principles and left his native country in a fit of indignation at its then intolerant government." Indignation indeed! When a relative urged that John leave at least one of his grandchildren behind, to continue the line, he responded, "No—no, I won't. I won't leave even a *hoof* of my family behind me!"[2]

Arriving in Pennsylvania, John settled his clan in Byberry Township, twelve miles up the Delaware River from Philadelphia, where a daughter and son-in-law who had come over with Penn owned five hundred arable acres. While the majority of colonizers struggled to survive in a harsh, inhospitable environment, the Rush family was at an advantage in that the local Native Americans who cleared it yearly by firing the grass and timber during hunting season had made their land arable. Thus the family prospered, albeit on a modest scale, from the outset, continuing the lives they had led back in England of country people whose lives and concerns were centered on their farms, their families, and their local community. Philadelphia's sole interest to John's family was as a market for their crops.

Though dedicated Quakers when they arrived in the New World— John would keep the faith for the remaining twenty years of his life— there was a gradual breaking away from the sect over the succeeding generations. It began with his wife, who became a Baptist in her eightieth year. This break from familial allegiance to the Religious Society of Friends, to give the Quakers their proper name, would prove to be, in a sense, fortuitous, in light of the intolerance, bordering on contempt, that Benjamin Rush cultivated for the predominantly pacifist sect during his revolutionary phase because of their opposition to warring against Great Britain. It was not that the Quakers opposed independence. Barring the rare exception, they simply opposed it by any means other than divine bestowal. Much as he accepted assiduously and unqualifiedly every aspect of the Lord, this was one thing that Rush believed could never be realized by His command. Praying for independence was one thing. Fighting for it was something else. Benjamin Rush was a firm believer in the old maxim: God helps those who help themselves.

The line of descent from John was through his eldest son, William, Benjamin's great-grandfather, who died in 1688 at the age of thirty-six, five years after the family's arrival in America. He left three children, of whom the eldest, James, Benjamin's grandfather, died in 1727 at the age of forty-eight, remembered as an industrious farmer, "uncommonly ingenious" gunsmith, and devout Presbyterian who left "a considerable property for that time," all of it debt-free. James bequeathed both the farm and the gunsmith business to John, a convert to the Episcopal Church, remembered by his son as "a man of meek and peaceable spirit," "agreeable and engaging in person and manners," and "exemplary in his life."

Benjamin's mother was Susanna Hall Harvey, whose lineage can be graced almost as far back as the Rushes. Her family migrated from England in 1685. Hall was the family name. Joseph Harvey was the name of Susanna's first husband. According to Benjamin, who doubtless got the story from Susanna, the marriage was "terminated [by Joseph's death] in three or four years by the extravagance and intemperance [for which read alcoholism] of her young husband."[3] Susanna was left with a young daughter, which she brought to her marriage to John Rush.

The marriage was by all accounts a happy one. According to Benjamin, who adored his mother, "She was a woman of a very extraordinary mind. It was full of energy. She had been well educated at a boarding School in Philadelphia, and was well acquainted with the common branches of female education. As a mother she had no superior in kindness, generosity, and attention to the morals and religious principles of her children."[4] In the family's stone house, which, greatly improved upon, stands to this day (though not owned by any Rush descendants), Susanna bore John seven children, of whom Benjamin, the fourth, as he later described it to John Adams, "made my first *unwelcome* noise in the world" on Christmas Eve, 1745. His birthday became 4 January 1746, when the Gregorian calendar was introduced into the colonies six years later.

Consistent with the penchant of the Old Trooper's descendants for moving over time from one sect of Protestantism to another until, it would seem, they had touched all bases, young Benjamin was baptized in the Church of England. But this would not remain a constant; during his lifetime Benjamin, in whose adult life and thinking religion would play a central role, himself moved through a number of the Protestant factions like a migratory animal in quest of the most gratifying habitat.

Four of Susanna and John's children survived to maturity; the others died in infancy. That Benjamin was one of the survivors is somewhat remarkable, since the year of his birth coincided with a particularly devastating epidemic of a disease known as *angina maligna*, probably modern diphtheria, which permeated the Pennsylvania countryside with, in the words of one chronicler of the times, "mortal rage. It swept all before it, baffling every attempt to stop its progress.

Villages were almost depopulated, and numerous parents were left to bewail the loss of their tender offspring."⁵ Two years later, John, having apparently lost interest in farming and tiring of the rural way of life, sold his house and moved his immediate family to Philadelphia where he became a full-time gunsmith.

From its founding at the junction of the Schuylkill and Delaware rivers where William Penn laid out a municipality of giant squares, to be subdivided into generous lots embraced with sufficient light and landscaping to prevent the development of grimy tenement dwellings, Philadelphia had by the time of Benjamin Rush's childhood evolved into the largest, most commercial city in the American colonies. Its approximately fifteen thousand inhabitants, chiefly Quaker and German, though immigrants of all religious persuasion were welcome, enjoyed physical, social, and cultural advantages equaled perhaps by Boston but certainly no other colonial city. This was owing in large measure to the man it would not be too wide of the mark to look upon, as did his fellow citizens, as the city's patron saint—Benjamin Franklin. It was this Boston-born Renaissance man of colonial times, eldest by a generation of the foremost Founding Fathers who, among other accomplishments, organized a street-cleaning system, a fire-fighting company, and a night watch; inspired a circulating library, a philosophical society, and a daily postal delivery service; invented the smokeless stove; and both regaled and edified the people with his inspired *Poor Richard's Almanac.* And books have been written devoted to his role in winning recognition at Europe's major royal courts for the American Revolution and subsequently the independent nation to which that war gave birth.

There was, though, the reverse side of the coin. Penn's vision of the City of Brotherly Love as "a green country town" was a metropolis—at least, what for the times could be so called—where hogs ran wild in the streets. A stream called the Dock Creek all but bisected the city like the rotting corpse of some gargantuan reticulated snake and emitted a horrific stench due to the habit of the stables and tanneries flanking it to use it as an open sewer. Filth accumulated in the streets until dispersed by the next rainfall. Flies, mosquitoes, bedbugs, and roaches were an especial source of discomfort, particularly in the summers. Though dreaded, they were accepted as an annual rite to be somehow gotten through, and somehow were. The heat in this city was excessive, since the brick houses and street pavements reflected the sun's rays. Awnings of painted cloth or duck were commonly used over shop doors and windows; at sunset, buckets of water were flung upon the pavements to cool them down. Water came from pumps in the backyards of dwellings; there were also public pumps at almost every fifty paces. A great number of the houses had balconies where in warm weather the men would sit in cool clothing and smoke their pipes.

To country-oriented mothers like Susanna Rush, it was a fact of life to be borne with forbearance and prayers to the Almighty for better times to come that young Benjamin and his contemporaries while roaming the streets in the manner of children down through history beheld adult brawls in which "little bastard" and "shitten elf" were the epithets of choice, and, *in extremis,* were resolved with the brandishing of knives and muskets. Still, the baser element never succeeded in diminishing Philadelphia's importance.

Its merchant aristocracy, professional class, and highborn elite could disregard the stink of Dock Creek, the hogs, the little bastards, and the shitten elves as they went about their business—the wealthier either in coaches or sedan chairs—and sought the comfort and salubrious ambience of their handsome, well-appointed residences or the satisfying social setting of their favorite taverns. It was in the taverns that one and all, regardless of socioeconomic status, found their entertainment. And here the word is used advisedly. Entertainment consisted of little more than general conversation, political gossip, and, perhaps, a bland joke or two, discreetly whispered. This was, after all, a city of Quakers, to whom the concept of frivolity was intolerable.

As the metropolitan center for the towns and hamlets situated within an approximately fifteen-mile radius, the city boasted, in addition to its many inns and taverns, its many churches, and its magnificent new State House on Chestnut Street where the Philadelphia Assembly met, a vast marketplace with countless sheds along a large portion of High (Market) Street and, to accommodate the city's southern section, one of comparable size on South Second Street at Cedar (South). To both came farmers from the surrounding counties to sell their produce, buy supplies, and hear the latest news of the day. For two shillings, they could amuse themselves and their children by going to see the large live lion at James Rorke's house on Water Street.

To the wharves on the Delaware, the city's outlet to the Atlantic, there came a steady stream of ships to on-load American produce for export and off-load every importable product not manufactured but in demand by the colonists—including slaves and indentured servants. These either found their place in Philadelphia's social structure or simply disappeared. John Howell, a tanner, advertised in the *Pennsylvania Gazette* (24 December 1745) for his servant, James Gardner, age about thirty, who had run off: "He is of pretty fresh complexion, middle stature, and round and full-bodied; He had on and with him, a dark homespun coat, with flat metal buttons, a half worn hat, a worsted cap. A light coloured cloth jacket, with pewter buttons, covered with leather, new black and white stockings, good shoes, two homespun shirts, and a pair of short trousers."

Benjamin's father prospered as a gunsmith in Philadelphia. Besides the house the family lived in, he owned two others in the city and a tract of land in suburban Warminster. His intense religiosity and honorableness as a businessman and private citizen was such that customers and neighbors alike measured a man's integrity with the catchphrase "He was as honest as John Rush." John's prosperity did not long survive the family's relocation to Philadelphia. Less than four years later he died, on 26 July 1751, at the age of thirty-nine. Though the cause has not come down to us—typhus or tuberculosis would be as good a guess as any, since no record survives of any accident—his last words, repeated mantra-like in his last hours, are said to have been "Lord! Lord! Lord!"

Susanna, at thirty-four, was now the sole support of the daughter by her first marriage, then about sixteen, James, twelve, Rachel, ten, Rebecca, seven, Benjamin, five and a half, Jacob, four, and the infant John, who died soon after his father. James was sent off to sea on the advice of physicians as an antidote to "a nervous disease" by which he had been "much afflicted"; he would die in his twenty-first year of yellow fever off the island of Jamaica. Jacob would go on to become one of the new nation's leading jurists. Rachel and Rebecca "married with good prospects and settled in Philadelphia." Both married twice. Rachel, to whom Benjamin was closest, died during the 1793 yellow fever epidemic. Rebecca, who had moved with her second husband to

Harrisburg, died five years later. Of Benjamin's half sister, it is known that she married and produced progeny, but no history of that branch of the family survived.

Susanna rented out the three houses she had inherited in the city, John's gunsmith shop, and the Warminster tract, and sold off John's tools and his slaves, retaining one as a servant. Still she lacked the funds to raise her family. Determined that her two sons still at home be educated, she opened a grocery and provision store, the Blazing Star, and was soon doing a thriving business. "Her industry and uncommon talents and address in doing business commanded success," recalled Benjamin. She later opened a second store across the street from the first that specialized in finer items like chinaware, which Rebecca would manage upon reaching young adulthood.[6] By then Susanna had married one Richard Morris, a distiller, whom Benjamin would recall as having been abusive to her throughout the sixteen years of the marriage that ended with his death. Determined never to be a burden to her children, Susanna purchased a small farmhouse outside the city before the Revolution, to which she retired after selling her business at war's end until Benjamin insisted she come live out her days with him and his family. She died on 2 July 1795, at age seventy-eight.[7]

Young Benjamin's education, both secular and religious, was begun at home by Susanna. Though a practicing Presbyterian, she instructed him in the tenets of the Episcopal Church, out of deference to her husband. When John died, Susanna took him to the Second Presbyterian Church in Philadelphia, whose spiritual leader, Rev. Gilbert Tennent, had been in the vanguard of the Great Awakening. As Paul Johnson points out in his monumental *History of the American People,* this spiritual movement which "proved to be of vast significance, both in religion and politics [and] was indeed one of the key events in American history [had] no obvious beginning or end, no pitched battles or legal victories with specific dates, no constitutions or formal leaders, no easily quantifiable statistics and no formal set of beliefs. While it was taking place it had no name."[8]

Briefly, the movement was a call for the sinners in colonial America to come back to religion. Led by the English evangelist George Wakefield, a band of ardent revivalists moved through the colonies and, by the force of their magnetism, their convictions, and their awe-inspiring personalities, stimulated religious zeal, achieved conversions, and increased membership in what was essentially a breaking away from stringent Calvinism. However, it wasn't long before their methodology and fiery emotionalism were being perceived as a threat to the established order, as they condemned ministers of being unconcerned and consequentially leading their congregants into the depths of spiritual annihilation.

This led to the splitting of many churches into factions. In New England, orthodox Calvinism was revitalized, with Congregationalist Jonathan Edwards emerging as the paramount theologian. Opponents of the revival preached against the conformist Calvinist doctrines of predestination, election, and original sin. In the Middle Colonies, of which Pennsylvania was the largest and economically most important, there were many Scottish and Scotch-Irish Presbyterians who also reaffirmed orthodoxy, which they insisted had been vitiated by the revivalist's emphasis on religious experience over force-fed dogma. The Reverend Gilbert Tennent, to whom Benjamin Rush's religious instruction and influence was entrusted by Susanna, had been one of Wakefield's most fervid fellow evangelists.

The Presbyterian Church in America had by now split into two factions. The "Old Side" (or "Old Lights") was, if possible, more Calvinistic than Calvin. They demanded doctrinal immaculacy and an inalterable adherence to the Westminster Confession of Faith established during the Cromwellian interregnum as the only acceptable standard for admission to the ministry. The "New Side" (or "New Lights") insisted that ministers who may have been pure in doctrine but were lacking in faith—"Pharisee Teachers" who preached the concept of brimstone and the fires of hell and damnation—had polluted too many pulpits.

The New Side, outraged by the demand that the church be governed by a hidebound synod made up exclusively of ministers imported from "home"—Ulster (Ireland) and Scotland—wanted to recast the American church. Here, it was argued, with congregations made up of many other immigrant nationalities, the local presbyteries should determine a congregation's affairs, not an all-powerful synod made up of a Scottish-trained clergy whose words would have little relevance for Americans who had fled the Old World for the religious freedom they believed was to be found in the New.

On accepting the Philadelphia congregation Tennent moderated his initially rigid Calvinist views. Indeed, he practically set the colony's Presbyterian Church on its ear. This endeared him to Susanna Rush, an advocate of the New Side. Figuring prominently in Susanna's thinking was the fact that her sister Sarah's minister husband, Samuel Finley, had been a protégé of Gilbert Tennent's father, William, and was a graduate of the school he opened in Bucks County north of Philadelphia known pejoratively by those who opposed his advanced views as the Log College. Finley was to become the first of four surrogate fathers who would influence Benjamin's religious and secular philosophy and his life's work both as a physician and a social reformer.

Having emigrated from Ulster in 1734 at the age of nineteen, Finley became the foremost acolyte of William Tennent, one of the primary opponents of Calvinism's pessimistic view of man's nature and destiny. Like Tennent, Finley posited that God offered regeneration to all who accepted Him unconditionally, regardless of their rank or race in society; that man was set on the road to spiritual happiness through regeneration alone, and not by wealth or political power or other "signs" of divine preordination and power; and spiritual happiness realized by the newborn man carried the unequivocal obligation to work with God to create Heaven on Earth.

These beliefs antagonized a large number of colonials who patterned their lives on practices in the mother country—a country which, Finley and his fellow Awakeners preached, God had abandoned as everlastingly corrupt and degenerate beyond salvation. They condemned "immoderate desires, fears, and cares about earthly things" as aspects of man's acquisitive instincts; praised the simple virtues of rural over city life; attacked the rich, arguing that men "grow in wickedness in proportion to the increase of their wealth"; and called for the equality of men. This led some to a denunciation of Negro slavery as a contravention of God's law—which would become for Benjamin Rush, as for other impassioned abolitionists, not so much a condemnation as a cause. Moreover, in a time when established churches flourished in most colonies, the New Siders called for religious liberty and toleration of all faiths. In tones resonant of the Old Testament prophets, they argued that God cared not about forms of worship, only that men worshipped from the heart.[9]

It is interesting to note that in the last year of his life Rush equated himself with "a character in the Old Testament which more nearly accords with mine. It is that of the prophet Jeremiah."[10] Here was the most vocal and most intransigent—and the one who suffered most for his labors—of all the canonical prophets in damning those who contented themselves with sacrifices and offerings to their Deity in the belief this was all that the Deity demanded in return for His favor and protection, when all that He truly demanded was man's probity and fidelity to the concept of monotheism and the moral principles of what evolved as Judaeo-Christianity.

After his ordination in 1742 by a New Side presbytery, Finley set out to awaken Connecticut. He was quickly evicted for preaching to a congregation not recognized by the civil authority. After wandering two years from pulpit to pulpit in the Northern and Middle Colonies, he accepted a call to Nottingham, some fifty miles south of Philadelphia near the Pennsylvania-Maryland border, in June 1744. Convinced that new schools must be established if the reformed church was to be stocked with a faithful ministry, he founded Nottingham Academy as a preparatory school for the College of New Jersey, the precursor of Princeton University, which the New Side Presbyterians founded in 1746, modeled on the Log College, to assure a steady flow of American-trained ministers into their church. While hoping, naturally, that his students would be drawn to the religious vocation, Finley recognized there were other honorable fields to enter for those who did not "receive the call from God." One was law, the other, medicine—or, to give it the term by which it was known at the time, "physic" (thus the noun *physician*).

It was to their uncle Samuel's Nottingham Academy in 1754 that Susanna sent eight-year-old Benjamin and seven-year-old Jacob to begin their formal education.

The school had at the time about fifteen students, all of whom lived dormitory style with the Finleys and their own eight children.

Though a Calvinist, albeit a decidedly less than uncompromising one cast in the John Knox mold, Finley exhorted his students to fight relentlessly the corruptions and temptations of a wicked world, eschew indulgence, and, above all, pursue meaningful lives. He saw as his primary goal the promotion of a boy's usefulness to society within the context of his religion. To that end, he insisted they learn arithmetic, geometry, and geography, in addition to Latin and Greek. These studies he considered essential for any professional career, be it the ministry, medicine, or the law. For that same reason he taught reading, writing, and speaking English "with great care and success." This was certainly the case with Benjamin, if one is to judge by the fame—one might say notoriety—he achieved as a prodigious pamphleteer, in addition to his enormous epistolary output in an age when everyone, notably men of great importance and accomplishment, would seem to have spent a good part of every day sitting at their desk, quill in hand. Finley also taught several of the arts and sciences (or, as they were then called, natural philosophy) but only lightly: "In these he was unfortunately tied down to the principles and forms that were common in the schools of that day."[11]

Also taught was practical agriculture, in a manner we would describe today as hands-on: "All his boarders shared in the labors of Harvest and hay making. I bear on one of my fingers to this day the mark of a severe cut I received in learning to reap," recalled Rush when writing his memoirs. "These exercises were both pleasant and useful. They begat health, and helped to implant more deeply in our minds the native passion for rural life. Perhaps it may be ascribed in part to their influence, that not a single instance of death, and not more than two or three instances of sickness occurred in the Doctor's family during the time I lived in it, which was five years."[12]

Impressed—and deeply influenced—even at this tender age by Finley's philosophy of education, Benjamin was truly inspired by his approach to religion, reflected in Finley's interpretations of the Bible. One sermon which remained in Rush's mind to the end of his days was on the words from Proverbs: "Madness is in their hearts while they live," subsequently printed (1754) under the title "Madness of Mankind." While Rush's life and thought, particularly during the Revolutionary period, were informed by Enlightenment ideas, as were those of Jefferson, Madison, and the other great thinkers among the

Founding Fathers, his ultimate disillusionment both with the new nation he would help to create, and the world itself, prompted him to fall back on the Gospel truths as interpreted by his uncle back at Nottingham. Or, as he told John Adams on 8 August 1812, not long before he died, "The present times have added many facts in support of his position."[13]

In the spring of 1759 thirteen-year-old Benjamin was adjudged by Finley sufficiently prepared to enter college. Given the family's finances, the logical choice would have been the College of Philadelphia, as having him live at home could save money. But Anglicans and Old Side Presbyterians controlled the college; and though it was now more than a quarter of a century since the schism created by the Great Awakening, the ill feelings it had engendered still flourished. While it would involve some sacrifice on Susanna's part, as the cost of educating Jacob would soon fall upon her and there were Rachel and Rebecca to care for, she accepted without demur Finley's suggestion of the College of New Jersey. It is testimony to his preparation at Nottingham that Benjamin, after a thorough examination, was admitted as a junior. Here he would come under the influence of the second of his four surrogate fathers and mentors.

The college had only three years previously relocated south to Prince Town—or Princeton, as it would soon be called—from its home in Newark mainly because students from the other colonies disliked being associated with a college bearing the name "New Jersey." The colonials had nothing against New Jersey, per se. They did not like the name of any colony to be associated with a school of higher learning. The reason for this is inexplicable, and need not detain us. The school's name change did not become official until 1896, but, consistent with early custom, it will henceforth be referred to in this narrative as Princeton. Nassau Hall, its main building at the time Benjamin Rush matriculated there, became synonymous with the school, affectionately referred to as "Old Nassau."

The name reflected the religious bias of its founders: It was the Protestant William of Nassau-Orange (the Netherlands) who at Parliament's invitation invaded England in 1688—the "Glorious Revolution"—deposed the openly Catholic James II, his father-in-law as well as his mother's brother, and as William III restored the Stuarts to the Protestant fold, from which the royal successors down to this day have never strayed. In the large faux Georgian building, the approximately fifty students and four faculty members lived, studied, and went about the business of education. The student regimen lasted throughout the year, with six-week breaks after the first and second semesters, respectively November to May and June to October.

The school day began before sunrise, when a servant pounding on the doors awakened the students. Prayers were at 5:30, followed by an hour of study, then breakfast, then classes from nine to one, followed by dinner, the main meal of the day. The boys were then free until five, when they attended evening prayers, followed by supper at seven and bedtime at nine. The only schedule variant was on Sundays, when everyone went to church at eleven, and heard a second sermon four hours later. Yearly costs, including tuition, room and board, books, travel, and incidentals, were about half of what it took to maintain a family of seven in Philadelphia. But Susanna gladly accepted the financial strain this imposed, since her sons would be properly educated in the New Side Presbyterian mode.

Even by the standards of the times, young Benjamin comes off as a bit of a prig. He declined to enter into dormitory life, especially card playing, which he held to be a sin of measurable magnitude: "Vices of the same species attract each other with the most force," he wrote years later when formulating plans for what he hoped would be a national university. "Hence the bad consequences of crowding young men (whose propensities are generally the same) under one roof in our modern plans of education." When he sent his firstborn son to Princeton, Rush had him lodge in the village with a private family, "for I considered a *college life* and *college society* to boys of his age as alike fatal to morals and manners" (emphasis in the original).[14]

Remarkably, given its having been founded to educate ministers for the Presbyterian Church, few courses were offered at the time toward that end. Its curriculum when Benjamin arrived was about what he had covered at Nottingham: mathematics, Latin and Greek, literature, a smattering of philosophy, but none of the natural or physical sciences. All that changed with the coming, a few months after Benjamin's, of the school's fourth president and second of Rush's mentors and lifelong influences: Samuel Davies.

Thirty-six at the time, and already in the preterminal stage of tuberculosis, the lowly born Delaware farmer's son, in Rush's words, "surmounted the disadvantages of scanty circumstances . . . by the strength and activity of a great and original genius. He was in most respects . . . 'a self-made man.' "[15] Caught up in the Great Awakening, Davies toured the colonies as an itinerant evangelical clergyman and secured his reputation as one of the great preachers of the day. Known as the "Father of the Presbyterian Church in Virginia," where he accepted a call to that colony's Hanover County whence he rode annually a five-hundred-mile circuit through the backcountry, Davies preached that public spirit and benevolence formed "a beautiful symmetry; they adorn, cherish, and perfect each other; they contain the substance of all obedience to the law, which is summed up in the Love of God, and the Love of Man."[16]

Rush's future abolitionist attitudes can be traced to Davies's feelings about the "neglected Negroes . . . these poor unhappy Africans are objects of my compassion." In 1758, the fiery preacher had the temerity to tell slave owners in Virginia, arguably the most resolute of the breed in all the colonies, "I have reason to conclude that making allowance for their low and barbarous education, their imperfect acquaintance with our language, their having no opportunity for intellectual improvements, and the like, they are generally as capable of instruction as the white people."[17]

Davies was as renowned for his secular learning as for his religious learning. Such was his reputation for classical literature, philosophy, and oratory that he was recommended to the trustees of the college even before undertaking a mission to Great Britain where he successfully solicited contributions to build and endow the school. Within months of assuming the presidency, he reshaped the college as Tennent had reshaped the church. Princeton now ceased its exclusivity as a training ground for the ministry. Davies increased the library to include secular masterworks, stiffened entrance examinations to keep out, to use an anachronistic phrase, "the frat boy, Joe College" type, and built up its science department while playing down the religious side. Young Rush had difficulties with the stress on Latin and Greek, for which languages he cultivated a lifelong distaste, as well as Davies's emphasis on metaphysics and the classics. He also rejected—though he was tactful enough to keep it to himself—Davies's conviction "that no government could be safe or durable where there was no kingly and aristocratic power, and that the British constitution included in it the perfections of every species of government without any of their imperfections."[18]

Despite his difficulties with Latin and Greek, and no great partiality for literature, it was Benjamin's "happy lot to attract a good deal of [Davies's] attention," having "discovered some talents for poetry, composition and public speaking, to each of which he was very partial . . . I hope I shall be excused in acknowledging that his mode of teaching inspired me with a love of knowledge, and that if I derived but little from his instructions, I was taught by him how to acquire it in the subsequent periods of my life."[19]

In addition, and of greater consequence in light of Rush's future accomplishments in innovative medical methodology, Davies taught him "the art of inquiry, in its most basic form, which another of Rush's teachers, Dr. William Cullen of the University of Edinburgh"—the third of that quartet of most influential men on the life of Dr. Benjamin Rush—"would later help to develop more systematically in Rush's thinking."[20]

Benjamin was fifteen years old when he was awarded a degree of batchelor of arts in September 1760. According to the *Pennsylvania Gazette* (9 October 1760) at his commencement exercises "MR. BENJAMIN RUSH . . . in a very sprightly and entertaining manner delivered an ingenious English harangue in praise of oratory." Of all the influences Rush took away from Princeton, probably none exceeded Davies's baccalaureate sermon (23 September 1770), which began, "Great and good characters are often formed by imitation . . . And if we would shine in any sphere, we must propose to ourselves some illustrious examples." Davies urged the graduates to hold as most precious a public spirit, for without it their lives would be "of little use to the community, and all the valuable ends of a liberal education will be lost upon you. . . . Bravely live and die, serving your generation—your own generation [but] be ambitious to survive yourselves [as] your own generation is the special and appropriate sphere of your usefulness."

Here it should be noted that in his comparatively brief presidency of Princeton, Davies taught—and influenced—many of the young men who, like Rush, would play leading roles in the great drama that was the American Revolution. Young as they were, Davies continued in his baccalaureate sermon to Rush's and his nine fellow graduates, they must realize that their time for work was brief, for "the day of life is short." For that reason, they must "seize therefore the flying moments," and above all "let religion be the source of your benevolence and public spirit." Ever the Calvinist, he warned that they "be not ambitious of self-government, but resign yourselves to the will of God," reminding them that anyone without a regenerated spirit and a new heart, "can never arrive at the finished character of good and great men." Lacking a spiritual rebirth, "it would be better for you to be Hottentots, or even the most abject and miserable creatures among the meanest and most noxious of the brutal tribes, than to be the sons of NASSAU HALL." A string of homilies climaxed in the sermon's peroration: Continue to study, otherwise "you will live your age backward, and be less wise at sixty than at twenty." When it came to choosing a profession, "follow Nature and consult the public good."[21]

Davies died not long after Benjamin left Princeton. Commiserating with Enoch Green, with whom he had formed a lifelong friendship at college, Rush said that the baccalaureate sermon "deserves to be printed in letters of gold in every young candidate's heart."[22] When the sermon was published, Rush purchased a copy, which remained a treasured part of his personal library until the day he died.

Benjamin was uncertain about a career when he entered college. During his last months prior to graduation, he gave much thought to the future, but was unable to arrive at any firm decision. Since he lacked family connections in the business world—his mother running a grocery store would hardly facilitate his entry into a world which at any rate he had no pressing desire to enter—that left but one of three fields in which an eighteenth-century college graduate had any chance of making a career: the church, the law, or medicine.

As for the ministry, while he believed that "every pursuit of life must dwindle into naught when Divinity appears," he could not see that profession for himself because of "my incapacity"—a vague reason he chose not to explicate. And since he "had an uncommon aversion from seeing such sights as are connected with its practice," medicine seemed out of the question. That left the law ("the babblative art"), in which he was encouraged by his classmates, all of whom were impressed with his reputation as an orator.

When Davies, who also considered Rush's oratorical and literary talents much more than "sprightly and entertaining," was told on being asked that law was his choice, he approved wholeheartedly, adding that he "believed I should make a better figure at the bar, than in the walks of a hospital." Davies's opinion "fixed my determination, and my mother in consequence of it applied to a Lawyer in Philadelphia to take me into his office" as an apprentice.[23]

Meanwhile, by way of a vacation Benjamin accompanied one of his schoolmates on a visit to his family in Maryland. On his return home, he stopped off at Nottingham to visit with Samuel Finley. Learning his nephew would be preparing for a law career, he told Rush "the practice of the law was full of temptations and advised me by no means to think of it, but to study physic. 'But before you determine on any thing (said he), set apart a day for fasting and prayer, and ask God to direct you in your choice of a profession.' I am sorry to say I neglected the latter part of this excellent advice, but yielded to the former.... On what slight circumstances do our destinies in life seem to depend!" There would be periods in his life when Rush regretted the choice he made, and actually considered abandoning medicine for law. "But providence overruled my intentions [and] I now rejoice that I followed Dr. Finley's advice. I have seen the hand of heaven clearly in it."[24]

It was thanks to Uncle Samuel Finley, who succeeded Samuel Davies as president of Princeton, that Rush was accepted as an apprentice by Dr. John Redman, Philadelphia's leading physician.

2

Apprenticeship

The University of Edinburgh was generally recognized as the world's foremost medical school, followed by the University of Leyden in Holland. But the first center devoted exclusively to medical learning in the American colonies was not formed—at Philadelphia—until 1765, a year before the conclusion of Rush's six-year apprenticeship. This was the College of Philadelphia; it would later evolve into the University of Pennsylvania. Already in operation for a decade was the Pennsylvania Hospital, America's first public hospital, which boasted the city's finest leading practitioners among its attending physicians, and the year-old Academy, also a teaching hospital with a notable faculty. When it came to medical care, primitive as it was by today's standards, Pennsylvania led all the other colonies. The personal apprentice system continued even after medical schools began to proliferate as the new nation expanded. No generally accepted norms of excellence were adopted until the opening decade of the twentieth century. Other than his apprenticeship, which included practical treatment and application, Rush's only *formal* training until he went to study abroad was attending the lectures, toward the end of his apprenticeship, by Drs. John Morgan and William Shippen, Jr. Both were also graduates of Rev. Samuel Finley's Nottingham Academy and the University of Edinburgh, both were leading lights in the first post-Redman generation of medical practitioners. Morgan lectured in the theory and practice of medicine. Shippen lectured in anatomy, surgery, and midwifery.[1]

Equally brilliant physicians and teachers, they quickly became competitive foes in the city's medical circles upon returning from their studies abroad. Without going at this point into their great feud years down the road during the Revolutionary War, in which Rush would play a paramount role, let it suffice to be said that Benjamin wisely attended the lecture courses given by both men and otherwise made sure he kept in the good graces of both. Morgan would remain Rush's lifelong friend and mentor. Shippen, who at first took a liking to him, would become during the war the only man Rush truly hated—so much so that, as we shall see, destroying Shippen's career and reputation became for Rush an obsession. In pursuit of that obsession, Rush almost succeeded in destroying his own career and reputation.

As a preceptor, Dr. John Redman could be overly rigorous. Though his nature precluded treating a pupil with undue severity, he did ride herd on them: "My master at this time was in the most extensive business of any physician in the city . . . and he kept [his pupils] constantly employed."[2] Rush was considered the most brilliant of all his master's apprentices over the years. This is reflected in the fact that after but a year Redman felt confident enough to place the sixteen-year-old Benjamin in charge of patients, instead of having him just stand by as an observer. This was quite possibly a first for medical apprentices.

Before we follow Rush into Dr. Redman's house in February 1761, where, as was the custom, he would live during his apprenticeship, let us learn a little about this devout Presbyterian, an alumnus of William Tennent's Log College, who would be the fourth father figure to, and great influence on, his then fifteen-year-old newest pupil.

A product of Philadelphia's apprentice system, Redman practiced in Bermuda for several years, and then served in the French and Indian War (1754–1763).* After the war, Redman went abroad to study, first at Edinburgh, thereafter at Leyden, where he came under the posthumous influence of the great Hermann Boerhaave. Boerhaave, who had died in 1746, taught his students—who would include half of Europe's

---

*This was the last of the four wars waged in North America from 1689 to 1763 between the British and French for control of the continent, with the assistance of Native American and colonial allies. In Europe it expanded into the Seven Years' War (1756–1763). While stripping France of its North America empire, the French and Indian War was of far greater consequence in that it caused the British to alter their relationship with their American colonies. To compensate for the war's cost, Parliament unilaterally imposed heavy taxes and import duties—thereby providing both the underlying and precipitating causes of the American Revolution.

leading physicians—the art of careful observation and, concomitantly, the careful recording of their observations. Another posthumous influence on Redman was Thomas Sydenham, known as the English Hippocrates. In the previous century Sydenham was the first to diagnose measles as a distinct disease, the first to distinguish between rheumatism and gout, the first to describe Saint Vitus' Dance, and the first to establish the psychic character of hysteria.

But there was a downside to Sydenham's theories, which influenced Redman and, by extension, Benjamin Rush. This was his insistence that disease resulted from an accumulation of "morbific matter" in the body that could be drained only by bleeding, purging, or sweating. Rush never abandoned his belief in bleeding—which, as can be imagined, often caused the patient's death quicker than the disease it was meant to ameliorate, and has, of course, long been discredited. If there was one major flaw in his otherwise flawless medical career, it was this practice, which earned him posthumously the pejorative cognomen "Dr. Vampire."

Returning to Philadelphia, Redman quickly became the leading practitioner of surgery and obstetrics. Surgery had not yet become, as it is today, a medical discipline in itself, owing mainly to the fact that it was so primitive, not the least of reasons being a general ignorance, by today's standards, of the internal workings of the human body, and the lack of anesthesia. Progress was being made to fill in the knowledge gaps. But such knowledge, like all technology, needed time to evolve naturally and at its own pace. Physicians of the times doubled as surgeons, though their procedures were, barring the occasional exception, generally limited to amputations, excisions, and dental extractions.

In his fortieth year Redman suffered from a subdiaphragmatic abscess, probably the result of amebic dysentery. He is believed to have been affected twice by the yellow fever epidemics that struck Philadelphia periodically. Because of his poor health, he gave up the practice of surgery and obstetrics. As dean of Philadelphia physicians and its leading medical teacher, Redman was elected first president of the College of Physicians. Despite his poor health, he would live on—and continue to teach—until the age of eighty-four. While his contributions to medical literature were rather scanty, his defense of the recently introduced use of variolation—direct arm-to-arm inoculation—prepared the way for vaccination, which was not discovered until 1796. But perhaps Redman's greatest contribution to the art of healing lay in his being one of the few who "with a few others temporarily filled the gap in the training of American physicians when medical schools and scientific discipline were unknown." In Redman, Benjamin Rush had the ideal preceptor—as did, by extension, every leading American physician down to the Civil War.[3]

Rush began his medical apprenticeship, as did all others, in Redman's apothecary shop. American physicians at the time made and sold their own prescriptions. The formulation was left to their apprentices while the doctors called on the patients; it was not unheard of for a doctor to see as many, often more, patients in their homes as he saw in his office. The materia medica was easy to master, as it included little beyond such drugs as laudanum and other opium preparations, mercury ointments, calomel, ipecac, magnesia, castor oil, Jesuits' bark or cinchona—the natural source of quinine—and a few others. And dosage was an unknown concept: It can be compared to an elderly grandmother of today teaching her daughter or granddaughter the recipe for a favorite family dish: "a little of this," "a pinch of that." A prescription that included opium might call for enough "to lie on a penknife's point"; instructions for the inclusion of mercury might include "a pretty draught" of the root "the size of a walnut."

Before seeking out the services of a physician and recourse to this kind of primitive pharmacopoeia, patients usually tried their own remedies passed down from generation to generation like heirlooms. Were one's foot trod upon by a horse, it was first soaked in cold spring water and then covered with "a cataplasm of cow dung." A sty on the eyelid? The doctor was called in with his lancet only after the application of a rotten apple proved ineffective. Should a nail be accidentally hammered into a hand or arm, the wound was dressed with rabbit fat. Rubbing with "spirits of wine" (brandy) was the primary treatment for painful corns. Initial attempts to combat asthma involved smoking a pipeful of what we, today, know as jimsonweed, which in itself posed a threat of sorts: While it could have some pharmaceutic benefit, it was exceptionally poisonous.

Cancer was treated by the application of a plaster consisting of sun-dried pokeberries, though obviously this involved only perceptible external cancers. Treatment of choice for dysentery was goldenrod; for consumption, magnolia berries steeped in brandy. More often than not, such folk medicine proved futile, and the physician was called in—assuming the patient was still alive. Depending on the ailment, and the extent of its progress, it was practically a presupposition that the physician could offer little more than palliation and prayer.

Certainly by modern standards, the primitiveness of the physician's pharmacopoeia was about on a par with the contents of his medical bag: no stethoscope, no clinical thermometer, no watch to count the pulse. There was, though—and here we speak of the physician's primary instrument—the lance, the principal use of which was to open a vein for bleeding "morbidic matters" from the patient's body. "Bleeding is proper at the beginning of all inflammatory fevers, as pleurisies, peripneumonias, etc.," according to a contemporary medical textbook. "It is likewise proper in all topical inflammations, as those of the intestines, womb, bladder, stomach, kidneys... rheumatisms, the apoplexy, epilepsy, and the bloody flux. After falls, blows, bruises, or any violent hurt received either externally or internally, bleeding is necessary." Indeed, it was easier, and quicker, to cite instances in which bleeding was *not* "proper"—if such an instance could indeed be cited. Another popular method of ridding the body of "morbidic matter" was to administer purgatives ("give the puke"), which is, of course, still practiced.

Leeches, which had been used for centuries—and, remarkably, seem to be making a comeback as a medical tool today, though nowhere as randomly and haphazardly as in times gone by—were by Benjamin Rush's day coming into disfavor. The quantity of blood being consumed by the leeches could not be precisely measured, and—perhaps worse—the leeches were often difficult to stop, and thus created more havoc than their vampirical craving was intended to mitigate. A more infallible—or less imprecise—alternative to leeching was cupping, second only in usage to lancing. Here, a bell-shaped glass with a syringe attached to the bottom was placed over the affected area. Heat applied to the outside of the glass created a vacuum that raised the skin, thus facilitating insertion of the syringe by means of which the intended amount of blood was extracted.[4]

*　　*　　*

After tending to his duties in the apothecary shop Benjamin Rush, who also kept Redman's records and account book up to date, accompanied his master on visits to patients and rounds at the Pennsylvania Hospital, where Redman was consulting physician. The building's elegance stood out in bold relief against—in a sense, was a mockery of—the misery it housed. Those who could afford it were treated at home. The hospital's patient population was made up of the poor, the aged, the insane, the moribund, and any others who had become unbearably burdensome to his or her family, or who had no family at all. That it was a venue of last resort, and a horrific one at that, prompted one contemporary physician to complain that the "strong smell of sores and nastiness rendered it insupportable even to me who have been pretty much used to such places." It wasn't long before apprentice Rush had learned to bleed, purge, and cup patients, dress wounds, and even assist in surgical procedures. Midway through his apprenticeship, he "covered" for Redman—and acquitted himself well—when Redman was incapacitated by illness. In time he achieved the distinction of being "admitted to see the practice of five other physicians besides [Dr. Redman's] own in the hospital."[5]

Disease nomenclature in the eighteenth century was as primitive as its treatment. Fits, convulsions, apoplexy, dropsy, pleurisy, and "scorbutic and scrofulous ulcers," "decays," and "flux" were given as causes of death. Designations of various ailments were defined by vernacular terminology. "Pleurisy" or "a pleuritical disorder" was a sign that a man's chest ached—and could well have indicated a heart attack. "Pulmonary consumption" was a sign of blood in the sputum—possibly tuberculosis. Any number of infections that could indicate diseases such as pneumonia, diphtheria, or scarlet fever were identified as "throat distemper" or "putrid sore throat." Typhoid or cholera might possibly be what was commonly called the "bloody flux"—though more often than not the "diagnosis" indicated dysentery. Common disorders of varying severity to which most people of the time fell victim that were otherwise unidentifiable by the physician were given the catchphrase "fever," of which there were variations. Those that came and went at regular intervals were "intermittent." Those that came and went with irregularity were "remittent." Those that came and remained constant were "continued," and could develop into "putrid fever." What we now identify as typhoid was termed "nervous fever";

typhus was called "hospital fever" or "jail fever," perhaps because it spread so often and so quickly where people were in close proximity in unhygienic surroundings. Any fever accompanied by chills was called an "ague," and here there was yet another variant: When the chills came every third day, the diagnosis was "tertian ague," and invariably indicated what we know as malaria. There were the occasional ailments that had been given specific names: smallpox, whooping cough, scarlet fever, and syphilis. Yellow fever, the disease that struck most epidemically, was commonly known as the "bilious remitting fever."[6]

It was Philadelphia's lot to suffer annually one or more of these fevers in endemic proportions. The worst year was 1762, Rush's second as an apprentice, when two epidemics struck. The first was smallpox. Most physicians had by that time accepted that inoculation—injecting a person or animal with a serum, antigen, or weakened form of a disease-producing pathogen in order to create immunity to and thus protection against the full effects of the disease—required up to six weeks of professional care, which only the economically advantaged could afford. Redman had sought to popularize a simplified, hence more affordable procedure, but his colleagues rejected this reform. As a consequence, the 1762 epidemic, especially among the poor, was "very mortal."[7]

Even while the smallpox epidemic was taking its toll, yellow fever made one of its periodic returns, to depart, as it always did, only with the first frost. Schools were closed, and those who could afford to, fled to the apparently immune countryside. One reason—conceivably the primary reason—Philadelphia was so often put at the mercy of this horrific disease was the erroneous belief entertained by physicians that it was randomly communicable. In the light of Rush's later groundbreaking work that led to the true cause and near eradication of the disease by physicians during the Spanish-American War, it should be noted that the disease was confined to tenements around the noxious Dock Creek, to squares of housing near the wharves that lined the Delaware River, and to the south part of town contiguous to a stretch of marshland. This supported the accepted contemporary theory that its cause was a contaminated miasma or effluvia that arose from the marshes and city water. Since Redman's practice was confined almost exclusively to the city's prosperous citizens, who lived outside the infected areas, his yellow fever victims averaged less than two dozen a day. Whenever he and his apprentices called upon an infected patient, he insisted that each chew a wad of tobacco to prevent swallowing saliva that could cause their bodies to ingest the disease. While this has a slightly absurd ring about it to modern ears, as does his insistence that no physician on an empty stomach should visit a patient, no less absurd-sounding was his insistence that the danger of contagion from a yellow fever victim was lessened considerably by plunging a hot iron into a bowl of vinegar in the sickroom. Ironically, it's quite conceivable that the fumes this created kept away mosquitoes—which in time would prove to be the transmitters of the yellow fever infection!

Rush wrote little about his six years under Redman's tutelage. Less than two pages in his memoirs are devoted to this period, and even here he speaks in generalities: "I read in the intervals of my business and at late and early hours, all the books in medicine that were put into my hands by my master, or that I [was able to] borrow from other students of medicine in the city." He also mentions keeping "a common place book" in which he records "every thing that I [consider] curious or valuable in my reading and in my master's practice."[8] Just about all of Rush's recollections of this period to survive are to be found in his letters to his Nottingham and Princeton chum Ebenezer Hazard. A letter dated 27 September 1762 in which Rush tells of the 1762 yellow fever epidemic is worth quoting from, less for what information it might impart than to illustrate his precociously grandiloquent literary style, which, mercifully, he would curb over time:

> Although I now indulge the pleasure of an epistolary conversation with you, yet it mortifies me to think that the constant hurry of my employment prevents me from entering on those minute friendly communications which have always been so agreeable to each of us.
>
> Our town has lately been visited with sickness of which numbers die daily—a solemn call to *prepare for Death!* You may perhaps reply, "Fine times for the physicians." Such a retort as this might only be adapted to those inhuman *monsters* who estimate their happiness by the miseries and infelicities of their fellow creatures; as for my part, I can assure you it awakens my compassion and calls forth every generous passion to sympathize with the afflicted.[9]

While Rush had little to share with Hazard of a substantive nature regarding his medical training, he had a few things to say on other matters. One letter reveals a preoccupation with religion that might seem to modern ears at first bizarre coming from an eighteen-year-old. But Rush, who had been raised within a strong religious background, and practiced daily devotions, should be judged in the context of his own time, and not ours:

> Religion is at a low ebb among us. Sinners are secure and dead ["and dead" may be a manuscript error that should read 'indeed'], and even the love of saints are cold. . . . Vice and profanity openly prevail in our city. Our Sabbaths are boldly profaned by the most open and flagrant enormities. Our young men in general (who should be the prop of sinking Religion) are wholly devoted to pleasure and sensuality, and very few are solicitous about the one thing needful. . . . We wrestle with powerful corruptions and temptations, but let us derive strength from the Rock of Ages. May the Son of God arise and shine upon our souls. May we be made to feel our vileness and undone situations, and earnestly cry aloud to Jesus till he opens our eyes to behold his all-sufficiency and fitness to be our Redeemer.[10]

A year later, having developed an interest in politics, Rush expressed his feelings about the Stamp Act that unified the colonists, played a major role in the rise of American nationalist sentiment, and was one of the primary causes of the American Revolution. Passed by the British Parliament in 1765 as a means of raising revenues in the American colonies to defray the cost of maintaining their military defense, the act required that all legal documents, licenses, commercial contracts, newspapers, pamphlets, and packs of playing cards be affixed with a tax stamp. Passed without debate, and arousing extensive opposition among the colonials, who argued that because they were not represented in Parliament they could not legally be taxed without their consent, it led to active opposition that ranged from attacks by mobs, organized by Samuel Adams's Sons of Liberty, on official stamp agents and their property; passage of protest resolutions by a number of the colonial assemblies; and agreement by colonial businessmen to stop importing British goods (the Non-Importation Agreements) until the act was repealed.

Criticizing Benjamin Franklin, then the colonial agent in London, for failing to denounce the act, and—a particular bête noire—the Quakers, Rush bemoaned that "Philadelphia is cursed with a set of men who seem resolved to counteract all our efforts against the Stamp Act, and are daily endeavoring to suppress the spirit of liberty among us. You know I mean the Quakers. They have openly spoke in favor of the Act and declare it high treason to speak against ye English Parliament."[11] In fact, Franklin did speak out against the act—after opposition coalesced in the British business community because of the substantial diminution in trade with the colonies. This led Parliament to repeal it in the following March. But the Declaratory Act, which confirmed the British government's right to pass legally binding acts upon the colonists, accompanied repeal. Hence the cry, "No taxation without representation!" that slowly but irrevocably transformed a desire for independence into a historical imperative. While the furor in America subsided, many a patriot chose not to forget. Included in that number was nineteen-year-old Benjamin Rush, in whom the Stamp and Declaratory acts planted an antagonism to the mother country that would remain steadfast, even expand exponentially.

Despite the rigid routine imposed upon him by Redman, Rush found time through his last two years of apprenticeship to wrestle with an ongoing anxiety over the state of his soul. In a letter to Hazard early in 1766, he defined himself as one of those madmen who "banish God from their thoughts, and plunge themselves into a gulf of sin, and thus ripen their souls for the torments of hell perhaps before they arrive at the age of twenty"—the age at which he had just arrived. Apparently the guilt over having, or so he thought, "banished God" from his thoughts had been within him from childhood—or perhaps instilled within him by Tennent, whom he revered—because he claimed that its high point came during his Princeton years. But since being apprenticed to Redman "my temper became more and more uniform, and I began to delight in reading religious books, in hearing good sermons, and in convening with pious people." In other words, he was arriving at his own interpretation of faith, instead of settling for the imposition of faith on him by others. Rush had more than medical tutelage to thank his mentor Redman for.

However, it wasn't easy for him. Rush was convinced that sin still dominated his soul: "This drove me sometimes to my knees, and made me importunate with God for a change of heart." Rush's "former state of security in sin" lasted until he heard a sermon by a college classmate by then preaching at Philadelphia, Samuel Blair. Blair's homily must have been the sort that would send an orthodox Calvinist fleeing screaming into the night, for it led to much private meditation on Rush's part that revealed "my exceeding aggravated guilt and insecurity." Allowing as how "Jesus Christ spoke to my soul as he did to the woman of *Samaria* when he told her that he with whom she lived was not her husband," he added, cryptically, "One particular *sin* lay heavy upon my conscience, which brought to my view *all the things that ever I did.*"

Apparently here, out of some inexplicable compulsion, Rush is confessing to Hazard that he had bedded a married woman. Whether this occurred during his college years or on one of the eleven days he admits to having been "absent from [Dr. Redman's] business" is unascertainable. The confession seems not to have cleared Rush's conscience—or the "particular *sin*" to have strayed very far from memory. More than thirty years later, in his autobiography—which he wrote primarily for his children—he reiterated the oblique admission to Hazard. Did he hope that by admitting it to his children Rush might at last obliterate whatever evil effect it might have had on his soul? We will never know. We do know, though, that while convinced, when writing to Hazard, of "being the chief sinner," Rush found his "heart more and more excited to an ardent, vehement desire about a *new nature* and an interest in Christ Jesus." That he now found his "mind more tender to sin of every kind" was tantamount to a conversion. He felt descending upon him what can be described as a spiritual peace.[12]

Before we leave Benjamin Rush's apprentice years and follow him across the Atlantic, where he became a full-fledged doctor, mention must be made of how, in the winter of his eighteenth year, he "was afflicted with a pulmonary complaint which continued, with occasionally a spitting of blood at longer or shorter intervals, until I was about forty years of age." The illness, not mentioned in his memoirs, was described in the last year of his life in response to one Vine Utley, a medical writer from Lyme, Connecticut, who had sent the preface to a medical work on which Utley requested his advice.

What Rush called "a pulmonary complaint" was probably a mild case of chronic pulmonary tuberculosis—then commonly called consumption—a leading cause of death in colonial America, exceeded only by periodic epidemics of smallpox. According to contemporary writers whose conclusions would find little favor with modern clinicians, the "pulmonary complaint" was particularly prevalent among the city's "fashionable women" because "they dance too much and then drink cold or iced water, or eat cold unripe fruit when they are hot; they drink boiling tea; they dress too lightly in winter and pay no attention to the changes of temperature so frequent in Philadelphia." Why Philadelphia was singled out, when consumption was a universal condition, is possibly because the observer chose to limit his study to that one city, perhaps on the theory that what sufficed for one sufficed for all. It was also believed that other contributory causes to the ailment included "eating too much meat" and "drinking too many spirits."[13]

Whether or not Rush subscribed to these theories, it is remarkable that until he rid himself of the disease he "lived chiefly upon vegetables, tea, coffee, and a small quantity of animal food. When most free from my disorder, I drank malt liquors and wine and took bark with advantage. In the paroxysms of my disease, whether induced by cold or any other cause," he bled himself and reduced his diet, "which generally relieved me in a few days." He also mentions in an aside that he had on occasion fallen victim to "several severe acute diseases, particularly pleurisy and bilious fevers" and "suffered likewise for months with vertigo and headache" both before and during the period under discussion. Then, going on to offer possibly more information about himself than solicited, an archetypical trait found throughout his voluminous correspondence, which in printed form runs to thousands of pages, Rush informs Utley that since his fifty-eighth year he has "enjoyed uninterrupted health, with the exception of now and then a catarrh, such as is common to persons of all ages in our country—" inflammation of the nasal or bronchial mucous membrane that causes an increase in the production of mucus, much like that in a common cold.

Advising that "through divine goodness" he was now sixty-eight and "possess[ed] the same facility in doing business and the same pleasure in study that I did when I was a young man," Rush wants Utley to know that he generally sleeps about seven hours a day, and spends from three to seven daily at his desk "according to the greater or less hurry of my business." Here he is doubtless referring both to his correspondence and his writing for medical journals or simply for publication on any number of topics covering the broad areas of medicine and politics—in particular, his fears for the direction in which the nation he had labored to found was heading. Returning to what keeps him fit, Rush says that he continues "to prefer tea and coffee with their usual accompaniment to all other kinds of aliment." He eats "sparingly of animal food, with the common garden vegetables of our country," followed by "one glass or glass and a half of old Madeira wine." He never drinks "ardent spirits in any way nor at any time. I see well with spectacles, and my hearing is unimpaired."

Then, in what can be interpreted either as a matter of pride or a matter of boasting, Rush goes on to note, "I appreciate the continuance and perfection of these two senses at 100,000 dollars a year"—truly an enormous sum for the times. He does, though, ascribe all credit where he believes it is due: "Blessed be God for them; without them life would be a living death." In the light of his lifelong genuine religiosity, we may suspect Rush was blessing God not for those hundred thousand dollars annually but for "the continuance and perfection" of his sight and hearing, both of which would accompany him to the grave.[14]

It was around the onset of his "pulmonary complaint" that the first of Benjamin Rush's extensive writings was published: "The Successful Minister of Christ Distinguished in Glory." Occasioned by the death of Gilbert Tennent, his admired pastor at the Secondary Presbyterian Church, and published under the byline "a young gentleman of Philadelphia" as a twelve-page addendum to the published eulogy by his uncle Samuel Finley, the essay comes off as a rather inconsequential compilation of just about every stylish banality of the period.

Still, it is a truly sincere commemoration by a teenager over the loss of a hero whose "tender soul" was stabbed with grief when "ruthless, bloodthirsty Indians" bearing "murdering hatchet" and "poisoned arrow" viciously grabbed infants "from their weeping, affrightened mothers' arms"; a hero whose "soul, like the setting sun, broke through the clouds of infirmity" in his declining years, whose insight "bloomed upon his silver locks, and while the cold hand of time snowed upon his head, his heart glowed with redoubled love for the church." Discernible among this veritable salmagundi of purple prose is the writer's evocation of the "old Puritan spirit" that had for "a series of years been asleep" but which "seemed to revive and blaze forth" in the now silenced Awakener "with a genuine luster."

Recalling how Gilbert Tennent in his powerful sermons thundered Jove-like when offended by any contravention of the Lord's commandments, Rush reminded the reader that "as he knew how to wound, so he knew how to pour the oil of consolation on the bleeding conscience." Rush wanted his idol to be remembered as one who "counseled, warned, and reproved them, with all the tenderness and solicitude of a father's heart." What is more, "it should never be forgotten that all men, notwithstanding color, social status, or economic condition, had equally free access" to this paragon among clerics whose "soul extended toward the human race."

Though he would ever more resort, on occasion, to formulaic locutions of the times, Rush would refine his literary manner. Still, the passions inherent in eulogizing Tennent would remain constant in all his published writings and personal correspondence, be they words of praise or castigation.

Rush planned to go abroad in 1765 to take a medical degree at the University of Edinburgh, encouraged by Redman, his mother—who agreed to underwrite the three years of study—and Dr. Morgan, who promised to use his now quite considerable influence in Philadelphia's medical circles to Benjamin's advantage upon his return. But, as he explained to Ebenezer Hazard (21 May 1765), Rush postponed the trip until the following summer, "in hope by hard study and longer attendance [as a Redman apprentice] on the practice of physic to fit myself better to make a figure in Europe and be of more use to society when I return." Not to cast doubt on the reason he gave Hazard, but two other factors should be mentioned: Redman's presumed suggestion that he improve his Latin and Greek before entering the academic world, and, perhaps of greater significance, the fact that he had fallen in love.

Benjamin had by now developed into "a comely young man above middle" (he was five feet, nine inches tall) with "highly animated" blue eyes and "an expressive face seldom seen in repose." He had a prominent forehead and an aquiline nose, but it was his head—"the diameter of his head from back to front was uncommonly large," said one contemporary—that impressed most observers. It was thought, to use the language of the age, that "the general traits of his physiognomy bespoke strength and activity of intellect." The young ladies of the town considered him quite good looking—his slender frame would thicken only with age—and he had no difficulty squiring around any that he chose. Busy as he was through the years of his apprenticeship, he managed to find time, though perhaps not as much as he would have preferred, to squire a respectable number. An attentive beau, rarely dull, he loved to talk, and needed no encouragement. Those who liked him spoke of Rush's "great powers of conversation." Those who didn't spoke of his propensity for talking "incessantly."[15] Recall John Adams's initial impression of Rush, quoted in the prologue to this book: "too much of a Talker to be a deep Thinker. Elegant not great."

Of all the objects of his affection, the one who doubtless played a role, albeit unwittingly, in his decision to postpone his trip abroad was Mary "Polly" Fisher. A year later, in a letter from Edinburgh to Thomas Bradford (15 April 1768), later the publisher of the *Pennsylvania Journal* and other newspapers, Rush described Polly as "the only woman I ever loved, and, I may add, ever shall. If ever I do marry, other motives of a sordid nature must influence me. *Love* never will." The marriage was forbidden by Rush's mother and stepfather, who gave him "unwelcome orders not to think of a wife for eight or ten years to come, as it would effectively shut the door against my providing for my sisters and their sons." Rachel and Rebecca had both recently become single mothers with three sons between them to raise. Moreover, Benjamin had to consider his younger brother Jacob, who had just graduated from Princeton and apprenticed himself to a Philadelphia lawyer, and might also wish to complete his education in London. There would, of course, be other women in Benjamin's life, and when he finally did marry it was truly for "*Love.*"

By the time he wrote the letter to Bradford, Rush had become "reconciled to my loss since I have been informed, not only from you but from other hands, that you have 'supplanted me in her affection.'" Bradford and Polly were married the November following the above quoted letter, and had a happy marriage that included numerous children that ended thirty-seven years later at Polly's death. They and Rush remained the best of friends. Bradford would publish a number of Rush's work, including his *Essays,* besides countless journalistic letters to the editor.

As he wrote in his memoirs, on the last day of August 1766—by which time Rush had more than exceeded Redman's expectations, was confident of a career under the aegis of the highly influential Morgan, and had presumably resigned himself to being denied "the only woman I ever loved"—Benjamin sailed for Liverpool on the *Friendship* "with a view of proceeding from there to Edinburgh in order to prosecute my studies in medicine."

3

Edinburgh

Rush's traveling companion was Jonathan Potts, who also intended to take his medical degree at Edinburgh but had to abort his studies and return home after a year when his fiancée's missing him had an adverse effect on her health.[1] Before sailing, the two students formed a friendship with a James Cummins. The young Scotsman was going to visit his parents in Aberdeenshire after losing both his fortune and his health trying to succeed as a planter in the West Indies. Rush recalled the fifty-one-day voyage as "stormy and dangerous. We were nearly lost on the coast of Ireland, and the next day narrowly escaped being wrecked . . . on the coast of Wales." Throughout the voyage he "suffered from seasickness. The only permanent relief I obtained was from Laudanum"—a solution of opium in alcohol that was a popular all-purpose medication for pain.[2] The trio arrived at Liverpool on 21 October 1776, and was entertained by several families to whom they had letters of introduction. On the twenty-fourth, Cummins died suddenly of a mysterious illness ("like a person in convulsions"). Rush and Potts "showed our respect for him by burying him at our own expense [which] was afterwards honourably reimbursed by his father."[3]

The day after arriving at Liverpool Rush wrote to Benjamin Franklin in London, where Franklin had been representing the colonies since 1764 and enjoyed the distinction of being the best-known and most highly respected American in Europe. Rush introduced himself and Potts as fellow Philadelphians "anxious to come under your patronage, as I well know your great love and partiality to the Province of Pennsylvania would readily include you to favor any one of its natives even though unknown to you." What he hoped Franklin would "favor" him with were a few letters of introduction. Regretting that due to time limitations he could not "do myself the honor of waiting upon you in person in London to intimate these my desires to you, I must therefore beg of you to write to such of your friends in Edinburgh, in behalf of Mr. Potts and myself, as you think will be most useful to us in the prosecution of our studies." The letter ended with a display of absolute sycophancy that will seem exasperating to modern ears but was perfectly in keeping with the times: "I hope, sir, you will excuse the freedom I have assumed in writing to you. During your stay in Philadelphia I was too young, and my confinement to study too close, to aspire after the honor of an acquaintance with you, although the high esteem I was early taught to entertain of that merit and learning, which have procured you to much reputation in the world would have prompted me to it."

Amused as well as flattered by such deference, Franklin dispatched letters at once to distinguished friends in Edinburgh, where the reputation he enjoyed was such that he had been given the freedom of the city while visiting there in 1759. One letter, to the eminent Scottish physician Sir Alexander Dick, requested that he be on the lookout for the two American students: "They are strongly recommended to me by many of my acquaintances as young gentlemen of ingenuity & application & excellent morals." And to the even more eminent Dr. William Cullen, he wrote that "from the character they bear of ingenuity, industry, & good morals, I am persuaded they will prove greatly under your learned lectures & do honor to your medical school."[4] The letters are not only fulsome, they suggest a knowledge of the two students that was rather exaggerated, since Franklin had never met them and probably never even heard of them.

But this was typical of Franklin when it came to aiding fellow colonials in establishing a foothold in Europe. The man who would emerge as the Nestor of the American Revolution very often offered gestures of assistance without being solicited, as when Rush arrived at London to begin his internship two years later. Franklin not only insisted on proffering an interest-free unsolicited loan, he initiated a friendship with the young physician forty years his junior that lasted until his death at eighty-four in 1790. Franklin became for Rush a role model as well as mentor, so much so that Rush planned a laudatory book of "Frankliniana" for which notes have survived, but which, regrettably, never appeared.[5]

On the last day of October, after a week sightseeing around Liverpool and attending to Cummins's interment in one of the city's Episcopal churchyards, Rush and Potts set off for Edinburgh by coach. They arrived there in the evening of 3 November after a journey whose worse moments had to have brought to mind memories of those storm-tossed days off the coasts of Ireland and Wales. Only the newest coaches of the day had springs. The two students rode in old coaches, over roads that were, more often than not, rock-strewn and pitted, and at times reduced to mud flats in which the horses would flounder and the coach sink to its axle.

After taking lodgings in the house of two maiden ladies named Galloway, Rush set about exploring the city that was to be his home for the two years he "consider[ed] as the most important in their influence upon my character and conduct of any period of my life." Edinburgh he would always look back upon as, notwithstanding his six years under Redman's tutelage, his birthplace as a physician.[6]

Comprising some eighty thousand inhabitants, the Scottish capital, about a third less than Philadelphia in area though twice its size in population, was called "Auld Reekie" by the natives because of the sooty smog that hung in the air most of the year. But Rush attributed the "reekie" to the crowded houses that subjected "the inhabitants to [sanitary] inconveniences, for as they have no yards or cellars, they have of course no necessary [out]houses, and all their filth of every kind is thrown out of their windows." Included in the filth was human waste—a not uncommon practice even in the more sophisticated city of London. The great diarist Pepys complains of having to "put my foot in a great heap of turds" while on his self-appointed rounds. The throwing in Edinburgh was "done in the night generally [and] carried away next morning by carts appointed for that purpose. Unhappy they who are obliged to walk out after ten or eleven o'clock at night." Noting that to be bombarded while abroad at night was "called here being *naturalized*," Rush notes facetiously that he "happily escaped being made a freeman of the city in this way," whereas his "unfortunate friend Potts" had "gained the honor before me."[7]

Rush also had some approving words to say about "the moral order which prevailed" among Edinburgians regardless of class:

Silence pervaded the streets . . . after 10 o'clock at night. The churches were filled on Sundays. I never saw a pack of cards in either a public or private house. Dancing supplied the place of insipid conversation in all large evening companies. Swearing was rarely heard in genteel life, and drunkenness was rarely seen among the common people. Instances of fraud were scarcely known among Servants. But integrity descended still lower among the humble ranks of life. I once saw the following advertisement pasted up at the door of the play house, "The gentleman who gave the orange woman a guinea instead of a penny last night is requested to call at the check office for it." This universal morality was not accidental. It was the effect of the parochial instructions of the clergy, who were at that time a regular and conscientious body of men. I have heard with pain that a great change for the worse has taken place in the morals and manners of the inhabitants of that once happy city. Nor was I surprised at it when I heard that the works of several of the most popular writers against Christianity were to be met with in the hands of journeymen mechanics of all descriptions.[8]

After settling into their lodgings, Rush and Potts presented their letters of introduction from Dr. Morgan to Cullen. These, in tandem with the one that Cullen had by now received from Franklin, sufficed to allow them to matriculate. They immediately obtained tickets of admission to the different lectures that would constitute their course of study.

Though the University of Edinburgh dated back to 1583, it took a century and a charter from King Charles II before a medical college was founded (1681). Forty years before Rush's arrival, the faculty of medicine had become part of the university, indeed, its most celebrated part. Even earlier the faculty had achieved fame for its line of preeminent anatomists, all named Alexander Munro—distinguished by the cognomens *Primus, Secundus,* and *Tertius*—whose successive birth dates spanned the century from 1697 to 1773. Rush studied with *Secundus,* for whom the Foramen of Munro, the opening that connects the ventricles of the brain, is named. Unfortunately, during this period the teaching quality of anatomy declined due to the scarcity of cadavers for dissection. This led to grave robbing by determined students, called with macabre ghoulishness "Resurrectionists."

Edinburgh's medical faculty was the world's most celebrated. Of these, two stand out in bold relief. One was Dr. Joseph Black, the discoverer of carbon dioxide, who had just succeeded the other, the aforementioned Cullen, in the chair of chemistry. Rush had been urged by Morgan to study with Black. This would qualify him for a teaching position in chemistry—a discipline to Rush's particular liking—at the College of Philadelphia upon his return. Cullen, who had just been elevated to the chair of the theory of medicine, was the school's star attraction. Through his writings and a succession of American students, his ultimate influence on the practice of medicine in the New World would complement his standing as the head of the British medical profession in the second half of the eighteenth century. Among his private patients and personal friends were just about all the major figures of the Enlightenment in Scotland, notably the great Scottish philosopher and historian David Hume. Cullen was quickly won over by Rush's enthusiasm, dedication, and application.

Unlike Rush's American teachers, including Redman, who were theological rather than scientific in outlook, Cullen was exploratory, skeptical, and tentative in methodology and nondogmatic in his thinking. His empirical approach to medicine, which represented a challenge to the received knowledge of the times, strongly supported the possibilities of medical speculation, as reflected in his recognition of the importance played by the nervous system in health and disease. His urging that medical systems be devised to conform with the advance in knowledge of each generation, instead of remaining fixed and immutable, took hold with Rush, who would go on to develop his own revolutionary theories. As an apprentice, Rush had already begun to question many of the archaic approaches by medical practitioners that would strike their modern counterparts as either purveyors of voodoo or itinerant snake-oil salesmen.

While influencing Rush in terms of medical methodology, Cullen exerted no lasting influence on Rush's philosophy. He could have, had Rush been receptive to his ideas. But Cullen was a product of the Enlightenment, which offered Newtonianism and Cartesianism as systems of thought. Rush, being a product of the Great Awakening, was an a priori thinker whose attitudes toward the world of experience, molded by Tennent, Finley, and Davies, were deeply theological. Admittedly, Rush would later acknowledge the thinking of Locke and

Francis Bacon in one of his many didactic essays, "On the Necessary Connection between Observation and Reasoning in Medicine." Still, his way of reasoning was ontological—the argument propounded by St. Anselm and others to prove the existence of God by pointing to God's essence as a perfect, necessary being—and deductive, more in the Continental tradition of Descartes than in the tradition of British empiricism. Rush was able to embrace Cullen's empirical approach to medicine. But Cullen's empirical approach to religion, rooted as it was in skepticism, found no favor in a young man steeped in orthodox Presbyterian sensibilities.[9]

"It is scarcely possible to do Justice to this great man's Character either as a scholar—a physician—or a Man," writes Rush in his *Scottish Journal* of the man who most influenced him as a physician, and, by extension, all American physicians who followed in Rush's path. "[I]n a word, I loved him like a Father, & if at present I entertain any Hopes of being eminent in my Profession I owe them entirely to this great man." But Rush did find "one thing however wanting in Dr. Cullen to constitute his Character a complete one, *viz.*: a Regard to religion."

Not that he found Cullen, whom he quickly came to all but worship, was in any way disrespectful of religious matters, let alone blasphemous. He was, admitted Rush, a man of "innate Dignity & Superiority of Soul," incapable of permitting his religious skepticism to give offense. It did, though, run counter to Rush's "absolutistic, Great Awakening mentality." Put another way, Rush was infinitely more concerned with, and impressed by, Cullen's approach to Aesculapius, the god of medicine, than to Yahweh, the god of monotheism. However, what proselytizing Cullen practiced was confined to his medical lectures—which, breaking with tradition, he delivered in English instead of Latin. And, unlike the preponderance of university icons, he interacted warmly, almost paternalistically, with pupils, particularly those he became fond of, like Rush. They were invited into his home for meals and general conversation. We can safely assume that all conversation was limited to medicine.[10]

In later years as a professor at the University of Pennsylvania, Rush, like Cullen, encouraged freedom of inquiry and discussion among his students. David Ramsay wrote that Rush would welcome criticism of his own theory of disease and urged his students "to think and judge for themselves, and would freely, and in a friendly manner, explain his principles, resolve their doubts, listen to their objections, and either yield to their force, or show their fallacy."[11]

From July 1769, when he returned to Philadelphia, until October 1789, when he was named to succeed the by then deceased Dr. Morgan as professor of the theory and practice of medicine in the College of Philadelphia, Rush considered himself the chief disciple of Cullen. Only with his election to the chair of the theory and practice of medicine did he feel constrained to formulate his own "System of principles in medicine," which had been evolving from his experience and thought as a physician.[12] Rush may have remembered on that occasion Dr. Cullen's advice to his classes:

> When a student has learned one system, if he cannot think for himself, he should keep to the system of his master as religious as he can, and allow no other views to disturb him; but if a student can think for himself, and every one believes that he can, he will no sooner have learned a particular system than he will be disposed to differ from it; he will immediately find that others also do so, and that the conflict of opinions is unavoidable. He will, therefore, wish to view matters in different lights, and, though he prefers no one Professor, yet, by comparing them, he becomes stronger in reasoning, and firmer in his own conclusions.[13]

However, even with the formulation of his own system, Rush's rebellion was more apparent than real, since the framework of his thought remained Cullenian. When Cullen died in 1790, Rush eulogized him before the College of Physicians at Philadelphia: "While Astronomy claims a Newton, and Electricity a Franklin, Medicine has been equally honoured by having employed the genius of a Cullen."[14]

Rush's attention to Dr. Joseph Black was overshadowed by his homage to Cullen, with good reason. In his late thirties, despite his accomplishments in chemistry, Black had not yet established himself as a famous lecturer. He was, moreover, only the brilliant student of Cullen, in Rush's view, and still not a towering figure in his own right. Rush was perceptive enough, however, with not a little encouragement from Dr. Morgan before leaving Philadelphia, to realize the value of Black's lectures in chemistry, which he attended twice and scrupulously recorded.[15] These, he knew, would fortify his appointment for the chemistry position at the College of Philadelphia, for which Morgan was promoting him.

As he did with Cullen, Rush confined his appreciation of the man's empiricism to his medical teaching. So persevering was he in his studies with Black that by the time of his graduation in 1768 Rush had become an expert in Black's system of chemistry, probably the best available at that time. Thus, in chemistry, as in medicine, Rush easily assimilated the elements of what may be termed the Edinburgh School of Baconian scientific method. Black's open-minded empirical techniques, like Cullen's, posed no philosophical difficulty for Rush as an a priori theological thinker. When he assumed the professorship of chemistry at the College of Philadelphia in 1769, Rush based his lectures upon his notes from Black's courses at Edinburgh. Rush's *Syllabus of a Course of Lectures on Chemistry* (1770), the first American-written text in chemistry, essentially followed Black's system.[16]

While it is true that Rush ultimately derived his understanding of nature from his Great Awakening teachers and personal religious experience, and never really comprehended the secular meaning of Enlightenment science as it was being taught at Edinburgh, he did acquire from his new studies the idea of secondary sources to explain natural events. At Nottingham and Princeton, Finley and Davies had trained him to account for all things by invoking God, the first cause. Their explanations of the physical world were supernatural, not natural. After studying at Edinburgh, Rush came to understand the distinction between primary and secondary causation, and how he could synthesize his Great Awakening view of God as the primary cause of the physical world with the Enlightenment doctrine of secondary, natural causes. His mature philosophy of animal life, published in 1799, shows this.[17] By then, Rush had adapted the idea of the Enlightenment to his theological mentality. Given the role he played in the nation's founding, and in particular the influence of the Enlightenment on those Founding Fathers, most notably Jefferson, who were the American Revolution's principal philosophers and articulators, one doubts it could have been otherwise.

Rush left no account of his student days at Edinburgh, other than his comments on personalities such as Cullen and Black in his correspondence, and fleetingly in his late-life memoirs and his *Scottish Journal.* On the basis of what has come down to us from other sources, however, and assuming he would have fallen in step with the custom of fellow students, we can picture his day beginning about seven A.M. After studying in his room all morning, he spent the afternoon in classes and touring infirmary wards, with an hour for dinner in midafternoon. Following a light supper at six, he devoted the evening to copying over and reviewing notes and doing some general reading, and was in bed by midnight. The routine, which varied only on Sundays, lasted from November to May. During the summer of 1767, though insecure in his command of German, he studied Spanish and Italian on his own, and French with a tutor—against the possibilities of a postgraduate European tour. He also struggled with Latin, which had always been a bane and was now a necessity: though Cullen's courses were in English, a custom quickly adopted by most of the other enlightened professors, all formal dissertations had to be written and delivered in Latin.

By the end of his first year Rush had won the praise of his professors and was invited to join the Medical Society. Founded by students in 1737, the society was by now so reputable that its membership included most of the university professors. It later evolved into the Royal Medical Society of Edinburgh. Writing to his Princeton classmate Jonathan Bayard Smith, Rush describes how "We meet once a week and dispute upon subjects in philosophy and the practice of physic. Each member is obliged to write a long dissertation in his turn upon a disease, or upon some of the animal functions, or any other subject, the president of the Society may propose to him, and is obliged to defend it publicly against all attacks from any person in the society." Rush spent his initial winter as a member "in prosecuting my favorite study, *Chemistry.* I know of no science in the world which affords more rational entertainment than this. It is not only a science of importance in itself, but serves as a key to a thousand other sources of knowledge."[18]

Rush also enjoyed great social success, meeting and enjoying the hospitality of leading members of the city's medical, social, and philosophical circles. Of these, the star attraction was David Hume, to whom Rush was introduced by Franklin's friend Sir Alexander Dick. "Mr. Hume's Appearance was no ways engaging—his Person was rather ungenteel and clumsy, he spoke but little, but what he said was always pertinent and sensible," Rush recorded in his *Scottish Journal.* A year later, on consideration, Rush added that Hume was "a Gentleman of the most amiable private Character, and much beloved by every Body that knows him." This was a considerable concession for Rush, a confirmed Whig, to whom Hume's Tory religious and political views ranged from objectionable to repugnant. Still, while a delegate to the Second Continental Congress, Rush employed the arguments expressed by the great Scottish philosopher in his *History of England.* He considered Hume's literary style nothing short of magnificent, and influential. He admitted to John Adams a quarter of a century and literally thousands of letters and published articles and essays later that by the means of Hume, along with some of Swift's works and Robert Lowth's *A Short Introduction to English Grammar,* published in 1762 and much reprinted and used in schools, "I learned to put words together."[19]

Of all the people Rush met at Edinburgh who most influenced his political thinking, pride of place goes to fellow medical student John Bostock, to whom he'd been commended by a mutual Liverpool acquaintance. Bostock, who would enjoy a distinguished practice at Liverpool until his death in his mid-thirties, exercised a strong influence in transforming what had been Rush's anger directed at Parliament over the Stamp Act into a confirmed republican enmity directed at the Sovereign, personified in George III. A friendship quickly blossomed when the two learned they shared the distinction of being descended from men who had served under Oliver Cromwell. Bostock, recalled Rush, "opened his mind fully to me, and declared himself to be an advocate for the Republican principles for which our ancestors had fought"—citing as inspiration the writings of Algernon Sidney, the seventeenth-century political rebel whose republican views provoked his execution for treason by Charles II. After being subjected to what would today be termed an ongoing rant by the fiercely antimonarchical Bostock in support of the compact theory of government, and the writings of Sidney and, closer to their own time, John Locke, whose philosophy would figure prominently in Jefferson's thinking when it came to composing the Declaration of Independence, Rush had to admit:

> Never before had I heard the authority of Kings called in question.
> I had been taught to consider them nearly as essential to political

order as the Sun is to the order of our Solar System. For the first moment in my life I now exercised my reason upon the subject of government. I renounced the prejudices of my education upon it; and from that time to the present all my reading, observations and reflections have tended more and more to show the absurdity of hereditary power, and to prove that no form of government can be rational but that which is derived from the Suffrages of the people who are the subjects of it.

The argument advanced by some historians that Rush exaggerated the suddenness of his conversion to republicanism, given his having ardently opposed the Stamp Act, does not quite wash. Like so many other Americans—in particular those who remained Loyalists when the Revolution began—his initial argument had been taxation without representation, and not condemnation of monarchy. Rush continues:

> This great and active truth became a ferment in my mind. I now suspected error in everything I had been taught, or believed, and as far as I was able to began to try the foundations of my opinions upon many other subjects. The sequel of my scepticism and investigations will appear hereafter. It has been said that there is no such thing as a solitary error in the human mind. The same may be said of truths. They are all related. . . . I shall only add in this place, that the change produced in my political principles by my friend Bostock had no effect upon any conversation or conduct. I considered the ancient order of things with respect to government as fixed and perpetual, and I enjoyed in theory only the new and elevating system of government I had adopted.[20]

In other words, the seeds had been planted; only in time, and the playing out of events during his post-Edinburgh years back at Philadelphia, would they blossom into a hybrid best described as a Physician/Political Revolutionist.

Young Rush was adept at, to put it anachronistically, networking. He met—and impressed—the leading Scottish men of influence, most notably the internationally celebrated evangelical divine, John Erskine, who "honoured me with many acts of attention and friendship."[21] He also became friendly with two of the city's most prominent bankers, William Hogg, who died just weeks after their meeting, and his son Thomas, with whose family Rush became particularly close. It was through Thomas Hogg that Rush was introduced to one of the landed gentry, David Leslie, the Earl of Leven. Rush was a guest several times at the Earl's estate, Melville, some twelve miles from Edinburgh.

There, in addition to forming lasting friendships with the Earl's sons Alexander and David, he became besotted with their sixteen-year-old sister Lady Jane.

Though he said nothing about her in letters to friends back home, the twenty-one-year-old Rush had plenty to say in his *Scottish Journal*. He was blinded by her radiance and left speechless by her beauty, which when blended "with all the additional strength which education, virtue, spotless innocence and sweetness of temper give, then its power becomes irresistible [and] when these amiable endowments meet in a person of high rank and fortune they strike us with something divine." She had "a complete knowledge of music," and when she sang Scottish airs it was with a lisp that left Rush as "overcome with delight" as when she spoke in impeccable French: "What Politeness! What an Address, what an Insinuating Manner does she possess! The Law of Kindness is written in her Heart, words like Honey drip from her Tongue. In a word Heaven is in her Eye—Grace is in her Look—in every Step there is Dignity and Love. Methinks She possesses Charms eno' to revive the Garden of Eden and restore the joys of Paradise itself."

While he dearly loved Lady Jane, and her affection for him was enough to guarantee a happy marriage, it all came to naught. Rush had other priorities: pursuing his studies, and returning home to assume the burden of family responsibilities and launch a career in medicine. The romance petered out before it got even properly launched. Rush seemed to have an innate faculty for falling madly in love with young ladies and suffering with equanimity and no lasting scars from the failure of matrimonial consummation. In fact, they maintained an epistolary friendship after Rush returned to America. Lady Jane went on to marry into the Scottish aristocracy. Rush would go on to further dalliances and one more great, ill-fated passion before finding the love of his life, Julia Stockton.

Ironically, Rush figured prominently during a mission that brought his future father-in-law to Edinburgh. Richard Stockton was a prominent New Jersey attorney and one of the wealthiest and most influential men in the colonies. When Rush's uncle Samuel Finley died while president of Princeton, the college's board of trustees chose the famed theologian John Witherspoon as his successor. Stockton, a member of the board, was sent to Scotland to officially inform him.

Witherspoon accepted the invitation to come to America, with some reservation. But after Stockton returned home, Rush learned that Witherspoon had decided to decline the offer. Rush took it upon himself to change his mind, encouraged from afar by Stockton. Rush "dined and supped frequently" with Witherspoon whenever he came to preach in Edinburgh, and was "charmed by his behavior. He appears to be Mr. Davies and Dr. Finley revived in one man. In point of genius he is equal to the first, and in knowledge I believe he is superior even to Dr. Finley himself, more specifically in the branch of knowledge that is nowadays so much admired, *viz.*, the Belles-Lettres. I have heard him preach twice and can truly say he exceeds any preacher I *have* ever heard since I came to Scotland. Indeed, I have heard few preachers in the course of my life that were equal to him."[22]

Sincere as his opinion of Witherspoon was, Rush's primary fear was that if he refused the Princeton presidency it would go to Dr. Francis Alison, an Old Side Presbyterian. On 23 April 1767, Rush wrote an impassioned letter to Witherspoon: "And must poor Nassau Hall indeed be ruined? . . . Recollect the pain you will give the friends of the College and the lovers of religion in America. They have had their expectations highly raised and their hopes much encouraged" by word that he would be coming. And now that he wasn't—and here Rush slyly implied a threat that the great preacher had to have given at least some consideration: "Their grief and vexation will be proportioned to their former hopes, and while they mourn over the forlorn, destitute state of the College, they will remember and mention your name (once precious to them) only by way of obloquy and censure."

When that failed to do the trick, Rush journeyed to Witherspoon's parish at Paisley, a few miles outside Glasgow, to make a personal appeal. It was then that he learned that the biggest drawback was Mrs. Witherspoon's fear of making an Atlantic crossing. Aided by Witherspoon, Rush succeeded in allaying her fears: "The Doctor with his family soon afterwards embarked for America. The College flourished under him for many years. He gave a new turn to education, and spread taste and correctness in literature throughout the United States."[23]

He did more. Witherspoon gave America perhaps its most articulate clerical spokesman, organized the American Presbyterian Church, signed the Declaration of Independence, was one of the leading Revolutionary patriots, and in his teaching and writings at the College of New Jersey combined Scottish Enlightenment philosophy with republican ideas of government.[24]

For his dissertation, obligatory for an M.D. degree, Rush chose to do research on fermentation, which involved four experiments—three upon himself, the fourth upon a friend—that called for imbibing and then regurgitating a full meal to test for remains of acid. His conclusion, which went against conventional wisdom of the times, was that "digestion is carried on *chiefly* by fermentation, and that the stomach stands in need of no other exercise, during this process, than its own gentle peristaltic motions, which serve both to mix the aliment and to discharge it from the stomach." He successfully defended his thesis, which was published a few years later in the *Pennsylvania Journal* (11 June 1772). By then his reputation for refusing to settle for established medical notions if more advanced ones could be proved—perhaps Cullen's greatest contribution to his medical philosophy—was rapidly gaining Rush a prestigious reputation in colonial America's medical circles that would be matched by his growing reputation in political circles.

On 19 June 1768, having successfully passed his final examinations, Rush "was admitted to the Degree of Doctor of Medicine" after taking an oath in which he and the other successful candidates "swore that we would never wantonly try experiments with any of our patients, nor yet divulge any thing that had been told us as a secret," whereupon "a cap was put on our heads and we were declared publicly Doctors of Physic."[25] Now considering himself "master of the science" of chemistry and convinced he "could teach it with confidence and ease," Rush felt more than confident that Morgan would, as he had promised, keep open the chemistry professorship at the College of Physicians pending his return. But he foresaw a problem with Redman, whose approval was obligatory; this despite his not being a member of the faculty, but because of his reputation among the city's medical establishment and his close ties with Rush. Redman was well enough acquainted with Cullen's overall empiricism to wonder how much he might have "infected" his orthodox Presbyterian apprentice.

Fearing that Adam Kuhn, who had recently received his M.D. from Edinburgh and returned to Philadelphia to become professor of botany, might wind up with the post Rush so sorely wanted, he wrote a harsh letter to Morgan (20 January 1769) reproaching Redman. Meanwhile, a letter was making its slow way across the Atlantic that would make the new Doctor of Physic realize that in attacking Redman for having learned, presumably through the more open-minded Morgan, that their young protégé had become in a medical sense a confirmed Cullenian, Rush had simply yelled ouch before being scratched. Even before Morgan received the letter, one arrived at Edinburgh from Redman in which he expressed his great affection for his former apprentice—his favorite among his "professional children." In a follow-up letter he expressed the opinion that the trustees should not promise a professorship "so long before the qualifications of a person could be certainly determined." Nevertheless, he assured Rush that he and Morgan would block all applications for the position pending his return to Philadelphia, adding reassuringly, "nor has the person you might suspect [i.e., Kuhn] (or any other) applied, well knowing from proper hints what he might expect if he had." To quote Rush biographer David Freeman Hawke, "Redman ended on a note of affection. Rush was justifiably convinced that the chair in chemistry he so coveted would be his. The father-son relationship of old had died, though; and when friendship resumed between him and Redman, it would be on Rush's terms, as equals."[26]

Thanks to the scientific teaching of Cullen and Black and, especially, the political rationalism of Bostock and Sidney—which helped the young American make sense of his colonial experience as a rebel against British authority—Rush came under the influence of Enlightenment liberalism with its Baconian empiricism and absolute trust in reason. But as one of the "Party for Jesus Christ," he rejected the extreme rationalism of the Enlightenment, accepting in his philosophy of reform certain ideas of the secular philosophers, like the ideas of social and physical science, progress, and benevolence. These he could accept because they were theologically consistent with his Great Awakening belief in God as the primary cause of all things. After leaving Edinburgh in 1768, Rush was to continue his education in the school of Enlightenment liberalism among the Whigs and philosophers of London and Paris.

Rush had planned to leave for London immediately upon receiving his degree, for further study, but delayed his departure in order to take an additional course under Cullen and spend more time with the Leven family and the fair Lady Jane. Shortly after the Cullen lecture ended, in September, Rush set out for London, convinced, somewhat melodramamatically, that, as he told his son James years later (19 March 1810), "The happiest part of my life is now over. My halcyon days have been spent in Edinburgh."

4

London and Paris

Relations between England and the colonies had deteriorated steadily while Rush was in Edinburgh. In 1767, the British Parliament passed the Townshend Acts, named for their sponsor, British Chancellor of the Exchequer Charles Townshend. The first measure suspended the New York Assembly for noncompliance with a law enacted two years earlier requiring all the colonies to adequately quarter British troops. The second, known as the Revenue Act, imposed duties on the import of glass, paints, lead, paper, and tea. The major complaint from America was articulated by thirty-five-year-old John Dickinson, a Maryland-born Philadelphia lawyer. In his *Letters from a Farmer in Pennsylvania to the Inhabitants of the British Colonies*, Dickinson argued "that we cannot be happy, without being free; that we cannot be free without being secure in our property; that we cannot be sure in our property, if, without our consent, others may, as by right, take it away; that taxes imposed on us by Parliament, do take it away."[1]

When the colonies resorted to nonimportation there were calls for appeasement in Parliament. The appeasement debate died, the Crown dissolved the Massachusetts legislature—the Bay Colony had been the chief instigator against England's American policies—and British troops posted in Halifax were ordered to occupy Boston. Two years later, in March 1770, British troops fired on American demonstrators. This was the so-called Boston Massacre that changed the question from *will* the colonials rebel to *when* will the colonials rebel?

In September 1768, as British troops were arriving at Boston, Rush arrived at London, "determined to spend a winter" in postgraduate studies, "although I never proposed [i.e., anticipated] any great improvement" over what he had already learned. Having attended "the lectures and practice of the great Dr. Cullen," he was "sure little knowledge can be acquired from the random prescriptions [i.e., knowledge] of the London hospital physicians." Still, he conceded there were a few from whom he might gain enough to justify his feeling that "as my reputation may be influenced by it, I shall follow them faithfully for some months."[2]

Wishing to be closer to the hospitals and lectures he planned to attend, Rush moved after a few days into a house in the Haymarket of a widow, Hannah Jeffries, where his cousin Thomas Coombe, in London to be ordained in the Anglican Church, also lodged. He immediately set out to acquaint himself with the city, visiting such popular tourist attractions as Westminster Abbey, the Tower of London, the British Museum, which he particularly enjoyed, and Parliament, which at the time was not in session. When he entered the House of Lords, he "felt as if I walked on sacred ground. I gazed for some time at the Throne with emotions that I cannot describe." Asking the guard if he might sit on it, and told that it was not "common for strangers" to do so, Rush "prevailed upon him to allow me the liberty. I accordingly advanced towards it and sat in it for a considerable time. When I first got into it, I was seized with a kind of horror which for some time interrupted my ordinary train of thinking. 'This,' said I (in the words of Dr. Young [presumably a paraphrase that has never been identified]), 'is the golden period of the worldly man's wishes. His passions conceive, his hopes aspire after nothing beyond this Throne.' I endeavored to arrange my thoughts into some order, but such a crowd of ideas poured in upon my mind that I can scarcely recollect one of them."

To put Rush's attitude here in its proper context, it must be realized that at this time the colonies, enjoying their own legislatures, believed they answered to the Crown, not to Parliament. In time, Rush, like all other pro-separation colonials, would come to hate the king as well as Parliament. This hatred began when George III followed the lead of a succession of politically myopic ministries, all of whom ignored the tradition of autonomous colonial self-government and began to treat the Americans as subjects of Parliament as well as subjects of the king. Whether events might have turned out differently if George III had surrounded himself with ministers who favored a fair and rational attitude toward the colonies is worth pondering.

From the House of Lords Rush went into the House of Commons. Here he could not say he felt as if walking on "sacred ground." To him it was "the place where the infernal scheme for enslaving America was first broached. Here the usurping Commons first endeavored to rob the King of his supremacy over the colonies and to divide it among themselves. O! cursed haunt of venality, bribery, and corruption!" In the midst of these reflections Rush asked where William Pitt stood when as prime minister he delivered his ringing defense of American resistance to the Stamp Act that led to its repeal. When the guide said, "Here, on this very spot," Rush "then went up to it, sat down upon it for some time, and fancying myself surrounded with a crowded House, rose up from my seat, and began to repeat" part of Pitt's great speech: "When the scheme for taxing America was first proposed, I was unhappily confined to my bed. But had some kind hand brought me and laid me down upon this floor, I would have bore a public testimony against it. Americans are the sons, not the bastards of Englishmen. I rejoice that America has resisted."

In describing the experience to his friend Ebenezer Hazard (22 October 1768), Rush expostulated: "O sir! How grand must have been the entertainment to have heard this once illustrious patriot declaiming with more than Roman eloquence in favor of his distant oppressed countrymen!" (Pitt lost a large part of his popularity when he accepted being named first Earl of Chatham and thus abandoned the House of Commons for the House of Lords.) So overcome was Rush by the moment and the memory, he "was ready to kiss the very walls that had re-echoed to his voice upon that glorious occasion, and to repeat again the enchanting sounds."3

Twice the size of Edinburgh, the sprawling London was for Rush a jolting adjustment after the Scottish capital. He found London "a rude change after the compact panorama of Edinburgh and the friendliness of his fellow students." This London, in which flourished the likes of such creative and intellectual giants as Hogarth, Christopher Wren, and Dr. Johnson, was also the London "of alehouses and taverns and gin swigging"—sights profoundly disagreeable to the orthodox Calvinists of the Scottish capital—"of elegant lords and their ladies and liveried footmen, of dim street lights and vice and cruelty and grime and public hangings, and the London of stately colorful processions." One procession Rush witnessed was the monarch he still respected but would soon come to loathe being driven ceremoniously through the streets of London to open a session of Parliament.[4]

Rush was soon pleasantly surprised to learn that his fear that he had little to learn in London was without foundation. London had some superb physicians—a few of them like Rush himself students of the revered Cullen—whose lectures and methodology contributed significantly to his already extensive medical knowledge and skills. Among the most noteworthy he singles out in his memoirs were the Hunter brothers, William and John, William Hewson, Mark Akenside, Richard Huck Saunders, and Sir John Pringle. William Hunter, renowned Scottish anatomist, surgeon, and obstetrician conducted with his even more famous brother John a school in anatomy where many of the best British surgeons of the period were trained. Hewson was also a brilliant anatomist whose experiments greatly advanced the knowledge and function of the human lymphatic system. Akenside, one of the physicians to Queen Charlotte, was principal physician at St. Thomas's Hospital, one of the two hospitals where Rush made rounds with his eminent teachers.

The other was Middlesex Hospital, where he found Dr. William Hunter's lectures "entertaining as well as instructing." Akenside, described by Rush as "distant and formal in his behaviour to the Students," was also exceedingly rough and cruel to the poor patients on his hospital rounds: "The most supercilious and unfeeling physician that I had then, or have since known." Huck Saunders ("Dr. Huck") was "the reverse of this. He was communicative and friendly. I owe him much for many civilities." It was Saunders who introduced Rush to Sir John Pringle, the founder of modern military medicine and a man of great influence in scientific circles. Pringle invited Rush "to attend a medical conversation party held once a week at his house [as well as] a similar meeting of Physicians at the Doctor's own house on another evening of the week, and [I] often dined with him in large and highly polished companies."[5]

The sixty-one-year-old Pringle was a walking almanac of attitudes and opinions that could be both attractive and off-putting, depending on the attitude and opinions of those who crossed his threshold. Well educated, an honored lecturer at just about all of Europe's leading universities and hospitals, Pringle had served with the British army in America and the West Indies during the French and Indian War. Despite his renown, Rush found him to be "so modest that he seldom spoke even at his own table without blushing. He was polite, correct, and just in his intercourse with the world." His "politicks," though, was something else. A "high-toned Royalist," he "never discovered any irritability of temper, except when he spoke against the claims of America, or the conduct of the opposition to" the government of George III. As Hawke notes, having once justified bribery among British cabinet ministers to obtain a staunchly royalist majority in the House of Commons on the grounds that "it was necessary to bribe the rascals in order to make them honest," Pringle was emphatic in his conviction that "the happiest people he had seen in his travels were those who enjoyed the least liberty."[6]

Rush wisely refrained from challenging Pringle's concept of "the happiest people" because it was in his nature to maintain the best possible relationship with anyone who could advance his career. Through Pringle, Rush met Dr. Maxwell Garthshore, one of London's most prominent accoucheurs, Gowin Knight, prominent physician and physicist who was also principal librarian of the British Museum, and George Fordyce, a leading teacher of medicine and chemistry and a member of Dr. Samuel Johnson's Literary Club. Additionally, Rush met several other respected members of the medical profession at Pringle's house, "from each of whom I always heard something that was capable of being applied to practical and useful purposes."

Through letters of introduction Rush was "taken up" by "the celebrated" Dr. John Fothergill, another friend of Franklin's and a fellow member of the Club of Honest Whigs. Rush, to whom Fothergill also took an immediate liking that was quickly reciprocated—not the least of their mutual attraction being their Whig politics—was invited by Fothergill to breakfast with him once a week. Rush not only enjoyed discussing politics but, even more so, medicine in all its ramifications with the famed physician who described facial neuralgia and "ulcerated sore throat."

Of all the important men Fothergill introduced Rush to, perhaps the one who had the most lasting influence was a physician three years his senior, John Coakley Lettsom. Lettsom had been raised in the

West Indies and was living with Fothergill while establishing himself in London. Both young men were remarkably alike in character and temperament; they liked to pursue the ladies, and balanced immense ambition with a comparable eagerness to leave the world on departing it at least a little better than they had found it on entering. Lettsom's influence on Rush would lead to his founding in post-Revolutionary America a medical society for physicians and the new nation's first humane society. This in turn paved the way for Rush's becoming the father of veterinary medicine. Moreover, Lettsom's sharing of his experiences on a West Indies plantation, where the horrendous effects of slavery were a constant sight, doubtless influenced the abolitionist views Rush was to express a few years later, putting him in the forefront of the earliest and most passionate advocates of manumission south of Boston.

The friendship between the two continued by mail until Rush's death, when Lettsom in his affectionately eulogistic "Recollections of Dr. Rush" (1815) captured the revolutionary passion that was a binding factor in their relationship. He recalled a visit the two made to a London "disputing society" at which one of the orators disparaged the spirit of rebellion already brewing in the American colonies by insinuating "that if the Americans possessed even cannon, they had not a ball to fire." Whereupon Rush jumped to his feet and shot back "that if the Americans possessed no cannonballs, they could supply the deficiency by digging up the skulls of those ancestors who had courted expatriation from the old hemisphere under the vivid hope of enjoying more ample freedom in the new one!"[7]

In addition to their weekly breakfasts, Fothergill was one of the physicians with whom Rush walked the wards of Middlesex and St. Thomas's hospitals. Built two centuries earlier under a charter granted by Henry VIII's heir, the ill-fated boy-king Edward VI, St. Thomas's was the larger of the two, having been expanded to meet the demands of the growing population. Every Thursday was "taking in day," when new patients were admitted for examination. Rush as a pupil assisted. In this way he was able not only to observe a variety of illnesses but also to observe the practical work of his masters in hopes of learning to emulate their skills.

Diagnostic procedures were primitive. Even counting the pulse and taking the temperature were not practiced, although Galileo had measured both.* Diagnoses were made by "looking, hearing, touching, smelling, and tasting and on inferences arrived at by intuition and experience and by happy guesses." Even more primitive than diagnostic procedures were therapeutic ones. "The kind and number of prescriptions written for the men, women, and children who crowded the out-patient department at St. Thomas's Hospital on Wednesday, Thursday, and Friday mornings were legion. It has been true in medicine, and it still is, that the less we know about a disease, the more remedies are used for it."[8]

But by then, reforms in diagnoses and therapeutics, like reforms in the pharmacopoeia, were slowly evolving, which Rush would employ in his own practice. Still, such practices as bleeding, purging ("the puke"), and blistering ("cupping") were held on to by the majority of his contemporaries. Letting go of the past was easier said than done. Even men of such eminence as Fothergill continued to include many of the old remedies with the new. "The test of a remedy was still purely pragmatic and empirical. Careful physiological investigations and the statistical methods and controls of modern medicine had not yet come into being. Rush himself grew up with these conventional eighteenth-century methods, and he was never able to rise above them."[9]

While Rush was in London, other reforms were underway that contributed greatly to the improvement in general health and personal hygiene. Due to the cheapness of cotton goods, clothing was introduced that could be washed. Theretofore, wives of the lower class had worn unwashable leather stays day after day for years, and quilted petticoats, stuffed with wool and horsehair, which were worn until they rotted. Also, iron bedsteads replaced the old vermin-infested wooden ones.

But the greatest innovation from a social point of view was the dispensary movement begun in 1750 that offered free medicines and medical advice for the poor. Prior to this time, medicine had been

---

*Though clinical thermometers had been first introduced by Fahrenheit in 1714, during the American Civil War there were no more than a half dozen used in the largest of the Union armies. Despite the fact that measuring blood pressure was first done in 1733 by Stephen Hales, it was not until the invention of the mercury sphygmomanometer in the 1880s and its acceptance in the 1910s that measuring blood pressure became a common clinical procedure.

practiced mainly among the upper classes. The poor led lives of degradation in vermin-infested, horrifically unsanitary cellars and tenements; and destitution led not only to prostitution and its inevitable by-product, venereal diseases, but bred disease as well, notably typhus (the "fever"), which was sporadically recurrent in London with devastating epidemics. These conditions, in tandem with a growing awareness on the part of social activists who refused to accept any longer the idea that the poor were foreordained to be looked upon as pariahs, precipitated establishment in 1750 of the first free dispensary.

As he had done at Edinburgh, Rush proved himself proficient in the art of networking. While he managed to work his way into what can be described as a Who's Who of London's elite, this should in no way be interpreted as an aptitude for scaling the social ladder. He did not have to insinuate himself into the city's principal medical, intellectual, and political precincts. He was invited in, on the strength of his intelligence and personality and a genuine eagerness to learn. Or, to put it in its most basic terms, Benjamin Rush can never be labeled a social climber. Benjamin Franklin was but one among the large cluster of the British capital's movers and shakers who took an immediate and lasting liking upon making the acquaintance of the young Philadelphian he had recommended to his Edinburgh acquaintances sight unseen.

Franklin treated Rush as a son and introduced him to a number of pro-American Londoners of prominence from all walks of life. Among these were the Dilly Brothers, Edward and Charles, publishers with a large trade in America in divinity treatises and general literature, who would become Rush's publishers. Rush was also introduced to a number of Franklin's literary friends. Franklin even "once took me to [George III's] Court with him and pointed at so many of the most distinguished characters of the nation. I never visited him without learning something."[10]

The twenty-two-year-old newly minted physician soon found himself socializing in the highest echelons of London's artistic and literary firmament. Among those who invited him into their homes and into their lives were the popular American-born Benjamin West (he painted a portrait of Rush), who during this period helped to organize the Royal Academy and, already a favorite at Court, would soon be appointed Historical Painter to the King; Sir Joshua Reynolds, then at the height of his fame as a portraitist; the Irish-born Oliver Goldsmith, who after practicing medicine in London turned to literature while in his thirties and achieved the extraordinary distinction of writing arguably the eighteenth century's greatest poem ("The Deserted Village"), greatest novel (*The Vicar of Wakefield*) and greatest play (*She Stoops to Conquer*); and the legendary, irrepressible Dr. Samuel Johnson.

In his correspondence from this period, Rush deals almost exclusively with the great men of medicine he met, and next to nothing of the great men of arts and letters. Only years later, in retrospect, did he recall those contacts. One such letter worth quoting from was to his friend James Abercrombie. A noted preacher prominent in Philadelphia's social circles with strong Tory inclinations who found it difficult reconciling himself to living in a republic, Abercrombie achieved notoriety after 1800 for his vicious anti-Jeffersonian sermons. In the letter, written a quarter of a century after the fact ("The day was to me one of the most memorable I passed while abroad, on account of the singular display which I witnessed both of talents and knowledge"), Rush describes "a memorable dinner" at the home of Reynolds at which he was seated between Samuel Johnson and Goldsmith.

During the dinner, Johnson, the great lexicographer and polymath, impressed Rush with his erudition on matters scientific. When one of the company raised the subject of the *anemone maritima*, which naturalists disagreed as to whether it belonged to the vegetable or animal kingdom, Johnson pronounced ex cathedra, "It is animal, for its ashes have been analyzed [by Johnson himself], and they yield a volatile alkali, and this we know is the criterion of animal matter as distinguished from vegetable, which yields a fixed alkali." Rush was "struck with this remark; for I did not expect to hear a man whose studies appeared, from his writings, to have been confined to moral and philological subjects decide so confidently upon a controversy in natural history." One can imagine how "struck" Rush was when, some years later, two of the century's greatest chemists, Lavoisier and Priestley, proved Johnson to have been right.

Also during the dinner, Goldsmith, "a man of gentle and unoffending manners," was treated by his friend Johnson "with great rudeness" when Goldsmith asked Rush "several questions relative to the manners and customs of the North American Indians." Johnson "suddenly interrupted him and said, 'There is not an Indian in North America who would have asked such a foolish question.'" Retorted Goldsmith, who could give as well as take, "I am sure there is not a savage in America that would have made so rude a speech to a gentleman."

But it was invariably Johnson who had the last word, no matter his verbal opponent. After dinner he became drawn into a dispute with Heaton Wilkes, brother of the notorious political agitator John Wilkes. Recent imprisonment for disparaging King George had led to a public demonstration in St. George's Fields by his supporters in which British soldiers dispatched to quell the riot killed a man. When Heaton Wilkes "condemned the conduct of government in very harsh terms" and said the mob could have been dispersed without firing a gun, Johnson snapped back: "That may be. Some men have a knack in quelling riots, which others have not, just as you, sir, have a knack in defending them, which I have not." Summing up his opinion of Johnson, whom Abercrombie idolized, Rush said: "I concur with you in your partiality to the genius and writings of Dr. Johnson," adding, by way of qualification, "after making some deductions from his character on account of his ecclesiastical and political bigotry."[11]

John Wilkes was the most vociferous of the surprising number in England who supported the American cause. Elected to Parliament in 1757 at the age of thirty-five, he began to publish five years later the vehemently anti-Tory weekly *The Briton,* an issue of which (23 April 1763), criticizing a speech of George III's, caused his imprisonment on the charge of seditious libel. Soon released on the grounds that his parliamentary privilege had been violated, he was shortly thereafter expelled from Parliament when an obscene parody *Essay on Women,* which he printed privately but apparently did not write, led to charges of libel and blasphemy. Visiting France and failing to return for trial made him an outlaw. When he returned to England five years later, such was his popularity in Whig circles that he was again elected to Parliament. Tried on the outstanding libel charges, he was convicted and incarcerated in the King's Bench Prison. Released the following year, Wilkes was again expelled from Parliament. His Middlesex constituents reelected him three times, and each time Parliament invalidated the results. The last time the seat was given to his defeated opponent, which caused riots among the lower- and middle-class Londoners who hailed him as a champion of freedom of the press.

After his release from prison in 1769, Wilkes campaigned extensively for political reforms while championing the cause of the American colonial revolutionists. He was believed to be the British agent for the Sons of Liberty. The powerful English merchant class, who were being hurt by the American reaction to the Townshend Acts (which is to say, the Non-Importation Agreements), joined in rallying to the slogan "Wilkes and Liberty!" With his popularity now at its peak, Wilkes was elected successively alderman of London (1770), sheriff of London in the following year, and lord mayor of London three years later, when he was simultaneously elected to the House of Commons and this time seated without opposition. Wilkes died in 1797, but his name lives on in the nation whose separation from Great Britain he so strongly advocated: The Pennsylvania city of Wilkes-Barre was named in his honor.

"While I was in Britain," Benjamin Rush recalled, "Mr. Wilkes was the object of universal attention. The nation was divided into his friends and enemies according as how they espoused or opposed the measures of the government. . . . My curiosity was excited to see the man that had so universally agitated and divided a nation." His curiosity was assuaged through the efforts of a friend, Arthur Lee, a Virginian who had received a medical degree at Edinburgh but was now studying law in London. Lee took Rush along to a dinner Wilkes gave in his prison apartment, to which he was entitled as a member of Parliament, attended by some fourteen or fifteen friends. "Mr. Wilkes abounded in anecdotes and sallies of wit. He was perfectly well bred. Not an unchaste word or oath escaped his lips. I was the more surprised at this, as he had been represented a monster of immorality."[12]

Before Rush left for Scotland, the Bradfords, publishers of the *Pennsylvania Journal,* had invited him to keep an eye out for stories they could use. Though several of his letters from Edinburgh were written with this in mind, only a few small excerpts were published. His account of the visit to Wilkes, in a letter to his brother Jacob, who was now launching what would prove to be a successful career as a lawyer, was run in full on 30 March 1769. One week later the *Journal* ran an even longer letter of Rush's to Jacob. In the first, Rush describes the controversial Wilkes as "one of the most entertaining men in the world. . . . He is an enthusiast for AMERICAN [sic] Liberty, and says if you can but preserve an equality among one another, you will always be free in spite of everything. . . . He spoke with as much virulence as ever against Scotland, for, you must know, all the Scotch members of Parliament, in both Houses, are against America."

In the second letter, which merits attention because of Rush's growing concerns with the worsening relations between America and Great Britain and his no-nonsense approach to confronting Parliament's economic stranglehold, Rush begins with the news that "Mr. Wilkes' affairs came before the House of Commons a few days ago; it is generally supposed they will expel him." (They did.) So far as Rush, like Wilkes's supporters, was concerned, "No reasons can be assigned" for the expulsion, except "that it is agreeable to the minds of the [king's] ministry." All of Wilkes's friends "are friends of America; some of them talk of seeking a shelter from arbitrary power in the peaceful deserts of America. Mrs. Macaulay, the celebrated female historian, talks of ending her days on the banks of the Ohio; she is employed in publishing a 5th volume of her *History of England,* in which she proposes to treat very largely of the settlement of the colonies. You may depend upon it, she will do ample justice to the rights of America."

Moving next to the "address of thanks" voted by Parliament to the king "for his care and vigilance" in sending troops from Halifax "to suppress" the people of Boston—a measure of the Townshend Acts— Rush expresses outrage that "affidavits are to be taken, and the persons found guilty [of anti-British actions and sentiment] are to be sent over here to be tried for their lives." Rush demands rhetorically, "Where now is the force or use of our penal laws? What mercy can we hope for when our accusers are our judges?"

There was, as he saw it, "but one expedient whereby we can save our sinking country, and that is by encouraging American manufactures. Unless we do all this, we shall be undone forever. There is scarce a necessary article or even a luxury of life but what might be raised and brought to perfection in some of our provinces." Grapes for wines could be grown. Sheep could be raised "with so little trouble that if a proper price was offered for wool, our farmers might raise many hundreds of them yearly without in the least hurting the cultivation of their grain." Mulberry trees were so plentiful "that we might raise silkworms in a few years to supply us with all the silk we want." In Pennsylvania alone the "materials" abounded for making china or porcelain. The popular Bohea and green tea from England could "be banished forever from our tables and buffets: a bowl of sage and baum tea is worth an ocean of both of them." The "grand complaint" of American laborers that they were not paid "sufficient prices for their work" Rush attributed to the fact that "we consume too little of their manufactures to keep them employed the whole year round; their wages therefore must of consequence be proportionately higher during the few months they do work." Let "American manufactures become general," he insisted, and "this complaint will have no foundation, and hundreds of artificers of every kind would be invited to come over from England and settle among us."[13]

It was also through Arthur Lee that Rush was brought into the literary and political circle that played the collective moth to the above-mentioned Whig historian Catharine Macaulay. Through her, Rush came to know and be known to such leading pro-American Englishmen men as her brother John Sawbridge and the Scottish teacher and philosopher James Burgh. Nonconformist in just about everything but her devout Anglicanism, Dame Thucydides, as she was known to her admirers, was being hailed for her multivolume history of England in which she used the Stuarts to defame the current royal incumbents, the Hanoverians. Rush found her "sensible and eloquent, but visionary in some of her ideas of government. I once heard her say laws were defective in not rewarding Virtue, as well as punishing Vice."[14]

While he accepted Macaulay's rejection of Thomas Hobbes's absolutist political philosophy in favor of republicanism, Rush took issue with her insistence that military officers should be able to serve in legislatures, and that taxes should be levied by an appointed senate. On 18 January 1769, he sat in the Pennsylvania Coffee House, a popular London gathering place for what might be termed "the Benjamin Franklin crowd," and wrote a letter to Macaulay arguing to the contrary. Military officers, he contended, should be excluded from national parliaments because, having fought in defense of their country and endured the hardships of war, they "naturally claim a superiority over the rest of their countrymen. They feel their own importance, they know how necessary they are to the support of the state, and therefore assume more to themselves than is consistent with a free government. Should they ever be provoked to it, their knowledge in arms and their popularity with the soldiers and common people would give them the great advantages over every other citizen, and would render the transition from democracy to anarchy, and from anarchy to monarchy, very natural and very easy."

That such thinking might have informed the antagonism Rush developed toward George Washington during the Revolutionary War, which was to earn him so much grief and obloquy, cannot be dismissed peremptorily, although, as we shall see, other, less philosophical causes lay at the root of their falling-out.

As to Macaulay's ideas on the levying of taxes being exclusively the purview of an appointed assembly, Rush "begged leave to observe" that he could not "help thinking that" the "exclusive right of taxing their country" should be reserved for the popularly elected legislative assembly: "They represent the greatest part of the people. They are supposed to be collected from all parts of the commonwealth and are therefore much better acquainted with the circumstances of the country. Besides, they (from their greater number) are naturally supposed to have more property in the state, and therefore have a better right to give it away for the purposes of government."

Conceding that "Perhaps I am wrong in both these observations," Rush "expect[ed] to be rectified by you, madam, who are so well skilled in the science of government. I am but a young scholar in the school of politics, although I have made great progress in the love of liberty; for this, let me assure you, madam, was among the first passions that warmed my breast." Far from "rectifying" Rush, Dame Thucydides was impressed with the letter, which she published in a second edition of her history—though, for reasons known only to her, she did not identify its author. When she visited America briefly in 1783, the two had an amiable reunion.

Having spent more money in Edinburgh than he had anticipated, Rush planned to return home on completing his studies in London, but decided instead to make a quick trip to Paris. This occurred quite likely at the suggestion of Franklin, who asked "how I was provided with money for my jaunt." Rush explained that he had enough. "Perhaps not," said Franklin, "you may be exposed to unexpected expenses." He gave Rush a letter of credit upon a Paris bank "for two or three hundred guineas."[15] Franklin also gave him letters of introduction to his "philosophical friends" among the French literati.

Rush left London on 16 February, arriving at Dover that evening. Sailing to Calais, he arrived at Paris by coach a few days later. After settling himself in a nondescript hotel, Rush presented his first letter of introduction, presumably at Franklin's suggestion, to the sixty-nine-year-old physician, botanist, translator Jacques Barbeu-Dubourg, Franklin's closest Parisian friend and most fervent admirer. Dubourg was France's staunchest admirer of everything American, not the least its desire for independence from England.

Rush was at once overwhelmed by this romantic idealist revolutionary whose vision of what must be accomplished to change the world for the better was not inhibited by the bounds of history, as was too often the case of such Whigs as Mrs. Macaulay. It was Barbeu-Dubourg more than any other philosopher who contributed to Rush's knowledge and understanding of the French Enlightenment.[16]

By translating the writings of Franklin and John Dickinson as well as those of Rush, whom he much admired from their first meeting, Barbeu-Dubourg did much to popularize knowledge of America in France. When the Revolutionary War broke out, he set himself up as an agent for the colonies to obtain French supplies and agitate for French intervention (which may well have been inevitable in any case, given France's traditional enmity toward Britain). As L. H. Butterfield observes in editing the Rush Letters, "Barbeu-Dubourg has had little attention from students of the period, but as a man of real scholarly attainment, a close observer of events, and an indefatigable friend of America, he does not deserve this neglect."[17]

Rush mentions favorably the other members of the so-called Physiocrats, a group of thinkers and writers on economics whose views on liberty of the individual and on taxation were in the forefront of intellectual agitation: "The members of this Society consisted of some men who bore an active part of the first years of the French Revolution. The seeds of the Revolution, it has been said by one of its enemies, were sowed by the meetings and publications of this Society."[18] Rush was both impressed by and in turn impressed these members, in particular Diderot, who "entertained me in his library." Rush, to whom the author-philosopher gave a letter to his fellow philosopher, Hume, makes no allusion in his memoirs to Diderot's *Pensées philosophiques*, which had been burned by the Parliament of Paris for its anti-Christian attitudes. To Rush's credit, such attitudes that an avowed Christian like he doubtless found offensive failed to mitigate his high opinion of Diderot. Anyway, the burning was more than twenty years in the past; besides, it's hardly probable that the two talked religion. Diderot's "conversation at the time [of their meeting] was general."

Rush's opinion of France's doctors did not approach his opinion of her thinkers: "Physic is not cultivated here by Men of Rank and Fortune, nor is the Profession look'd upon so liberal in this Country, as it is in England or America." Having "conversed with several of the principal physicians in Paris," he wrote in his *French Journal*, Rush was "sorry to find them at least fifty years behind the Physicians in England & Scotland in Medical Knowledge."[19] While he "visited all the public hospitals in Paris but without entering myself as a pupil in any of them," he was particularly impressed with the charitable institutions for the relief of the poor and the sick." This planted in Rush's mind the idea that eventually led to his founding the first free dispensary for the indigent in the new American nation.

Rush found a number of characteristics that were shared by the French ("the most civilized of any nation in the world") and the Indians ("savages") of North America, notably their practice of taking their main meal in the evening, and the "fond[ness] of ornamenting their faces by means of paint." He observed that French women took "no pains to conceal the practice," sometimes taking out "their boxes in their carriages in the streets of Paris, and paint[ing] their faces by means of a pocket looking glass, in the presence of many hundred passing spectators." But this was not intended as an attack on the ladies' moral behavior, merely an observation. Like the American Indians, Rush further noted, the "people of rank and fortune among the French are very fond of fishing and hunting." Yet another trait shared in common was that the French "seldom address[ed] each other by their proper names." It was "not uncommon" for a Frenchman when addressed by his name in company to say "Sir, I am much obliged to you for putting me in mind of my name, but I assure you I had not forgotten it."[20]

To Rush's consternation, while few countries could equal France for varieties of soil and climate, and the ideal conditions for agriculture, "yet, because of the neglect of cultivation, an acre of ground in the most fruitful part of the country produced no more than did an eighth of an acre in most parts of England." He ascribed this to the contempt in which agriculture and farming "had always been held in France, by the vast number of parks reserved for hunting, the short leases granted to farmers, and the want of enclosures for fields and the lack of encouragement from the Crown." Reflecting wisely that civilization of mankind and agriculture are inextricably linked, he noted philosophically in his *French Journal:* "It is owing to this that the American Colonies, have in so short a Space of time arisen to such a Pitch of Grandeur & Riches, . . . where Agriculture is encouraged, there will be Riches, where there are Riches, there will be Power, and where there is Power, there will be Freedom and Independence."

Like all tourists, Rush visited the major churches, public buildings, and various royal palaces, including Versailles. There he saw pass before him in procession Louis XV ("the most sensible looking fool in Europe"), followed by his grandson the Dauphin, the ill-fated Louis XVI ("dull in his intellects and vulgar in his manners"), and the latter's equally dull and vulgar brothers and eventual successors in the post-Napoleonic era, the future Charles X and Louis XVIII. On a subsequent occasion, though he does not indicate the palace where the incident took place, Rush joined some visitors and courtiers in one of the favorite indulgences among the era's European royalty: graciously permitting visitors to stand in silence respectfully and watch them dine.

After watching the king and his mistress Madame Du Barry, Rush fairly shouted into his *French Journal*, "Let such as maintain [the] Divine Right of kings come and behold this monarch, sitting at [table] with a common Prostitute, picked up a few years ago from the Streets of Paris . . . and then let him declare if they can, that they believe him to be [the] Lord's anointed!" Rush also noted that while there were parliaments in France, they were "mere Courts of Justice, and have no Power of any Kind as a legislative Body." Though they had at one time been "as free and independent as our own," they now existed only at the "King's Pleasure"—the same fate, he was convinced, that awaited America's provincial legislatures unless the people resolved to emulate "the true Whig" John Wilkes and other, earlier like-minded heroes in their opposition to arbitrary government by George III's Parliament.

"Having gratified [his] curiosity to its greatest extent in Paris," Rush set out for London on 21 March, arriving at Calais on the twenty-fifth and crossing the Channel the next day, landing at Dover. Leaving Dover on the twenty-seventh, he arrived at Dartford that same evening. Their concern raised by the "suspicious conduct of a man who rode several times around the post chaise in which I was, with a lady and gentleman," and the conviction that his intention was to rob them, the three insisted that the postillon hold up for the night. "This apprehension was not without its use, and probably was the means of saving a life"—a newborn life. As they were proceeding along the road to London next morning female cries were heard coming from a copse at the side of the road. Jumping out to investigate, Rush realized the woman was in labor, "and in ten minutes with the assistance of the lady who was with me in the carriage, I delivered her of a fine boy." Shortly thereafter, the new father showed up "with two old women whom he had picked up in the neighbourhood." All crowded into the coach, and drove to a little village about a mile and a half back, where mother and infant were left "in a comfortable house, with as much money as was sufficient to support her for several days."

When, on arriving at London, Rush mentioned the incident to his landlady, Mrs. Jeffries, she "sent her a bundle of clothes for her Child, and sundry other things which are necessary and comfortable to women in this situation." It was not until two years later that Rush learned that the mother had come looking for him at Mrs. Jeffries's house to thank him and let him know she had named the little boy Benjamin in his honor.[21]

One of Rush's first acts after arriving at London was to call upon Franklin and tell him he'd had to spend only about ten percent of the loan: "He seemed pleased and requested that I would pay them when convenient to his wife in Philadelphia," which Rush did "with the first money I earned after my arrival." Mrs. Franklin refused at first to accept the money, since her husband had made no mention of the loan in any of his letters. But she finally did so at Rush's insistence—a mark of the young doctor's character that endeared him even more to Franklin: "It attached me to him during the remainder of his life, and it has, since his death, disposed me to respect and love all the branches of his family."[22]*

Rush stayed on in London for two months, visiting the hospitals as an observer, and visiting friends, of whom by far the one he most admired and sought out was Franklin. It is also possible that he made a trip to Scotland to deliver the Diderot letter to Hume, and to see once again and bid yet another final farewell to the fair Lady Jane Leslie. None of this is mentioned in either his memoirs, his *Scottish Journal,* or any of his correspondence, and is thus no more than conjecture. Hume could have been visiting London at the time, where Diderot's letter would have been delivered.

On 24 May, Rush left London in a post chaise, arriving that evening at Gravesend. After a two-day wait for a westbound ship, he embarked upon the *Edward:* "The last view I took of the white cliffs of Britain from the stern of our ship was an affecting one. All the ancient and modern glory of that celebrated and highly favoured island rushed upon my mind. I enjoyed in silence this pensive retrospect of the first country in the world, 'till distance snatched it for ever from my sight."[23]

Thus did Benjamin Rush sever his physical ties with the mother country. Little did he know that in seven years, as a signer of the Declaration of Independence, he would sever his political ties as well, along with those of his posterity, with "the first country in the world."

Unlike his first Atlantic crossing, Rush suffered only one day of seasickness, though he does admit that he "was never perfectly well" for the remainder of the voyage. While he found his fellow passengers congenial, they were all royalists; beyond pleasantries, there was little

*Rush might be slightly exaggerating here. One doubts he could have "loved" Franklin's illegitimate son William, royal governor of New Jersey, who remained a British Loyalist, something even his own egalitarian father could not come to terms with. William was arrested (24 June 1776) on orders of the Congress and imprisoned for two years, after which he was allowed to exile himself to England, where he spent the remainder of his eighty years, permanently estranged from his famous father.

about them to mitigate the monotony felt by one such as he, who in any event found confinement to a small ship for seven weeks not only near-claustrophobic: "My mind was equally restless and unsettled." To make matters worse, his books, in which he had always found pleasure, had been sent ahead. "I was obliged to borrow such books as I could procure from the ship's company."

One of the passengers, an attorney, happened to have with him the first three volumes of Blackstone's *Commentaries on the Laws of England* (the fourth had not yet been published), which a grateful Rush "read with uncommon attention and pleasure." In addition to the Blackstone, the bible of the legal profession to this day, he had access to Foster's *Crown Law:* "To the reading of these books I ascribe in part the relish for political science which I felt in the beginning of the American Revolution."

Since the books, in particular Blackstone's, were unequivocally Tory, stressing the supremacy of Parliament, the "relish for political science" they provoked in Rush was probably his way of saying they afforded him for the first time a full comprehension of that principle of paramount parliamentary authority which he condemned as asserted in the Declaratory Act of 1766 and which he would later reject unequivocally in his attack upon the Pennsylvania Constitution of 1776 and in his condemnation of the Articles of Confederation. (The Declaratory Act asserted the right of Parliament to legislate for the colonies in all matters, a concept rejected by many of the colonials, who refused to accept that they were not represented in that body ["No taxation without representation!"].)

Though already republican in principle, Rush had not yet considered the problem of governmental organization along republican lines, except perhaps for the views expressed in that Philadelphia Coffee-house letter to Mrs. Macaulay. From his own study of seventeenth-century history, Rush knew that the rights of creating a constitution was extended to all "Commonwealthmen," and not reserved for the select few. In Blackstone's *Commentaries* he found added material for the ideal "balance-of-power" constitution favored by Commonwealthmen. Of equal consequence, it helped give Rush a more practical direction to the "natural rights" philosophy of the Enlightenment and the Whig ideology which he had been exposed to—one might say inundated in—while abroad. As Donald D'Elia, one of Rush's foremost twentieth-century interpreters, has so eloquently put it, "Rush now began to see and condemn British colonial policy in the wider perspective of English law, English history, and the 'rights of man.' In a sense, then, as the *Edward* drew nearer to the colonies, Rush's political thought became less speculative and more concrete. His republicanism, conceived in skepticism and accordingly tentative and incomplete, was now taking on the flesh of American political reality."[24]

When the *Edward* reached New York City, Rush "viewed the American shore with a rapture that can only be conceived by persons who have been in my situation"; that is to say, away from his native land for an extended period. His friend Ebenezer Hazard met him at the pier. "The first refreshment I tasted after I came on shore was a dish of tea with bread and butter." Though it was hardly the first such meal he had had in the past three years, the fact that he was having it on American soil "had a relish to me which I never before perceived in food of any kind and such as is perceived after enormous hunger, and in the convalescent state of a fever." Apparently Rush did not take in many of the sights. Of all that he saw during his brief stay that he saw fit to recall in his memoirs, "Three things struck me in the appearance of the people I saw in the streets of New York. 1, They had less color; 2, they walked less erect; and 3, they moved with a less quick step than the citizens of London."

Anxious to see his family, and not overly impressed with New York—"The evening and day after my arrival, I felt an uncommon depression of spirits"—Rush took the stage for Philadelphia, pausing at Bristol to meet his brother Jacob and Jonathan (Bayard) Smith, a Princeton classmate and soon-to-be fellow-laborer in the vineyard of rebellion, both of whom accompanied him into Philadelphia. There he was received by "my dear mother and sister" Rebecca, who had lost her husband.[25]

Having left home three years previously practically apolitical, Rush had become a republican in Edinburgh, largely through the influence of Bostock. During his less than six months in London, under the spell of Pitt's "more than Roman eloquence," he morphed into a rebel, largely through the influence of Wilkes, Macaulay, and all their fellow

Whigs who were antagonistic to the British government's uncompromising attitude toward its American colonials. By the time Dr. Benjamin Rush returned home, he was primed for the rebelliousness that would metastasize him as the colonies moved imperceptibly toward irrevocable separation.

5

Philadelphia Physician

Benjamin Rush took a house on Arch Street between Front and Second, sharing it with Jacob, who was finishing his apprenticeship, and Rebecca, who would stay on as Benjamin's housekeeper until her second marriage seven years later. (Their mother owned her own home across the street from the grocery store.) When Jacob left for London a few months later to complete his studies, Benjamin and Rebecca moved to a more preferable house on Front Street near Water that had a commanding view of the wharves along the Delaware River and the constant ferry traffic and of cargo vessels bringing in cotton, tobacco, spices, and slaves from the South and from the West Indies. It was here that Rush brought his bride in 1776 and here they lived until the birth of their first child four years later.

In launching a medical career the twenty-three-year-old Rush faced three seemingly insurmountable obstacles: "The principal means which introduce a physician into business" in the colonies, he recalled in his memoirs, were "the patronage of a great man," the "influence of extensive and powerful family connections," and the "influence of a religious sect or political party." As regarded the first factor, "I had no hopes, for I was unknown to any of the [business moguls] who were called great in our city"—so much so that when Rush's name, with his professional title, "was mentioned in one of the first circles of the city, a few days after my arrival, one of the company asked whether I was a Doctor of Divinity or Physic."

As for "extensive and powerful family connections," Rush's claim that "From this quarter likewise I had nothing to hope. My family connections were few, and without power or influence in the city" derived from the fact that his father had been a gunsmith and his mother ran a grocery store. Social snobbery was as prevalent in Colonial America as it is in twentieth-century America. As for lacking "the influence of a religious sect or political party," being a staunch Presbyterian made Rush ipso facto "the object of the jealousy, or hatred" of the Quakers and Episcopalians, who between them possessed the greatest part of the city's wealth and influence.[1]

While on target when it came to the Episcopalians, who considered Presbyterians beneath their notice, Rush was being slightly unfair to the Quakers, who dominated in numbers and political power not only in Philadelphia but throughout the entire province. They accepted without persecution or prejudice not only people of all nationalities but of all religious persuasion. Indeed, Pennsylvania—whose eponym, Admiral Sir William Penn, founded the state under charter of the Crown—"was the first large community since the Roman Empire to allow different nations and religious sects to live under the same government on terms of equality."[2] Like the Episcopalians, they had, in Rush's words, "long been in the habit of confining their business chiefly to persons who belonged to their Society, or who favored their views in politicks." The Presbyterians, it will be recalled, were themselves divided between Old Style and New Style; and the Old Style, whose doctrines the entire Rush family disavowed, were the dominant, more influential of the two factions.

Compounding the situation, Rush had to compete with a number of excellent physicians already well established. In addition, a number of medical quacks no more qualified to practice medicine than the traditional snake-oil salesmen of the not-yet-settled American West, were both a competitive force to Rush and a physical threat to the community as a whole. Their nostrums and methods were not only life-threatening, they were often life-taking.

Over time, Rush's reputation would became such that even a number of Quakers accepted his ministrations, along with some of Philadelphia's aristocrats representing other denominations, and he would manage to negotiate the chasm between the Presbyterian sects. Many patients, though, regardless of religious orientation, would abandon Dr. Rush when he became a pronounced patriot, either out of loyalty to the mother country, or if Quakers, out of their traditional abhorrence of war: "They took literally the commandment, 'Thou shalt not kill,' and so ran afoul of war-waging governments."[3]

Consequently, at the outset, because Rush had, he writes with all due modesty, "a natural sympathy with distress of every kind," and his "natural disposition made this mode of getting into business agreeable to me"—and, no mean consideration, because he had little choice, Rush confined his practice to the city's poor. Fortunately, it was a considerable patient pool. Between his birth and his return from abroad, Philadelphia had more than doubled its population, from some 13,000 to 28,000, making it the largest metropolis in America. The times favored any qualified physician: The city's annual death rate was one in every twenty-five citizens.

In the month Rush began his practice, a scarlet fever epidemic broke out among the city's children. This was followed a few months later by an epidemic of croup, which also struck mostly children. The next winter brought with it an influenza epidemic, followed a year later by an epidemic of measles that struck all the colonies, and, a year after that, a periodic smallpox epidemic that left three hundred dead in Philadelphia alone. There were, in addition, frequent outbreaks of cholera morbis during the summer months; chronic fever (called at the time "nervous fever") in the fall of the year, especially in the densely settled sections of the city; dysentery throughout the year; and, of course, recurrent epidemics of influenza and the more devastating yellow fever.

High as the mortality rate was, it is remarkable that these epidemics were not more sweeping, given the hygienic conditions of the times. Street gutters served as open sewers. The closest home access to running water was a pump in the yard. Bathing was done in the summer months, in tin-lined wooden tubs, with the same water being used successively by the entire family, starting with the mother, then the father, then the daughter(s), then the brother(s). And this was among the well-to-do families. The poor seldom bathed at all, and thus were victim to almost perpetual lice infestation. Public baths, while frequented occasionally, were looked upon as immoral by the Quaker majority. Cleaning of the streets was a rarity. Cesspools were seldom emptied—often for years. Instead of emptying them, the people dug pits to keep them from filling up; pits so deep that the water flowed into nearby wells. Flies and mosquitoes were ever present. So, too, were diseased gums, due to the lack of dental care, primarily among the poor. Dr. Rush had plenty of patients to keep him busy. And here let it be noted that, in addition to being the first American to write on *cholera infantum*, he was the first to recognize focal infection in the teeth. (Focal infection is a bacterial infection in one part of the body that might cause symptoms elsewhere in the body.)

With his growing practice among the indigent, and a concomitant growing reputation—he was among a small group who formed a Society for Inoculating the Poor without charge against smallpox—Rush began to prosper. Other physicians called upon him from time to time for consultation, at a fee. He took on apprentices, for which, as was not his own case with Redman, he charged a fee. That he did so should not be interpreted as mercenary. He was financing his brother Jacob's studies in London, in addition to supporting his two now unmarried sisters and their small children. He took on no less than seven apprentices at one time, boarding them dormitory style in a neighboring barn. Though only in his twenties, he looked after them as would a father. Not only did he train them, but he willingly offered medical advice when they themselves went into practice; it endeared their master to them for life.

It wasn't long before Rush was making greater financial strides than he had dared anticipate. In less than six months he was living on a scale of comfort which can be gauged from published reports of a robbery he suffered in March 1770, when thieves broke into his house and made off with, among other items, "six new-fashioned silver tablespoons marked with a wolf's-head crest, a common sized chased cream pot, a pair of tea tongs, together with a half-dozen tea spoons."[4]

Rush "led a life of constant labor and self-denial." Mornings he received patients in his office, which in keeping with the tradition of the times was in his home. Afternoons were reserved for house calls: "Nearly every street and alley in the city was visited by me every day. There are few old huts now standing in the ancient part of the city in which I have not attended sick people." Often he "ascended the upper story of these huts by a ladder, and many hundred times have been obliged to rest my weary limbs upon the bedside of the sick (from the want of chairs) where I was sure I risqued [*sic*] not only taking their disease but being infected by vermin. More than once did I suffer from the latter." Attesting to his dedication, when no other help—a relative or a neighbor—"was attainable," he remained within the vermin-infested sickroom "of these abodes of poverty and misery" to administer personally prescriptions, "particularly bleeding and clysters [purges or enemas], with my own hands." While his days were occupied with medicine, Rush's evenings were given over to study and writing. He "seldom went to bed before 12 o'clock, and many many [*sic*] times have I heard the [night] watchman cry 3 o'clock before I have put out my candle."5

With all that he had to occupy his time and energies, it's understandable that Rush's social life was minimal. "Now and then I gave a dinner or a supper to a stranger, and to a few young merchants in my neighbourhood." These were, more often than not, Scotsmen, whom he seems to have preferred because "some of them possessed Education and Sentiment." Also he "mixed freely in female Society, and occasionally spent afternoons in the company of ladies upon parties of pleasure both in town and in the country."6

At first, Rush made his rounds on foot, but as his income increased he rode in a sedan chair, accompanied by the servant he had acquired, a freed slave. Slaves, especially in the Middle Colonies, were able to purchase their freedom, and often went on to achieve success in the business world. Moreover, while imported slaves were sold in Philadelphia, locals did not purchase them in the same numbers they were bought in the Southern Colonies, where the main cash crops—cotton and tobacco—were dependent upon slave labor. The Quakers, after all, dominated Pennsylvania. And no sect of people was more opposed to slavery until the Boston abolitionists coalesced.

Occasionally on his rounds, Rush would stop off at the old London Coffee House on the corner of Front and High Streets, which functioned as an informal social club. There the city's—and often the province's—movers and shakers made social connections and transacted business. Assurances had been given by the proprietor "as a Christian to preserve decency and order . . . and to discourage the profanation of the sacred name of God Almighty by cursing, swearing &c." Furthermore, he "covenants that under a penalty of £100 he will not allow or suffer any person to use, play at, or divert themselves with cards, dice, back-gammon, or any other unlawful game."7

Apparently the proprietor and his distinguished clientele, which included Pennsylvania's governor and members of the legislative

Assembly, did not consider it "a profanation of the sacred name of God Almighty" that the London Coffee House, given its proximity to the Delaware wharves, was one of the public places were the latest incoming cargo of blacks was displayed for sale. For example, "The firm of Allen and Turner advertised the sale of some likely Negroes from the Barbados, including a likely breeding Negro woman. Messrs. Willing and Morris advertised for sale 170 Negroes just arrived from the Gold Coast."[8]

What Rush observed of the slave market, plus what he had already observed in Liverpool, along with an inherent abhorrence to the idea of slavery, resulted in the most controversial of his many compositions, *An Address to the Inhabitants of the British Settlements in America, upon Slave-Keeping.* He wrote it in support of a petition being circulated that the Pennsylvania Assembly increase the duty on imported Negro slaves, hopefully as a means of reducing the traffic if not, as many hoped, stopping it altogether. This was the first of Rush's numerous published essays that helped establish his reputation throughout the colonies as a reformer, an outlook hailed in New England and vilified in the South.

Rush branded as totally fallacious the claim of some "that by treating slaves well, we render their situation happier in this country than it was in their own." Fallacious not because the blacks were not all that well treated in their own home, if only because it was their own rulers who sold them into bondage, but because they were not treated all that well in this country. Rush points out that "even the ox is entitled to his reward for 'treading the corn.' But how great then must be the amount of the injustice which deprives so many of our fellow creatures of the *just* reward of the labor!" Then asking, "What steps shall we take to remedy this evil, and what shall we do with those slaves we already have in this country?" Rush admits:

> This is indeed a most difficult question. But let every man contrive to answer it for himself. If you possessed an estate which was bequeathed to you by your ancestors, and were afterwards convinced that it was the just property of another man, would you think it right to continue in the possession of it? The voice of all mankind would make him for a villain who would refuse to comply with this demand of justice. And is not keeping a slave after you are

convinced of the unlawfulness of it—a crime of the same nature? All the money you save, or acquire by their labor is stolen from them; and however plausible the excuse may be that you form to reconcile it to your consciences, yet be assured that your crime stands registered in the court of Heaven as a breach of the eighth amendment.

Rush goes on to argue that the "first step to be taken to put a stop to slavery in this country, is to leave off importing slaves" by having the colonial assemblies "unite in petitioning the King and Parliament to dissolve the African Company"—the "incorporated band of robbers [by whom] the trade has been chiefly carried on to America." Along with petitioning against this hideous grievance, he urges that "such of our countrymen as engage in the slave trade, be shunned as the greatest enemies to our country, and, let the vessels which bring the slaves to us, be avoided as if they bore in them the seeds of that forbidden fruit, whose baneful taste destroyed both the natural and moral world."

As for those slaves either too old or too infirm "to be set at liberty," Rush suggests, "for the good of society," that they "continue the property of those with whom they grew old." This may sound callous. But consider that even after the Civil War and enactment of the Civil War amendments (the Thirteenth, Fourteenth, and Fifteenth) many of the old and infirm slaves, and even some of the younger ones, fearful of entering a life with which they could not cope, forewent freedom for the security of the only life they had known. When it came to the young slaves, Rush suggests they "be educated in the principles of virtue and religion—let them be taught to read and write—and afterwards instructed in some business, whereby they may be able to maintain themselves. Let laws be made to limit the time of their servitude, and to entitle them to all the privileges of freeborn British subjects. At any rate let retribution be done to God and to society." Then asking "my countrymen" to "rouse up your indignation against slave-keeping," Rush, in some of his most impassioned writing, asks that they "consider the many complicated crimes" involved in the institution:

Think of the bloody wars that are fomented by it among the African nations, or if these are too common to affect you, think of the pangs which attend the dissolution of the ties of nature in those who are stolen from their relations. Think of the many thousands who perish by sickness, melancholy and suicide, in their voyages to America . . . and see them exposed there to public sale. Hear their cries, and see their looks of tenderness at each other upon being separated. Mothers are torn from their daughters, and brothers from brothers, without the liberty of a parting embrace. Their master's name is now marked upon their breasts with a red hot iron. But let us pursue them into a sugar field, and behold a scene still more affecting than this. See! the poor wretches with what reluctance they take their instruments of labor into their hands. Some of them, overcome with heat and sickness, seek to refresh themselves by a little rest. But, behold an overseer approaches them. In vain they sue for pity. He lifts up his whip, while streams of blood follow every stroke. Neither age nor sex are spared. Methinks one of them is a woman far advanced in her pregnancy. . . . Behold one covered with stripes, into which melted wax is poured—another tied down to a block or a stake—a third suspended in the air by his thumbs—a fourth obliged to set or stand upon red hot iron—a fifth,—I cannot relate it. Where now is law or justice? Let us fly to them to step in for their relief. Alas! . . . See here one without a limb, whose only crime was an attempt to regain his liberty—another led to the gallows for eating a morsel of bread, to which his labor gave him a better title than his master—a third famishing on a [hangman's] gibbet—a fourth, in a flame of fire!—his shrieks pierce the heavens—O! God! Where is thy vengeance! O! humanity—justice—liberty—religion!—Where, where are ye fled.

Published in Philadelphia in 1773 over the pseudonym "By a Pennsylvanian," it was reprinted in Boston and New York in the same year, and two years later in Connecticut. By then it had spread throughout New England, thereby endearing Rush—whose identity as the author had long been an open secret—to those provinces at the center of the abolitionist movement. A second edition was brought out in Philadelphia also in 1773, supplemented by *A Vindication of the Address, in Answer to a Pamphlet Entitled, "Slavery Not Forbidden in Scripture, or a Defense of the West India [sic]."* This was Rush's response to an attack on his original *Address* by a Richard Nesbit (or Nisbet) of St. Kitts-Nevis.[9]

Obviously his *Address* cost Rush a number of patients among slave owners and their sympathizers. It led to a diminution of his patients, and thus his income, as well as of social and professional acceptance in Philadelphia society. But he didn't care. Like any dedicated reformer, let alone one who, as it were, practiced his religion as well as preaching it, Benjamin Rush never hesitated to put principle before pecuniary and social considerations.

On 1 August 1769—coincidentally, the day he saw his first patient, a Miss Lydia Hyde, whom he charged three shillings for medical services that have gone unrecorded—Benjamin Rush was unanimously chosen by the College of Philadelphia's board of trustees professor of chemistry. He was the first man in America to hold that position. He was also the youngest of the five-man faculty. The others were John Morgan, founder of the college, and professor of the theory and practice of medicine, arguably the most esteemed physician in the colonies, who thus kept his promise to hold the position for Rush provided he acquitted himself well in his studies at Edinburgh; William Shippen, professor of anatomy, surgery and midwifery; the highly respected Adam Kuhn, professor of materia medica and botany; and Thomas Bond, a protégé of Benjamin Franklin, whose opinion of this professor of clinical medicine was such that he selected Bond to represent the medical profession in the American Philosophical Society, which had been founded in 1743 and flourishes to this day.[10]

The college grew slowly. During the first decade of its existence, twenty-eight graduates received bachelor's degrees, of whom four received the M.D. degree in 1771 after presenting theses. After 1789, its successor, the University of Pennsylvania, terminated the practice of granting bachelor's degrees in medicine, and granted only M.D. degrees to their students—a practice that became universal in American medical schools twenty-three years later, during the War of 1812. In lieu of a general admission policy, students paid for the courses, which were also open to nonmedical students.[11] Both Shippen and Rush advertised, perhaps out of personal ambition, but mainly to involve and educate the general public in scientific matters. Of the two, Rush advertised more widely—even beyond the bounds of his own province. In the Virginia capital at Williamsburg readers of the Virginia Gazette learned that on September 4, 1771

A COURSE of *lectures and experiments* on *chemistry* will commence on *Monday* the *28th of October*, at 3 o'clock in the afternoon by BENJAMIN RUSH, M.D., professor of chemistry in the college of *Philadelphia*. In these lectures and experiments, it is proposed to deliver not only the chemical history of the various bodies in nature, such as *salts—earths—inflammables—metals—waters*, &, with their application to medicine; but also to explain and illustrate most of those curious principles in nature and art, which depend upon chemical principles. The whole will be taught in such a manner as to be intelligible to the private Gentleman and enquiring artist [i.e., artisan], as well as the student of medicine. *The price of a ticket six pounds.*

Rush also conducted a course in domestic science at a recently opened academy for young ladies of Philadelphia's aristocracy. There he lectured on such matters of concern for future homemakers as keeping their houses cool and clean and ridding them of insects and vermin, on materials for making dresses, on the use of soap, starch, and dyes, on foods and condiments, even on means of preserving female beauty. He introduced this course of lectures by stating that he would teach the young ladies economy and frugality and thereby qualify them "to shine as wives, mothers, and mistresses of families." Rush would later come to believe that women deserved as much exposure to other than domestic concerns as that enjoyed by men, thus placing himself in the forefront of the movement for higher education for females.

By now, Rush had published his *Syllabus of a Course of Lectures on Chemistry*, the first such text to be written by an American. A plethora of papers would follow on many subjects which the author, serving as his own agent, and an accomplished one at that, made sure were reproduced in local newspapers as well as journals and periodicals both in America and in London. Along with his medical talents, eloquence, and great personal charm, the wide range of Rush's lectures at the college that often transcended the subject of chemistry and a growing reputation for his controversial medical theories that flew in the face of established belief "held me up to public notice now and then in the newspapers [much of which Rush himself generated], and made my name more familiar with the public ear much sooner than it would have been. It was likewise an immediate source of some revenue."[12]

But there was a down side. A number of the city's established physicians had taken a dislike to him and refused to send him referrals. This was primarily because he openly and vigorously espoused the comparatively revolutionary approach to medical treatment and methodology practiced by Dr. Cullen instead of the rather archaic system of Holland's Herman Boerhaave, whose theories governed the practice of medicine in Philadelphia through the 1760s. According to Boerhaave, now dead thirty years, diseases in general were the result of "morbid acrimonies, and other matters in the blood"; the physician must be constantly on the lookout for the discharge from the patient's system of these so-called morbid causes of the fever.

"This matter," notes Rush, "was looked for chiefly in the urine, and glasses to retain it were a necessary part of the furniture of every sick room. To ensure the discharge of the supposed morbid matter of fevers through the pores," patients were confined to their beds in sickrooms that were all but sealed against the introduction of fresh air. Spirit of sweet water and, in perilous cases, Virginia snakeroot were the diuretics of choice. Bloodletting was usually resorted to in cases of pleurisy and rheumatism. "Purges or vomits began the cure of all febrile diseases, but as the principal dependence was placed upon sweating medicines, those powerful remedies were seldom repeated in the subsequent stages of fevers. Opium was used mainly to alleviate pain. Warm and cold baths were prescribed sparingly."[13]

Condemning the Boerhaavian theory that fluids of the body were the source of diseases, Rush from the very outset of his career in Philadelphia established himself as the paramount champion of the theory advanced by Cullen, his beloved Edinburgh teacher, that the cause of disease lay in the nervous or vascular system. This theory held that "sedative powers"—solids—reduced the brain's energy, thereby producing a general weakness of the body. To restore the brain's energy, the heart, and the larger arteries as a sine qua non to a successful attack on a disease, the physician must attempt to increase their activity. Thus, the prevalent practice of practically strapping the patient to the bed and subjecting the ailing body to purging and sweating and above all enveloping the patient in what amounted to fetid air was as anti-Cullenian as a physician could possibly get. And that was the route followed by the overwhelming majority, the Boer-haavians, all of whom not only opposed but also openly condemned this upstart Rush.

We shall deal at length with Rush's groundbreaking innovations in causation and cure when we come to the great 1793 Philadelphia yellow fever epidemic. For now, it is enough to say that to so many backward-looking physicians, including many prominent throughout the colonies, he was the arch-Cullenian, ergo, the arch-villain. Such was the controversy, Cullen's system—and Rush's championing of it—was openly condemned in the press: "The system of Dr. Cullen was calumniated and even ridiculed in the newspapers with my name connected with it. Perhaps my manner of recommending it provoked this opposition, for I know by experience as well as observation that an indiscreet zeal for truth, justice, or humanity has cost more to the persons who have exercised it, than the total want of zeal for any thing good, or even zeal in false and unjust pursuits."[14]

The reader can well imagine how the opposition was provoked when at a dinner party attended by a number of medical students, Rush offered the toast, "Speedy interment of the system of Dr. Boerhaave, and may it never rise again!" Once this became public to the Philadelphia medical fraternity—and we can assume it became public by the next sunrise—the reaction was not unlike one that might have rocked the Presbyterian fraternity if at a public convocation of Old Style and New Style, Rush had offered the toast, "Speedy interment to the misguided Old Style fanatics, and may they remain buried in perpetuity!" Still, Rush enjoyed the satisfaction of noting, years later, "However unpopular and offensive the System of Dr. Cullen was when first broached by me, I lived to see it adopted by all the physicians who had opposed it; nay more, I lived to see it adhered to and defended with great obstinacy when an attempt was made to alter and improve it twenty years afterwards."[15]

Rush's self-confident individualism—and an innate unwillingness to concede he might be wrong—fueled the attitudes that embroiled him in bitter controversy not only with older colleagues, who found the young upstart offensive and a menace to the practice of medicine, but also with many of his elders—and not a few of his contemporaries—who were not themselves physicians. Just as his antislavery pamphlet earned him the enmity of the city's slaveholders, and his pro-revolutionary politics would in time provoke Philadelphia's large Loyalist population, so his reformist views on women's education and the humanity of treating the mentally ill and impaired as victims of physical disorder instead of shutting them away in asylums as if they were human embarrassments to be cast out of society would earn him the enmity of traditionalists.

But at this point in his career, the main thrust of Rush's energies was directed to medicine, to which his work in chemistry played handmaiden. To quote one of his leading biographers in the twentieth century, Dr. Carl Binger, "Rush was more the teacher, the advocate, the patriot, and even the propagandist than he was the creative student." Notwithstanding experiments he had performed as a student at Edinburgh, such as his thesis on digestion, Rush was now more concerned "with popularizing chemistry as an applied science which could contribute much to improving life in the Colonies." While he did perform some experiments to find the best vermifuge to expel worms or other parasites from the intestines, and others to bring into disrepute a then popular fake cancer cure, his contribution to chemical science, at least in the prewar phase of his professorship, could in no way be considered substantial. Dr. Oliver Wendell Holmes, Sr., commented that Rush was an observant man, but not a good observer, while one commentator ascribes it to "his constitutional inability to concentrate on any single one among his innumerable enthusiasms." Adds Binger, in summation, Rush "was, in fact, an insatiable accumulator of facts with an almost evangelical gift for teaching."[16]

Lack of equipment and of funds to import the necessary chemicals kept Rush's demonstrations to a minimum. He was, however, able to demonstrate the production of hydrogen, and a few other such efforts. But while he proved adept as a teacher, he was not keeping up with the latest advances. Whether this was because of his wide range of interests, his private practice, his extensive writing, or, as some commentators suspect, his use of his position at the college to further his career—or perhaps a combination of reasons thereof—is difficult to determine.

In his first medical publication in America (in the *Pennsylvania Journal,* 14 October 1769), published within the year in London under the title *Dissertation on the Spasmodic Asthma of Children,* where it was well received, Rush dealt with the cause and cure for what was then called "hives," a corruption of "heaves"—a description for the heaving action of the lungs as the patient struggles for breath, the condition we know today as croup. Basing his conclusions on bedside observations, autopsies, and the available literature, Rush succeeded where most men of science fail: rendering the subject matter at one and the same time comprehensible to the general public as well as a contribution to contemporary medicine.

In a follow-up piece seven months later (9 August 1770), Rush was the first to stake out a methodology that only in our own time has gained widespread acceptance in the medical community—preventive medicine: "Obviating diseases is the business of physic as well as . . . curing them." Explaining that no effective remedies had been found for those made sick by drinking cold water, he suggested holding the cup in one's hands until the chill had moderated or, even more efficacious, mixing some spirits with the water, as "this infallibly prevents the water doing any harm."

On 2 November 1770, Rush read before the American Philosophical Society a four-page essay whose importance lay in the bold brand of medicine he was determined to practice despite the antagonism he knew it would earn him among the traditionalists. The case involved a child of three or four who became violently ill after ingesting some thorn apple, more commonly known as jimsonweed, which grew profusely in the family yard. In a subtle attack on a favorite target, Boerhaavian medicine, Rush charged that first removing "obstructions" in the blood with emetics, purging "all superfluous juices and fluids" by dosing the patient with mercury "to promote salivation," and otherwise taking pains "to free the more open passages from impurities" accomplished little more than to argue down Boerhaave's thesis that the eruptions on the child's skin which accompanied her violent fever and "delirium tremor in the limbs could be ameliorated."

Resorting to more aggressive measures, and thus restoring the child's health to the degree that "all her complaints vanished, and in a few days she appeared well," Rush concluded by expressing the belief that Philadelphia physicians were quite possibly practicing too mild a brand of medicine. Perhaps "it should be our practice to increase the doses of our vomits [emetics], or to give substance as will destroy the life, or [poison], of those things we would wish to expel from our stomach."[17] Here was truly a revolutionary concept that pointed two decades down the line to Rush's theories on medical management, manifested in the horrendous 1793 yellow-fever scourge, that would set in stone his reputation worldwide.

Rush seemed to relish the controversy he was creating, though he did not relish the consequences. Colleagues were no longer seeking his advice or making referrals. In addition, the influential Shippen was keeping students from attending his lectures. While Shippen's views toward Rush's "new medicine" doubtless played a major role in his antipathy, one cannot dismiss the belief that Rush's warm relationship with, and mentorship by, Shippen's archantagonist, Morgan, was a contributory factor. Rush, though, treated the matter philosophically, writing to brother Jacob in London (24 January 1771), "Better, infinitely better, is it to be at eternal variance with a man of his cool malice and treachery, than to have any connections with him." It's doubtful that even Clio the Muse of History could have foreseen that Rush's dismissal of Shippen would in time come back to haunt him.

Besides being a prolific correspondent—his published letters run to more than two thousand pages, and a goodly number unpublished are scattered round the world in university and private collections—Rush published prolifically in his areas of primary interest: medicine, followed by politics, with a good sprinkling on abolition, education, and other areas of social reform. Here was one man who subscribed to the doctrine of publish or perish—or, at the very least, be forgotten by future generations. He antagonized the medical establishment, but found favor with his patients, and interested observers, with some of his ideas, which revealed him to be far ahead of his time when it came to ideas ancillary to the practice of medicine but which nevertheless put him on the cutting edge.

This becomes apparent in his *Sermons to Gentleman upon Temperance and Exercise*. (When published in London by the brothers Dilly, the title was changed to *Sermons to the Rich and Studious, on Temperance and Exercise* "as it is more applicable to such persons than to gentlemen in general.") The paper, from which Rush withheld his name because "he seeks nothing from his countrymen but the pleasure of doing them good," was in fact three essays dealing with gout, diet, and proper physical exercise.

In the first, published 26 December 1771 in the *Pennsylvania Gazette,* Rush, while hoping that not all imbibers will become afflicted with gout, advises that wine be given to the sick; to those dwelling in low marshlands ("The moisture of such places obstructs perspiration, and brings on a general laxity of the system"); and to the elderly. Wines should, though, be withheld from children, as they were in no need of stimulants; from studious people ("Thinking is a stimulus to the constitution, and wears out the springs of life behind the most laborious exercise of the body"); and from those below the age of forty. One suspects that Rush is doing a bit of leg-pulling in this first essay, which he concludes by advising that "the groans" emanating from the chamber of one suffering the agonies of gout is attributable to the melancholy fact that "death, the last friend of the wretched, refuses to come at his call."

In the second essay, published in the *Gazette* on 9 January 1772, he posits theories on diet that have found much favor of late among health-food faddists, such as abjuring a diet of highly seasoned foods for people "in the full vigor of health and youth." While he finds the ingesting of spices acceptable for the elderly and for those living in tropical climates, where they "obviate the relaxing powers of heat and moisture," the diet for most Americans should be bland and simple, and well balanced, with vegetables predominating, especially in warm seasons and warm climates. Contending that people consumed too much, he advised one "hearty" meal daily: "food . . . may be said to be taken in too large a quantity, when we do not feel light and cheerful after it." In Rush's day it was customary to take the main meal at noon. He preached taking it in the evening for the twofold yet interrelated reasons that "Sleep is always natural after eating, Nature loudly calls for it," and "digestion has been lately proved to be carried on chiefly by FERMENTATION, to which rest, everybody knows, is so essentially necessary it cannot take place without it."

The third, and most modern "sermon," which strongly advocates exercise, was published by the *Pennsylvania Packet* (17 February

1772) after the *Gazette* declined to run it—probably because it was a time when little if any attention was given to the need of formal exercise and athletics in daily life. Insisting that exercise is necessary for the preservation of not only one's physical well-being but also one's mental vitality as well, the author advocated the indulgence of "active" exercises: walking ("It promotes perspiration, and if not continued too long, invigorates and strengthens the system"); running (though "too violent to be used often"); dancing ("a most salutary exercise [that] inspires the mind with cheerfulness, and this, when well founded, and properly [limited to once a week], is another name for religion," though one should not "expose one's self" to cold air after doing so); fencing, "which not only exercises most of the muscles but also stimulates the brain"; swimming, which Benjamin Franklin also found to be highly beneficial, as it not only exercises the limbs, it also "serves to wash away the dust which is apt to mix itself with the sweat of our bodies in warm weather"; and, finally, "TALKING, which also includes reading aloud, singing, and laughing." Passive forms of exercise, such as riding, either on horseback or in a coach, and sailing were recommended only for those "with a weakness of the nerves, such as hysteric and hypochondriac disorders." Extended journeys were also recommended "for ill patients to stimulate mind and body: to cold climates for those suffering chronic hysteria or epilepsy, to warm climates for hypochondriacs and consumptives."

Attesting to the antagonism he had by now raised in the medical community, the "sermons" were "well received before it was known who was the author of them"—a bit of knowledge Rush himself could well have circulated, given his propensity for self-advertisement. He "heard of a physician who commended them in high terms when he believed they were written by another person, and abused them as extravagantly when he discovered that they came from my pen."[18] Other physicians followed suit, which was perfectly fine with Rush. He was happy for the free publicity generated by the book and its subsequent controversy in some quarters.

He was not happy, though, when his paper on "hives" was rejected by the Royal Society; nor, for that matter, his next paper, dealing with intestinal worms. Rush remained convinced until his dying days that his research constituted a contribution worthy of his admittance to that august group. That he failed to win admission to the Royal Society, despite the high repute in which he was held by a number of London's leading physicians, was arguably the greatest frustration of his life.

By 1773 the troubles Rush was having with the medical community, the Quakers, and just about everyone else became common knowledge. Inhibited from enjoying the fruits of his profession he felt he deserved at this point in his career, he considered moving to London. But medical friends in London advised that such was the competition there that Rush could not expect to do any better financially in London, and possibly worse.

From Charleston came an offer to relocate there to take over the practice of the city's most distinguished physician, Dr. Alexander Garden, who was retiring because of ill health. Rush was assured that being a Presbyterian would not prejudice the Anglican elite against him. Furthermore, his income would be more than twice what he was currently making in Philadelphia. But a Charleston friend discouraged the idea on the grounds that some thirty-odd established physicians in the city would be competing for what they might get of Garden's practice. Better, advised Chalmers, to remain in Philadelphia, where he was confident Rush would in time be appreciated and emerge as a leading member of the medical profession.[19]

Writing to his friend Barbeu-Dubourg in Paris as if the Charleston offer was his for the taking, his friend's warning to the contrary, Rush decided he was "too attached to [Pennsylvania], this dear province where one owes one's ease only to free and honest toil, to be tempted to exchange it for a [province] where wealth has been accumulated only by the sweat and blood of Negro slaves."[20]

In fact, despite the antagonism he aroused, his income was now on the rise, what with his private practice, his courses at the college, his publications both at home and in England, and his appointment as one of the physicians at the city's almshouse, House of Employment (later the Philadelphia General Hospital). To his friend Elihu Hall he was able to write on 10 November 1774, "My business has increased greatly within these two years, so much so that I have much less leisure than formerly to promote my studies." From a low of 43 patients in February 1772 it rose by October to 99; and after a slump of two months, his patient load rose from 78 in January 1773 to 86 in the following month. Rush was now in a position to rescind a vow made as he stepped ashore from the *Edward* on his return from Europe that no woman might "tempt him to perpetuate matrimony" until he was financially secure enough to be tempted. In fact, he had met the young lady he was determined to make his bride.

Benjamin Rush was now not only ready to become a husband and father, he was poised to become one of the nation's Founding Fathers.

6

Marriage and Politics

Benjamin Rush's feelings for Polly Fisher and Lady Jane Leslie would seem to have been not so much true love as infatuation. The following is what he wrote of Sarah Eve, the first woman to whom he proposed marriage.

> Her understanding was strong, her imagination brilliant, and her taste correct. These were improved by an intimate acquaintance with some of the best political and prose writers in the English language. Her disposition was amiable; a person who had lived with her from a child, declared that she had never once seen her angry, or heard a hasty word from her lips. Her manners were polished. They were not put on, and laid aside, like a part of a dress; she was always alike captivating, even in her most careless moments, and in the society of her most intimate friends. Her person was elegant, her face had a happy mixture of the happy and beautiful in it; her voice was soft, and her elocution was flowing. Her sentiments were often original, and always just; it was impossible for her to speak upon any subject without gaining the attention of company. Such were her unaffected displays of good sense, modesty, and good humour, that no one, I believe, ever left her without emotions of love, esteem, or admiration.

The words appeared not in his memoirs or any of his many letters to friends with whom he liked to share comments on affairs of the heart, but in an encomium—significantly, unsigned—in the Philadelphia Packet on 12 December 1774 under the title, "A Female Character."

Were Rush's anonymity and his failure to mention her in his memoirs or correspondence indicative of a desire to close immediately and forever a painful episode in his life? The idea remains open to conjecture. So do a few others, such as, was their love affair all that profound, or has tradition exaggerated what may have been no more than a strong friendship? In a letter dated 24 September 1774 to Lady Jane, Rush admits to squiring other girls around town; and this in the same month he and Sarah Eve became affianced.

Would the marriage have been a successful one? If it is true, as the old adage would have it, that opposites attract, speculation on its success would resound with certainty. But an adage, it must be conceded, is a traditional means of expressing something taken as a general truth, not a metaphysical certitude. What we know of Sarah Eve's attitudes—and she had more than her fair share, the preponderance of them contrary to those held by Rush—were recorded in her "Journal of Miss Sarah Eve While Living Near the City of Philadelphia in 1772–3," from which her words below are taken.[1]

Attractive, stately in bearing, and fashionable in dress, the redheaded Sarah was the daughter of a sea captain, Oswald Eve, whose residence was a farm some two miles from Rush's home on the Delaware. Four years younger than the twenty-seven-year-old Rush when they first met in 1773, Sarah had become friendly with Mrs. Rush, often taking tea with her at her grocery shop and dining occasionally at her home. Their friendship was of recent vintage, as it was not until four years after his return from Europe that Rush became aware of her. Now that he was financially secure enough to take a mate, Rush made it a point to be present, his hectic schedule permitting, whenever she dropped by his mother's house for a social visit. By early 1774, the visits were turning into an active courtship. They planned to be married sometime around Christmas.

How could Rush have allowed himself to fall in love with a girl like Sarah Eve, who was overly concerned with pleasure but held opinions that to an archetypical puritanical gentleman of his times were considered neither becoming nor agreeable in the bride of a professional man upon whom success was at last descending? There was, for example, her attitude toward the ministry, which Rush considered a sacred calling: She could not understand why "such an exemplary man as Mr.

Duché," a prominent clergyman, "should sit every day and have his hair curled and powdered by a barber."

And then there was her lack of comportment when it came to such conventions as young ladies being expected to walk sadly by the biers of contemporaries during funeral processions: "Foolish Custom for girls to prance it through the streets without hats or bonnets!" And her dislike of fairly harmless masculine advances: "One hates to be always kissed, especially as it is attended with so many inconveniences; it decomposes the economy of one's *handkerchief*, it disorders one's *high roll*, and it ruffles the serenity of one's countenance."

Of course, these opinions were confined to Sarah's diary. Still, a girl—especially a girl of Sarah's caliber—will reflect in social conversation, albeit more temperately, opinions and feelings she will confide to her diary less inhibitedly. Rush knew that he had chosen for a bride one he might possibly have passed over had he approached the matter intellectually. But when it came to Sarah Eve, the heart, not the head, informed his decision. He was madly in love with her. Or at least he believed himself to be, if we are to judge by the attention he danced on her despite a hectic professional life. Rush knew what he was getting. Rush also knew what he was *not* getting. And that was a dowry. Sarah's father had commanded one ship and owned shares in at least twenty-five others, but had met with financial reverses five years previously and gone off with his two sons to the West Indies, where he was still trying to repair his fortunes as a merchant in Jamaica.

The question now obtrudes: Why did Sarah agree to become Mrs. Benjamin Rush? Though he is mentioned frequently in her diary—always as "Mr. Rush" or "B. Rush"—it is in an inconsequential context. Did she genuinely love him? Or did she not perhaps see in marriage to him a means of helping her impoverished family? Rush was now earning £900 a year, a goodly sum that placed him in the upper tier of the middle class. What patients he had lost by his attack on slavery had been offset by those who agreed with him, and lauded his continued attacks on the institution. He was now well known and respected not only in Philadelphia but also throughout the colonies for the role he was rapidly assuming as one of the most fervid and articulate among those calling for separation from England.

Here, again, is one of those questions that can only be speculated upon. For tragically Sarah, who around the time of their engagement in September 1774 came down with a lingering illness believed to have been tuberculosis, died three weeks before their wedding date.[2] Remarkably, Rush submitted to her father a bill for professional services rendered Sarah Eve. Surely an unseemly act by a physician caring for his betrothed on her deathbed. (Lee paid the bill.) As a physician watching Sarah's health decline rapidly, Rush must have at least suspected that if the wedding went through, theirs would have been a cruelly abbreviated marriage. Is it possible that his going ahead with the plans was not so much an act of intention as an act of charity? The point is moot. Sarah was dead. And within the year, Rush would fall in love with his future wife, to whom he would give absolute love and connubial loyalty for the remaining thirty-eight years of his life.

Actually, it was not so much a meeting as a reunion. A dozen years before, on the day Rush was awarded his degree from Princeton, he came upon a child who had lost her way in the commencement crowd. Taking the four-year-old in his arms, he delivered her safely to the nearby estate of her concerned father.[3] The child was Julia Stockton. Her father, Richard, a law graduate of the College of New Jersey when it was located at Newark, went on to build a successful career before the bar; it was so successful that he was able to persuade its trustees to relocate the college to his hometown of Princeton and become one of its leading and most influential benefactors. It was Stockton who had urged the selection as the school's president of Rev. John Witherspoon, who, it will be recalled, Rush, when a student at Edinburgh, had persuaded to accept the position.

In August 1775, eight months after his unrealized marriage to Sarah Eve, Rush went to Princeton to visit Witherspoon and Stockton, with whom he had become reacquainted during the First Continental Congress in the previous year. Rush "was conducted by him to his house [Morven], where I was kindly entertained as his guest for several days." The scintillating conversationalist with the good looks, fetching mien, and engaging manner of that now sixteen-year-old heiress he had carried to her home on his graduation day "soon attracted my attention. . . . From this moment I determined to offer her my hand." Soon after he returned to Philadelphia, Rush wrote the Stocktons seeking permission to court their daughter, which "request was politely granted. After several visits my suit was blessed with success."[4] On 11 January 1776, at Morven, the two were married by Witherspoon. Six months later the bride's father and her husband would share the distinction of being the only father-in-law and son-in-law pair to sign the Declaration of Independence.

Attesting to the success of the marriage, Rush was able to write toward the end of his life: "Let me here bear testimony to the worth of this excellent woman. She fulfilled every duty as a wife, mother, and mistress with fidelity and integrity. To me she was always a sincere and honest friend. Had I yielded to her advice upon many occasions, I should have known less distress from various causes in my journey through life. . . . May God reward and bless her with an easy and peaceful old age if she should survive me. . . ."[5] God complied. Julia survived Benjamin by thirty-five years, dying in 1848 at the age of ninety.

Rush's great love for, and dependence upon, Julia is evident by his numerous letters to her ("My Dearest" is a typical salutation) during the many periods they were apart due either to her many visits to Morven, be it to bear their children or escape the periodic yellow fever and smallpox epidemics that were almost a way of life in Philadelphia, or when he was serving with the Continental Army. A typical lament *de coeur*, only four months after their marriage, when Julia was visiting with her parents and Rush was consumed not only with his medical practice but his activities in the cause of independence:

> I did not know till since we parted how much you were a part of myself, and I feel some abatement of my affection for my country when I reflect that even she has deprived me of an hour of my dear Julia's company. I have more than once forgotten that you were out of town, and have come [home] prepared to entertain you with an account of everything I had seen and heard . . . when alas! The first steps I took in passing through the entry convinced me of my mistake. A melancholy silence reigns through every apartment of our house. Every room and piece of furniture proclaims that you are gone, and sympathizes with me in lamenting the absence of their mistress.[6]

Two days later, acknowledging having heard from her ("My Dearest Life, I have wept over both your letters"), he describes his involvement with the Second Continental Congress, and wants her to know "My heart glows with an affection for you at this instant so tender, so delicate, and so refined that I want words to express it." He anticipates the pleasure they will share when independence has been achieved and "we have no third person to break in upon our sweet house of social and conjugal happiness."

The couple had thirteen children. Four died in infancy. Of the others (three girls, six boys), three are worthy of note. John (1777–1837), the firstborn, followed his father into medicine, and was commissioned as a surgeon in the United States Navy, but resigned after two years as a result of an emotional reaction to naval life that led progressively to clinical insanity. This condition, which was never made public, led his sorrowful father to devote himself to the study of insanity, and to the contention that victims of mental derangement were deserving of clinical treatment, where possible, instead of, as was customary for the times, being condemned to sequestration from society.

James, the seventh child (1786–1869) also followed his father into medicine, but retired after a few years of practice to follow his scientific and literary interests. His chief work, highly regarded in its time, was a study of the physiology of the voice. Upon the death of his heiress wife, Phoebe Ann Ridgway, James used his bequeathed wealth to found the Ridgway Library, now a branch of the Philadelphia free library system. William, the last born (1801–1864), also pursued a medical career.

But it was the third born, Richard (1780–1859), who was the most distinguished son. Admitted to the bar at the age of twenty, within ten years he had commenced a career that brought him national renown, serving as Attorney-General of Pennsylvania and Comptroller of the U.S. Treasury (1811), Attorney-General of the United States (1814–1817), acting Secretary of State (1817), Minister to Great Britain (1817–1825), Secretary of the Treasury (1825–1829), and U.S. Minister to France (1847–1851), thus earning Richard Rush the distinction of having served in high capacity six American Presidents (Madison, Monroe, John Quincy Adams, Jackson, Taylor, and Fillmore).

Of the many letters Rush wrote to his wife, the overwhelming preponderance relate his activities and experiences attendant upon his role in the run-up to and actual playing out of the American Revolution. Julia could almost have predicted this. By the time of their marriage her husband was in the maelstrom that was the labor pains preceding the birth of history's first pure constitutional democracy. He had entered that maelstrom around the time he began courting Sarah Eve in earnest.

At the time Rush went abroad to study, repeal of the Stamp Act seemed to suggest a dramatic abatement of antagonism between England and her American colonies. But this proved to be illusory. During his stay at Edinburgh, influenced by passage of the Townshend Acts and the philosophical arguments of his friend John Bostock, Rush's "attachment to political justice was much increased by my adopting republican principles. Thus prepared, I took an early but obscure part in the controversy between Great Britain and the American colonies in the year 1773."

Early, perhaps. But hardly obscure. "Having published several pieces in the newspapers in favor of the claims of my country, which attracted notice," Rush soon found himself "admitted into the confidence" of such rapidly rising nationalists as John Dickinson, author of the aforementioned *Farmer's Letters*; George Clymer, "a cool, firm, consistent Republican who loved liberty and government with an equal affection," and who, beneath a façade of manners "that were cold and indolent . . . concealed a mind that was always warm and active towards the interests of his country"; and the universally respected and trusted Charles Thompson, "a man of great learning and general knowledge, at all times a genuine Republican."

Heading the roster of those Rush mentions proudly as having been "admitted into the confidence" of, perhaps the most memorable was the Quaker merchant Thomas Mifflin, a member of the First Continental Congress, Quartermaster General in the Continental Army, president of the Congress in 1783, delegate to the Constitutional Convention of 1787, and, for the last nine years of his life, governor of Pennsylvania. According to Rush, "he possessed genius, knowledge, eloquence, patriotism, courage, self-government and an independent spirit, in the first years of the war [and] was extremely useful in the gloomy winter of 1776 by rallying the drooping courage of the militia of his native State, which he did by riding through all the populous [counties], and exhorting them to turn out to check the progress of the British army."

Adding that Mifflin's "influence was much promoted by an elegant person, an animated countenance, and popular manners," Rush suggests that this man, who was from the very beginning one of George Washington's senior aides, would have held greater appeal for posterity if he had "fallen in battle, or died in the year 1778." By the time he was elected governor of Pennsylvania in 1791, the man whom Rush the Patriot had so admired had turned into an object of wretched scorn to Rush the Puritan: "a very immoral character [who] lived in a state of adultery with many women during the life of his wife, and had children by some of them . . . much addicted to swearing and obscene conversation. His political character was as bad as his moral. He had deserted his friends and joined with the men who slandered them. . . . He lived beyond his income, and was much in debt." That so erstwhile a paragon won the majority of the votes both in Philadelphia and throughout the state is attributed by the moralistic Dr. Rush to the assumption "The Quakers generally supported him."[7]

Though busy with his medical practice and his lectures, Rush "was not idle at this time with my pen. I wrote under a variety of signatures [i.e., pseudonyms], by which means an impression of numbers in favor of liberty was made upon the minds of its friends and enemies."[8] Doubtless because they were published pseudonymously, only a few have come to light. One, though, that has, and the one which further spread Rush's reputation beyond the bounds of Pennsylvania was a letter, "To His Fellow Countrymen: On Patriotism," published in the *Pennsylvania Journal* over the name "Hamden" on 20 October 1773. It was prompted by Parliament's passage of the Tea Act, and through it Rush can be said to have played no small role in instigating the Boston Tea Party that occurred eight weeks later.

Following the Boston Massacre, the colony's merchants, anxious for a restoration of peace and trade, organized to combat what they termed "the unbridled Spirit of Mob Violence," which resulted in the curbing of further violence. By way of appreciation—and due in large measure to the influence of British merchants—Parliament rescinded all the Townshend duties except the three-pence tax on tea. This posed little problem, since most of the tea being consumed in the colonies was being smuggled in, mostly from Dutch sources. Normally, tea imported into England was taxed for reshipment to the colonies, which tax was added to the selling price in America. In May 1773, in order to relieve the British East India Company, which had a virtual monopoly on the legal colonial tea trade, from going into bankruptcy because of maladministration, Parliament removed the duty on tea entering England and allowed the company to be its own exporter to America, thus eliminating the middlemen.

Britain's trade policy toward her overseas colonies was characteristically obtuse and the plan to rescue the East India Company from bankruptcy can be likened to the great American wit Will Rogers's flippant suggestion for eliminating the menace of German submarines to Allied shipping during World War I: "All you have to do is to heat the Atlantic to 212 degrees. Then the subs will have to come up and we can pick them off. Of course, somebody's going to want to know how to heat up the ocean. I'm not worrying about that. That's just a detail, and I'm a policy maker."9

On the surface, the new arrangement would have worked to the colonists' advantage in that it added no new duty, but eliminated one. If enforced, the East India Company would have been enabled to undersell the Dutch smugglers and thus give the colonial consumers cheaper tea. But to the radicals, led by Samuel Adams's Sons of Liberty, it still violated the principle of self-government and further congealed the hated concept of taxation without representation. By this time, the Americans were being kept apprised of what was happening not only in Boston but throughout the colonies through the Committees of Correspondence, which ensured that pertinent—one might say properly inflammable—newspaper articles were given wide circulation. One such article was Rush's "Hamden" letter of 20 October 1773.

Addressing himself to "My Countrymen," Rush begins on a philosophical note: "Patriotism is as much a virtue as justice, and is as necessary for the support of societies as natural affection is for the support of families," and insists that love of country ("The Amor Patriae") is both a moral and a religious duty. It comprehends not only the love of our neighbors but of millions of our fellow creatures, not only of the present but of future generations." This virtue, he went on, constituted "a part of the first characters in history," and he cites the "holy men of old" who were "endowed with a public spirit" that was in equal proportion to their religious spirit: "What did not Moses forsake and suffer for his countrymen! What shining examples of Patriotism do we behold in Joshua, Samuel, [Judas] Maccabeus, and all the illustrious princes, captains, and prophets amongst the Jews!"

After citing further historical personages whose "benevolent virtue sometimes goes beyond humanity and extends itself to the very soil that gives us birth"—Joseph, for example, ordered that upon his death in Egypt his brothers "inter his bones in his own country," and Themistocles insisted he be "removed from Persia after his death in order that [his remains] might mix with his native dust in Greece, although he had been banished from that country"—Rush comes to the main thrust of his letter:

The design of this attempt to rescue patriotism from obloquy is to prepare the way for calling upon you to show whether the opposition you formerly gave to the British Parliament in their attempts to tax the American colonies was founded upon resentment and party rage, or whether it flowed from a well-informed zeal in the cause of liberty. You have heard of the machinations of the enemies of our country to enslave us by means of the East-India Company. By the last accounts from Britain we are informed that vessels were freighted to bring over a quantity of tea taxed with a duty to raise a revenue from America. Should it be landed, it is to be feared it will find its way amongst us. Then farewell American Liberty! We are undone forever. All the images we can borrow from everything terrible in nature are too faint to describe the horror of our situation. But I rely too much upon the virtue which has hitherto distinguished my countrymen to cherish a thought that this will be the case. *Let us with one heart and hand oppose the landing of it* [author's italics]. The baneful [tea] chests contain in them a slow poison in a political as well as a physical sense. They contain worse than death—[they contain] the seeds of SLAVERY. Remember, my countrymen, the present era—perhaps the present struggle—will fix the constitution of America forever. Think of your ancestors and of your posterity.

Sam Adams's Sons of Liberty and their supporters, who were by now organized throughout the colonies, took Rush's words to heart.

In December 1773 British ships bearing large consignments of tea began to arrive in the four main ports. The cargo at Charleston was off-loaded—and put under bond in a damp warehouse. At Philadelphia and New York, the ships' masters were persuaded, under threat of bombardment from shore batteries, to turn back without entering the harbor. At Boston, the two ships were permitted to enter the harbor. The East India Company, deciding to play it safe, had consigned their tea to merchants such as the sons of Governor Hutchinson, who were known to hate the Sons of Liberty as much as they revered their king.

But that was not the reason the ships were permitted to anchor. Sam Adams wanted to make a more dramatic statement of protest. Toward that end, he had devised a plan, whose backing he sought by convening the colony's regional Committees of Correspondence at the Old South Meeting House. After hearing Adams out, the convention sent a message to Governor Hutchinson demanding that the ships return home immediately and take their tea with them. The wily Adams knew the request was illegal, as the ships had already entered the customs limits. When the governor's refusal was read out to the convention, Adams jumped up and said, "This meeting can do nothing further to save the country." At that point, as if on cue, a mob disguised as Mohawk Indians and Negroes rushed down to the waterfront and dumped all 342 enormous chests of the precious cargo into the harbor.

This Boston Tea Party was an act of calculation on Adams's part to provoke the British government into imprudent acts of retaliation. As soon as word of how the tea was "received" in the colonies reached London, the cabinet went into immediate session to consider how to deal with the "late proceedings" at Boston. Lord North, the prime minister, wished to avoid further infuriating the, by now, easily infuriated Americans. But his king was furious, as was the English public.

North realized that unless something was done his government would fall. Parliament joined the king and his subjects in reasoning that since appeasement had twice failed—by rescinding the Stamp Act and the odious Townshend Acts—England had no choice but to take punitive measures. Despite warnings from such prominent figures as philosopher-statesman Edmund Burke and the highly respected General John Burgoyne that retaliation would only further enflame the Americans, Parliament passed the Coercive ("Intolerable") Acts. King George III wrote to Lord North, "The dye is now cast. The Colonies must either submit or triumph."

To quote the preeminent American historian Samuel Eliot Morison, "That is why this comic stage-Indian business of the Boston Tea Party was important. It goaded John Bull into a showdown, which was exactly what Sam Adams and the other radical leaders wanted."[10]

The First Continental Congress, comprising fifty-five delegates from twelve colonies—Georgia declined to attend—convened on 5 September 1774 in Carpenter's Hall. (Canada, technically an American colony and thus included in the equation, had been invited, but decided to go its own way under British duress.) The delegates represented all classes—doctors, lawyers, politicians, merchants, farmers, and hunters—and ranged the spectrum of opinion, from conservative southern plantation owners like Virginia's George Washington and Richard Henry Lee, both of whom hoped the English would be "reasonable," to moderates like Pennsylvania's John Dickinson, who strongly favored conciliation, to firebrands like Virginia's Patrick Henry and Massachusetts' Sam Adams. All had one thing in common: hatred of British oppression. Elected unanimously as president of the Congress was Peyton Randolph, the fifty-three-year-old Speaker of the Virginia House of Burgesses who had rallied the opposition of these legislators against the Stamp Act.

The intention of this Congress was not to plan for war, but, rather, to debate the extent to which the colonies should carry their resistance to Great Britain. Most of the delegates, reflecting the majority consensus in their respective provinces, hoped to achieve a redress of grievances. The radicals, preferring an immediate break with England but realizing they were in the minority, could only hope Parliament would stand firm and as a result precipitate a volte-face among that majority consensus. As it turned out, Parliament reacted just as the radicals anticipated—indeed hoped.

Thus it can be posited that it was the British themselves and not their American colonists who started the Revolution.

*   *   *

The British strategy of dividing the Americans was to use the destruction of tea and the ensuing Intolerable Acts to isolate what they saw as the radical Massachusetts patriots from more moderate Americans in the southern and the mid-Atlantic colonies. They nearly succeeded. Even before the opening session was called to order, all the members had divided into two camps: the radicals, led by Samuel Adams, and the conservatives, led by Joseph Galloway of Pennsylvania. The Adams camp scored a victory on 18 September when, by a slim margin, the Congress approved the Suffolk Resolves, which urged formidable opposition to Great Britain.

Galloway then came up with his so-called Plan of Union. This called for creation of an American parliament to replace the existing provincial legislatures with significant powers of taxation and legislation, subject to approval of a governor-general to be appointed by the Crown. This was Galloway's conciliatory compromise with the view expressed by Thomas Jefferson in a pamphlet titled "A Summary View of the Rights of British America." Intended to influence the Virginia delegates to the Congress, Jefferson denounced all parliamentary legislation as acts "of arbitrary power . . . over these states."

The delegates then adopted policies favored by the more radical Patriots, as they were now becoming popularly known. On 14 October a resolution was passed called the Declaration of Rights and Grievances. Denying the power of Parliament to tax the colonies, it presented King George with a list of grievances and declared the Crown's colonial policy "unconstitutional, dangerous, and destructive to the freedom" of America. Six days later, the Congress voted to establish a Third Nonimportation Movement. To implement this boycott, which included pledges against exportation and consumption as well as importation, the Congress created a Continental Association made up of committees from each colony to enforce the boycott of British imports and institute a ban on exports if Parliament did not repeal the Intolerable Acts. Among these local committees were the Committees of Correspondence and the Committees of Safety. These measures were to remain in effect until all colonial grievances had been addressed.

The delegates declared that they had written both measures as loyal Englishmen. In the first document, they expressed the hope that "their fellow subjects in Great Britain" would restore the relationship they had previously held with the colonies. The resolution for the Continental Association opened with the phrase "We, his majesty's most loyal subjects . . ."

The Congress adjourned seven weeks after convening, on 26 October, realizing they could do little more at this point than play a waiting game. Their last resolution was to the effect that if King George failed to respond favorably to their petition, a second congress would reassemble at Philadelphia on 10 May 1775.

During that first Congress, Rush entertained and was in turn entertained by those attendees now legendary among the Founding Fathers. John Adams and he cemented the friendship that would last until Rush's death. George Washington noted in his diary that he dined at Rush's home on 17 October.[11] Rush recalls a "long evening" he spent at the home of Thomas Mifflin, one of the Pennsylvania delegates who kept Rush abreast of what was happening during the secret sessions. Also attending were Washington, the two Adamses, "and several other gentlemen who acted a conspicuous part in the American Revolution." As they sat around after dinner discussing events of the day, "several of the company looked forward to the probable consequences of the present measures, and state of things." John Adams said that he foresaw no redress of grievances by, nor any reconciliation with, the mother country. To support this pessimistic view, he offered a toast, "Cash and Gunpowder to the Yankies!" Adds Rush: "The war which [Adams] anticipated, it was expected[,] would begin among the New Englandmen who were then called Yankies both by their friends and enemies."[12]

For the six months between the adjournment of the First Continental Congress (26 October 1774) and the battles of Lexington and Concord (19 April 1775) Rush "continued a spectator only of the events which passed in our country." The events of 19 April, however,

gave a new tone to my feelings, and I now resolved to bear my share of the duties and burdens of the approaching Revolution. I considered the separation of the colonies from Great Britain as inevitable. The first gun that was fired at an American cut the cord that had tied the two countries together. It was the signal for the commencement of our independence and from this time all my publications were calculated to prepare the public mind to adopt that important and necessary measure.[13]

7

Patriot

In the second week of March 1775, while browsing in Richard Aitken's bookstore, Dr. Rush was introduced to a stranger Aitkin had hired temporarily to edit his *Pennsylvania Magazine or United States Monthly Magazine* until he could establish himself as a freelance political journalist, poet, and polemicist. The thirty-seven-year-old stranger, Thomas Paine, son of an Anglican mother and a Quaker father, lacked a rounded education but was an accomplished autodidact. After working for his father from the age of thirteen, he went to sea at nineteen, returned to civilian life, and held a number of jobs. His last was as collector of taxes from smugglers he tracked down as a sort of bounty hunter. Indicative of his sense of social commitment, he was fired for publishing a document that called for an increase in wages as a means of reducing corruption in government service. His first wife had died, he had legally separated from his second, and career-wise he seemed to be on a treadmill to oblivion. In a word, his life was a mess. On the advice of Benjamin Franklin, whom he met and befriended and who provided him with letters of introduction, Paine emigrated to America, arriving at Philadelphia in November 1774.

Paine told Rush he hoped "to teach a school, or to give private lessons upon geography to young ladies and gentlemen." This struck a responsive chord in Rush, who was interested in establishing a school for young ladies whose curriculum would embrace much more than simply how to become a homemaker. A few days later Rush read an essay, "African Slavery in America," that had appeared in the 8 March 1775 issue of the *Pennsylvania Journal*. In it the pseudonymous author, "Justice and Humanity," attacked cogently the justification by those who insisted slaves could be legitimately traded on the market as commodities. He insisted they were "*an unnatural commodity* . . . and as the true owner has a right to reclaim his goods that were stolen, and sold[,] so the slave, who is proper owner of his freedom, has a right to reclaim it, however often sold." But it was Christian justification of slavery that drew the author's sharpest condemnation:

> Christians are taught to account all men their neighbours; and love their neighbours as themselves; *and do to all men as they would be done by; to do good to all men; and Man-stealing is ranked with enormous crimes* [emphasis in the original]. Is the barbarous enslaving [of] our inoffensive neighbours, and treating them like wild beasts subdued by force, reconcilable with all these *Divine people?* Is this doing to them as we would desire they should do to us? If they could carry off and enslave some thousands of us, would we think it just? One would almost wish they could for once; it might convince more than Reason, or the Bible.

Paine's solution: immediate emancipation of all slaves. Let the Americans set an example for the rest of the world. Former masters should provide for old and infirm slaves unable physically to exploit their freedom. All other freed slaves should be offered a choice of land grants, low-rent allotments, or gainful employment "so as all may have some property, and fruits of their labours at their own disposal." Admirers of the essay assigned to its author the honor of being the first American abolitionist. But the reader knows that that honor rightfully belongs to Benjamin Rush, whose *Address to the Inhabitants of the British Settlements in America, upon Slave-Keeping* had been published two years earlier, and whose very arguments "Justice and Humanity" appeared to be echoing.

The tract "excited [Rush's] desire to be better acquainted" with its author, whose first published essay it was. Learning that "Justice and Humanity" was in fact the same Mr. Paine he had met in Aitken's bookstore, Rush invited him to visit a few days afterward: "Our subjects were political." Rush "perceived with pleasure" that Paine "realized the independence of the American colonies upon Great Britain, and that he considered the measure as necessary to bring the war to a speedy and successful issue." Thus was Paine prepared to go further at this time than even such men as John Adams and George Washington, who, like so many delegates to the First Continental Congress, hoped that Parliament would acquiesce in a peaceful resolution of the colonials' demands—if for no other reason than that the colonials, themselves divided on the issue, were hardly in a position to take on a powerful Great Britain. They lacked not only a singularity of purpose and acceptable cohesion but also an army, a navy, and a capacity for manufacturing needed war matériel.

Rush and Paine were of the same mind. The outlook for redress by the British of the colonists's grievances was grim. Their first petition to the king had been debated and rejected by Parliament, as had William Pitt's Motion for Conciliation. In early February, the House of Lords passed a proposal to declare Massachusetts in rebellion, thereby hoping to score the twofold purpose of punishing the New Englanders, whose seditionist activities against the Crown were the most overt, and driving a wedge between the Bay Colony and the other provinces.

Even before the first Congress adjourned, Rush was convinced of the inevitability of war. His conviction was borne out from news coming out of England. Though the present Parliament still had a year to run—British law required a general election be held at least once every seven years—the Americans' reaction to the Intolerable Acts had prompted dissolution of the Parliament and a new election. This resulted in King George III now enjoying a sizable majority in Commons that allowed his new government, led by the uncompromising Lord North, freedom of action for the next seven years. When Parliament reassembled in November 1774, its first act was to endorse the king's position that, with the New England colonies "in a state of rebellion," "blows must decide" whether they were to be subject to or independent of the Crown.

By year's end, the ten nonproprietary colonies whose legislatures were ordered dissolved by royal fiat had established provincial congresses. All were extralegal, and all were composed mainly of the same men who had sat in the regular assemblies. It was these local congresses that approved the proceedings of the First Continental Congress and elected delegates to the second. This despite orders that went out to all colonial governors in January 1775 to prevent the election of delegates to that second Congress. A month later, three generals—Sir William Howe, Sir Henry Clinton, and John Burgoyne—set sail with reinforcements for the army already on station in the colonies under the overall command of General Thomas Gage.

In that same month, with an ill-prepared America moving toward war, a joint stock venture, the United Company for Promoting American Manufacturers, was organized; three weeks later, on 16 March, Rush was elected president by unanimous vote of all the subscribers. No one seriously thought he would actually direct company affairs. His election was a confirmation of the hope that a man so capable of articulating his views in print would engender popular support for what to many seemed at first blush to be less a practicable project than a visionary one. Rush set out at once to disabuse them of that notion.

In his "inauguration speech," Rush began with the admission that what optimism he once held for reconciliation with England had now evaporated. Of more immediate concern, woolens, cottons, and linens were a considerable part of the embargo that the Congress had placed on British goods. And it was imperative that Americans establish woolen, cotton, and linen factories of their own: "I am far from thinking that the Non-Importation Agreement[s] will be so transitory a thing as some have supposed. The same arbitrary ministers continue in office, and the same arbitrary favorites continue to abuse the confidence of our sovereign." Rush foresaw at least two or three years of resistance by the colonials before the British "came around." His battle cry: Continue the embargo, and foster home industries!

Many Pennsylvania families were already manufacturing in their own homes sufficient woolens and linens to meet their needs. Take special pains to breed and care for the sheep, Rush urged, and American wool would equal in quality that of the English; within five years there would be enough wool in Pennsylvania to clothe all its inhabitants. Cotton could be imported from the southern provinces and the West Indies on terms that would enable the Philadelphia manufacturer to undersell British cotton cloth. Additionally, since Americans wore cotton cloth so extensively, a cotton industry must be established. It would concurrently serve an important ancillary purpose: strengthening political union through commercial intercourse between the northern and southern provinces. And then there was the economics of it all: The more than £250,000 annually that went from Pennsylvania alone to pay for British-made cloth could be kept at home. Also, manufacturing—not only of cotton but also of other products the colonials needed from England—would increase local employment while decreasing Britain's exports to the Americans.

Moving from the practical to the philosophical, Rush viewed resistance to Britain as a holy crusade with the welfare not only of the colonials but of all mankind at stake: "America is now the only asylum for liberty in the whole world." God, he suggested, through the problems with Britain, was seeking "to show the world this asylum, which, from its remote and unconnected situation with the rest of the globe, might have remained a secret for ages." His listeners, he maintained adamantly, must accept as irrefutable that Britain was determined to enslave that "asylum"—America: the land of liberty. "By becoming slaves, we shall lose every principle of virtue. We shall transfer unlimited obedience from our Maker to a corrupted majority in the British House of Commons." As a consequence, "We shall cease to be men, We shall be *slaves*." And let it not be forgotten, he added, noting the moral advantages to be derived from home manufacturing, that the ships that brought in goods also brought "European luxuries and vices." By denying these ships admittance to American shores, liberty would burgeon for "a people who are *entirely* dependent upon foreigners for good or clothes must always be subject to them."

There were, he conceded, arguments raised against manufacturing. It would "draw off our attention from agriculture." Not so, he argued. Two-thirds of the work could be done by women and children. In rebutting the argument that manufacturing was "hurtful to population," Rush proved—certainly not for the last time in his career—how far ahead of the times he was in his perceptions: "I believe that many of the diseases to which the manufacturers in Britain are subject are brought on not so much by the nature of their employment, but by their unwholesome diet, damp houses, and other bad accommodations, each of which may be prevented in America."[1]

A house was shortly leased and by the fall of the year four hundred women were employed. This initial attempt to manufacture cotton cloth, which first introduced the flying jenny into the country, established confidence that the new nation need not have to rely solely on the import of manufacturable goods and, what is more, could itself manufacture products for export. "President" Rush had served the purpose for which he had been named. His speech, which would have its desired effect, ended his association with the company. His name never appeared among the list of subscribers or among the company officers. In the words of David Hawke, "While the United Company moved from one crisis to another, mainly for the lack of a good manager, Rush had joined other flanks in the resistance movement."[2]

That Rush was in the vanguard of those who would settle for nothing less than separation even if it came to war, is obvious from his recollection that even before his "interview" with Paine he had "put some thoughts upon paper upon this subject, and was preparing an address to the inhabitants of the colonies upon it." However, he had "hesitated" as to the timing: "I shuddered at the prospect of the consequence of its not being well received." Mentioning the subject to Paine, Rush suggested he write a pamphlet on it. "I suggested to him that he had nothing to fear from the popular odium to which such a publication might expose him, for he could live anywhere, but that my profession and connections, which tied me to Philadelphia, where a great majority of the citizens and some of my friends were hostile to a separation of our country from Great Britain, forbade me to come forward as a pioneer in that important controversy."[3]

Rush "observed the public mind to be loaded with an immense mass of prejudice and error relative to" the idea of American independence. "Something appeared to be wanting, to remove them beyond the ordinary short and cold addresses of newspaper publications." What he had in mind for Paine was a vehicle for "preparing our citizens for a perpetual separation of our country from Great Britain by means of a work of such length as would obviate all objections to it." Paine "seized the idea with avidity and immediately began his famous pamphlet in favor of that measure." Even though the armed struggle had begun—it was now the first summer following the Battles of Concord and Lexington—Rush warned Paine that two words must be sedulously avoided in the writing "by every means as necessary to his own safety and that of the public." The words: "*independence* and *republicanism.*"[4]

Rush's warning was provoked by a piece for the *Pennsylvania Jour-*

nal (18 October 1775) titled "A Serious Thought." In it Paine, this time over the pseudonym "Humanus," equated "the horrid cruelties exercised by Britain in the East Indies, her persecution of whites and the murder of the Indians in the American colonies," and her despoiling "the hapless shores of Africa, robbing it of its unoffending inhabitants to cultivate her stolen dominions in the West." His conclusion: "When I reflect on these, I hesitate not for a moment to believe that the Almighty will finally separate America from Britain. Call it independence or what you will, if it is the cause of God and humanity it will go on."

Rush found the words alarming. He was realistic enough to know that the Americans were not yet in a position to fight. There was no telling but that the mighty British army, and European mercenaries it was in a position to purchase, might descend upon America's shores en masse before the colonials were of one mind and in a position to offer more than token resistance. Perhaps of greater consequence, he warned Paine, there had been little change in public opinion over the preceding twelve months. Among many, if not a majority, of the delegates to the First Continental Congress there had been an unqualified desire for reconciliation, as witness the petition and declaration of grievances to the Crown. Indeed, delegates had assured their "fellow subjects" in England and worldwide of their unwavering adherence to "the duty we owe to ourselves and posterity, to your interest and the general welfare of the British Empire," concluding with an appeal that the people of Great Britain oust their iniquitous politicians and "furnish a Parliament of such wisdom, independent in public spirit, as may save the violated rights of the whole Empire from the devices of wicked ministers and evil counselors."[5]

Even now, in September 1775—five months after "the shot heard 'round the world"—while General Washington and his Continental army were contesting the more powerful British army for control of Boston, the New York Assembly was petitioning King George to rid himself of his odious ministers and reminding him respectfully "that the grandeur and strength of the British Empire" was dependent "essentially on a restoration of harmony of affection between the mother country and her colonies."[6] Such an expression could not have aroused much surprise, coming as it did from the one colony that was the epicenter of Tory support in America, the one colony whose Loyalists, as they are better known in American history, totaled in the aggregate more than those of all the other provinces combined.

But New York did not stand alone. Two months later, when news reached Philadelphia that George III had by royal proclamation threatened "condign" punishment for the insurgents and a blockade of colonial ports, the Pennsylvania Assembly ordered its delegates in Congress to push for yet another redress of grievances and to "utterly reject" any proposals that might further isolate the Americans from Great Britain. Similar instructions came two weeks later from the New Jersey Assembly to *its* delegates. Shortly thereafter the Maryland convention instructed its delegates in Congress to push, if humanly possible, "for a reconciliation with the mother country."[7]

All this had little influence on Paine's thinking as he worked on his pamphlet through the winter of '75. As his leading American biographer, John Keane, writes,

> Always headstrong, Paine was not intimidated by such nostalgia for the sovereign mother country. He may have been "a fool or a fanatic," but his conviction that talk of conciliation was sickly was soon to change the course of modern history. Paine began to take his cue from the popular emotions that had already been aroused by the battles of Lexington, Concord, and Bunker Hill ... He was simply convinced that Americans were no longer in love with Britain and that they feared a comprehensive conspiracy against their liberties. He therefore decided to reject the advice given him by Rush. If anything, Rush's warning encouraged him, strengthening his conviction that, in politics, words count and that, chosen carefully, words can sometimes disarm tyrants."[8]

Paine brought to Rush the first draft of the manuscript's opening section around the end of September. From time to time, he would appear at Rush's home to read passages as he composed them and solicit the latter's editorial suggestions. When it was completed, in December, Rush showed the manuscript to Samuel Adams, Benjamin Franklin, who had returned to America, and David Rittenhouse, the Patriot and astronomer famous for his observations on the transit of Venus in 1768. All, Rush knew, "were decided friends to American independence." All would join Rush in using their influence to see the finished product disseminated throughout the colonies.

Paine wanted to call his essay "Plain Truth." Rush "objected to it and suggested the title of 'Common Sense.' This was instantly adopted, and nothing now remained but to find a printer who had boldness enough to publish it." Rush gave the manuscript to one Robert Bell, "an intelligent Scotch bookseller and printer in Philadelphia, whom I knew to be as high-toned as Mr. Paine upon the subject of American independence." Bell "at once consented to run the risk of publishing it." And a risk it was. Were word to get out, via the Loyalists, British officials could not only ban its publication but also arrest Bell on charges of sedition. The "effects" of *Common Sense* when published

were sudden and extensive upon the American mind. It was read by public men, repeated in clubs, spouted in Schools, and in one instance, delivered from the pulpit instead of a sermon by a clergyman in Connecticut. Several pamphlets were written against it, but they fell dead from the press. The controversy about independence was carried into the newspapers, in which I bore a busy part. It was carried on at the same time in all the principal cities in our country. I was actuated by the double motives of the safety of my country, and a predilection to a Republican form of government which I now saw within her grasp. It was a blessing I had never expected to possess, at the time I adopted republican principles in the city of Edinburgh.[9]

But we have gotten ahead of the story. *Common Sense* was published on 8 January 1776, six months before the Declaration of Independence. Its chief effect was to bring the non-Loyalist fence-straddlers around to the inevitability of separation from Great Britain. But by then the American Revolution had begun, if not in name, then certainly in spirit.

On 22 March 1775, six days after Benjamin Rush's address to the United Company for Promoting American Manufactures, the British Parliament, having already rejected the American petition for a redress of grievances, rejected Edmund Burke's motion for reconciliation. A similar motion, by David Hartley, was rejected five days later.[10] By that time orders had gone out to General Gage, now governor as well as military commander of Massachusetts, to dissolve the colony's assembly, which was then meeting illegally at Lexington, and arrest its leading members and seize the arms being stockpiled by the colonial militia. On 16 April Paul Revere rode from Boston to Lexington to warm Samuel Adams and John Hancock that Gage intended to arrest them.

Hancock, whose inherited mercantile fortune made him the Bay Colony's wealthiest citizen, had recently been elected a delegate to the upcoming Congress. Both men, only informal guests at the Lexington assembly, were most wanted by Gage: Adams, because he was the colony's most outspoken agitator for independence; Hancock, because he was the first colonial to defy the British in his own name. Eight years earlier, when British customs officers boarded his new sloop *Liberty*, he had them held belowdecks while he had a cargo of smuggled Madeira wine off-loaded with forged papers. A suit against him for £90,000 was still pending. That suit would be made moot by the events of 19 April.[11]

This was not Paul Revere's celebrated "midnight ride." That came two days later. Learning that a detail of some seven hundred men had been dispatched under the command of Major John Pitcairn to dissolve the illegal assembly, arrest its leaders—in particular, Adams and Hancock—and then move on to destroy the patriot munitions at Concord seven miles away, Revere rode at breakneck speed to Lexington. Arriving there around midnight, he conducted Adams and Hancock and the other leaders into the woods for safety. Along the way, Revere aroused the countryside, as did other riders who had fanned out from Boston in all directions. By daybreak, Minute Men from as far away as New Hampshire and Connecticut were on the march. When Major Pitcairn and his Redcoats reached Lexington after an all-night forced march from Boston, they found their way blocked by perhaps seventy Minute Men.

The British halted. Major Pitcairn ordered the Minute Men to "Disperse, ye rebels, disperse!" Whereupon one of the rebels, whose identity remains unknown to this day, fired a shot from behind a stone wall. This precipitated the firing of muskets on both sides and in all directions. By the time the Minute Men were dispersed, eight of their number lay dead on the village green. Adams and Hancock emerged from their hiding place in the woods. According to tradition, Adams exclaimed exultantly—though one wonders how he could have been heard above the clamor—"This is a glorious day for America!" Here, at long last, was what he had been laboring toward for years: a bloody confrontation that would precipitate independence. Then he and Hancock rushed off to join the rest of the Massachusetts delegation preparing to leave for Philadelphia.

The Redcoats continued on to Concord, where they came under fire from waiting colonial militiamen shooting from behind buildings, trees, and hedges. Major Pitcairn and his men were forced to retreat to Boston in disorganized flight, leaving behind 273 casualties; American losses were fewer than 100. The battle was not only a great victory for the colonials; it was a great morale booster as, in the immortal words of Emerson,

> *By the rude bridge that arched the flood,*
> *Their flag to April's breeze unfurl'd,*
> *Here once the embattled farmers stood,*
> *And fired the shot heard round the world.*

When the "local version of an unprovoked massacre of peaceful farmers," to quote historian Samuel Eliot Morison, reached London eleven days before Gage's official report, a great furor was raised against the North government. Full details were reported in the Paris press: "Here were troubled waters in which [the vehemently anti-British] France might fish with profit." In Italy, the leading Venetian newspaper ran an account of *La Grande Scaramucia a Concordia*.[12]

The Second Continental Congress convened on 10 May, sharing with the Pennsylvania Assembly what was then called the State House but would later be known as Independence Hall. Unlike the first Congress, all the provinces were represented at the second. The delegates now totaled sixty-five. Included among its illustrious newcomers in addition to Hancock were George Clinton and Robert R. Livingston from New York (whose twelve-member delegation was the largest, while Georgia's, with but one man, was the smallest), Benjamin

Franklin from Pennsylvania, and Thomas Jefferson from Virginia. Among the equally illustrious returnees were Connecticut's Silas Deane and Roger Sherman, Delaware's Caesar Rodney, the two Adams cousins and Robert Treat Paine from Massachusetts, Pennsylvania's Edward Biddle and John Dickinson, and, representing Virginia, Patrick Henry, Richard Henry Lee, George Washington, and Benjamin Harrison, the future father and great-grandfather of United States presidents. Hancock was elected president in place of the ailing Peyton Randolph, who was five months away from death.

Before the Congress could begin to tackle the main issue before it—unanimity on whether to push immediately for separation, as the radicals urged, or pursue further attempts at reconciliation, which a near majority of the delegates favored—startling news came out of the north.

On the very day Congress convened, Ethan Allen and eighty-three of his Green Mountain Boys crossed Lake Champlain from the Vermont side, captured the undermanned Fort Ticonderoga on the inland route to Montreal, and forced the British surrender of Crown Point. This opened the invasion route to Canada while at the same time affording the possibility of stemming any projected British move down into the colonies from that direction. Indicative of the twisted personality that would see him emerge in time as an American traitor and spy for the British, Benedict Arnold, who reached the scene in time for the mopping-up operation, all but claimed exclusive responsibility for the mission's triumph.

In that triumph lay yet a larger indication—the extent to which the colonies were divided even as, led by the Congress, they began to wage what the Crown termed "rebellion" and "insurrection" but what was in fact all-out war for independence. Vermont ("Green Mountain") was not one of the original thirteen Colonies but a territory disputed by New Hampshire and New York known as "the Hampshire Grants." While New York regarded Allen and his men as outlaws, he had been asked by Connecticut to enter that province without permission. (In 1791 Vermont became the first state to join the Union after independence.)

This inter- and intracolonial conflict over independence versus accommodation became apparent immediately upon news of Lexington and Concord, when a civil war of sorts broke out in Virginia and North Carolina between the pro-Patriot Whigs and pro-British Tories.

And even those siding with the Patriots, let alone those actually engaged in battle, the hard-liners like Sam Adams and Patrick Henry excepted, adopted the mind-set that they were not fighting the king's army but the "ministerial army," hoping—at this point decidedly unrealistically—that George III would realize he was being horrendously misled by terrible counselors. In other words, the majority in Congress hoped that the determination with which their army fought would somehow persuade the Parliament to bring down Lord North's myopic ministry and turn for leadership to someone like the Earl of Chatham, whose immediate reaction on learning of the events at Concord and Lexington was "I rejoice that America has resisted!" But for the colonials to budge King George and Lord North was like expecting a flea to budge an elephant—and an obdurate elephant at that.

Congress was in the curious position of seeming to behave like a two-headed hydra, its two heads irreversibly opposed in aim and intent: While seeking a nonviolent approach to resolving their grievances, they pursued a more bellicose approach. Almost fourteen months were to elapse between the start of the war and the Declaration of Independence.

As he had during the first Congress, Rush spent as much time as he could away from his medical practice and teaching to circulate among the delegates. He renewed old acquaintances and cultivated new ones. Of the latter, the one with whom he formed the most lasting relationship was Thomas Jefferson, a fellow Virginian of another of Rush's closest "old acquaintance" friends, Charles Lee. Rush and Jefferson met at a party at Mullens Tavern on the banks of the Schuylkill River celebrating George Washington's appointment by Congress (15 June) to command the newly created Continental army.

The appointment was made at the urging of John Adams, who reasoned shrewdly that naming a Virginian to this highest position would ensure solidarity between the Northern and Southern colonies, of which the largest, wealthiest, and most important was Virginia. To Jefferson, described by Rush as possessing "a genius of the first order" and "not only the friend of his country, but of all nations and religions," Rush wrote in fond reminiscence a quarter century later on the eve of Jefferson's election as president,

I shall always recollect with pleasure the many delightful hours we have spent together, from the day we first met . . . to the day in which we parted. If the innocent and interesting subjects of our occasional conversations [through the mails, during the postwar era] should be a delusive one, the delusion is enchanting. But I will not admit that we have been deceived in our early and long affection for republican forms of government. They are, I believe, not only rational but practicable.[13]

Among the relationships Rush renewed, the three most important were with the Adams cousins and Charles Lee, Jefferson's fellow Virginian, who became Washington's second-in-command with the rank of major general. Rush often visited with them at Mrs. Yard's Boarding House, where they lodged. His close friendship with the three would enable Rush to serve as a go-between once the war began, collecting gossip from the Congress directly from the Adamses, until his own election to that body, which functioned behind closed doors, and military gossip passed by mail from Lee with the army during the siege of Boston (July 1775–March 1776), passing along what he gleaned from one to the other. Given the intense rivalries among the Founding Fathers, Rush thus at first served a useful purpose. Only later in the war would his alarming penchant for indiscretion create problems, particularly with General Washington.

When, during the previous year, Washington "was generally spoke of as commander in chief of the American army"—an indication of the thinking prevailing during the first Congress despite the overwhelming hope that it would not come to rebelling against the mother country—Rush "informed him that his appointment would give universal satisfaction to the citizens of Pennsylvania and hoped he would not decline it."[14] "Universal satisfaction" to the Pennsylvanians? Surely Rush was indulging his occasional impulse to hyperbole. The *independence-minded* Pennsylvanians, perhaps. But the province's Tory leaders were decidedly in the minority.

Testimony both to Rush's standing in the community and the regard in which Washington and the other delegates held him was his attendance at the party celebrating Washington's selection. Rush recalled,

The first toast that was given after dinner was "The Commander in chief of the American Armies." General Washington rose from his seat, and with some confusion thanked the company for the honor they did him. The whole company instantly rose, and drank the toast standing. The scene, so unexpected, was a solemn one. A silence followed it, as if every heart was penetrated with the awful, but great events which were to follow the use of the sword of liberty which had just been put into General Washington's hands by the unanimous voice of his country.

The battles of Lexington and Concord were prologue. The Revolutionary War started at Bunker Hill on 17 June 1775, two days after Washington was named commander in chief. Having left Philadelphia with his staff on the twenty-third, he was en route to Boston to take command of the New England militia, which Congress had absorbed into the Continental army, when he heard the exciting news.

On 12 June, General Gage, whose forces in Boston now totaled ten thousand with recent reinforcements, plus the sailors and marines in Admiral Thomas Graves's fleet lying offshore, had issued a proclamation to the "infatuated multitudes" who "with a preposterous parade . . . affect to hold [his] army besieged," and promised to pardon all who agreed to lay down their arms. (Excepted were Sam Adams and John Hancock; apparently Gage did not realize they were already in Philadelphia.)

There was something almost pathetic about Gage's proclamation, since the Americans had the British hemmed in on all sides except Charleston and, of course, the harbor. It was their fortifying of the hill on the night of 16–17 June 1775 that precipitated the first real military confrontation between untested colonial troops and British regulars. The Redcoats won at Bunker Hill (more properly Breed's Hill), though at a cost of 1,054 killed and wounded out of 2,200 engaged; American losses were 441 out of an estimated 3,200 engaged. What may have been a tactical victory for the British was for the Americans a strategic and moral one. This is borne out by the comments of the two British generals, Gage, and Sir Henry Clinton. Said the latter: "A dear bought victory—another such would have ruined us." Wrote

Gage to his superiors in London: "Those people shew [*sic*] a spirit and conduct against us [that] they never shewed against the French."[15]

Washington assumed command of the Continental army on 2 July at Cambridge and began at once an astonishingly successful job of turning some fifteen thousand undisciplined colonials into an army that invested Boston until the following March, when the besieged British were forced to evacuate the one strategically vital city in the New England colonies that King George III had insisted had to be held.

Back in Philadelphia, on the day after Washington assumed command in Boston, Dr. Benjamin Rush became directly involved in the war effort.

Great Britain had by now forbidden shipment to the colonies of gunpowder, without which no eighteenth-century nation could go to war.

As luck would have it, in November 1774, a month after the close of the First Continental Congress, Rush had begun to "prepare the public mind" for a possible war. With his knowledge of chemistry he had, through experiment, produced from a half-pound of dry tobacco stalks an ounce of saltpeter (potassium nitrate)—an essential ingredient for making gunpowder. Two months later he published "An Account of the Manufactory of Salt-Petre," with a brief follow-up piece on the art of making common salt, using the pseudonym "A Manufacturer." The two short articles were combined as one in the *Pennsylvania Magazine* (June 1775) and then reprinted and widely circulated under the title, "Several Methods of Making Sals-Peter [sic]."[16] Concurrent with Washington being named commander of the Continental army, Congress published the two essays as a pamphlet, with a brief introduction by Benjamin Franklin.

The day after Washington arrived at Cambridge, Rush, along with several others, was chosen by Pennsylvania's Committee of Safety to supervise building of a "saltpeter manufactory"—actually the conversion of a house on Market Street—to supply the obligatory gunpowder. On that same day, the Committee voted to build a fleet of "row galleys"—gunboats—to defend the city against any British invasion up Delaware Bay. When the galleys were completed in September, Rush was appointed the fleet's physician-surgeon.

He accepted the appointment with a notable lack of enthusiasm. It was around this time that the top medical post in the Continental army—Director General of Hospitals—had become vacant when Congress removed the incumbent, Dr. Benjamin Church, on charges of spying for the British. Though Rush may have wanted the position—the suggestion to that effect was made by a former apprentice now serving with the American forces besieging Boston—his name seems not to have come up for serious consideration. The post went to his mentor, Dr. John Morgan. Rush was content with his less demanding responsibilities as Pennsylvania's fleet physician, "for he rarely exaggerated his talents as an organizer or as a leader of men."[17]

On 6 July, the Congress, having previously approved an issue of $2 million in bills, passed a Declaration on Taking Up Arms. This was tantamount to a declaration of war, though it was not made openly. Hope still prevailed among the majority of the delegates that reconciliation might still be effected. Two days later, toward that end, came yet another petition to the king—the so-called Olive Branch Petition. Drafted by John Dickinson, its key paragraph read as follows:

> Attached to your Majesty's person, family and government with all the devotion that principle and affection can inspire, connected with Great Britain by the strongest ties that can unite societies, and deploring every event that tends in any degree to weaken them, we solemnly assure your Majesty, that we not only most ardently desire the former harmony between her and these colonies may be restored, but that a concord may be established between them on so firm a basis, as to perpetuate its blessings uninterrupted by any future dissentions to succeeding generations in both countries.

After passing additional appropriation bills, and organizing a postal system, Congress went into recess on 1 August to await the king's response. It was during this lull in activity, while awaiting completion of the Pennsylvania fleet, that Rush made the visit to Princeton that resulted in his courtship and eventual marriage to Julia Stockton.

Though the delegates could not have known it, due to the time it took for communications to pass between Philadelphia and London, the king refused to receive the messengers bearing the petition; he had by then heard of the expedition Congress had ordered launched at Canada under the command of General Richard Montgomery. On 23 August, George III proclaimed the existence in the colonies of a general rebellion, and vowed "utmost endeavors" should be made "to suppress such rebellion, and to bring the traitors to justice."

Congress reassembled on 13 September. Learning of the king's reaction to the Olive Branch Petition, Congress organized a number of secret committees. Among them was one for the importation of gunpowder from other European powers to supplement that being turned out at Rush's saltpeter manufactory, and one for intercepting armed British vessels attempting a blockade of American ports. "Our Congress continues firm and united. It will be to no purpose for Lord North to amuse the nation with offers of an accommodation to the colonies," wrote Rush on 29 October 1775 to Thomas Ruston, a childhood friend and schoolmate who on obtaining his medical degree at Edinburgh, married an heiress, and was now practicing in London. "Nothing short of a *total* repeal of all the acts complained of last year will now satisfy the most timid of the delegates." Reflecting an atmosphere among the delegates that would not, despite Rush's exuberance, be realized until the publication of *Common Sense* two months hence, he insisted: "A majority of them I believe will now insist upon much greater privileges, and as they are determined to ask everything hereafter with the sword in their hands, they will not be refused."

Word was expected "every hour to hear that the standard of American liberty is planted in the heart of Quebec." (The word that Congress would in fact "hear," though not for weeks, was that Montgomery had indeed taken Montreal, but the siege of Quebec, under the command of Benedict Arnold, resulted in a rout and Montgomery's death on the last day of the year.) General Gage's army, Rush's war communiqué to Ruston continued, "are still prisoners in Boston." (In fact, Gage had earlier informed London that offensive operations could not be conducted from Boston and been relieved by Sir William Howe on 10 October. British contact with the outside world was, of course, through the harbor, which the Americans lacked a navy to blockade.)

With the city now under siege by Washington's army, Rush advised

Ruston, the British troops "spend their time there in the most ignoble and miserable manner. . . . They execrate us, for they *hate* us. We laugh at them, for we *despise* them. I cannot describe the wonderful spirit which prevails over the continent, and nowhere more than in" Pennsylvania, where Congress had ordered the raising of a regiment to join the Continental army at Cambridge, Washington's base of operations, for which "[h]undreds offered themselves immediately as soldiers, and thirty young men, lads of the first families of the province, solicited at once for commissions." As for General Washington, he

> has astonished his most intimate friends with a display of the most wonderful talents for the government of an army. His zeal, his disinterestedness, his activity, his politeness, and his manly behavior . . . have captivated the hearts of the public and his friends. He seems to be one of those illustrious heroes whom providence raises up once in three or four hundred years to save a nation from ruin.

Rush's high praise of Washington strikes a rather discordant note, knowing as we do that he would in time be part of the Conway Cabal that a few years into the war sought to remove Washington from his command.

Also significant is Rush's praise here of General Charles Lee— "There is not a king in Europe that would not look like a *valet de chambre* by his side. . . . He has infused a spirit of order and subordination in the army which were greatly wanted before he accepted of [*sic*] a command of it." Lee would go on to acquit himself admirably in battle at Boston, in the South, and around New York, but because of disobeying orders in the Battle of Monmouth, he would be cashiered from the army "for misbehavior in the face of the enemy." Yet Rush, who admitted Lee was "addicted to many private vices," "was obscene, profane, and at times impious in his conversation," and whose "avarice discovered itself in every transaction of his life" and "appeared to have no affection for any thing human," ever after condemned his courtmartial. But despite that supposed lack of affection "for any thing human," Lee had many friends and admirers among the Patriots, not the least of them Rush; the two carried on a brisk correspondence from 1774, when they first met, until 1781, on the eve of Lee's death.

As Rush wrote in his memoirs, Lee "was useful in the beginning of the war by inspiring our citizens with military ideas and lessening in our soldiers their superstitious fear of the valor and discipline of the British army."[18] That alone earned him the undying loyalty of Rush. As much could not be said for Washington, whose anti-British enthusiasm was not commensurate with Lee's even after accepting command of the colonial army. Like so many others, Washington hoped that success at Boston would convince Parliament that conciliation was the only alternative to continued rebellion. And like so many others, Washington still toasted "His Majesty, the King" while dining with his staff. The mind-set among so many of the colonials that their true enemy was Parliament and not King George III was still operative.

On 7 November, the House of Lords rejected the petition that the king had refused to read. Nine days later, the House of Commons rejected an impassioned proposal by Edmund Burke for reconciliation by a vote of two to one. On the twenty-ninth, the Congress approved an additional $3 million in bills of credit. On 3 December, Lieutenant John Paul Jones first raised the official American flag, aboard Commodore Esek Hopkins's flagship *Alfred*. Washington would follow suit atop a hill near Boston on New Year's Day. While the flag carried thirteen stripes to symbolize the union of the colonies, it still displayed the Union Jack in the canton as a symbol of union with Great Britain. This flag raised by Jones and Washington would not be replaced by the Stars and Stripes until June 1777. That it still carried the Union Jack indicated the division of opinion still permeating the American colonists on separation versus reconciliation.

It was in the vital middle colonies that division of opinion was most pronounced. Between November 1775, when a second petition to the King was rejected, and January 1776, the provincial congresses of New York, New Jersey, Pennsylvania, and Maryland instructed their delegates in Congress to hold out against independence. Then there were the many exporters of American goods and importers of British goods who though not all that much in love with the mother country feared that separation would impose economic hardship; those who feared that the colonials were in no position to take on the powerful British army (despite the problems the British were facing in Boston); and pacifists, like the Quakers, who while not Loyalists, shared the view of the many Whigs who opposed rebellion on philosophical grounds.

Suddenly the dynamic of the Congress, and the provinces its delegates represented, took an abrupt shift—as Rush had hoped for and foreseen—with publication in the first week of the new year of the fifty-page pamphlet whose composition he had instigated and named and for which he had arranged publication.

8

Founding Father

On 18 February 1776, a month after his marriage, Rush was elected to Philadelphia's Committee of Inspection and Observation. It was also a month since publication of *Common Sense;* and there were many, and powerful, colonials who would never accept breaking away from England. Rush entered active political life determined to reverse that stand. The committee—comprised initially of forty-three members, but soon expanded by degrees to an even hundred—was one of a network created throughout the colonies to implement the resolutions of the First Continental Congress. From the committee's inception it was controlled by the so-called gentlemen of the city—the largely Quaker aristocracy who for a half century had controlled Philadelphia's, and thus Pennsylvania's, politics. As it increased in size, so did its influence.

Rush's election was orchestrated by the city's merchants, tradesmen, craftsmen, and other Whigs—self-styled "friends of America"—who just happened to make up the vast majority of his patients, and who, like Rush, were considered outsiders by the powerful Quaker majority. Many had been read out of their Quaker affiliation; that is to say, they were denied permission to attend meeting. Rush considered himself ostracized by his colleagues, and rightly so, being the only member of the college medical faculty denied a staff appointment to the Pennsylvania Hospital. All the men who backed him "shared a strong desire to remake America, to purge it of ills that they had diagnosed. They had not yet got around to specifying neither what the ills were nor whether they agreed how they should be exorcised. At the moment they were obsessed by the issue of independence."[1]

A few days before their election to the committee, Rush and his fellow ideologues asked their insurgent counterparts in the outer counties—populated predominantly by the Scotch-Irish, who resented bitterly the Quaker domination of the Assembly—to select delegates for a Provincial Convention to meet in Philadelphia. Its purpose, deliberately couched in vague terms, was to take "into consideration the present state of the province." In fact—and the outraged, predominantly antiseparationist hard-liners *knew it to be fact*—the instigators, now known as the Independents, had one goal for the convention: compel Pennsylvania to accept the idea of independence.

The Pennsylvania Assembly, dominated by the three eastern counties of Bucks, Philadelphia, and Chester, was no more obsessed with the idea of independence than any of the other twelve provincial legislatures. It would be enough for them, as for so many Americans, if Parliament were to cease their taxation without representation and eliminate such odious legislation as the Townshend Acts. And now here had come, in the words of one of their own, "a body of men from whom [we] expected to derive the firmest support": a number of "violent wrongheaded people of the inferior class . . . chief promoters of this wild scheme" that was "opposed by the few *gentlemen* [italics in the original] belonging to the committee—but they were outvoted by a great majority."[2]

The "schemers" had already petitioned the Assembly to change the instructions of its delegates in Congress so that they might vote for independence, should the question arise. Its refusal to do so was what prompted the insurgents to appeal to the back counties, where proindependence sentiment was strongest, and whose counties were clearly underrepresented in the provincial legislature. Seizing upon the discontent in the back counties, the Independents sought to get the Assembly to revise representation along more evenhanded lines. Their ultimate aim was that once the back counties got their share of the seats, the Independents would be in a position to bend the legislature to their will. When the Assembly balked at the idea, this second rebuff resulted in the call for the Provincial Convention.

Public pressure, stirred up by the Independents, influenced the committee to agree to a compromise whereby membership in the forty-one-member Assembly was expanded to fifty-eight—four seats to go to the city, thirteen to the back counties. The compromise stopped the "mouths of those violent Republicans."[3] They "were appeased because they were convinced that the people would fill all seventeen seats with men who shared their views on independence. It pleased the Assembly because it righted a long-known wrong [i.e., disproportionate representation throughout the province] and at the same time fended off, for a while at least, the most serious threat to its existence that the legislature had faced. The question of amending Pennsylvania's instructions to its delegates to Congress had been bypassed. The decision was left up to the men the people would send to the enlarged Assembly."[4]

Where, one may ask, was Rush throughout all these maneuverings? No doubt behind the scenes. In his memoirs he says merely that he "took an active part both in [the committee's] debates and business." Given his reputation and talent as a writer, it's no leap of the imagination to assume he helped to draft the circular letter to the county committees explaining why, consonant with the compromise worked out with the Assembly, it was rescinding the call for the Provincial Convention. Equitable representation in the Assembly—the Independents' first priority—had been achieved, thus "further need for a convention ended." This is no way suggested abandonment of their goal to maneuver the Assembly toward supporting independence. Rather, it reflected the more realistic attitude of one step at a time. Rush and his fellow insurgents were dedicated revolutionists. But they were also realists.

Many wondered if the overconfidence of the Independents that they would eventually gain control of the Assembly ought not be relegated to the level of idealism in lieu of reality. After all, in generously acceding to their main objective of equitable representation, the committee would have little excuse to remonstrate regardless of any future legislative action. No record survives of Rush's feelings on the matter, or on that of any other of his fellow Independents. But from our knowledge of his determination to force the province to support independence, we may assume he was confident that somehow, in some way, the Independents would bring the majority of the electorate around.

Such confidence was bolstered by the fact that within a month Washington's Continentals would force the British to evacuate Boston. Three weeks later American ports would be opened to trade other than with the British. And besides an emission of $4 million in bills of credit approved by Congress on the day before Rush's election to the committee, an additional emission of $5 million was approved. More and more of the holdouts both in Congress and throughout the colonies had decided to accept independence. Of greater consequence, all the provinces that had earlier instructed their delegates to hold out for compromise with England were now being prevailed upon to instruct their delegates to take the opposite course.

Unless Pennsylvania, which was America's economic keystone (thus its nickname, the Keystone State), was persuaded to go along with the idea, America could not hope to push for separation. Though the Independents had scored a victory in one of the nastiest elections in American colonial history, they still could not gain control of the Assembly. The dominant faction, now known as the Moderates, reflected public opinion in the colony. And since Pennsylvania beat the drum by which the Middle states marched, moderates in New York, New Jersey, Delaware, and Maryland were emboldened to hold out for reconciliation.

Then came an abrupt shift in opinion. It was said that it was at this point that the fight for independence took on an inexorable life of its own.

First came news that mercenaries in the hire of King George III were en route to America. This was the king's response to Congress's last petition that he send peace commissioners for the purpose of effecting "harmony." Wrote Benjamin Franklin's son-in-law, the merchant Richard Bache, "You will see by the papers what a formidable armament we are to expect—45,000 *commissioners,* at least, of different nations, that is to say, Hessians, Hanoverians. . . ."[5]

All his life, Rush would deride as "absurd and frivolous reasons" that it took such news to bring so many over to the revolutionary cause. Recalling how one man told him, "I am now for independence, since the King of G. Britain has employed Hessian mercenaries to assist in subjugating us," Rush told John Adams in later years, "Foolish man! As if there was any difference between being killed by a Hessian and a British bayonet!" Rush also retained an abiding contempt for the "hundreds" who advocated separation

> only because the Indians were let loose upon our western settlements, as if the British decrees and attempts to enslave us were rendered more absolute by that single link in the chain that was contrived to bind us. Few, very few, consented to our becoming an independent nation from the influence of causes and motives that rendered our reunion with Great Britain as impracticable after what had passed on both sides in 1774 and 1775 as the reunion of a body dissevered from its head by the stroke of an ax. Still fewer were actuated by a prospect of the future and permanent safety, happiness, and prosperity of our country. Indeed, we were conducted with our eyes obliquely directed, and backwards, in spite of ourselves, to the haven of peace and independence. We are the causes of our own misery in most cases, but our happiness came to be forced upon us by the kind and invisible hand of heaven."[6]

Barely had the news of the coming of the Hessians been absorbed when word arrived in the city on 6 May that two British men-of-war, the *Liverpool* and *Roebuck*, were coming up Delaware Bay from their patrolling stations at the mouth of the Delaware "for no good purpose." The alarm guns reverberating throughout the city signaling that an attack was imminent "put the town into some consternation for a short time."[7] When it was realized that the ships still lay several miles downriver and any attack, if that was their purpose, would not come that day, the "consternation" abated and Congress remained in session. In the hope that the alarm guns might panic the timid delegates, John Adams asked Congress to recommend that all colonies that had instructed their delegates not to vote for independence repeal or suspend those instructions, if only for a time. The motion was defeated. Through the next day the muffled boom of firing cannons between the British ships and the Pennsylvania navy's galleys could be heard throughout the city.

The following evening brought heartening news. The city's galleys now surrounded the *Roebuck*, which had been forced aground. But the *Roebuck* drifted free on the high tide, and the fighting resumed on 9 May, this time farther upriver, closer to the city. Instead of rushing to take cover, thousands of Philadelphians ran to the shores to watch their galleys lob shells from all directions at the slow-moving warships, which, adding to their disadvantage, were unable to maneuver with the facility they would have enjoyed were the battle fought on the open seas. The fighting, in which casualties were sustained on both sides, came to a halt around seven o'clock in the evening when the British, as if conceding to a draw, slowly turned back and, to the relief of those manning the galleys and the applause of those on shore, headed downriver to their patrolling stations some ninety miles away.

As the fleet's physician-surgeon, Rush spent the evening tending to the wounded in the galleys. The day's encounter marked the beginning of his direct participation in the war.

Less than twenty-four hours later, with verification that the Hessians were on their way and the city shaken from its complacency by the brief naval battle, John Adams rose in Congress to offer the so-called May Resolutions calling upon each state "where no government sufficient to the exigencies of their affairs have been hitherto established, to adopt such governments as shall, in the opinion of the representatives of the people, best conduce to the happiness and safety of their constituents in particular, and America in general." Adams was astonished when John Dickinson, speaking on behalf of the Pennsylvania Assembly, supported the measure wholeheartedly—and then went on to add that of course it did not apply to *his* province, as it already had a government "sufficient to the exigencies of their affairs."

Dickinson's argument: The liberties and rights the colonials were now fighting to preserve were already well protected in Pennsylvania by the 1701 Charter of Privileges, which, among other factors, gave its Assembly—the governing body of a proprietary province as distinct from a royal province—the right to initiate all legislation. With Dickinson's unanticipated blessing, Adams's resolution easily passed. But given Pennsylvania's position, it was like letting loose a toothless tiger.

Refusing to be outmaneuvered by Dickinson, Adams fell back on the tradition that all-important resolves of Congress must contain a preamble before being presented to the public. Using this device effectively to plug any loopholes in his resolution, Adams in his preamble said that "it appears absolutely irreconcilable to reason and good conscience, for the people of the colonies now to take the oaths and affirmations necessary for the support of any government made under the crown of Great Britain, and it is necessary that the exercise of every kind of authority under the said crown should be totally suppressed. . . ."

The obvious target of the preamble was Pennsylvania. Its Assembly still took oaths of loyalty to the Crown, the king's justice was still practiced in its courts, and the official tone of the province still supported George III's authority. When the preamble came up for debate on 15 May, Dickinson's fellow Pennsylvanian James Wilson defined what he saw as the preamble's purpose: "In this province if that preamble passes, there will be an immediate dissolution of every kind of authority; the people will be instantly in a state of nature. Why, then, precipitate this measure? Before we are prepared to build a new house, why should we pull down the old one, and expose ourselves to all the inclemencies of the season?"[8]

When the final vote was taken, six voted aye (the four New England provinces plus Virginia and South Carolina), four voted nay (North Carolina, New York, New Jersey, and Delaware), Pennsylvania and Maryland abstained, and Georgia stayed away.

Rush was convinced—and rightly so—that success of the drive for independence in Pennsylvania, without whose support the entire colonial effort would be doomed, depended upon a select few, himself included. "Our cause prospers in every county of the province," he told his wife.

> You have everything to hope and nothing to fear from the part which duty to God, to my country, and to my conscience have led me to take in our affairs. The measures which I have proposed have hitherto been so successful that I am *constrained* [emphasis in the original] to believe I act under the direction of providence. God knows I seek his honor and the best interests of my fellow creatures supremely in all I am doing for my country. General Mifflin and all the delegates from the independent colonies rely chiefly upon (*me*) Colonel [Thomas] McKean and a few more of us for the salvation [BR's euphemism for independence] of this province. It would be treason in any one of us to desert the cause at the present juncture.[9]

The "measures" Rush alludes to were nothing less than a concerted drive by him and the "few more of us" to push Pennsylvania toward independence by boldly plotting to stage a revolution in the state government. Only weeks earlier, the city had voted down the insurgent Independents' slate of new candidates for the Assembly. The few conciliatory Independent incumbents had been reelected, but their numbers were negligible. They had not yet become firebrands like the Rush faction. But attitudes were changing, what with news of the coming of the Hessians and the river battle. Whether they liked it or not, Philadelphians were now convinced they were in a shooting war, with their property and their very lives at stake.

It was traditional among politicians of the period that regardless of how much ill will was generated by contending sides during an election campaign, all was forgiven and harmony prevailed once the results were in. The loser would, of course, continue to act in opposition. But he would confine his opposition to the parameters of the prevailing political framework.

After the May Resolutions, though, the tradition was ignored by the Independents, their sense of insurgency exacerbated by their defeat at the polls two weeks previously. Convinced that the drive for separation would drop dead in its tracks unless they could force Pennsylvania into line, Rush and his obdurate fellow agitators organized a mass demonstration to demand a change on the Assembly's part seeking to resolve the conflict with an England that was now on record as determined to resolve the conflict on the Crown's terms.

General Washington had arrived in the city, on the heels of his Boston success, to receive further instructions from Congress. When Rush "waited upon" him, he was encouraged by Washington's support for doing whatever it took to get the most important province behind the independence movement. Rush was further encouraged by Charles Lee, and by word from brother Jacob, then in Maryland, that seven thousand men had "risen in arms" in that other holdout province "to compel their convention to declare independence." "I trust the spirit of God himself moves me to declare that I will never desert the cause I am embarked in, till I see the monster tyranny gnash its impotent teeth in the Province of Pennsylvania," Rush wrote to Julia, who was visiting her family at Princeton.[10]

The mass demonstration—for which Rush had been so busy planning that he all but ignored his patients—took place on the twentieth of May. Despite a steady rainfall, an estimated six to seven thousand people crowded into the walled yard behind the State House, where Congress was meeting on the first floor and the Pennsylvania Assembly was about to convene on the second. The crowd was a hostile one, eager to embrace the resolves offered by various speakers condemning the Assembly's competence to rule because the majority of voters loyal to the Crown had elected its members.

Among the resolves—which had been prepared mainly, it is believed, by Rush—the first, which was passed unanimously by the mob, said that the Assembly's instructions to the Pennsylvania congressional delegation "have a dangerous tendency to withdraw this province from that *happy union* with the other colonies, which we consider both our *glory* and *protection*." The second said the Assembly would be assuming arbitrary power if it sat at this session "since it lacked the authority of the people." (When one man voted nay, he was "abused and insulted" by some of the crowd, whereupon he "thought it prudent to vote with the multitude.") Next, it was unanimously agreed that, Dickinson's avowal to the contrary, the incumbent provincial government was *not* "competent to the exigencies of our affairs." Finally, the crowd voted to call the previously postponed Provincial Conference of county committees to formulate plans for a constitutional convention, consonant with John Adams's May Resolutions.[11]

It was tacitly agreed that the Assembly would continue to function while the source of governmental power would be orderly transferred from the Crown and proprietors to the people.

But not so far as the Assembly was concerned.

An ad hoc committee comprising Rush and a few others was charged with determining the time and method of calling the convention to draw up a state constitution and, what's more, elect an Assembly of men who would strongly support the independence movement. Impetus was added as word spread that Virginia's delegates in Congress had received instructions to propose independence by congressional resolution. Still, the Pennsylvania Assembly dithered by asking that Congress clarify the meaning of the May Resolutions.

From a historical view, this was a critical moment.

Should Congress agree that the Assembly, after eliminating all traces of the Crown's authority in Pennsylvania, was qualified to run the province's affairs, the revolution would have lost the requisite unanimity. To Richard Henry Lee of Virginia, one of his closest friends in Congress, and leader of the Southern faction pushing for independence, Rush got off a hasty note (22 May) warning that the Assembly's seemingly innocent request revealed "a design to enslave the people of Pennsylvania. I conjure you . . . not to desert us in this trying exigency. Four-fifths of the inhabitants of our colony will fly to the *ultima ratio* before they will submit to a new government formed by the present assembly. Please to circulate the papers you will receive herewith among *all* the Southern delegates tomorrow morning."

The papers, written in large part by Rush, reflected the will of his fellow Pennsylvanians, who would now settle for nothing less than separation from England.

In addition to Lee, who went about "working" the southern delegates, the Adams cousins helped block the Assembly's request for clarification. On the twenty-fourth, a memorial composed by a committee of Independents, including Rush, was sent to the Congress, its purpose to discredit the Assembly altogether:

> This situation of our province requires vigor and harmony in the direction of both civil and military affairs, but these can never be obtained when a people no longer confide in their rulers. . . . The committee have too much confidence in the wisdom of your body, to believe (when informed of the true situation of the province) that you meant not to include the assembly thereof in your recommendations to "assemblies" to form new governments.[12]

The overwhelming majority of Moderates in the Assembly were determined to hold their ground. By now they had in circulation a remonstrance reminding Pennsylvanians that Congress had "no right to interfere in their or any other province's politics"; thus "the representatives of the people are left as the sole judges whether their governments be 'sufficient for the exigencies of their affairs.'" Much promoted throughout the colony by the Quakers, it harvested some six thousand signatures. Despite their efforts and those signatures, the Moderates realized little return for their effort. Rush advised his "dearest Julia" in a letter dated "Friday, June 1st, 1776," that

It gives me great pleasure to inform you that our cause continues to prosper in nine out of ten of the counties in our province. Two emissaries from the [Moderate] party were detected at Lancaster and York with the Remonstrance. One of them fled; the other was arrested by a county committee and obliged to go off without getting a single convert to toryism. The Remonstrance was burnt as a treasonable libel upon the liberties of America in Reading in Berks county. Many hundreds who signed it in Philadelphia county have repented of their folly and scratched out their names. A German we are told in Oxford township ... came up to the man who by a direct falsehood had prevailed upon him to sign the Remonstrance, and begged him to erase his name. The man refused it. The German in a passion took the paper out of his hands and tore it into a thousand pieces, saying at the same time, "Now, sir, you [dare not] tell me d——d lies again." The Remonstrance had 86 names subscribed to it.

Rush also advised Julia that "Dr. Franklin's arrival [from London] gives great spirits to the independents. His enmity to the proprietary [Tory] party has always kept pace with his love of freedom. The noise they are now making is nothing but the *last* convulsion of expiring ambition and resentment."

And quite a convulsion it was.

On 7 June, by which time the Georgia delegates had returned to Congress with full powers to vote for independence, as had North Carolina's, and South Carolina had expelled her royal governor, Richard Henry Lee rose in Congress and moved

That these United Colonies are, and of right ought to be, Independent States, that they are absolved from all allegiances to the British Crown, and that all political connection between them and the State of Great Britain is, and ought to be, totally dissolved.

That it is expedient forthwith to take the most effectual measures for forming foreign alliances.

That a plan of confederation be prepared and transmitted to the respective Colonies for consideration and approbation.

After a day of debate, consideration of the resolution was postponed by a vote of seven colonies to five because the New York, Pennsylvania, Delaware, and South Carolina delegates, lacking instructions by their provincial congresses, were not prepared to vote.

Still, Congress forged ahead as if universal acceptance was a foregone conclusion.

On 11 June, a committee of five, consisting of Thomas Jefferson, John Adams, Benjamin Franklin, Roger Sherman, and Robert R. Livingston, was appointed to write a Declaration of Independence. At the suggestion of Adams, and with the concurrence of the others, Jefferson was assigned the task of preparing the first draft. The final draft, which included many alterations by Adams, Franklin, and Jefferson himself, was presented to Congress for consideration on 28 June.

Meanwhile, on 14 June, the same day the Pennsylvania Assembly adjourned without having accomplished anything during its three-week session, Philadelphia's Committee of Inspection and Observation chose twenty-five delegates—among them Benjamin Rush—for the Provincial Conference called for by the Independents, to convene in four days. It was hoped that Benjamin Franklin would preside, but he became immobilized by an attack of gout, and the leadership passed to Thomas McKean. The delegates unanimously proposed annulment of Pennsylvania's proprietary form of government, called for a convention to frame a new constitution for the province, and replaced the conservatives in Pennsylvania's delegation to the Congress.

One of the replacements was Benjamin Rush. He resigned as physician-surgeon of the galley-fleet and took his seat on Congress on 22 July. By then, Congress had unanimously approved Lee's resolution for independence, and debated and approved the Declaration of Independence. Printed copies were sent next day to the former British American colonies—now independent states—and to the army. On 8 July it was read from the balcony of what was now known as Independence Hall. Eleven days later Congress voted to have it signed. A copy for that purpose was ordered engrossed on parchment. The actual signing was weeks away.

On 30 July 1776, describing the Congress and what lay ahead for the newly forming nation, Rush asked Dr. Walter Jones, a close friend and fellow delegate from Virginia, rhetorically,

What shall I say of the august Assembly of our States? It is a wide field for speculation. Here we behold the weakness of the human understanding and the extent of human virtue and folly. Time will meliorate [*sic*] us. A few more misfortunes will teach us wisdom and humility, and inspire us with true benevolence. The republican soil is broke-up, but we still have many monarchical and aristocratical weeds to pluck up from it. The history of the Congress that will sit in the year 1780 will be the history of the dignity of human nature. We have knocked up the substance of royalty, but now and then we worship the shadow. O! Liberty, liberty, I have worshipped thee as a substance and have found thee so. The influence of the declaration of independence upon the senate and the field is inconceivable. The militia of our state pant for nothing more than to avenge the blood of our brave countrymen upon our enemies.

On the day after his election to Congress, as he wrote his wife on 23 July, Rush delivered his first speech, "about ten minutes upon a question that proved successful." Under debate were the Articles of Confederation. (It would take until 1 March 1781 before Congress resolved the "debate" and all thirteen states ratified them.) Rush said a few words regarding the proposed mode of state representation in Congress. His first recorded speech in Congress came on the first day of August, on the same question. This time he held forth at some length on the proposal that each state, its size notwithstanding, be entitled to cast but a single vote in Congress.

Rush argued that the vote should be based on population: Voting by states would "tend to keep up colonial distinctions [and] promote factions in Congress and in the states. It will prevent the growth of freedom in America. We shall be loath to admit new colonies into the confederation." Finally, he insisted, "The voting by the number of free inhabitants will have more excellent effect, that of inducing the colonies to discourage slavery and to encourage the increase of their free inhabitants." Realizing that the delegates from the small states suspected his views were informed by the fact that he represented one of the largest states, Rush sought to disabuse them of their suspicion in his concluding words: "I would not have it understood that I am pleading the cause of Pennsylvania. When I entered that door, I considered myself a citizen of America."[13]

The delegates were impressed with Rush's erudition, his eloquence, and, as would prove out over time, his prescience. But they were not persuaded by his argument. The decision that the states should cast ballots as single units became a part of the Articles.

Rush's speech did, however, arouse interest in those delegates who did not know him as did Adams, Franklin, Hancock, and a few of the others. Five days later he would be assigned to a committee investigating defective gunpowder being made for the army. A day later he was added to the Medical Committee, whose current responsibility was to accelerate the flow of medicine to army hospitals.

Before recording Rush's signing of the Declaration of Independence, mention must be made of a commendable burst of passion on his part before the Provincial Congress that sent him to the Continental Congress, as they reflect a most commendable aspect of his character.

After calling for test oaths by all voters to prove that they would "support a government in this province on the authority of the people only," it was agreed by the majority that an oath of religious conformity should be required of any man who would stand for election to Pennsylvania's forthcoming constitutional convention. Every potential candidate must "profess faith in God the Father and in Jesus Christ His eternal Son, the true God, and in the Holy Spirit, one God blessed for evermore [and must] acknowledge the Holy Scriptures and of the Old and New Testament to be given by divine inspiration."

To his everlasting credit, Rush, "the chief and zealous oppressor" of such an oath, insisted that there were numerous good men who did not believe in the divinity of Jesus as the Son of God. Hastening to add, "I am not one of that class," he went on to argue that no man "whose morals were good should be exempted because he would not take that declaration."[14] Benjamin Rush was a zealous Christian. But he was equally zealous in his belief that no man should be judged simply by how he worships God but, rather, how he conducts his life consonant with the will of God. The deputies passed the oath almost unanimously. Rush refused to openly condemn them for doing so. He knew there were times when it behooved him not to swim against the tide. Besides, he had made his views known.

The embossed copy of the Declaration of Independence was signed on 2 August 1776; Rush's neat signature stands between those of Benjamin Franklin and Robert Morris.[15] Rush would ever after

> recollect the pensive and awful silence which pervaded the house when we were called upon, one after another, to the table of the President of the Congress [John Hancock] to subscribe what was believed by many at that time to be our own death warrant. The silence and the gloom of the morning was interrupted, I well recollect, only for a moment by Colonel [Benjamin] Harrison of Virginia, who said to Mr. [Elbridge] Gerry [of Massachusetts] at the table, "I shall have a great advantage over you, Mr. Gerry, when we are all hung for what we are now doing. From the size and weight of my body I shall die in a few minutes, but from the lightness of your body you will dance in the air an hour or two before you are dead," This speech procured a transient smile, but it was soon succeeded by the solemnity with which the whole business was conducted.[16]

Part Two

1776–1813

9

Dr. Rush Goes to War

With the "official commencement" of the American Revolution came good news and bad. The good news: The British attempt to take the major Southern port city of Charleston had failed. The bad news: A new British army of thirty thousand men had arrived in the largest fleet yet to invade the New World. Commanded by General Sir William Howe's brother, Admiral Richard Howe, it was dispatched by Prime Minister North to capture New York City, seize control of the Hudson River Valley, and then ascend the Hudson to join forces with General Sir Guy Carleton's army in Canada. The strategy was to isolate the radical New Englanders from the rest of the colonies. Assuming that this tremendous show of force would break the back of the rebellion, North gave General Howe authority to negotiate an end to the affair.

Washington, having forced Howe to evacuate Boston early in 1776 and correctly anticipating the British would attempt to capture New York City, quickly brought the Continental army down from Boston and set about building up Manhattan's defenses, reinforced by militia from Connecticut, New York, and Pennsylvania. He spread three of his divisions along the island, placed one across the East River on Brooklyn Heights, under command of General Israel Putnam, and dispatched another, under General John Sullivan, to Long Island (on the site of what is Brooklyn's Park Slope section).

With his army safely encamped on Staten Island, Howe decided to launch his attack on Brooklyn Heights, the most isolated of the Americans' positions. On 22 August he put ten thousand troops ashore at Gravesend Bay in Brooklyn, and commenced the attack through Jamaica and Bedford Passes before dawn five days later. By noon he had forced the outnumbered Americans to retreat, with a loss of about a thousand men and two generals. British casualties were about four hundred. When Howe did not press the attack on Brooklyn Heights, Washington crossed the East River that night from his Manhattan headquarters to assume direct command. Within forty-eight hours it appeared likely that the British fleet would move upriver and cut off the American troops in Brooklyn from the main body of the army in Manhattan. On the night of 29–30 August, Washington took advantage of a heavy fog to extricate his forces from Long Island and move them back across the river to Manhattan.

He sent word to Congress that he was "obliged to confess my want of confidence in the generality of the troops. Till of late, I had no doubt in my own mind of defending [New York], nor should I yet, if the men would do their duty. But this I despair of."[1] Obviously, much of the blame for the disaster could well attach to the fact that Howe had outsmarted Washington. But this is of minimal consequence, given the added cause for "despair": The militias were deserting in great numbers ("in some instances by whole regiments") in the face of overwhelmingly superior British forces. On 15 September, Washington abandoned New York City and retreated northward toward Harlem Heights.

With New York City secure in British hands, General John Sullivan, one of the two captured senior officers, was sent on parole to Philadelphia with Howe's request that Congress appoint a committee to meet with him at his headquarters on Staten Island "to confer upon peace with Great Britain." Rush joined with John Witherspoon and John Adams in violently opposing any such mission. The tone was set by Adams after the proposal had been raised for debate, when he muttered in a stage whisper to Rush, who always sat next to him when Congress was in session, that he wished "that the first ball that had been fired on the day of the defeat of our army, had gone through [Sullivan's] head." Rising to speak, Adams reined in his criticism of Sullivan slightly by calling him "a decoy duck, whom Lord Howe has sent among us to seduce us into a renunciation of our independence."[2]

But where Adams spoke with asperity, and the few others opposing the proposal "spoke with uncommon eloquence," it was Rush, in this his first major speech before the Congress, who spoke with the most passion. Arguing that the emerging nation was "far from being in a condition to make it necessary for us to humble ourselves at the feet of Great Britain," he conceded "We [have] lost a battle, and a small island but the city and State of New York [are] still in possession of their independence. But suppose," he hypothesized, "that State had been conquered; suppose half the States in the Union except one had been conquered, still let that one not renounce her independence; but I will go further: should this solitary state, the last repository of our freedom, be invaded, let she not survive her precious birthright, but in yielding to superior force, let her last breath be spent in uttering the word *Independence*."[3]

His passion was of no avail. Taking their cue from one of the delegates who threw Rush's words back at him—he "would much rather live with *dependence* than die with *independence* upon his lips"—Congress voted to honor Howe's request. The committee, made up of Adams, Franklin, and South Carolina's Edward Rutledge, representing, respectively, New England, the middle and southern states, met with Howe at his headquarters 11 September on Staten Island. Much as Howe, reflecting Lord North's attitude (if not King George III's), wanted an end to the rebellion, his power to make peace was conditional on the Declaration of Independence being rescinded. The Americans considered the idea closed to further discussion, and returned to Philadelphia after three hours.

"In the course of the interview many clever things were said on both sides," Rush reported in a letter to his wife on 14 September 1776. "When his Lordship asked in what capacity he was to receive them, Mr. Adams said, 'In any capacity your Lordship pleases except in that of *British subjects* [emphasis in the original].' His Lordship said that nothing would mortify him more than to witness the fall of America and that he would weep for her as for a brother. 'I hope,' said Dr. Franklin, 'your Lordship will be saved that mortification. America is able to take care of herself.' "

Rush was of the same opinion, though, as he wrote Julia on 18 September, three days after Washington evacuated New York, "Our affairs in New York wear a melancholy aspect in the eyes of most people." But not in Rush's. In fact, he "not only expected but *wished*" [emphasis in the original] that Howe would gain possession of New York, for just as Rush had "seen molasses wasted on a board on purpose to collect together and destroy all the flies of a house," so, he predicted, would General Howe "attract all the [Loyalist] tories of New York and the adjacent states to his army, where they will ripen as the tories of Boston did for banishment and destruction. The continent in the meanwhile will be purged of those rascals whose idleness or perfidy have brought most of our present calamities upon us."

Then switching to a mode redolent of an Old Testament prophet warning that ultimate victory for the righteous must be preceded by moral regeneration, he added, "But further, I think we stood in need of a frown from heaven. I should have suspected that our cause had not been owned as a divine one if we had prospered without it. It is, you know, through difficulties and trials that states as well as individuals are trained up to glory and happiness." His faith, though, was "now stronger than ever." He was beginning "to hear with pleasure an outcry among some people that there is no dependence to be had upon the arm of flesh. But," he conceded, "the worst is not over—we must be brought lower. I predict a defeat or another disgraceful retreat. We stand in need of it. We must all be taught that 'Salvation is not to be hoped from the hills, or from the multitude of the mountains.'"

Rush was correct. The worst was not over. But his prediction of "a defeat or another disgraceful retreat" was wide of the mark.

Before Washington could properly solidify his position at Harlem Heights, Lord Howe threw a large force into the area, and Washington and his army retreated to White Plains on 21 October. There they hastily fortified Chatterton Hill, on the west side of the Bronx River. A week later, Howe threw some 13,000 British and Hessian troops against Washington's approximately same number of men. Despite poor morale from defeats and desertions, the Americans offered surprisingly strong resistance. Though the British captured Chatterton Hill after severe fighting, Howe, assuming that the Americans were still too strong, decided to wait for reinforcements before pressing his advantage.

This proved to be a tactical error of epic proportions.

Washington drew his beleaguered forces back to a well-fortified position about two miles north of White Plains. Because of a storm

Howe hesitated in continuing the attack, and the Americans were able to withdraw in unhurried, orderly fashion. The bulk of the army went north to guard New England while Washington and several thousand troops crossed the Hudson River into New Jersey, where they took up positions at Fort Lee and Hackensack. American casualties in the Battle of White Plains totaled about 200, the British 300.

But the true significance is that Howe lost an opportunity to destroy the Continental army and thus win the war in this single battle!

It must be said in Howe's defense that he was a naturally cautious commander who did not want to take any military risks that might result in heavy casualties, as it would take six months for reinforcements to arrive from England. Moreover, he was personally sympathetic to many of the American demands and truly hoped to negotiate a settlement of the conflict. As a result, his failure to undertake a pursuit of the disorganized American forces gave them much-needed time to regroup.

Washington and his Continental army may have escaped destruction, but their troubles were only beginning. Howe also crossed the Hudson. On 20 November he entered the abandoned Fort Lee. Within two weeks the Americans were in full retreat across New Jersey and into Pennsylvania. While waiting for supplies and reinforcements to arrive, Howe made plans to pursue Washington across the Delaware River and then take possession of Philadelphia.

On 12 December the Congress adjourned, to reconvene in Baltimore on Christmas Eve. Rush took advantage of the adjournment to take his wife, pregnant with their first child, to stay with the family of a kinsman, Colonel Hall, on the Susquehanna in Cecil County, Maryland. He sent his mother and sister Rebecca to Rush Hill, the small house outside Philadelphia where Susanna planned to live out her days when she felt it was time to give up the grocery store, and removed part of his furniture and all of his books to the safety of a patient's home in Darby.[4]*

Then, on 20 December, by which time the streets were all but

---

*The house later became Howe's headquarters. Interestingly, the British commander wrote his dispatches to England on one of Rush's mahogany tea tables; the ink marks he left on the table were the only damage done to Rush's property.

deserted, the shops shuttered, and the flight of so many inhabitants had transformed Philadelphia into the semblance of a ghost town, Benjamin Rush went off to war as a physician-surgeon. He joined the Philadelphia militia, which had been ordered to reinforce the Continental army, now encamped four miles from the Delaware River about ten miles above Bristol. Rush was "resolved to stand or fall with my country."[5]

On Christmas morning, after spending the night at a farmhouse nearby, Rush rode out to General Washington's headquarters with Joseph Reed, a prosperous young Philadelphia lawyer who had gone to Boston in 1775 as Washington's military secretary and was now the army's adjutant general. Reed was highly critical of the Continental troops, in particular their cowardice, especially among the New Englanders, compared to the bravery of the British. Moreover, he did not stint in criticizing Washington as a military chieftain, ascribing most of the blame for the way the war was going for the Americans to the leadership of a man he dismissed as "only fit to command a regiment."[6]

Extreme as Reed's evaluation was, it was symptomatic of the anxiety felt by many at the highest levels of the war's management, just about all of whom felt they were not getting the full support of the Congress. Prompted by Reed's analysis and his own view of the "rag tag army" to which Washington's forces had been reduced by losses on the battlefield and the desertion of so many militiamen, Rush took it upon himself to rectify the situation if humanly possible. Over the following days, in a flood of letters to Richard Henry Lee, then with the Congress in Baltimore, he "begged leave to suggest things" that had "occurred" to him, offering advice on just about everything.

He urged that Lee use his influence to fine anyone who refused to accept the by now inflated Continental currency "severely": "Pray don't let the matter be neglected." He expressed grave concern about the paucity of enlistments from the New England states, where an "excessive rage for privateering" (war profiteering) was rampant. He criticized the lack of funding for spies: sending money to compensate them should not be "debated and postponed in the usual way for two or three weeks" but "done in an *instant.*" He was alarmed over lack of winter clothing among the majority of the troops, in particular the militiamen, and the fact that the total of regulars was now a miserable twelve hundred. Congress must deal immediately with the "clothing and officering of the army," an army which "must consist of seventy or eighty thousand men, and they must be fit for the field before the first day of May next." The time for caution on the part of Congress had passed. "The *vis inertiae* of the Congress has almost ruined the country." And, in words that would subsequently raise eyebrows in the light of his own future concerns regarding Washington's leadership, Rush insisted that the general "must be invested with dictatorial power for a few months, or we are done."[7]

At army headquarters that Christmas morning, Rush "passed an hour" with Washington "in private." The general "appeared much depressed, and lamented the ragged and dissolving state of his army in affecting terms." Rush "gave him assurance of the disposition of Congress to support him, under his present difficulties and distresses. While I was talking to him, I observed him to play with his pen and ink upon several small pieces of paper. One of them by accident fell upon the floor near my feet. I was struck with the inscription upon it. It was 'Victory or Death.' "[8]

That evening, Rush was ordered by the Pennsylvania militia commander, General John Cadwalader, to tend to the sick and wounded at Dunk's Ferry. It was from here that Cadwalader planned to take his troops across the Delaware to join Washington next morning in an attack on the Hessians encamped on the Jersey side of the river. However, large ice floes precluded the crossing, and Cadwalader and his staff, which included Rush, returned to Bristol in the middle of the night in a heavy snowstorm. Not until the next morning was it learned that Washington had managed to cross the Delaware successfully above Trenton "and that he had surprised and taken 1000 Hessians" as well as control of "that place" which would become the state capital. Cadwalader's militia crossed to the Jersey shore that afternoon, spent the night at Burlington, and then moved on to Crosswicks, a village southeast of Trenton, where they remained a few days while Washington worked out his next plan of action. Rush now had "reason to believe" that in his Christmas Day "interview with Genl. Washington, he had been meditating upon his attack upon the Hessians . . . for I found that the countersign [password] of his troops at the surprise of Trenton was 'Victory of Death.' "[9]

It was also at Crosswicks that Rush learned that his father-in-law was now a prisoner of General Howe. Stockton, who had apparently returned to his home instead of going with the Congress to Baltimore, perhaps to secure the estate, had been captured—it is believed through the treachery of a Loyalist relative—at the home of a friend in Monmouth, on the Jersey shore, where he had taken refuge when Morven was taken over as British headquarters at Princeton. He had been severely treated, dragged to British headquarters at Amboy in bitter weather, and there thrown into a dungeonlike jail. Rush asked his friend Richard Henry Lee, with the Congress in Baltimore, to propose that Congress pass a resolution in Stockton's favor: "They owe it to their own honor as well as to a member of their body." Congress formally protested Stockton's treatment, and he was shortly thereafter exchanged for a British prisoner and returned home, his health as well as his fortune shattered.

While the Philadelphia militia was encamped at Crosswicks, Rush rode into Trenton to spend the day with a few friends among the regular army officers at the headquarters of the Scottish-born Brigadier General Arthur St. Clair, briefly a medical student at the University of Edinburgh: "It was a day," Rush recalled in his memoirs, "which I have ever since remembered with pleasure." Rush dined and spent the afternoon with Brigadier General Hugh Mercer, also born in Scotland, and formerly an assistant surgeon of a Highland regiment before emigrating to America and distinguishing himself in the French and Indian War. Following the war, he practiced medicine in Virginia before joining Washington's army. Rush was particularly impressed with General Mercer's comments, made "with great composure," that "he would not be conquered, but that he would cross the mountains and live among the Indians, rather than submit to the power of Great Britain in any of the civilized states." Sadly, he would never be faced with that option, dying of wounds suffered at the Battle of Princeton despite attempts by Rush—at the express order of Washington—to personally do everything in his power to save this talented, highly esteemed officer.

That evening word was received that Howe's army at Princeton intended to attack the American posts at Trenton and Crosswicks. A council of war was called immediately at Washington's quarters to determine what steps should be taken to oppose the British. Specifically, should the Pennsylvania militia at Crosswicks be drawn to Trenton, or left where they were to create a diversion? General Henry Knox, afterward Secretary of War and of the Navy in President Washington's cabinet, but at this time colonel (later brigadier) of a regiment of the Continental artillery, suggested that as Rush was connected with Cadwalader's corps,

> I should be called into the council, to give an opinion on the question. I was accordingly sent for, and heard from General Washington a brief state of the controversy. He then asked my advice. I said that I was not a judge of what was proper in the business before the council, but one thing I knew well, that all the Philadelphia militia would be very happy in being under his immediate command, and that I was sure they would instantly obey a summons to join his troops at Trenton. After this information I retired, and in a few minutes was called in again and requested by Genl. Washington to be the bearer of a letter [of instructions] to General Cadwallider [Rush's erroneous spelling]. I readily consented, and set off for Crosswicks at ten o'clock. . . . The weather was damp and cold, the roads muddy, and the night extremely dark.[10]*

It was around one in the morning when Rush awakened Cadwalader to deliver Washington's message. "He instantly arose, and set his brigade in motion. We reached Trenton about 7 o'clock in the morning." At St. Clair's headquarters, an exhausted Rush "begged the favor of his bed for a few hours." Barely had he fallen asleep when St. Clair awakened him with the news that the enemy was advancing on Princeton. "What do you intend to do?" asked Rush. "Why, fight them," replied St. Clair with a smile. "He then took down his sword, and girded it upon his thigh with a calmness such as I thought seldom took place at the expectation of battle. I followed him out of the room,

---

*Why Cadwalader did not attend the war council is not known; perhaps the messengers sent out to summon the participants could not find him.

and mounted my horse in order to join the Philadelphia militia . . . a little below Trenton, and rode slowly along with them towards the enemy . . . In the afternoon a cannonade began in which several soldiers were wounded. All was now hurry, confusion and noise. General Washington and his aids [*sic*] rode by the Philadelphia militia in all the terrible aspect of war." In the midst of the action, General Knox passed Rush and shouted out to him, "Your opinion last night was very fortunate for us." Firing between the two armies continued for several hours. Toward evening the Americans "retired and left the British in possession of Trenton."[11]

What followed—Rush's initiation into battle—was harrowing. The first soldier he treated was a New England soldier whose right hand "hung a little above his wrist by nothing but a piece of skin. It had been broken by a cannon ball." Rush directed him to a home on the river that had been expropriated for a hospital, which by evening had about twenty other wounded. Their wounds were dressed by Rush, a Dr. John Cochran, "and several young surgeons under our direction. We all lay down on some straw in the same room with our wounded patients. It was now for the first time war appeared to me in its awful plentitude of horrors. I want words to describe the anguish of my soul, excited by the cries and groans and convulsions of the men who lay by my side. I slept two or three hours."[12]

Around four o'clock Dr. Cochran went up to Trenton "to inquire for our army. He returned in haste, and said they were not to be found." Rush procured some wagons, in which he had the patients put, and then, leading the caravan on horseback, rushed off to Bordentown, "to which place we supposed our Army had retreated." There they "heard a firing [and] were ignorant from whence it came, 'till next morning." It was then they learned that General Washington and his troops, while en route to the highlands of Morris County "thro' a circuitous rout[e] that had been pointed out to him the night before"— hopefully to avoid another confrontation with the numerically superior enemy—had in fact met and defeated the British at Princeton. Rush and his party left immediately for Princeton, passing "over the field of battle still red in many places with human blood" where they found a number of wounded belonging to both sides.[13]

Among them were General Mercer and a British officer, a Captain McPherson. Mercer had had his horse shot out from under him. The

British, believing they had taken Washington, called on him to surrender. Mercer became so incensed he tried to strike the Redcoats with his sword, and was viciously attacked. Feigning death, he was carried from the battlefield to the house of one Thomas Clark, a Quaker, which had been appropriated by the British as a repository for their wounded. On hearing next day that Mercer was still alive, Washington dispatched Dr. Rush, accompanied by his own aide, Captain George Lewis, under a flag of truce to Lord Cornwallis, commander of the British forces in the area, seeking permission to attend to Mercer.

Permission was granted, and Rush was able to report that "the General is considerably better and there are reasonable hopes of his recovery. I have attended him since yesterday [6 January] and [as ordered by Washington] shall not leave him till he is out of danger. He is wounded in seven places with a bayonet. One of these wounds is in his forehead, but the most alarming of them are in his belly." Rush stayed with him until the tenth, when he and the British surgeon agreed that, though weak "from loss of so much blood that it had passed through the bed and stained the floor," Mercer would survive.[14] But a small bayonet wound under his right arm that had initially gone unnoticed, became infected and Mercer died after two days of agonizing pain.

While attending to Mercer, Rush learned from McPherson that his dear friend from his Edinburgh days, William Leslie, the brother of Lady Jane, had fallen in battle near Princeton. His body had been thrown into a baggage wagon and carried along with the American forces to Pluckamin [today Pluckemin], a village some thirty miles north of Princeton. In Leslie's pocket a letter was found from Rush in which he had "requested if the fortune of war should throw [Leslie] into the hands of the American army, to show the letter to General Washington or General Lee, either of whom would, I expected, indulge him in a parole to visit Philadelphia, where I begged he would make my house his home." The letter was taken to General Mifflin, who obtained permission to have Leslie buried "with the honors of war" in the churchyard at Pluckamin."[15] Writing to Lady Jane some years after the war, Rush says that the letter "was carried to General Washington, who politely ordered him a coffin and afterwards buried him with the honors of war—a mark of respect to an enemy at that time very uncommon in our army."[16] Apparently Mifflin "obtained permission" from Washington, which protocol would have required. After the war, Rush had a stone placed over the grave.

Rush's revulsion for the British reached new heights when he arrived at Princeton to find it "indeed a deserted village. You would think it had been desolated with the plague and an earthquake as well as with the calamities of war," he wrote to Richard Henry Lee (7 January 1777). "The College and church are heaps of ruin. All the inhabitants have been plundered." There was a reunion with his father-in-law, Richard Stockton. His estate had been stripped of its furnishings, its barns emptied of grains, which, along with all the livestock—cattle, horse, hogs, and sheep—had been carried off by the British. His losses "cannot amount to less than five thousand pounds," an enormous sum for the times. Stockton himself was a broken man both physically and spiritually.

In a follow-up letter a week later, Rush described the horrors inflicted by the enemy. When an American officer, having received a wound in the side during the Battle of Trenton, saw the enemy advance toward him and begged for assistance, a British soldier "stopped, and, after deliberately loading his musket by his side, shot him through the breast. Finding that he was still alive, he stabbed him in thirteen places with the bayonet, the poor youth all the while crying for mercy." When the British were forced to retreat, "either the same or another soldier," realizing the American officer was still alive, "struck him with the club of a musket on the side of the head. He languished a week in the greatest anguish and then died (I declare it upon my honor as a man and a physician) of the wounds." Rush also informed Lee—which he hoped the Virginian would pass on to the other delegates—that "the savages murdered" the Rev. John Randolph, chaplain of the Pennsylvania militia, while he was trying to reach the American lines on the night of 2 January, "after he had surrendered himself and begged for mercy."

On 11 January, judging his patients out of danger (including General Mercer, who died unexpectedly four days later), Rush left Princeton to return to Congress, thus ending what can be termed his unofficial tour of duty with the Continental army, unofficial in that he had served without pay as a civilian physician. After spending a few days in Maryland with his pregnant wife, where he had sent her for safety, Rush then left for Philadelphia to ascertain that his property and belongings were safe, before going on to rejoin the Congress at Baltimore.

From Philadelphia, he wrote two letters (14 January 1777) to Richard Henry Lee. In the first, cited above, he told of complaining to British officers (presumably American prisoners) "of the hard fare of our prisoners in New York," and was asked, "Why do not the Congress appoint a commissary and send provisions to them?" Indeed, the enemy had done that for the Hessian prisoners at Princeton. Rush wished that "the attention of Congress could be roused in behalf of our poor fellows" being held by the British in New York: "They are confined in churches without firewood. Twenty have been thrown out in a day to putrefy in the streets. It is a prostitution of language and truth to attribute a fiber of humanity to General Howe's heart." Hoping to join Lee in Congress "in a few days," Rush concludes the letter: "I forgot to mention before that I left our army not only in high spirits but in good health. The medical department must undergo a revolution."

In the second letter, written a few hours after the first, Rush told Lee that he had "heard of the removal of Dr. Morgan and Dr. Stringer from the medical department." Five days earlier, Rush's mentor Dr. John Morgan and Dr. Samuel Stringer had been dismissed peremptorily by Congress, without giving any reason, from their posts as directors general of army hospitals east of the Hudson and of the northern department, respectively. It is believed that what lay behind the dismissals was contention between the two physicians, and that both behind and ahead lay the unending feud between Drs. Morgan and Shippen.

Rush now tacitly asked Lee to use his influence with Congress to secure him both positions: "I beg you would suspend the filling up their places till I have the pleasure of seeing you." Then picking up on his suggestions that Congress see to it that American prisoners received the proper attention they deserved, Rush told Lee that he had "taken some pains to acquire from a surgeon in General Howe's army a perfect knowledge of the methods of taking care of the sick in the British military hospitals."

Much as he despised the enemy forces, Rush had to admit that "from conversing with the surgeons of the British army as well as from my own observations, that the care of the sick is a matter that engages the attention of even their general officers." In retreating from Princeton, Lord Cornwallis left five privates and a surgeon to tend to the wounded men he'd been forced to leave behind. Rush was "sorry to say nothing of this kind was done by our generals." Moreover, Rush pointed out, every British army captain was "obliged to visit the sick of his company at least once a day to see that they want for nothing." In view of the fact that "sickness sweeps off more men than the sword in all armies," Rush argued, "I cannot help thinking that it is as much the duty of a good officer to save his men by tenderness in the one case as it is by ... [*sic*] in the other." Six months later Congress got around to adopting Rush's suggestion, appointing a commissary general for prisoners.

Rush arrived at Baltimore the last week of January. Much as he desperately wanted Julia by his side, he was "convinced" that she "had acted very wisely in determining not to accompany me." Apparently, Julia had considered doing so, but in view of her advancing pregnancy, decided to move instead closer to Philadelphia, staying now at the home of Benjamin's sister Rachel and her husband, Rev. Joseph Montgomery, each of whom was the other's second spouse. In this first letter to Julia from Baltimore (24 January 1777) Rush's gratitude for her decision not to accompany him was informed by the difficulty "in procuring tolerable lodgings," the fact that "the rain which fell yesterday has rendered the streets so very muddy that they are impassable," and the exorbitant cost of living, which he felt was outrageous. "Every article of provision, clothing, and the common conveniences of life are 100 percent higher in this place than in Philadelphia," he added in a follow-up letter one week later. "I associate only with delegates and attend only to the business of the Congress."

In his letter of 24 January, Rush mentioned to his wife, almost in passing, that he had "been told since my arrival here that our [Pennsylvania] Assembly intend to leave me out in the next appointment of delegates [to the Continental Congress] as a punishment for opposing their new government. Welcome this storm of popular rage! I shall kiss the rod that smites. I never was so weary of public life and never languished more for the sweets of domestic life than since I parted last from you." The one consolation he had was that his brother Jacob was also in the city "and perfectly harmonizes with me in complaining of Baltimore."

Also "harmonizing" with Rush, and on matters of greater import than Baltimore's lack of charms, was John Adams, who had returned from a brief visit home to see his family. Their relationship was further bonded by a number of factors, among them the Pennsylvania constitution, which had been promulgated the previous September. In brief, the moderate Whigs of Pennsylvania, who had led the country to the brink of revolution, had lost political control to a much more radical group including the Philadelphia proletariat, the Scotch-Irish and German immigrants, and the farmers, who felt it necessary to overthrow the old form of provincial government in order to bring the province into the Revolution. Out went all the moderate Whigs with the exception of Robert Morris. The constitutional convention set up in July 1776 promptly assumed the functions of the Assembly and went on to frame a radical constitution that provided for a unicameral legislature, a weak plural executive (Supreme Council) without a veto on legislation, and a Council of Censors, with each county equally represented, to convene every seven years, with extensive supervisory powers over the executive and the judiciary. This constitution was bitterly opposed by the so-called Republicans or "anti-Constitutionalists," among whom one of the most active was Rush.

Rush's initial reaction to the 1776 charter was, remarkably, rather temperate: "It is thought by many people to be rather too much on the democratic order, for liberty is apt to degenerate into licentiousness as power is to become arbitrary." But this optimism soon diminished because of Adams's opinion of the charter: "You were my first preceptor in the science of government," Rush admitted to Adams years later. "From you I learned to discover the danger of the Constitution of Pennsylvania."[17]

Adams, on reading the first printed copy, had exploded to Rush: "Good God! The people of your state will sooner or later fall back upon their knees to the King of Great Britain to take them again under his protection, in order to deliver them from the tyranny of their own government!"[18] Rush later told Adams he repeated the remark, made in confidence, only "to friends I can trust." In fact, he had had it inserted in a brief paragraph in the *Pennsylvania Evening Post* of

2 November 1776. Adams had merely lost his temper. By this characteristic indiscretion, Rush would lose much more; specifically, his political career, by making it known how he felt about the charter, which he proceeded to do at every opportunity, though knowing full well that his position as a delegate to Congress was dependent upon the sufferance of an Assembly controlled by men who favored it and were thus the targets of his denigration.

At one point, while Congress was sitting, Rush leaned over and asked Adams in a whisper "if he thought we should succeed in our struggle with G. Britain," to which Adams replied: "Yes—if we fear God and repent of our sins." On another occasion, when asked by Rush if he thought the American people were "qualified for republican forms of government," Adams said, "No—and never should be till we were *ambitious to be poor.*"[19]

Adams also shared Rush's views on returning the Congress to Philadelphia, now that the threat of invasion had passed. In a letter to Robert Morris (8 February 1777), back in Philadelphia, whose letter to Congress four days previously advocating such a move precipitated a debate that was defeated because one state "was accidentally unrepresented for a few minutes," Rush requested that Morris "urge the necessity of our returning to Philadelphia in your next letter." He cited a litany of reasons: Congress's absence was depreciating the money there. Moreover, "the want of a sufficient number of boarding-houses [and] the constant accession of strangers who have business with the Congress and who create a fluctuation in the quantity of provisions brought into the town, have rendered the price of living and transacting business of all kinds here three times as high in this place as it is in many parts of the continent, and nearly twice as high as in Philadelphia." There were "other considerations which ought to influence us. Our return will have the same effect upon our politics that General Washington's late successes have had upon our arms. Its operation perhaps may not be confined to the continent. It may serve our cause even in the Court of France."

In a later debate, Rush and Adams spoke as one in opposing Congress's imposition of price controls, even though inflation was running rampant throughout all the colonies. In a long, characteristically impassioned speech, Rush noted that price controls had been tried in Philadelphia when he served on the Committee of Inspection and

Observation, and failed. Could it hope to succeed on the continental level, where the problem of enforcement was insurmountable, he asked rhetorically. To inflict an unenforceable law on the people would diminish Congress's authority and prestige. Resorting to an analogy he knew best—medicine—he said, "The continent labors under a universal malady. From the crown of her head to the sole of her feet she is full of disorders. She requires the most powerful medicines. The resolution before you is nothing but an *opiate*. It may compose the continent for a night, but she will soon awaken to a fresh sense of her pain and misery."[20]

On 19 February, the two stood as allies when Congress debated the question of ceding to Washington the power to appoint all general officers. Insisting that control of the army must remain vested only in Congress, and that granting the commander in chief such powers would undermine "the virtuous principles of republican government," Rush warned sardonically that if the motion were passed, he would "move immediately afterwards that all the civil power of the government may be transferred from our bands into the hands of the army, and that they may be proclaimed the highest power of the people."

Rising in support of the people's representatives retaining the sole authority to create all officers above the rank of colonel, Adams dismayed the Congress by making Washington, and not the principle, the focus of his objections. He was "distressed" that some members were "disposed to idolise an image which their own hands have molten. I speak here of the superstitious veneration which is paid to General Washington. I honour him for his good qualities, but in this House I feel myself his superior. In private life I shall always acknowledge him to be mine."[21]

As Rush biographer David Freeman Hawke notes perceptively, though both Rush and Adams spoke out forcefully against the right of an American commander in chief to appoint the army's general officers, "Adams had managed shrewdly to do what Rush forever would fail at when discussing Washington—to distinguish between the man and his office. Rush's failure [to follow Adams in this regard] helped to ruin him politically and would blot his reputation with historians into the twentieth century."[22]

On 20 February, the day after the debate, Rush spoke out against a letter received by Congress from General Charles Lee, now a prisoner in New York, expressing General Howe's desire for another peace conference. The timing, he argued, could not have been worse, with American commissioners in the midst of negotiations to secure aid from France. Should the French learn that the Americans were even willing to consider a negotiated end to the war, they would not enter it. Furthermore, Rush argued, what was doubtless behind Howe's invitation was that Britain was now "alarmed with the fear of a French war." The Congress unanimously sided with Rush.

On that same day, following weeks of debate, a motion to raise the interest rates on loan certificates (government bonds) by two points, to 6 percent, was defeated, much to the disgust of Rush and Adams, and the delight of Richard Henry Lee. His objection to raising the interest rate was rooted in the Virginian's fear that the certificates would be grabbed up by the Northern mercantile interests, thus concentrating the nation's debt in that area and giving the North a tight hold on the national government's financial policies once independence was achieved.

The votes by states defeated the motion, fueling Rush's feelings about "the impropriety of each state having a separate vote." Those favoring the motion represented two-thirds of the nation's population; but it had been defeated by seven members representing five small states. "This unjust mode of representation I hope will be altered in the [Articles of] Confederation," he wrote Robert Morris two days later. "If it is not, it will end sooner or later in the ruin of the continent. We shall attempt the important question once more before we adjourn to Philadelphia. If we fail, we are undone. Another emission of money will in my opinion be a public fraud which no *state-necessity* can justify. The loss of two or three provinces would not hurt our cause so much as the news of our bankruptcy." As it turned out, Rush was crying ouch before he'd been properly pinched. A few days later Congress reversed itself and voted to raise the interest rates to 6 percent. Rush later boasted, "This resolution brought immense sums of money into the treasury."[23]

On 27 February, the Medical Committee, chaired by Dr. Rush, submitted its revised version of a plan drawn up primarily by Dr. Shippen for reorganization of the Continental army medical department. Washington, who usually accepted proposals affecting his command with a letter of acknowledgment without comment, went out of his way to urge acceptance of the Shippen plan, which owed much to the British hospital system. Though it called for higher pay for physicians and surgeons, Washington saw no alternative to attracting able medical men into his army; and it was imperative that the best men be available for his soldiers. Despite Washington's enthusiasm, and his not too heavily veiled warning that failure to impose it would be detrimental not only to the army but to the entire revolutionary cause, Congress tabled the plan until it had relocated to Philadelphia. For this was the last day the Congress sat in Baltimore, having voted to reconvene in the Pennsylvania capital on 4 March.

It was also the last day Rush sat in Congress.

In electing a new delegation for Congress, the Pennsylvania Assembly had ousted Rush; this was payback for his attacks on the new state constitution, in print as well as privately. Having immersed himself in the writings of Montesquieu, Bolingbroke, and other great thinkers on political thought in quest of a solution for the defects of the new charter, Rush had published his *Observations upon the Present Government of Pennsylvania in Four Letters to the People of Pennsylvania,* in which he postulated a thesis that anticipated the United States Constitution of a decade later: that the framework of every democracy must include a bill of rights, a constitution, and general laws.

His state's new constitution, he insisted, was something of an unworkable hodgepodge, with departments muddled unsystematically. He called on his fellow Pennsylvanians to unite and create a form of government that was more efficient and more workable. Describing as dangerous the unicameral legislature—"all governments are dangerous and tyrannical in proportion as they approach to simplicity"—he importuned for a second legislative chamber, "inasmuch as each body possesses a free and independent power, so that they mutually check ambition and usurpation in each other." This was basically the same argument that would echo ten years later when the concept of a bicameral versus unicameral legislature was being thrashed out by the framers of the United States Constitution.

Given his denunciation of his home state as "a tyranny," Rush's dismissal from Congress could hardly have come as a surprise; as already noted, he had written his wife in the previous month that he expected as much. But whether, as he told Julia, he "never was so weary of public life and never languished more for the sweets of domestic life than since I parted last from you," is questionable. Much as he loved Julia and missed her terribly whenever they were apart, the idea of retiring into private life, where he could enjoy a thriving medical practice, was something Benjamin Rush could never entertain until independence had been won and the new nation safely launched.

10

Physician General in Washington's Army

Rush's dismissal from Congress, while not entirely unexpected given his well-aired criticism of the Pennsylvania Assembly, must have been a profound humiliation. Still, his only reaction, both privately and in print, was that he "was not offended nor mortified . . . for I wished to hold a station for which I was better qualified, and in which I could be more useful to my country." This was more than mere sour grapes. He was a physician, and knew he was a good one: "The American army had suffered greatly in the campaign of 1776 from the want of [systematic organization], and perhaps knowledge, in the management of the medical department. I wished to introduce order and oeconomy [sic] into our hospitals."[1]

After the Congress adjourned in Baltimore, Rush went directly to the farm of his friend Elihu Hall and took his pregnant wife to stay with his mother and sister Rebecca at Rush Hill, eleven miles outside Philadelphia, where he stayed on. Much as he would have preferred to have her at home, there remained the possibility that the British might attempt to take the city when the summer campaigning resumed. Rush was not so much passing time as marking time. Now outside the political maelstrom, with no patients to fill his days and on which to hone his medical skills, and otherwise rusticating with no companionship save a family of women, all of whom he dearly loved but none of whom could quench his intellectual and philosophical thirst, Rush turned his thoughts to the realization that the "romance" of revolution had given way to concern about the direction politics must take in a republic. On 18 March 1777, a month after his removal from Congress, the *Pennsylvania Packet* published a dissertation that reflected the disillusionment gleaned from his months in that body.

The idea for the article was suggested by Thomas Paine, who in his second *Crisis* essay had promised that at a later time he intended "to distinguish between the different kind of persons who had been denominated Tories; for this I am clear in, that all are not so who have been called so, not all men Whigs who were once thought so. . . ." Its actual composition was precipitated by Carter Braxton. A delegate from Virginia, Braxton had told the Congress in no uncertain terms that he detested all New Englanders, in particular their laws, their governments, their manners, and their religion. Rush detested the Virginian's attitudes; thus, his essay, which divided Americans into five classes, four of them pejorative to those who fell within the given parameters.

Topping the list, which translated to lowest in Rush's opinion, was the Rank Tory—the Loyalist—who esteemed slavery, loathed liberty, the Congress, and Continental currency, and craved "unconditional submission to Great Britain." Next came the Moderate Man, whose yearning for the status quo ante bellum was suffused with a Braxton-ian "connection with men who held offices under the old government" as well as by ties with the Church of England, complemented by an unappeasable keenness for luxuries; who loved the Rank Tory and abhorred everything about New England and its people.

Faring little better in Rush's opinion were the Timid Whigs: men of little faith, who overestimated British power and underestimated America's capacity for survival. What these Whigs did to undermine the war effort by their doubts, the Furious Whigs, as Rush termed them, accomplished by violence. They hated the Tories even more than they hated the British, and were prepared to suspend justice in order to expose and punish them: they "should be tomahawked, scalped, and roasted alive." Worse, as Rush viewed them, they were "all cowards and skulk under the cover of an office, or a sickly family, when they are called to oppose the enemy in the field." Only the Staunch Whigs, among whom he numbered himself—"friends to liberty from principle"—won the author's approbation. Inexorable foes of Great Britain whom no misfortune could thwart, they stood for "order and good government," ruled with justice and mercy, and were unshaken in their faith that victory would be theirs: "They esteem the loss of property, of friends, and even of life itself as nothing when compounded with the loss of liberty." Six days after the essay appeared, Rush left Julia at Rush Hill with his mother and sister and returned to Philadelphia.

He took a room in a boardinghouse run by a Miss Leonard and made a halfhearted attempt to revive his medical practice. He was still marking time, on the assumption that instead of merely rushing off to offer his services to the Continental army, he should wait until called to active service in a ranking position of authority. When, on his last day in Congress, he presented Dr. Shippen's plan for reorganizing the army's medical department, it seems to have been with the expectation that he would join the service under Shippen. While he was no great fan of Shippen—in time he would come to hate him above all other men—Rush was not prepared to be just another of the numerous army medical officers lacking influence. He kept abreast of what was going on in Congress, now caught up in the highly contentious ongoing attempt to bring forth the Articles of Confederation that were a sine qua non presupposing the thirteen United States were to defeat the British and achieve irrevocable and irreversible independence. Also, he saw a few patients, managed to collect money owed by earlier patients, and continued to sound off on a few matters that were almost obsessive in nature, particularly the Philadelphia Tories and the Pennsylvania Assembly, whose members he deemed "the only *unaccountable body of men* that ever existed in a free country."

On 2 April 1777, writing to Anthony Wayne to congratulate him on his promotion—the letter in which the preceding quotation appears—Rush starts off on a high note: "The Court of France has declared herself to be our friend and is now giving us such aid as must inevitably involve her in a war with Great Britain in the ensuing year. Spain will probably act in conjunction with her. All the ports in the Mediterranean are open to our vessels. In a word, all the powers of Europe are in our favor, Russia and Portugal excepted, and it is to be hoped that France and Spain will effectually prevent Great Britain receiving any succors from those two allies."

Next came the fearful news that General Howe's army, "after being cooped up" in winter quarters, was "at last in motion." Some believed

Howe was about to make his move against Philadelphia up the Chesapeake; others believed it would be up the Delaware, still others, up the North River. At any rate, the time was "now past when the sight of a few frigates or red coats threw our whole country into a panic." The Philadelphians were "preparing to receive" Howe's army: the colonials with musketry, the Tories with open arms. But, Rush assured Wayne, should the British "possess themselves of our city, we expect to check their progress through the country." In a burst of bitter irony, he went on, "If the Tories only who have invited Howe to Philadelphia could suffer, it would be wrong to attempt to oppose him. They deserve more than the most complicated calamities of war from his hands." Whether Howe would in fact inflict such "complicated calamities" upon the Loyalists is a question Rush declines to discourse upon. Besides, his concern was with "the poor women and children" who would suffer the consequences of invasion: "Few of them I believe will fly for safety into the back parts of our state, owing to the difficulty of procuring tolerable accommodations, so much have the country families been crowded with refuges from this and the neighboring cities."

Concluding in a philosophical vein—"A happy constitution is a most powerful inducement to press on a soldier [in] the toils and dangers of a campaign"—Rush "anticipates the pleasure with which [Wayne] will forget them both in the perfect security he will enjoy hereafter for his prosperity, liberty, and life." He wishes that he could "animate" Wayne "with such prospects in our native province," but regrets that "you will find when you lay down your arms and seek to refresh yourself under the shade of your own vine and fig tree, that the one will want fruits and the other leaves to support and shelter you against the rude influence of slavery."

Behind the bravado of the letter to Wayne lay a dispiritedness on Rush's part that was given added fuel when, about this time, General Horatio Gates passed through the city. During a conversation between the two, Rush mentioned Joseph Reed's already cited comment that Washington "was only fit to command a regiment." Gates responded that Patrick Henry "had said the same thing of him when he was appointed commander in chief." Rush was impressed by this comment of a fellow Virginian of Henry, whom he liked and respected. It was also around this time that Rush's friend, Mifflin, a senior Washington aide, disparaged the general with the observation that "he was totally unfit for his situation, that he was fit only to be the head clerk of a London countinghouse."[2]

On returning from Baltimore to Philadelphia, Congress took up the plan Rush had presented to reorganize the army's medical service, which it approved on 7 April. Four days later Dr. William Shippen, having seen his archrival, Dr. John Morgan, removed, was named the new Director General of the medical department, and Dr. Benjamin Rush was named a surgeon general, one of a number, for the Middle Department, which extended from the Hudson to the Potomac rivers. During his less than a year in the position, Rush would start—and lead—the controversy over the maladministration of the army hospitals that, while rooted in justification, would prove anew his predilection for the occasional act of self-destructive tactlessness that seemed to be less psychological than congenital. It would involve the jealousy-induced hatred between Morgan and Shippen into which Rush thrust himself, a controversy that will be dealt with further along in this narrative.

Rush was willing to go on active duty at once, but wished to remain free until the birth of his child. Despite his insistence that she remain at Rush Hill in light of the threatened invasion by Howe, Julia came to join him in Philadelphia anyway on the nineteenth. Rush allowed her to stay only a short while before sending her back to Elihu Hall's farm at Mount Welcome, which he considered a safer refuge than even Rush Hill.

While the revised plan for the Medical Department eliminated the kind of intramural squabbling and grab for power that had developed under Morgan's leadership by increasing the Director General's authority, clarifying his influence over deputies, and providing sufficient funds to pay physicians and surgeons, purchase medical supplies, and establish hospitals, the plan was flawed. Congress had failed to create the post of commissary general. This would have relieved the Director General of administrative and organizational concerns, leaving him free to concentrate exclusively on medical matters. Moreover, Congress insisted on interfering in the department's affairs, maintaining tight control over appointments, and consistently undermining the Director General's authority by countermanding any orders that did not meet with its approval. The final approval regarding important medical concerns resided in the hands of often mutually antipathetic politicians among whom there was not to be found a single practicing physician.

Compounding the problems facing the medical department were two further factors for which neither the department itself nor the Congress bore responsibility. As Rush biographer David Hawke notes, "America lacked a physician of sufficient *stature and character* [emphasis added] to impose his views on the department and Congress. Yet even if a Washington had been unearthed among the nation's physicians he would have been swamped and defeated by the illness that pervaded the army in 1777. A head count in July revealed 3,745 sick in the Continental army and nearly every hospital bed occupied— this, several weeks *before* Howe unleashed his attack on Philadelphia."[3]

In its 22 April 1777 edition, the *Pennsylvania Packet* gave over the entire first page to Rush's chef d'oeuvre in the area of military medicine: "To the Officers in the Army of the United States: Directions for Preserving the Health of Soldiers." This pioneering contribution to military hygiene has proved over time to be one of Rush's most influential writings on any subject. Proceeding from the proposition long established down through history that "a greater proportion of men perish with sickness in all armies than fall by the sword," due to deplorable sanitary conditions both in camps and hospitals, in conjunction with improper hygiene in matters of dress, diet, personal cleanliness, and encampments, he posits that "the munificence of the Congress and the skill of physicians and surgeons will avail but little in preventing mortality from sickness among our soldiers without the concurrence of the officers of the army." It was "absolutely necessary" that they "enforce the most salutary plans and precepts" for preserving the health of those under their command.

Getting down to particulars, Rush begins by lamenting that constraints on our foreign trade and paucity of domestic manufacture necessitated that America's soldiers be clothed in linen: "It is a well-known fact that the perspiration of the body, by attaching itself to linen and afterwards by mixing with the rain, is disposed to form miasmata which produce fevers." Urging the banishment of linen shirts from the army—"besides accumulating putrid miasmata, it conceals filth and prevents a due regard being paid to cleanliness"—he notes that "among other causes of the healthiness of the Roman armies" was that their soldiers wore flannel shirts next to their skins. He also cites from personal experience several instances where the "yearly visits" of epidemic fevers have been "stayed in the State of Pennsylvania, in places most subject" to such disorders "by nothing else but the use of flannel shirts."

Turning to the matter of hair—"being long uncombed [it] is apt to accumulate the perspiration of the head, which by becoming putrid sometimes produces diseases"—Rush offers "two methods of guarding against this evil." One is to comb and dress the hair daily; the second is to cut it short at the neck. Since the former is "attended with delays often incompatible with the duty of a soldier," the latter is to be preferred.

As for the diet of soldiers, this "should consist *chiefly* of [well-cooked] vegetables." He supports this argument with the observation that if "every tree on the continent of America produced Jesuits bark [the cinchona bark, from which quinine is extracted]," it would not suffice to "preserve or restore the health" of soldiers who eat two or three pounds of meat in a day. He also cites the dangers inherent in flour being "rendered unwholesome by an error in making it into bread," and urges the use of wheat in its place. Recalling the benefits the Roman armies derived from using wheat instead of flour, which could easily be rendered harmful by dampness or careless handling, he notes that Julius Caesar kept his army in optimum condition by feeding them with wheat only, prepared by being husked and well boiled and eaten as a porridge in lieu of bread: "If a little sugar or molasses is added to wheat prepared in this manner, it forms not only a most wholesome food but a most agreeable repast."

Next turning to alcoholic spirits with what some saw as advocating temperance, others as advocating remedial logic, Rush attacks the "common apology for the use of rum in our army" as being necessary "to guard against the effects of heat and cold." He maintains "in no case whatever does rum abate the effects of either of them upon the constitution. On the contrary, I believe it always increases them. The temporary elevation of spirits in summer and the temporary generation of warmth in winter produced by rum always leave the body languid and more liable to be affected with heat and cold afterwards.

Happy would it be for our soldiers if the evil ended here!" The use of rum, he maintains, gradually wears away "the powers of the system," thereby laying "the foundation of fevers, fluxes, jaundices," and just about every other disease found in military hospitals.

He describes as "a vulgar error" the common supposition that fatigue derived from violent exercise or hard labor was "relieved by the use of spirituous liquors." Noting that the "principles of animal life are the same in a horse as in a man," and horses "undergo the severest labor with no other liquor than cool water," Rush tells of "many instances where even reapers have been forced to acknowledge that plentiful draughts of milk and water have enabled them to go through the fatigues of harvest with more pleasure and fewer inconveniences to their health than ever they experienced from the use of a mixture of rum and water." Again falling back on historical empiricism, Rush points out that hard alcoholic beverages—except wine, and that only for medicinal purposes—were unknown to the ancient Roman soldiers. Their canteens were filled only with vinegar, "and it was by frequently drinking a small quantity of this wholesome liquor mixed with water" that they were able to "sustain tedious marches through scorching sands without being subject to sickness of any kind." Admitting, however, that there may be medical instances "in which a small quantity of [even] rum may be useful," he cautions that it will be "of the most essential service if it be mixed with three or four times its quantity of water."

Rush finds that "too much cannot be said in favor of CLEANLINESS" in the context of the soldier's body, his clothes, and his food. He should be "obliged" to wash his hands and face at least once a day, and his whole body twice or thrice weekly, especially in summer; cold baths, he adds, again citing the example of the Roman soldiers, were part of the military discipline "and contributed much to preserve their health." Cleanliness should also extend to the soldier's clothes, with frequent changes "indispensably necessary." Unless "a strict regard is paid to this article, all our pains to preserve the health of our soldiers will be to no purpose." As for the soldier's food, "Great care should be taken that the vessels in which he cooks his victuals should be carefully washed after each time of their being used."

Moreover, too many soldiers "should not be allowed on any pretense whatever" to sleep in the same tent or quarter, as this would lead to so-called jail fever, with the resultant "perspiration and respiration of human bodies brought into a compass too narrow to be diluted and rendered inert by a mixture with the atmosphere." Also, the straw or hay that comprised the soldier's bed should be changed often, and his blanket exposed every day to the sun, thereby preventing "the perspiration from becoming morbid and dangerous by accumulating upon it." All commanding officers should "take the utmost care" never to allow a soldier to sleep "or even to sit down in his tent" while wearing wet clothes, nor to lie down in a wet blanket upon damp straw. Too, the environs of each tent and of the camp in general "should be kept perfectly clean of the offal of animals and of filth of all kinds," which should be buried or carefully removed daily "beyond the neighborhood of the camp."

Rush's fourth concern was the formation of an encampment, especially if it became necessary to locate beside a river. He deemed it the duty of the quartermaster to determine "from what quarter the winds come" at the time: "If they pass across the river before they reach his army, they will probably bring with them the seeds of bilious and intermitting fevers," especially in the fall of the year. It was also the duty of the commanding officer of a division or detachment of the army, Rush insisted, "to avoid as much as possible exposing his troops to *unnecessary* fatigue or watchfulness," and perform the "daily exercises of the manual and maneuvers (which contribute to the health of the soldier), as well as marches, in the cool of the morning and evening in summer." Sentries should always be provided with proper coats, and "be *often* relieved in very hot, cold, and rainy weather," and, Rush added in a subsequent edition the following year, always be given "a hearty meal" before going on duty in cold weather. After noting that the fire and wood of smoke, "as also the burning of sulfur and the explosion of gunpowder," is singularly efficacious in "preserving and restoring the purity of the air," Rush concludes these directions

by suggesting two hints which appear to be worthy of the attention of the gentlemen of the army. Consider in the first place that the principal study of an officer in the time of war should be to save the blood of his men. An heroic exploit is admired most when it has been performed with the loss of a few lives. But if it be meritorious to save the lives of soldiers to preserve them by skill and attention in the field, why should it be thought less so to preserve them by skill and attention of another kind, in a march or an encampment? And on the contrary, if it be criminal in an officer to sacrifice the lives of thousands by his temerity in a battle, why should it be thought less so as to sacrifice twice their number in a hospital by his negligence?—Consider in the second place that an attention to the health of your soldiers is absolutely necessary to form a *great* military character.

Falling back on historical precedent as he often did to validate an innovative suggestion, Rush pointed out that but for "this eminent quality, Xenophon would never have led ten thousand Greeks for six-teen months through a cold and most inhospitable country, nor would Fabius have kept alive that army together with which it conquered Hannibal and delivered Rome."

In warmly acknowledging receipt of the article as first printed, General Nathanael Greene urged Rush, in a letter dated 3 May 1777, that it be reproduced in pamphlet form; he would do all within his power to ensure the implementation of its ideas throughout the Conti-nental Army. On 5 September 1777, the Board of War "ORDERED, that Doctor B. RUSH be requested to re-publish, in a small Pamphlet, certain Directions for preserving the Health of Soldiers; published in the *Pennsylvania Packet,* No. 284, with such Additions and Alter-ations as he shall think proper." The pamphlet was not published until after Rush's resignation from the army; he referred to it in a letter to Greene as "my last legacy to my dear countrymen in the line of my profession."[4]

At the urging of Greene ("Your own reputation, the protection of the country, and the success of the campaign[s] are dependent upon the health of the army") Washington instituted some of Rush's sug-gested reforms: latrines and slaughter pens were to be located with more care relative to the soldiers' encampments, and the men were told to bathe more often and eat more vegetables. Unfortunately, any full-scale implementation of Rush's suggested improvements had to be put aside, due to the accelerated activities on the battlefield. Neverthe-less, Rush had achieved a dramatic breakthrough in the area of mili-tary hygiene. Admittedly, the essay made no lasting contribution to medical science in the clinical sense. It does stand, though, as one of the many innovations, not only in medicine but in other areas as well, that substantiates his pioneering contributing to mankind's leap in the betterment of social as well as clinical enrichment.

Though remaining at Philadelphia until Julia had given birth, Rush did not neglect his medical duties. While writing his essay, he was attending in the military hospital, which had been the House of Employment, adjacent to the Philadelphia Almshouse, whose inmates manufactured wool, hemp, and flax for the army. In early May "a fatal fever"—also termed "putrid fever" by Rush, and in all probabilities either typhus or typhoid fever—was, in his words, "generated . . . by our sick being too much crowded." Among the many casualties were a number of the attending physicians and hospital corpsmen. Rush pleaded with the army medical director, Shippen, to make "more rooms for the sick. This was denied." In Shippen's defense, it must be admitted that there were few empty buildings available for conversion to hospitals, and billeting the infected soldiers among the city's population would have put too many more lives at risk. But Rush could only see, and barely accept, the suffering of the men "shivering with cold upon bare floors without a blanket to cover them, calling for fire, for water, for suitable food, and for medicines—and calling in vain," which he blamed on Shippen. The coming of summer "lessened the evils which were experienced from the want of air in our hospitals, for it was easy to ventilate them by means of open doors and windows." The epidemic abated. So, too, Rush's feelings about Shippen. But only for the time being.[5]

Another factor, this one political in nature, that Rush continued to obsess over was the state's new constitution, in particular its unicameral structure; the fact that it had not been submitted to popular ratification, but simply activated by the convention that drew it up; the requirement that voters take an oath not to act in any manner "prejudicial or injurious" to the new government; that all assembly members must attest to the belief in one God and that the Old and New Testament were "given by divine inspiration"; that there was no provision for amending the constitution; and that any change in the fundamental law of the state could be effected subject not to the will of the people but to two-thirds of the Council of Censors voting to convene a new constitutional convention.

In a 2 April 1777 letter to Anthony Wayne, Rush condemned the Pennsylvania Assembly, whose "domestic tyranny cost me my seat in Congress." He wished he could "add here that the Declaration of Independence had produced the same happy effects in Pennsylvania that it has in the rest of the united [sic] States." But the Philadelphians, "intoxicated with the *musk* or first flowings of liberty," had formed a government "that is absurd in its principles and incapable of execution without the most alarming influence upon liberty. The wisest and I believe the major part of the people are dissatisfied with it, but they have suspended all opposition to it for the present, as the enemy are now at our gates."

The Pennsylvania Assembly might have had it in for Rush, as witness its removing him from the state's delegation to the Continental Congress. But the Congress was less interested in Rush's politics than in his medical expertise. On 1 July, it promoted him to fill the vacancy of physician general of the Middle Department, thus making Rush the chief medical officer of the area that was the primary locus of the Continental army's fighting under the personal command of Washington. Rush was now the third-ranking officer in the army medical department after Shippen, to whom he would report personally, and the latter's deputy, Dr. Thomas Bond, Jr. Son of the eminent Philadelphia physician who had opposed Rush's medical theories, Bond, whose service throughout the war in a number of medical posts was commendable, would enjoy Rush's admiration and respect—until Bond became a strong Shippen partisan in the administration of the army's hospital department. Like many a man whose confidence in his convictions is not subject to doubt, Rush, barring the odd exception, neither forgot a friend nor forgave an enemy.

On 24 July, after joining Julia, now back at Mount Welcome where three days later she delivered their first child, John, Rush prepared once again to join up with Washington's forces. Meanwhile, the first anniversary of the Declaration of Independence had come around. It was celebrated by the normally staid Philadelphians with an uncharacteristic display that seemed to be more an attempt to compensate for the general mood of depression with the war's progress than pride in having launched the world's first attempt at democratic government since the failed attempt two and a half millennia ago in Greece known to history as the Age of Pericles.

At noon, all vessels in port, their yardarms a veritable symphony of flags of every color fluttering in the breeze, prepared to fire their guns, while the city's taverns were the settings for sonorous orations and toasts being offered and downed as if the Lord had decided this was to be the last day man might thus indulge himself. At four in the afternoon, every available cannon in the city united with those guns in the harbor to fill the air with a volley that doubtless came perilously close to causing permanent hearing loss not only in Philadelphia but in the surrounding towns and hamlets. Two hours later came a parade by the militia up one street and down the other "with great pomp, tho' many of them were barefoot and looked very unhealthy." This was followed in the evening by a great display of fireworks, "and those people's windows were broken who put no candles in."[6]

Within two weeks the elevated mood of the city darkened appreciably when word was received that Britain's General Burgoyne had accepted the surrender of Fort Ticonderoga by General St. Clair. St. Clair's public apology, published throughout the states, blamed the disaster on the fact that his troops were only half supplied with arms, and even less ammunition. Two weeks later, on 31 July, at six in the morning, the darkened mood became absolutely stygian when the din of the city's alarm guns was followed immediately by word that General Howe's armada ("about 200 sail") was preparing to move up Delaware Bay. The message was erroneous, but the alarm was no less justified. Instead of moving up Delaware Bay with the large army he had brought down from New York, Howe continued down to Chesapeake Bay where he planned to disembark his troops at the north end and march them overland to Philadelphia.

It was at this time that Rush arrived at Morristown, where Washington was headquartered, to report for service. While the army was encamped there, Rush was stationed at Princeton, from which he moved constantly among the military hospitals scattered throughout New Jersey supervising the attending physicians and their staffs.

Though he wrote John Adams (8 August 1777) that "Dr. Bond, the assistant director, cannot be too much commended for his humanity and zeal in doing his duty," Rush couldn't find much to say about Shippen, whom he would never forgive for having replaced Rush's mentor, Dr. Morgan, as chief of the army's medical department. His dealings with Shippen were, for now, limited to weekly reports on the patient population and conditions among the troops.

In the letter Rush reveals the disparity of feelings between himself and Adams about what a year of independence had accomplished. The disparity lay in what had prompted both men to join the revolutionary movement at the outset. Adams had done so with a spectacular lack of confidence for the future of the states. He was not convinced that breaking away from the mother country would cause the colonials to replace with virtue the sloth and corruption he ascribed to them. Rush had gone into the revolution with the diametrically opposed conviction. With the Declaration of Independence a year old, Adams saw no reason to dispense with his negative feelings. Rush, on the other hand, though admittedly disillusioned that a year of independence had yet to see realized the revolution he had hoped for in the hearts of people, nevertheless refused to abandon his dream that the war would introduce "among us the same temperament in pleasure, the same modesty in dress, the same justice in business, and the same veneration for the name of the Deity which distinguished our ancestors." Indeed, he hoped that the war would last until this desired end was achieved. ("A peace at this time would be the greatest curse that could befall us.")

Rush admitted to seeing "a gloomy cloud hanging over our States." Where it was his initial fear that the Tories would undermine the cause for which the revolutionary war was being fought resolutely by the Americans against immeasurable odds, he now saw as the true enemy within, his own political soul mates, the Whigs. But not all. There were, he told Adams pedantically, five classes of Whigs. Four were motivated by differing principles: love of power, resentment, interest, a love of the military life. The fifth class—the class of Whigs whose ideology he embraced—was motivated solely by the love of liberty. Expressing the wish that "this class of Whigs prevailed more among us," and insisting that the "time is now at an end when danger is to be apprehended from the Tories," Rush warned Adams, "If we are undone at all, it must be by the aristocratic, the mercenary, the persecuting, and the arbitrary spirit of our own people"—that first four categories of Whigs. But Rush refused to abandon hope. He was "sure" that the gloomy cloud hanging over the states "will descend only in fertilizing rains upon" the fifth class of Whigs, "for they have not forfeited their birthright by their vices." Rush closed his letter rejoicing to learn that Congress had relieved Philip Schuyler as commander of the northern forces with one of his favorite generals (and one of the Continental army's most outstanding), Horatio Gates: "he belongs to the 5th class of Whigs."

Rush was with the army when, on 24 August, having ascertained that Philadelphia was Howe's objective, Washington moved his force of about eleven thousand troops through the city, from which they were ferried across the Schuylkill, and headed southward in the hope of throwing back the British and thus to save the new nation's capital. On 11 September they joined battle with Howe's eighteen thousand troops at Brandywine, near Chadds Ford, some twenty-five miles southwest of Philadelphia. The British made a frontal feint at the Americans preliminary to a full-scale attack on its right wing. The surprise attack on the American right, led by the British general Lord Cornwallis, forced the Americans, under Nathanael Greene, to fall back. Washington ordered a withdrawal to Chester. Official British casualties totaled about 600 but are estimated much higher; American, about 900 killed and wounded and 400 men taken prisoner.

Rush "attended in the rear" during the battle "and had nearly fallen in the hands of the enemy by my delay in helping [remove] the wounded." Two days later, under a flag of truce granted by Howe at Washington's request, Rush "went with several surgeons into the British camp . . . to dress the [American] wounded" taken prisoner in the battle.[7] The experience left Rush impressed with the manner in which the British tended to their men—both the wounded and the healthy regulars—and disgusted with the way the Americans tended to theirs. As he reported in a long letter to Adams a few weeks after the visit (1 October 1777), he was "struck upon approaching General Howe's line with the *vigilance* of his sentries and pickets," and how the Redcoats "pay a supreme regard to the cleanliness and health of their men."

After Brandywine, British soldiers were strictly forbidden to touch any of the blankets that had belonged to the dead or wounded lest they should become infected. Though they carried blankets as part of their kit even in battle, "such was their laziness" that many slept on the cold and dew-ridden ground rather than troubling to untie and open them. One of the officers informed Rush that it was "his business every night before he slept" to make sure that "no soldier in his company laid down without a blanket." Great pains were taken to assure that the army was well provided with vegetables. In a dig at the corruption that seemed to permeate the Continental army, Rush noted that in Howe's army the deputy quartermasters and deputy commissaries were "composed chiefly of old and reputable officers, and not of the [American] vagrants and bankrupts." There was "utmost order and contentment in their hospitals," and the American wounded "we brought off from the field were not half so well treated as those whom we left in General Howe's hands."

In addition to superior medical attention, every ten men were allotted an orderly, and officers went so far as to ascertain that their surgeons properly tended to not only their own wounded but also the Americans. "You must not attribute this to their humanity," Rush advised Adams. "They hate us in every shape we appear to them." Their care of the American wounded "was entirely the effect of the perfection of their medical establishment, which mechanically forced happiness and satisfaction upon our countrymen." It would take Rush "a volume" to tell Adams "of the many things I saw and heard which tend to show the extreme regard that our enemies pay to discipline, order, economy, and cleanliness among their soldiers."

How different was the situation in the American army, where, after arriving at the headquarters of a general without being challenged by a single sentry, Rush "saw soldiers straggling from our lines in every quarter without an officer, exposed every moment to be picked up" by the enemy, and heard of two thousand men who "sneaked off with the baggage of the army to Bethlehem." An officer admitted they would probably not be missed for several days because sergeants instead of officers made the daily head count. Rush was convinced that "General Washington never knew within 3,000 men what his real numbers were. I saw nothing but confidence and languor in all the branches and extremities of the army." The American hospital "opened a continuation of the confused scenes I had beheld in the army. The waste, the peculation, the unnecessary officers, &c. (all the effects of *our* medical establishment), are enough to sink our country without the weights which oppress it from other quarters."

Taking aim at a target that would grow with each passing week— Dr. Shippen—Rush condemned the system that "was formed for the Director General and not for the benefit of the sick and wounded," The sick suffered, but no redress could be had for them. "Upwards of 100 of them were drunk last night. We have no guards to prevent this evil." In Howe's army, by comparison, "a captain's guard mounts over every 200 sick. Besides keeping their men from contracting and pro- longing distempers by rambling, drinking, and whoring, guards keep up at all times in the minds of the sick a sense of military subordina- tion." Insisting that a soldier "should never forget for a single hour that he has a master," Rush expressed the fear that "one month in our hospitals would undo all the discipline of a year, provided our soldiers brought it with them from the army." Urging that Adams, in his posi- tion as a leading member of Congress, "let our army be reformed," Rush bemoaned, "we are on the brink of ruin." He was "distressed to see the minions of a tyrant" (i.e., King George III) "more devoted to his will than we are to a cause in which the whole world is interested. New measures and new men alone can save us. The American mind cannot long support the present complexion of affairs. Let our army he reformed."

By the time Rush wrote this letter, events had been reduced to a "slough of despond" when word was received that on 26 September at ten in the morning British troops, against a cacophonous rendition of "God Save the King," had marched through Philadelphia, the side- walks crowded only with the Loyalists sympathetic to the Crown. Throughout the preceding week those supporting the American cause had fled to the homes of friends and relatives in the countryside. Eight days previously, Congress had fled to Lancaster, but finding the city overflowing with refugees, and fearful that Howe's army might carry the invasion inland, moved on to York and there reconvened.

On 4 October, counting on the element of surprise, Washington engaged the British encampment at Germantown, just north of Philadelphia. What appeared at first to be a prelude to victory soon degenerated into yet another rout due to predawn confusion within the American ranks. Washington deemed it prudent to leave Philadelphia to Howe, who by subsequently capturing Fort Mifflin (16 November) and Fort Mercer four days later completed British control of the Delaware River.

It was losing the Battle of Germantown that prompted Rush's pessimistic view that the new nation was "on the brink of ruin," and "New measures and new men alone can save us." About the only good news from the field was that on 17 October, following his defeat at the Second Battle of Bemis Heights—also known as the Battle of Saratoga—Burgoyne surrendered his entire force to General Horatio Gates. Ten days earlier, Rush's spirits had hit rock bottom following a visit to Washington's temporary headquarters at Bethlehem, where they had been established on the route to winter encampment at Valley Forge.

To Rush it seemed to be not so much an army headquarters—let alone of the commander in chief—as a second-rate carnival of inebriates and stumblebums ad-libbing stopovers while striving to keep one step ahead of a pursuing posse: "Dined with the commander in chief of American army—no wine—only grog—knives & forks eno' for only half the company—one half the company eat after the other had dined at the same table. The General gave the head of his table to one of his aids-de-camp, and sat 2nd or 3rd from him on his left. The commander in chief at this time the *idol of America*—governed by Gen. Greene—Gen. Knox & Col. [Alexander] Hamilton, one of his aids, a young man of 21 years of age."

Singled out by Rush for particular animadversion were four major generals: his future good friend Greene ("a sycophant to [Washington], timid, speculative, without enterprise"); John Sullivan, who, it will be recalled, had while a prisoner of Lord Howe brought the British leader's peace proposal to Congress ("weak, vain, without dignity, fond of scribbling in the field, a madman"); William Stirling ("a proud, vain, lazy, ignorant, drunkard"); and Adam Stevens, whom Rush had admired till he turned up drunk at the Battle of Germantown ("a sordid, boasting cowardly sot"). "The troops dirty, undisciplined, & ragged, guns fired 100 a day, pickets left 5 days & sentries 24 hours, without relief; bad bread; no order; universal disgust." At Valley Forge Rush would find the "encampment dirty & stinking, no forage for 7 days—1500 horses died from ye want of it. 3 ounces of meal

& 3 pounds of flour in 7 days, Men dirty & ragged. The commander-in-chief and all yᵉ Major Generals lived in houses out of yᵉ Camp."[8]

Thus Rush's condemnation of the American generals (at the time there being but two grades, brigadier and major): "The fashion of blaming our soldiers and officers for all the disorders of our army was introduced in order to shelter the ignorance, the cowardice, the idleness, and the drunkenness of our major generals"—that is to say, the army's top commanders.

Rush urged Adams in a letter dated 31 October 1777—and, by extension, Congress—that if the army could not rid itself of these tosspots ("if the blood and treasure of America must be spent to no purpose—if the war must be protracted through their means for two or three generations—and if the morals and principles of our young men must be ruined through their examples") then two resolutions must be passed: "If any major or brigadier general shall drink more than one quart of whiskey, or get drunk more than once in twenty-four hours, he shall be publicly reprimanded at the head of his division or brigade," and "that in all battles and skirmishes the major and brigadier generals shall not be more than five hundred yards in the rear of their respective divisions or brigades upon pain of being tried and punished at the discretion of a court-martial." Only a mental defective could have missed the point that in indicting the army's top brass, Rush was tacitly indicting the man who not only tolerated them but surrounded himself with them: the commander in chief.

Ironically, the one officer for whom Rush could find no fault was the forty-two-year-old Thomas Conway, with whose intrigue—the so-called Conway Cabal—Rush would shortly become involved, however peripherally, to the impairment of his reputation. An Irish-born soldier of fortune educated in France, Conway was a colonel in the French army when the American diplomat Silas Deane recruited him to serve in the American Revolution. On his arrival in America in 1777 Conway was given the rank of brigadier general, and acquitted himself admirably in the battles of Brandywine and Germantown. When he applied for promotion, Washington opposed the application as being unfair to officers with longer service. Conway threatened to resign from the army.

Rush wrote to Adams (13 October 1777), "For God's sake, do not suffer him to resign. [He is] the idol of the whole army. Make him a major general if nothing else will detain him in [the country's] service. He is entitled to most of the glory our arms acquired in the late battle [i.e., Germantown]. But his bravery and skill in war are not his only military qualifications. He is exact in his discipline and understands every part of the detail of an army. Besides this, he is an enthusiast for our cause." Conway was given the rank of major general and made inspector general of the Continental army two months later.

If Washington had even the remotest idea of the dust-up Conway would soon create, he would have probably sent him packing back to France. Despite his promotion, the seeds of Conway's disillusionment had by then been sown, as had those of his champion, Rush. Rush now took to openly criticizing Washington's leadership, albeit for Adams's ears only. Citing Horatio Gates's victory at Saratoga—"your way to take the command of the army which captured General Burgoyne, can never pass from my mind," Rush would recall to Gates a quarter of a century after the fact[9]—Rush compared his and Washington's leadership style: "I have heard several officers," he wrote Adams (21 October 1777), "who have served under General Gates compare his army to a well-regulated family."

Washington's "family," on the other hand, was "an unformed mob." Gates, "on the pinnacle of military glory, exult[ed] in the success of schemes planned with wisdom and executed with vigor and bravery." Washington, conversely, was "outgeneraled," more than twice "bested" in battle, and "forced to give up a city the capital of a state [as well as the new nation's capital], and after all outwitted by the same army in retreat." Equating Washington, quite hyperbolically, with the biblical Golden Calf, Rush warned Adams in no uncertain terms, "If our Congress can witness these things with composure and suffer them to pass without an inquiry [into Washington's leadership in the field], I shall think we have not shook off monarchical prejudices and that like the Israelites of old we worship the work of our hands."

From attacking Washington by name, and now having worked himself into a lather, Rush railed at the Continental army's miserable medical department: "Our hospital affairs grow worse and worse. There are several hundred wounded soldiers in this place who would have perished had they not been supported by the voluntary and benevolent contributions of some pious Whigs. The fault is both in the establishment and in the Director General [Shippen]. He is both *ignorant* and *negligent* of his duty."

Mercifully for Rush, Adams kept to himself the worst criticism to date of Washington either on paper or verbally, as well as his friend's opinion of his superior, Dr. Shippen. This act of mercy would soon prove to have been, in a sense, wasted effort. Rush would need no man to air his negative opinion of both men. He would manage that quite nicely all by himself.

Dr. Rush's Private War

Benjamin Rush was a congenital victim of two major personality flaws: impetuousness and a proclivity for indiscretion. Thus it came about that while Washington and his generals were waging war against the British on a number of fronts, Rush was waging a war of his own on two fronts: against the army's medical department, and against Washington and his favorite generals.

The second issue, which was subordinate to the first in Rush's list of priorities, will be discussed further along. As for the medical department, there is no question that Rush was in the right in his attacks on the handling of wounded and sick American soldiers. Whether, as it could be argued, the entire problem could have been obviated if Congress had not insisted on interfering in an area where it had no right to, but had limited itself to enacting appropriate legislation in terms of funding and staffing, is in fact moot. Indeed, whether things might have been different if the medical director had been anyone but Shippen—even if it were Rush's choice, Morgan—is equally moot.

It must be conceded that Shippen, like Morgan, was a brilliant physician. As director of the medical department, though, he was a disaster. But then, the ultimate fault is attributable to Congress for putting Shippen in so high a position of authority. Still, Shippen must share a large portion of the blame, to judge by so much of his behavior of a nonclinical nature that was downright reprehensible. Rush would succeed in bringing Shippen's professional misbehavior to light when their whole entanglement wound up eventually before a military tribunal—and would learn that trying to triumph over Shippen was not unlike trying to nail gruel to a wall.

Rush would have been well advised to tolerate Shippen as his superior and confine himself to what he did best—tending the sick and wounded—and limiting his barrage of letters to Adams and a few other members to seeking their influence to mandate Congress's improvements in the medical department. But Rush considered Shippen, and with good cause, one who must be brought down; and in pursuit of that objective, as in a number of others, Rush was incapable of backing down. Even were Shippen a paragon of a man—which he wasn't—Rush was determined to bring him to grief. That he brought more grief upon himself than upon his nemesis is almost beside the point.

To put the whole mess into proper perspective, it is necessary to backtrack to Rush's return from Europe as a newly minted physician, when Morgan and Shippen were the star attractions in Philadelphia's medical establishment. Both were of the patrician class, both were justly celebrated for their medical talents, both enjoyed the advantages of birth, position, and wealth. And both were arrogant prima donnas.

While studying at Edinburgh they had exchanged thoughts on the state of medical education in the colonies. Later, by then a successful practicing physician, Shippen formulated in greater detail the founding of a medical school in Philadelphia, for which he presented his proposals at a special meeting of the trustees of the College of Philadelphia on 3 May 1765. Morgan, who had brought back with him a brilliant reputation after years of medical lecturing in Britain, France, and Italy, was elected professor of the theory and practice of physic at the college. At the college's first commencement exercises, he delivered his famous "Discourse upon the Institution of Medical Schools in America," in which he called for establishing the medical school. He gave little credit to Shippen for having conceived the idea, thereby earning his undying enmity. An apology might have resolved what could well have been defined as an unintended slight. But Morgan was not the apologizing kind. Besides, he wanted full credit for the idea, whereas half the credit, at most, was all he deserved. Rush felt morally indebted to Morgan for having gotten him the first professorship in chemistry at the college, and had his own axe to grind with Shippen. But he steered clear of the controversy.

When war broke out, Dr. Benjamin Church, the first director of the medical department of the army, patterned his administration on the British army's: complete separation of responsibility for supply procurement and the direction of medical administration. Church's tenure was brief. Congress court-martialed him, ostensibly—never proved—for "holding criminal correspondence with the enemy," and discarded his system before it could even be properly put into effect, for no other reason than that it was British. Morgan was named by Congress to succeed Church (17 October 1775) and given the two hats of director general of the military hospitals and physician in chief to the American army.

Immediately upon joining Washington at Cambridge, from where the newly created Continental army was fighting to evict the British from Boston, Morgan was appalled to find not only the hospital but the entire army medical establishment either perilously short of or totally lacking in medicines or appliances. Exacerbating the situation, dissension was rife among the medical officers. As a prelude to correcting the overall situation, Morgan tried to mitigate the friction that had arisen but with little success. Establishing proper hospital protocol was at this time all but impossible. Washington's army, a young one comprised of militia unused to discipline, lacked proper clothing and stores of all kinds that Congress was unable to provide. Moreover, after the loss of New York that followed success at Boston, the situation became aggravated. The disheartened, disorganized army was now in full retreat across New Jersey. Still, Dr. Morgan sought to correct the abuses he found and relieve the sick and injured, even to the extent of personal funding.

But his prodigious efforts can be compared to the mythical cleansing of the Augean Stable. And Morgan was no Hercules. Compounding his problem was the opposition of the regimental surgeons, most of whom were unschooled beyond apprenticeship, many of them no more than family physicians of the officers and selected by their regimental colonels, who in turn were not appointed by Congress but by the various colonial legislatures. This led not only to defiance of Morgan's authority but also to the constant demand that requisitions for drugs be filled without justifying the need for their intended use. In one six-week period, for example, one regimental surgeon requisitioned—and received—a disproportionate hundred gallons of rum and an equally disproportionate amount of rum and sugar. Since this was way beyond the needs of his patient population, it can be conjectured that the surgeon and his friends had a high old time.[1]

Knowing he could not count on Congress—or a militarily preoccupied General Washington—to combat such waste and inefficiency, Morgan arbitrarily gave permission for the regimental doctors to ameliorate sore throats and minor intestinal upsets and tend to minor wounds, but insisted, on pain of draconian measures, including court-martial, that the serious cases be removed to the central hospital serving the current area of combat. (Under Church, battalion medical officers retained their own cases and drew what stores were needed from the director.) Moreover, he lectured them on discipline, and went so far as to insist that his own staff physicians take examinations to prove their competence. This resulted in the resignation from the army of some, mostly those who could never take the examination to prove just how incompetent they truly were. Many who remained became Morgan's enemies, as did a preponderance of the regimental surgeons, who were not expected to be as knowledgeable in matters medical as physicians; they were little more than a step or two above what we today know as trained medical corpsmen.

While stationed as a physician with the army in New Jersey, Shippen solicited Morgan's influence to be appointed director of the "flying Camp" in that state. The flying camp was a force of some ten thousand troops from the middle states organized to meet any emergency that might arise in protecting the region from a vantage point on the Jersey side of the Hudson River. At that time all the activity was taking place in New York, where the flying camp refused to become engaged. Though disliking him as a man, Morgan respected Shippen as a physician and helped him secure the appointment, despite an angry exchange between the two as to who would hold ultimate authority.

Conditions in the field were appalling, and not only in the middle states, which saw the heaviest action between Washington's and Howe's armies. In the Northern army alone, some five thousand men fell victim to smallpox between 1 April and 8 August in the first year of the war. By February 1777 the disease had spread so rapidly that Washington, fearful lest it spread throughout the whole army, ordered the inoculation of all troops in his command and all recruits upon induction despite the prior issuance of a general order prohibiting the procedure. Nevertheless, the troops in New Jersey were falling victim to camp or putrid fever (in all probabilities typhoid) in large numbers.

By the first week in September nearly a quarter of Washington's troops were hospitalized.[2]

On 22 November 1776, while Rush was still a member of Congress, the medical committee was asked to examine a number of soldiers who had come into the city from the flying camp with what was probably typhoid. He describes their arriving in open wagons, without officers or surgeons. Many had died along the way from hunger and cold. No arrangements had been made for their care on arrival. By the end of December, according to one gravedigger, the soldiers were dying so rapidly and in such numbers that he could not "dig graves for them all, and so [dug] a large hole fifteen feet square and ten feet deep, and so [buried] them in two tiers, and that the highest coffin [was] almost five feet underground." One day alone saw the burial of fifty victims; by month's end, the fever had spread into the civilian population, this at a time when smallpox fever had begun to spread throughout the city. In sum, Rush charged, "there were buried in potter's field from November 1776 to March 1777, betwixt a thousand and eleven hundred soldiers, the chief of whom belonged to the flying camp."[3]

Three and a half years later, testifying at Shippen's court-martial, Rush would irrationally hold him singularly responsible for the catastrophe by failing to foresee it. Such was his hatred for Shippen by then, Rush apparently forgot—or perhaps chose to forget—that six days after Congress called for an investigation of the soldiers' conditions, he had written to Shippen: "I am bound in justice to your fidelity, to inform you, that every person who comes from the camp, speaks in the most respectful terms of your conduct towards the sick and wounded under your care."[4]

The Congress's Committee on Medical Affairs was of no help in Morgan's attempt to improve the army's medical system. Its head was Samuel Adams, who had little time, less energy, and no applicable knowledge to deal with medical problems. All that the committee managed to do was interfere with everything Morgan was striving to accomplish. It undermined his authority, forced political appointments on him, and left unanswered his barrage of letters seeking instructions. With no real chain of command and an unfulfilled urgent need for supplies, the entire medical system was in a state of collapse.

And everyone was pointing the finger of blame at everyone else. All that Morgan could do, against a rising tide of opposition, was express his contempt for the regimental medical officers and insist on the total respect of his subordinates and on the most stringent military discipline, all the while striving round the clock with his own hands to save the sick and dying.

It was around this time Morgan learned that Shippen, who had never forgiven being slighted by Morgan in connection with the establishment of a medical faculty at Philadelphia, was plotting against him. It wasn't long before he learned that Shippen was trying to get possession of all the supplies Morgan had collected for the army through great effort and stored in Newark. Even worse, Shippen was using his influence to remove his rival. And that influence was considerable. Having married into the prominent Lee family of Virginia, Shippen's two brothers-in-law, Francis Lightfoot Lee and Richard Henry Lee, were important members of Congress. Moreover, there is evidence that he falsified reports to Congress that made his own record appear superior to Morgan's. Learning of Shippen's maneuverings against him, Morgan called on Washington at his headquarters near Trenton to lodge a complaint. Washington, who had his hands full trying to keep his bedraggled army together and prevent the collapse of the Revolution, urged that Morgan "lay the matter before Congress, that some steps may be taken to remedy this irregularity and inconvenience, and that I may know what I have to depend upon."[5]

On 18 November Congress ordered that "Dr. Morgan take care of the sick and wounded of the army of the United States, as are on the east side of the Hudson River, and that Dr. Shippen take care of such of the said sick and wounded as are on the west side." Shippen's politicking and those presumably bogus reports had paid off. With Washington's army now in New Jersey, Congress had thus made Shippen the commander in chief's principal medical officer. His first act was to demand Morgan's supplies stored at Newark. Morgan refused the demand and rushed off to Philadelphia to lay his case before Congress. Outside Independence Hall, where Congress was in session, he met Samuel Adams—who advised that he resign from the army! Morgan demanded a congressional inquiry and the opportunity to vindicate himself. Adams, who was well up on the whole medical department chaos, thanks to a stream of letters from his friend Dr. Rush, put him off, on the grounds that Congress was heavily engaged, but assured Morgan that it would grant him an investigation in due course.

Due course never came for Morgan. On 9 January 1777, the Congress ordered his dismissal from the army. Shippen's triumph was complete when on 11 April 177 he was appointed to succeed Morgan. He was now the Continental army's number-one medical officer, answerable directly to General Washington.

It was at this time that Rush assumed his administrative responsibilities as Physician general of the Middle Department of the Continental Army.

Some critics would claim—a claim heatedly denied by Rush—that his antipathy toward Shippen dated from Shippen's disapproval of certain data that Rush as a young teaching physician had offered the students in his chemistry course. Also, that Shippen and his father, also a prominent physician, were from the aristocracy of Philadelphia physicians, which would hardly have gone down well with a man of Rush's background; that Shippen, ten years Rush's senior, had, as Rush saw it, failed to help him get established when he returned from study in Europe; that Shippen was married to the sister of Richard Henry Lee, once a friend of Rush's but no longer, as a result of the dispute in Congress over raising the interest on loan certificates; and that Shippen was a close friend of Washington.

Much as he came to detest Shippen, Rush insisted that any man, himself included, be judged on the evidence, and personal enmity be excluded from consideration. We may take him at his word that, notwithstanding his insistence that the British army medical system was the only practical one (and one that Congress would in time adopt for the Continental army) and the American one was, at this time, a muddled, even life-threatening mess, Rush "reluctantly accepted the commission of Physician general of the military hospitals under it, and entered upon my duty with a heart devoted to the interests of my country."[6]

After leaving Washington's headquarters in October, Rush went off to inspect the hospital at Reading. There he "found the wounded soldiers in the most distressed condition" and so deficient in clothing "that most of them lay for several weeks in the same shirts in which they were wounded." When he prescribed Madeira wine for one of the patients, an orderly informed him that only port was available; the several pipes of Madeira in the hospital stores were Shippen's personal property.[7] Outraged, Rush asked three staff members to join him in signing an affidavit against the medical director, and was overheard to remark, "We will bring the Shippens down; they are too powerful and have reigned long enough." He also wrote to John Adams that if Congress did not reform the medical department, "I shall trouble you with my resignation, and my reasons shall afterwards be given to the public for it." He was now bombarding Adams with letters offering his suggestions—indeed, demands—for reorganization of the medical department, and openly attacking "the ignorance, the cowardice, the idleness, and the drunkenness" of many of the major generals in general, and Shippen in particular ("He is both *ignorant* and *negligent* of his duty"), and bemoaning the wretched state of the ill and wounded ("Our hospital affairs grow worse and worse").[8]

Adams was sympathetic, and may well have voiced these concerns to fellow members of the Congress. But Congress was not only confident of the manner in which *it* was supervising the affairs of the medical department, it had many other problems confronting it, ranging from the management of the war to attempting to secure foreign loans to seeking a consensus on the Articles of Confederation.[9]

Justified as Rush was in his condemnation, he was beginning to obsess about it to the point where it is possible that in a face-to-face talk with his friend, Adams might have managed to calm him down. But the two men were both too busy in their respective areas of responsibility to have such a meeting. Rush dashed off to Adams the following resolutions, which "would remedy many abuses and prove the means of saving the lives of hundreds before the campaign is over": that all senior physicians and surgeons be furnished by Shippen and his deputy with such medicines, stores, and accommodations "as they shall require," with said requisition to be made in writing and to be used afterward as a voucher for the expenditures of the director general; that all accounts of Shippen for medicines, wines, stores, etc., "be certified by the physician or surgeon general before they are possessed." This resolution, Rush stressed, was "of the utmost importance, and I have *good reason* to say will save thousands on the conti-nent"; and that "all returns of sick, wounded, and of officers of the hospital" be transmitted to Congress's Medical Committee by the physicians or surgeons or general. "The reason of this is plain. They can have no interest in making out *false* returns, and the returns from them will always be a check upon the expenditures of the director general."

Rush concludes, "Should [Adams] think it worth while to read any parts of this letter" to any of his colleagues, "it will perhaps give some weight to them if you conceal the name of your friend and humble servant, B. Rush."[10] Not that Rush cared what Congress thought of his criticism. But there *was* Shippen's relationship to the two Lees, influential in themselves and as members of the powerful Virginia del-egation and among other delegations from the southern states. This, too, is moot. Unwilling to take on the southern delegates with Con-gress now divided along so many lines on so many issues, it is doubt-ful Adams would have introduced resolutions so condemnatory of the medical director had they come from Washington himself.

Rush next moved on to inspect the hospital at Burlington (9 November) and left the next day for Red Bank to establish a hospital in the neighborhood of the American forts—Mifflin and Mercer—on the Delaware. Fort Mercer, on the Jersey side at Red Bank, and Fort Mifflin, on Mud Island, had been blocking British shipping on the river for the two months since Howe had taken Philadelphia, thus denying him much needed supplies and reinforcements. Watching the barrage of Fort Mifflin, Rush found it "impossible to do justice to the officers and soldiers who defended it." He describes witnessing for a day "their patience and fortitude under the most complicated dangers and sufferings . . . Britain in the height of her glory when she fought for liberty never saw her sons perform more gallant exploits than the ragged sons of liberty performed who fell in defense of that island."[11]

Rush returned to Burlington on 12 November; five days later he went to Princeton to visit his wife, who had returned to her father's home there with her newborn son: "He is so good-tempered that he seldom or never cries. He spends his whole time in sleeping, eating, and pulling his mama's caps and handkerchiefs to pieces."[12] Rush had planned a brief stay with Julia and the baby, mainly to check out the hospital there. He then planned to join General Greene, who was rushing with a force to engage Lord Cornwallis, who had come from Philadelphia with two thousand troops to take Fort Mercer, which was blocking the British fleet. But Greene was delayed by bad timing, and Fort Mercer had to be evacuated due to the horrendous British shelling. This enabled Howe to secure his hold on Philadelphia. The British were now in complete control of the Delaware River.

Rush stayed on in Princeton for the next six weeks visiting the hospitals, which were quartered in Nassau Hall and the First Presbyterian Church, whose pews and gallery the British had ripped out for firewood while occupying the town. The average weekly patient population was from 500 to 600. Plans to commandeer the Quaker meetinghouse and the huge mansion of a Tory who had fled came to naught. Rush did manage to mitigate the overcrowding somewhat by billeting the ambulatory patients with farmers on Princeton's outskirts.

Rush's main problem was that of discipline. To Nathanael Greene he wrote (2 December 1777) that there were in the hospital some five hundred sick and wounded soldiers, many with complaints "so trifling that they do not prevent their committing daily a hundred irregularities of all kinds." With the physicians and surgeons lacking the authority "to prevent or punish them," he begged Greene to "send immediately two or three officers, or even one if more cannot be spared, to take command in this place. The sick cannot be governed without military authority." But Greene could not spare even one man.

On the same day, Rush repeated his request in a letter to Shippen: "We suffer so much every hour from the want of an officer to command in this place that I . . . request that you would procure one for us. A hospital cannot be governed without one." Having made the request, Rush went on to reiterate the need for the Continental army to emulate the British approach to management of their ill and wounded—an approach that the medical director agreed with Congress should not be considered: "An officer of rank and reputation is always stationed near the hospitals in the British army. He is called a MILITARY INSPECTOR." Had Rush stopped there, it's possible—though only possible—that Shippen might have entertained his request. But Rush now proceeded to poach on Shippen's area of responsibility by asking, indiscreetly albeit with the best intentions,

Is not this the time to lay in stores for next year? Every day increases their scarcity and high price. Suppose you send Dr. Bond to New England for that purpose. 100 pipes of wine, 50 hogsheads of sugar, and 100 [ditto] of molasses will not be too much for us. Perhaps Dr. [Isaac] Foster [of Massachusetts, deputy director of the eastern medical department] may spare some of his linen, sheets, &c, with which he abounds. What do you think of a magazine of Indian corn—a most wholesome and agreeable diet for the sick? It is rising and perhaps will not be to be had in the spring?

What Shippen thought was that Rush believed he could do the job of medical director better: "Dr. Shippen had taken pains to represent my complaints of the sufferings of the sick as intended to displace him," Rush wrote six days later to William Duer, an influential New York delegate to Congress. In truth, Shippen was completely misreading Rush's motives. Rush was ambitious for many things, but power was not one of them. After reiterating to Duer all that he had written to John Adams on the need to reorganize the entire army medical department along the British plan, firstly by creating a quartermaster general to handle all nonmedical matters, such as procuring of supplies and supervising hospital management, thus allowing the medical director to concentrate on the care and management of the ill and wounded—"These ample and *incompatible* powers [now] lodged in the hands of *one* man appears to be absurd as if General Washington had been made quartermaster, commissary, and adjutant general of your whole army"—Rush wanted Duer, and by extension the Congress, to know:

No man can suspect I wish for any alteration in the system from a desire of holding a higher or more lucrative office in it than the one I have received from the Congress. I would not accept the directorship of our hospitals upon its present footing for the riches of India. On the contrary, I am resolved to retire as soon as the campaign [in New Jersey] is closed, since I cannot act agreeable to the dictates of my conscience and judgment,

Moreover, he wanted it understood that he did "not mean by this comparison of our [present] plan with the British system to hint anything to the prejudice of the present director of our hospitals." (Did he assume naïvely that Adams had not shared Rush's letters of complaint about "the present director" with Duer?) If, Rush continued, Shippen "possessed the abilities of a Bacon, the industry of a Boyle, and the integrity of Aristides, he could not execute one half of the extensive powers" given the medical director by Congress.

> The sufferings of the sick from the want of medicines, stores, and bedding, their irregularities from the want of officers to command and guards to watch them, *most* of the mortality, and ALL the waste, peculation, negligence, and ignorance which have prevailed in our hospitals during the whole of this campaign are to be in part charged to the very nature of our establishment.

As for Shippen's suspicions that Rush was plotting to replace him, he concluded: "[T]o show that I aimed only at the happiness of my distressed countrymen and the honor of my country, I shall seal my disapprobation of our medical establishment as well as of its administration with my resignation. A battle is inevitable. Nothing but a desire of assisting the poor fellows who are to suffer in it detains me a moment in the department."[13]

Five days later, in a follow-up letter to Duer, Rush admitted that, far from "hint[ing] anything to the prejudice" of Shippen, he was in fact indicting him. (Did this come as any surprise to Duer? One doubts it.) At this point his differences with—indeed, his contempt for—the medical director reached the point from which Rush could not retreat. Having "heard with great pleasure" that Duer was "about to new-model the army," Rush pleaded, "For God's sake, do not forget to take the medical system under your consideration." He then went on to reiterate his by now familiar charges: "It is a mass of corruption and tyranny. . . . It would take up a volume to unfold all the disorders and miseries of the hospitals. . . . Old disorders are prolonged, new ones are contracted, the discipline of the soldiers . . . is destroyed, the [patients] are plundered, and the blankets, clothes, shoes, &c., of the soldiers are stole[n] for exchange in every tavern and hut [Rush was writing from Princeton] for spirituous liquors."

He had "witnessed these things for six months," and complained "to the Director General, to the Congress, and to the generals of the army to no effect." Now zeroing in on Shippen, Rush said that on complaining to him about the overcrowding of too many sick in one house, Shippen replied "he was the *only* judge of that, and that my *only* business was to take care of all he sent there." Meanwhile, Shippen had yet to go "*inside* of a hospital or to expose himself to the least danger of being infected by a fever" that had already carried off six surgeons contracted in the hospitals, "and there is scarcely one who has not been ill to a greater or lesser degree with it." Comparing Shippen unfavorably with Dr. Jonathan Potts, Rush's friend and fellow student at Edinburgh, who "has confined himself *solely* to the purveying business," and Dr. [Malachi] Treat, a former surgeon in the British army who had "introduced the British system in its *most minute parts* into the hospitals" of the army's Northern Department, of which he was physician general, Rush wishes "some members of Congress (not related to Dr. S——n)"—a not too subtle dig at the Lee brothers and their supporters in Congress—"would visit our hospitals" and see for themselves the chaos rampant within. Shippen, Rush goes on to charge, had handpicked physicians and surgeons willing to play the moth to his flame, "and has made some of them dependent upon his will."

Yet he was convinced that Duer "will not find more than *one* man" in the entire medical department "who does not reprobate our system and who will not ring peals of distress and villainy in your ears much louder than anything you have heard from me." Additionally damning Shippen by praising his assistants, and to assure his complaints would be brought before Congress, Rush ends with: "You may make any use you please of this letter and *my name* with it."

Over the next few weeks Rush took New Jersey governor William Livingston on a tour of the state's army hospitals, leading Livingston to write Washington on Christmas Day his observations, which reflected Rush's influence. Next day, Rush wrote a long letter to Washington that began with an apology for bypassing his superior, the director general, but only because he believed the commander in chief had not been adequately briefed on the deplorable state of the army hospitals. In the original draft of the letter, as given in his memoirs,

Rush makes it obvious upon whose shoulders—Shippen's—the blame must be laid.[14] In the final draft, the one that went off to Washington, Rush wisely reined in his characteristic penchant for indiscretion and took pains to avoid attacking Shippen, whom he knew was looked upon most favorably by the commander in chief.

He reiterates what had by now become a mantra of many parts. Overcrowded, and thus hygienically perilous hospitals: "I have seen 20 sick men in one room ill with fevers and fluxes large enough to contain only 6 or 8 well men without danger to their health." Scanty medical stores for the sick: "and these are too often withheld from them from the want of checks upon the officers of the hospital whose business it is to provide and administer them. Beef and bread are by no means suitable diet for men in fevers." The want of clothing and bed linens: "Nothing but a miracle can save the life of a soldier who lies in a shirt and blanket which he has worn for four or five months before he came into the hospital." And a need for guards to guarantee discipline, as in the British system: "The men [go] out when they please [and] catch colds, they sell their arms, blankets, and clothes to buy rum or provisions that are unsuitable for them, they plunder and insult the [local] inhabitants; while within doors they quarrel and fight with each other, disobey their [medical attendants] and thus defeat the most salutary plans that can be contrived for their recovery." Rush buttresses this point with the argument that "An officer with a suitable guard at every hospital I am sure would save many hundred lives and many thousand pounds to the continent every year." (The Americans still used the British monetary system.)

Rush then sums up his petition with the bald statement, "The medical establishment is a bad one. It gives the director general the most *incompatible* offices." Referring yet again to his belief that the salvation of the army's medical department lay in adopting the British system, he notes that the offices held by the medical director "are held by no less than *three* physicians in the British hospitals, who are all independent of each other and who, by checking each other, perfectly secure to the sick all the good offices and medical stores that are intended for them by the government."

When Rush did not receive a response from Washington by 2 January, his self-imposed deadline, he left Princeton determined to present personally his complaints to Congress, which was still meeting at York ("I thought it my only duty"). He had no way of knowing that on the preceding day Congress's first order of business of the new year was to hear his letters to Duer read aloud; also, a committee had been appointed, headed by John Witherspoon—who would be sympathetic to Rush—to look into the matters raised by the letters.

Washington finally replied to Rush on 12 January, informing him that the substance of his letter of 26 December, with another from Governor Livingston on the same subject, had been forwarded to Dr. Shippen. Though Washington had been made aware of Rush's low opinion of Shippen (as had everyone else), this was not an act of malice but of protocol. These were problems to be addressed by the medical director. Deploring the lack of provisions and of discipline in the hospitals, Washington told Rush he had ordered "a discreet Field Officer to visit the principal Hospitals" and report back directly to him. He added the assurance that he was prepared to do everything in his power to render "the situation of these unhappy people who are under the necessity of becoming the inhabitants" of army hospitals "as comfortable as possible."[15]

Washington's letter, while rather vague in response, was at least well intentioned as far as it went. For Rush, though, it did not go far enough. Worse, it came ten days too late. For by then Rush had triggered a dynamic that would culminate in his resignation from the Continental army. And in the light of his innovative, indeed revolutionary ideas on not only military patient management but also confronting health problems in general, his determination to see them put into force, and Shippen's behavior which, as will be seen, was simply appalling, the Continental army rather than Dr. Benjamin Rush would come out the loser.

12

Dr. Rush Quits the Army

Rush took six days to travel from Princeton to York, stopping the first night at Rush Hill to check up on his mother and sister. The next day he reached Washington's winter encampment at Valley Forge, "where I saw similar marks of filth, waste of public property, and want of discipline which I had recently witnessed in the hospitals." While having breakfast at the quarters of General John Sullivan, he was told by his host, "Sir, this is not an army—it is a mob." At this point "a new source of distress was awakened in my mind, I now felt for the safety and independence of my country as well as for the sufferings of the sick under my care. All that I had heard from General Stevens, Colonel Reed, Mr. Mifflin, and some others was now revived in my mind."[1] Translation: While holding Shippen responsible for the deplorable state of the army medical department, he believed Washington should be held responsible for the deplorable state of the army.

On 5 January 1778 Rush moved on to Lancaster, where he remained two days checking on the conditions of the major army hospital there. At Lancaster he found many friends who had fled inland to the west when Howe's troops took Philadelphia. On 8 January Rush reached York, the temporary national capital. Located ninety miles west of Philadelphia: "a pleasant village [which] contains above 500 houses. Most of the inhabitants are Germans." These so-called Pennsylvania Dutch were joined now by the many Philadelphia families who had fled there along with the Continental Congress.[2] One who did not flee there was John Adams, who had been elected (28 November 1777) joint commissioner to France to replace Silas Deane. In a letter to James Searle on 21 January 1778, Rush described York as "this noisy, crowded town," to which he had come "to request a 'dismission' from the hospitals." He knew that the Congress—now down to twenty-one members who met in the village's dingy courthouse—"will not grant it till I point out the abuses which prevail in them." In his letter to Julia, Rush "found such a general disposition among the members of Congress to correct the abuses and reform the system of our hospitals" that he "readily yielded to the solicitations of my friends in suspending my resignation."

Rush was heartened to learn that Congress's Medical Committee had urged that the sick be supplied with clothing and blankets, that an inspector had been ordered to visit the hospitals and report back to the delegates, and that both he and Shippen had been summonsed to appear before Congress "to answer for the many complaints that are made against his management of his hospitals." Rush told Julia it would be "a disagreeable task to accuse him publicly of ignorance and negligence of his duty" (though he did not find it disagreeable to do so in his correspondence to Adams, Duer, and Greene, which was now common knowledge to the delegates). "But the obligations I owe to my country preclude all other ties." He promised Julia he would "act strictly agreeable to the dictates of my conscience, and if the system is altered and Dr. Shippen can be restrained by proper checks from plundering the sick"—among Rush's charges was that the medical director withheld medicinal rum and wines from the patients in order to stock his own cellars—he would not resign his commission: "This resolution is taken not only from a sense of duty and a love for my country, but in consequence of the advice of some very worthy members of Congress, who assure me that a contrary step will be ascribed to a want of perseverance or to downright disaffection."

Rush was even more heartened to learn that several members of the Congress concurred with his negative—indeed, basement-level—opinion of Washington, whom he had at the outset of the war hailed as the nation's future savior. At Washington's suggestion, a Board of War was organized in the previous November, intended, in Rush's words, to effect "a reformation of every department of the army." But, as he told Julia, "it is feared no great things will be accomplished by this measure."

That's because his friend, General Horatio Gates, had been named to head the board, which included another friend, General Mifflin.

Both men were on bad terms with Washington, especially Gates, who was in effect Washington's superior in his capacity as head of the war board. The two were now practically irremediable enemies mainly because of a remark made by General Conway, another anti-Washingtonian, in a letter to Gates: "A great and good God has decreed that America shall be free, or the——and weak counselors would have ruined her long ago." Even any village's local idiot would have figured out that the blank space indicated "commander in chief"—General Washington.

Rush savored the remark and passed it on to Adams, who was no great admirer of Washington and most likely shared it with a few of the other members who felt likewise. The remark quickly spread like the proverbial wildfire both within and outside Congress. Historians are divided on whether it soon reached Washington's attention through the grapevine, or arrived there via Rush's notorious letter to Patrick Henry with which we shall deal momentarily.[3]

The chilly atmosphere at Washington's headquarters was raised a degree or two when Gates and the rest of the board "set off to the army immediately" to seek ways of reform, and Conway took off to pursue his mission as the army's inspector general. Rush told his wife pessimistically that there was "great uneasiness to all the true Whigs, who foresee from General Washington's coolness to [Gates and Conway] a continuation of all the calamities under which we have groaned for these two years in the middle states." However, he was confident that Congress would continue to "act a prudent part. They consult General Washington in everything, but they are determined to support the authority and influence of [these two top-ranking officers], Gates and Conway."[4] Whether Rush was deluding himself or actually believed this is arguable. If it was a matter of confidence on Rush's part, it was a confidence that soon proved to have been misplaced.

While awaiting that scheduled confrontation with Shippen before Congress, Rush committed what was arguably the greatest indiscretion of his life, and inarguably the most deleterious to his reputation. On 12 January—concealing his authorship by not signing the letter—he wrote to his old acquaintance from the calling of the First Continental Congress and now governor of Virginia, Patrick Henry, detailing his dispirited feelings about the war. Recalling how Henry had "first taught us to shake off our idolatrous attachment to royalty, and to oppose its encroachments upon our liberties with our very lives," Rush expressed the fear that "America can only be undone" not by the British but "by herself." Congress was offering only "weak counsels and partial remedies applied constantly for universal diseases." The army—and here he quotes what he'd been told by General Sullivan—is "a *mob. Discipline unknown,* or *wholly* neglected. The quartermaster's and commissaries' departments filled with idleness and ignorance and peculation." The military hospitals he found to be crowded with six thousand sick "but half provided with necessaries or accommodations," and more were currently dying in them in one month than perished in the field during the entire last campaign. No effectual measures were being taken to halt the depreciation of the currency. The spirit of the people was "failing through a more intimate acquaintance with the causes of our misfortunes—many submitting daily to General Howe, and more wishing to do it only to avoid the calamities which threaten our country."

But with all that, was the revolutionary cause desperate? "By no means. We have wisdom, virtue, and strength *enough* to save us if they could be called into action." The problem was not the caliber of the troops but of their leaders. And, Rush implied, with a commander in chief possessing qualities of military leadership not found in the present one. "The Northern Army has shown us what Americans are capable of doing with a GENERAL [i.e., Horatio Gates] at their head. The *spirit* [emphasis added] of the Southern Army"—the army under Washington's personal leadership—"is in no ways inferior to the spirit of the northern." Of the mere handful of capable generals, a Gates or a Conway "would in a few weeks [manage to] render them an invincible body of men." Admittedly, Conway, having accepted the newly created office of Inspector General of the Continental army, was determined to reform abuses. "But the remedy is only a palliative one," Rush fears, quoting Conway's remark ("A great and good God hath decreed America to be free . . .").

Advising Patrick Henry that he "may rest assured of *each* of the facts related in this letter," Rush identified himself only as "one of your Philadelphia friends," and cautioned that even a "hint of his name, if found out by the handwriting, must not be mentioned [even] to your most intimate friend. Even the letter *must* be thrown in the fire." However, "some of its contents ought to be made public in order to awaken, enlighten, and alarm our country. I rely upon your prudence and am, dear sir, with my usual attachment to you and to our beloved independence, yours sincerely."

Rush's perturbation over what was to him—as well as to others more qualified to make a value judgment in matters military—a failure in Washington's leadership is reflected in a letter to Adams ten days later. Washington, of course, did not deserve to bear full responsibility for his army's failures in the middle states. Even Rush conceded that tacitly, as is evident in his wholesale condemnation of the miserable medical department and the Congress's management—rather, mismanagement—of its true responsibilities. But, to use a modern locution, it was on Washington's "watch." And then, of course, there was the fact that while confronted with the same problems, the Northern army had acquitted itself brilliantly during Gates' watch.

In his letter to Henry, Rush had equated the new nation with the ancient Israelites following their exodus from Egypt: "[W]e have only passed the Red Sea. A dreary wilderness is still before us, and unless a Moses or a Joshua are [*sic*] raised up in our behalf, we must perish before we reach the promised land." To Adams he wrote on 22 January 1778, "I am daily looking for some *great* military character to start up, perhaps from the plow, to save the country." Typifying the kind of leader he longed for, Rush cited such historical exemplars as Sweden's Gustavus, Holland's Prince Maurice, and Portugal's Braganza. "Does providence refuse us such genius to prevent that danger to liberty which the fascination of great military talents produces upon vulgar minds? If so, let us adore his [i.e., God's] wisdom and be patient under the blunders of all our generals. Rome," he goes on, with the determination of a carpenter driving the last nail into a coffin that will hold the remains of his greatest enemy, "was on the eve of ruin when Pompey alone could make war on Mithradates, destroy the [Mediterranean-infested] pirates, bring corn [from Egypt, known to the ancients as the "breadbasket of the Mediterranean world"] to Rome, and oppose the invasion of Caesar. General Gates's success [at Saratoga] has rescued this country in a degree from its idolatry to *one* man."

Well, not quite. Washington was still, as Rush had referred to him ironically, "the *idol of the people*," if not of all his commanders. But that is not what should engage our attention. What should is the twofold question: Why did he not reveal himself as author of the letter to Patrick Henry, and why did he commit so colossal a blunder as to write Henry in the first place? A blunder so colossal that he makes no mention of it in his autobiography; one he would regret having made for his remaining thirty-five years. But such was his nature. While Benjamin Rush was incorruptible, he was opinionated and impetuous, given to scolding and being importuning. Here was one instance when, as can occur in the lives of all men, be they highborn or low, a volatile letter should have been set aside to be examined next day after the writer had considered his words, instead of being sent off with the ink barely dried.[5]

But back to why Rush concealed his authorship of the letter to Patrick Henry.

There is more than a semantic difference between an anonymous letter and an unsigned letter. The purpose of remaining anonymous is to conceal the writer's identity; the purpose of not signing is to keep the writer's identity from being seen by unauthorized people. This was especially so during the revolutionary period, when letters were carried by messengers or couriers and could easily fall into the wrong hands and thus compromise the writer. If Rush wished to conceal his identity completely, he could have had the letter copied by another hand. But he wrote it in his own, assuming that, since he had written other letters to Henry, the Virginia governor, as well as others with whom Rush corresponded, would recognize his handwriting and could circulate the letter without worrying that his identity would become known, were it to fall into unfriendly hands. Then again, as yet another Rush biographer has suggested, "That Rush expected the letter to be published by a local newspaper was apparent, and that may have been the compelling reason he did not sign it."[6]

As for why Rush aired his views to Henry, he regarded him as a friend. Gates had told him that Henry had a low opinion of Washington's military capabilities, and doubtless would be receptive to any criticism of the commander in chief. Rush further assumed that Henry, now focusing on his own state, might like to know the current views of those close to the Congress. And he hoped that being Virginia's governor, Henry might use his own considerable influence to undermine Washington's reputation in his home state.

Rush's reasons were logical. But logic does not enter into the equation. Patrick Henry was not prepared to abide an insult to his state's leading citizen. Moreover, as commander in chief of the Virginia militia by virtue of his gubernatorial status, Henry apparently felt a responsibility to and kinship for Washington, his criticism of the previous year notwithstanding. Therefore, Henry did not react as Rush had dared hope he might. Instead, he sent the letter on to General Washington, claiming (perhaps legitimately) not to know who the author was. Washington, having received so many faultfinding reports from Rush, recognized his handwriting at once. "This man has been elaborate and studied in his profession of regard for me," he wrote Henry.[7] Thus his feeling of betrayal by a man who had once lauded him.

The timing of the letter intensified Washington's rage over Rush's treachery. Its arrival coincided with the exposure of the so-called Conway Cabal.[8]

Named for General Thomas Conway, probably because he was the instigator, the scheme, which some historians doubt even existed outside the minds of Washington and his senior staff, involved a number of army officers and members of the Continental Congress who allegedly hoped to replace Washington as commander in chief with General Gates. Gates's ambition was doubtless fed by the high esteem in which the public held him because of his victory over Burgoyne at Saratoga—although, as historians agree, the credit he took belonged in equal if not greater share to Generals Philip Schuyler and Benedict Arnold. The many statements criticizing Gates's leadership that had come to Washington's attention, and the rather considerable correspondence he had received, including Rush's unsigned letter via Patrick Henry, fed Henry's suspicions about Gates and Conway. And here it should be noted that, suspicions at the time notwithstanding, it's rather doubtful that Rush had any part, indeed, any knowledge, of the plot. To quote Rush biographer Carl Binger, "As for Benjamin Rush it may safely be claimed that conspiracy and intrigue would have been wholly out of character. If he was opinionated and impetuous, he was also incorruptible."[9]

Still, Rush openly favored Gates and Conway, as well as Charles Lee. And given his well-aired feelings about Washington, plus the valid suspicion that he would not have minded seeing Gates assume supreme command of the Continental army, made him—in Washington's eyes as well as history's—guilty by association. In the event, Washington succeeded in turning public opinion against Gates, who now had to defend himself before Congress. All the other participants repudiated their connection with the alleged cabal. Conway bore the brunt of the blame and was forced to resign his commission. Gates was allowed to retire to his Virginia estate.

Having openly criticized Washington and openly supported men whom Washington banished from his headquarters, Rush paid a heavy price for his indiscreet letter to Patrick Henry. That he considered Lee and Gates to be the Continental army's best generals can be taken as evidence that Rush should have stuck to his medicine and left the choice of military leadership to the professionals. Gates was recalled by Congress in 1780 and given command of the army of the South. Due in part to his poor leadership, his forces suffered a disastrous defeat near Camden, South Carolina (16 August 1780), by the British under Lord Cornwallis, and was replaced by General Nathanael Greene. After the war Gates returned to his Virginia estate. In 1790 he freed his slaves and moved to a farm in present-day New York City, where he died sixteen years later.

Lee's career collapsed when he was court-martialed, at Washington's insistence, for disobeying orders and retreating before General Sir Henry Clinton's forces at the battle of Monmouth Court House. On 18 June 1778 the British army under Clinton evacuated Philadelphia and retreated across New Jersey bound for New York, followed closely by Washington and the American army. Ten days later Washington ordered Lee to attack the rear of the British forces. Lee attacked but, after some minor skirmishing, ordered a general retreat. When Washington arrived, he rallied the demoralized troops and checked the advance of the British troops. Clinton's army fell back and during the night withdrew to Sandy Hook, New Jersey, and boarded transports for New York. The defeat of the British, whose losses outnumbered the Americans', was a political success for the Continental army because it boosted the morale of the troops and increased public support of the war. When Lee refused to accept his court-martial sentence of suspension from command for one year, he was cashiered from the army.

As the date for his confrontation with Shippen before Congress rapidly approached, Rush grew increasingly apprehensive. On 19 January

Shippen addressed a letter to Congress in which he denied all of Rush's charges—and "wondered" who had authorized Rush's trip to York ("there may arise some cause of complaint at Princeton from his long absence from his duty without leave at this important period"). This was the medical director's circumlocutory way of making Congress aware that the physician who had made so many heinous charges against him—was indeed out to destroy him—had committed the military transgression of taking it upon himself to visit Congress, and to demand that either his charges be upheld or he would resign his commission, without seeking the permission of his superior—the medical director.

Rush's increasingly uneasy state vis-à-vis the coming confrontation is revealed in the fact that he was preparing in his mind for defeat and making plans to retire to Princeton, "secluded from the noise and corruption of the times and spending my time in the innocent employments of husbandry on a farm in Jersey with an amiable wife and rosy boy," as he put it to John Adams, now back in Massachusetts preparing to depart for Europe. To a friend and fellow Whig, James Searle, he wrote that if Shippen triumphed, "I expect, if not *banished* for the negligence, inhumanity, injustice &c., which have prevailed in our hospitals during the last campaign, to retire to a small farm in the neighborhood of Princeton, where I shall remain till I can get back to Philadelphia."[10]

On 25 January, consonant with the requisite formalities of the occasion, Rush wrote a brief note to the president of the Congress, Henry Laurens, that since the "Director General of the military hospitals had contradicted the assertions in my letter to General Washington in a *public* letter addressed to the *whole* body of Congress," he would "esteem it a particular favor" if Congress would "indulge me with the privilege of a *public* hearing, in order that I support the claims I have made of the abuses which prevail in our hospitals."

The following day, after hearing Rush's letter, the delegates denied his request for a public hearing; instead, his and Shippen's letters to the Congress were given to a committee of five, headed by John Witherspoon, to investigate the charges. Witherspoon, it will be recalled, was the preacher Rush had persuaded to come to America and head Princeton. He and the four others were all friends of Rush, which encouraged him to expect a sympathetic hearing. Convening immediately following its creation, the committee invited Rush to detail his charges against the medical department on the following afternoon (27 January), which Shippen would be asked to rebut the next morning.

There was nothing new in Rush's complaints, merely a reiteration at greater length of what he'd written Washington and a few others. He was quite persuasive, and it would seem that he was going to carry the day over anything Shippen might offer in rebuttal. But then, as he neared the end of his presentation, Rush made an egregious tactical gaffe.

He went from criticizing the hospital system, and Congress's failure to define the director general's authority, to a personal denunciation of Shippen: because he "required no vouchers for the expenditure of hospital stores, which gave the commissaries and stewards of the hospital the most unlimited opportunities to defraud the public . . . there was nothing to prevent the Director General from converting all the stores of the hospital to his own use." Indeed, "while our sick were suffering from the want of Madeira wine at Reading," Shippen "had sold six pipes upon his own account which he had transported thither among hospital stores in public wagons." Rush now seemed to be speaking only out of hostility toward Shippen, his superior, thus undercutting the effect of what he had testified to earlier.[11] Perhaps realizing he had blundered, Rush

> concluded my complaints by declaring that I was not actuated by the least personal resentment against Dr. Shippen; that my complaints arose from the purest affection to my country; and that while some members of Congress affected to ascribe all the abuses and distress of the hospital[s] to a want of harmony between Dr. S. and myself, I had only to beg the public's pardon that I had lived so long in harmony with him; and that to have harmonized any longer would have been high treason against my country.

In his rebuttal, Shippen denied almost all of Rush's accusations: Overcrowded hospitals were a concomitant aspect of heavy campaigning, which, as had the most recent, produced a torrent of casualties; scarcity of supplies was also normal in wartime, and medical supplies were no worse than the paucity of supplies in arms and ammunition faced by Washington on the battlefield. Shippen did, however, admit to selling six pipes of wine, but pled "as a precedent for making money by the directorship of the hospitals that of Dr. [James] Napier, [who] made a large fortune during the [French and Indian War] by being director general of the British hospitals in [North] America."[12]

Asked by Witherspoon for proof of the charges he had leveled against the administration of the hospitals and particularly against Shippen, Rush responded that

> my business and only wish was to get an alteration made in the hospital system and to have the purveying business taken out of Dr. Shippen's hands—that I did not come there to detect rogues—that that was the business of Congress—but that if the Congress would send a committee to the hospitals or order a court of inquiry to be held, I would produce proofs of all the facts I had related and of many more of a more heinous nature. This proposal had no effect upon the committee. They treated the complaints I made of the sufferings of their brave soldiers with neglect, and were easily persuaded to believe that all their misfortunes arose from a misunderstanding between Dr. S. and me.[13]

While Congress was considering the committee's findings, Rush was reassured by friends among the delegates that he had won the match, and Shippen told several delegates that the choice must be between him and Rush. Anxious to resolve the issue between the two, Witherspoon told Rush of Shippen's ultimatum, that the two could never work together, and that one of them must resign—and that by consensus Rush was the one.

Rush insisted he could work with Shippen once Congress had effected changes it had promised in the director general's authority. Witherspoon's response: Rush had made so many enemies in Congress because of his complaints about Shippen, his resignation was the only solution. It's possible that Witherspoon was exaggerating the number of Rush's enemies in Congress in order to force his resignation and thus settle the dust raised by the two senior physicians. Though personally fond of Rush, Witherspoon made it explicit that Rush must choose between suffering the humiliation of being cashiered or resigning his commission without prejudice.

Rush was not about to go without a fight: "I answered that I was very indifferent about the number of my friends or enemies in Congress," that he had accepted a commission "to serve the army and my country," and that should be the only consideration. Standing firm, he told Witherspoon, "Do not think to terrify me into a resignation by the fear of being dismissed by the Congress [which had] suffered enough in the opinion of the public by dismissing Dr. Morgan without a trial. I dare you to dismiss me in the same manner." Changing tactics, Witherspoon told Rush he had "been deceived with respect to the alterations to be made in the hospital system, that no material changes would be made in it, and that the purveying business would not be taken out of Dr. S.'s hands." This "had the desired effect": Rush "saw no prospect of doing my duty or of giving satisfaction to my country while Dr. Shippen had the charge and direction of the hospital stores."[14]

An hour later, bitterly hurt by the attitude of the man whom he had earlier brought to America and who had, as he chose to see it, apparently "defected" to Shippen, Rush wrote to the president of Congress, "Finding it impossible to do my duty any longer in the department you have assigned me in your hospitals in the manner I would wish, I beg the favor of you to accept the resignation of my commission."[15] The resignation was accepted unanimously. Not even one of his former colleagues or any of his friends among the delegates who had a few days earlier promised their support, spoke out in his defense. The bitterness of this pill was heavily coated with the sweet knowledge that Rush knew he was in the right, and that fighting Shippen turned more on the medical director's influence in Congress, thanks in large measure to his relationship with the two powerful Lee brothers and his own relationship with Washington (who could hardly qualify as being sympathetic to Rush).

Might the outcome have been different if John Adams, now en route to his new assignment in Europe, had been in Congress to speak out for his friend? (Rush himself suggests that it might have: "My complaints were dismissed as groundless, factious, &c., and the Director General was honored with approbation of the Congress. Had you been there, I am sure matters would have taken another turn.")[16] Adams certainly carried more weight in the middle and northern states than did the Lee brothers, and the demographics of the Congress suggests he might well have enjoyed more overall influence. As soon as Rush had written him that he had come to York "to lay down my commission" if he could not persuade the delegates to favor him over Shippen in the hospitals dispute, Adams had urged that he not do so: "Men who are sensible of the evils in the hospital department are most likely to point them out to others, and to suggest remedies, Patience! Patience! Patience! The first, the last, and the middle virtues of a politician."[17] But "Patience! Patience! Patience!" was to Benjamin Rush an alien concept.

Stunned, depressed, and disgusted with the way in which events had played out, Rush left York the moment his resignation was accepted. He arrived at Lancaster the same day, knowing that his cause had been a just one, albeit a rebuffed one, and not quite knowing his next move. At Lancaster he received a reply to the idea he had made in confidence to Witherspoon of joining a proposed expedition planned by the Board of War to invade Canada under the joint command of Conway and the Marquis de Lafayette. Witherspoon told him, in a letter dated 2 February, "I have mentioned to some Members what you proposed to me about the Expedition . . . but they seemed to be at a Loss what station or Character you could sustain." Rush took this as a further rebuff and abandoned the idea. There is doubt he would have followed through with it even if he had had Congress's support. But the question is moot, since the expedition was aborted.

Rush also wrote General Greene on 1 February, with what seems suspiciously like a somewhat monumental lack of conviction, "I am not disgusted or distressed with the opinion of our superiors concerning the case of my complaints or of my resignation." Averring that his "dear country, freedom, and independence are words as big with charms to me as ever," he said he would "therefore join the army in the spring as a volunteer [with the Pennsylvania militia when Washington mounted a new campaign], and while there are 500 men in arms in America I shall never keep back the mite of my labors and life from the service of my country and posterity." No record has survived of Greene's response; but knowing as we do what Washington now thought of Rush—which was precious little—it's probable that any response would have suggested that Rush think twice before carrying through with his offer.

Rush devoted much of the first of two weeks he spent in Lancaster to preparing a revision of "To the Officers in the Army of the United

American States: Directions for Preserving the Health of Soldiers," of which the Board of War had requested an edition of four thousand copies ("my last legacy to my countrymen in the line of my profession"). Also from Lancaster, on 1 February 1778, Rush wrote what can only be dismissed as an extraordinary letter to Shippen, responding to a letter from Shippen transmitted through a mutual friend, Dr. James Fallon, a senior army hospital physician near Valley Forge. Shippen's letter has been lost to history. In his response, Rush reminds Shippen that he received the message via Fallon after he had submitted his resignation: "I think it proper to mention this circumstance lest you attribute that step to any fear I entertained of suffering by a court-martial." He wants Shippen to know he "had nothing to dread from that quarter." Moreover, by this letter he was taking the "opportunity of informing you that nothing but the remembrance of an early connection with you, a tenderness for your worthy family, and in particular an affection for your amiable and promising son, Tom" (a friend of Rush's youth, from whose early death Shippen never recovered)

> prevented my collecting and producing vouchers [i.e., verified documentation] of the abuses of our hospitals which would ultimately have ended in your dishonor. The illiberal censures you passed upon my conduct before the committee of Congress did not force from me several anecdotes of your conduct (properly attested) that would have shown more than 100 other things [constituting] the extreme danger of the medical system. The one I mentioned (a *suspicious* one only) was intended to show that nothing but a change of the system would do justice to the sick, be safe to the directors our purveyors, and agreeable to the surgeons.
>
> You have supposed that I am busy in traducing you. Far from it. I declare solemnly I feel no personal resentment against you, and that a superlative regard to the comfort and lives of our soldiers and the honor of the department were my only motive in appealing to General Washington and in complaining to the Congress of the abuses in the hospitals.
>
> I have been *advised* to publish the accounts I have written and delivered of the said abuses with proper vouchers, which I could collect by hundreds. But I have declined it. I have no revenge in me.

What would the inhabitants of Pennsylvania in the neighborhood of the hospitals—what would the surgeons—what would the military inspector say to the following extract of your letter to Congress of the 18th of last month: "No fatal disease prevails in the hospitals, very few die, and the hospitals are in very *good* order"? Think of these things. If you can establish the truth of these assertions before next spring, I shall be satisfied and bless the day I left the department.[18]

The letter closes with a wish for Shippen's "health, peace of mind, and as much happiness as you wish yourself."

The operative phrase here is "I have no revenge."

In fact, Rush's revenge was obsessive. His main reason for staying on at Lancaster was to gather enough evidence against Shippen to confront that obsession. He discovered from an examination of the medical director's records that only twelve patients were reported having died at the Lancaster hospital in December, and a similar low number in the following month. Still, Rush obtained from a carpenter an affidavit that thirty-two coffins had been delivered to the hospital in December and thirty-three in January. Visiting the hospital and inspecting the coffins, Rush informed General Greene: "From their weight and smell, I am persuaded they contained hospital patients in them," and blasted outright Shippen's obviously falsified hospital records, adding with bitter irony, "if they were not dead I hope some steps will be taken for the future to prevent and punish the crime of burying the Continental soldiers alive."[19]

There was more. While at the Lancaster hospital Rush wrote on 9 March to a friend in Congress, Daniel Roberdeau, that a senior surgeon had been ordered by Shippen "to make use of *one* of the pipes of Madeira [he had stored] for the sick in the hospital," but that when the surgeon went to use the wine, a friend of Shippen's came with an order from the medical director that the wine had been set aside as "the Doctor's private property," and that, moreover, two pipes from the stock had been sold for £800—which sum had wound up in Shippen's pocket. He also told Roberdeau that while in Reading a few weeks earlier to gather additional evidence at the hospital there of "the director general's peculations," he was told by Dr. Jonathan Potts, the friend from his Edinburgh days, that Shippen had "sold several hogsheads of brown sugar," intended for use in the hospital, to "a person in Reading" for personal gain.

Rush next moved on to Allentown and then Bethlehem, in both of which army hospitals he collected even more incriminating evidence from the physicians and surgeons. According to Shippen's records at the Bethlehem hospital, the patient population in December was 320, of whom only 21 died; yet one of the resident physicians gave an affidavit that in that month 420 patients were admitted, of whom "above 40" died. After returning to Princeton to spend a few days relaxing with Julia and their son and visiting the military hospital there to gather further evidence against Shippen, Rush wrote to George Washington on 25 February a letter that he hoped would suffice to commence court-martial proceedings against Shippen.

He begins by expressing the belief that he should think it "inexcusable" that he had resigned his commission "without informing your excellency" that he was "compelled" to do so "by the prevalence of an opinion" among the delegates that "the distresses and mismanagement of the hospitals" was the result of a "want of harmony" between Dr. Shippen and himself. "Next to the conviction of my own mind that this was *not* the case, I wish to have it known to your excellency that *none* of them originated in that cause." Rush allows that he was "so anxious" to "cultivate harmony with Shippen while in service" that he laid none of the abuses which prevailed in the hospitals directly at his door. But since his "obligations to living in harmony" with Shippen as an army medical officer "have now ceased, justice to my country, a regard to the honor of the army, as well as duty to your excellency, call upon me to lay the following facts before you."

These began with the Finley affidavit, and quite an affidavit it was! His charges against Shippen, supported by three other of the hospital physicians, included adulterating wine administered to the patients to such a degree "as to have none of the qualities or effects of Madeira"; making it "common practice" to deduct a third, sometimes more, sometimes less, from the orders for wine, sugar, molasses, "and other stores ordered for the sick by the surgeons"; denying the patients venison, poultry, or wild fowl "(unless purchased by themselves)," even though "*large* Quantities of those articles" were purchased by the hospital's assistant commissary, "by *order* of the Director General"; that Shippen had set foot in the hospital only once during his six weeks in the village of Bethlehem, "although the utmost distress and mortality prevailed in the hospital at that time"; that "a putrid fever" which raged for three months in the hospital "was greatly increased by the sick being too much *crowded* and by their [lacking] blankets, shirts, straw [matting for beds], and other necessaries for sick people"; and that the mortality rate, among not only the patients but also the medical officers and civilian "inhabitants of the village," was beyond excuse. Rush added that "vouchers of the same kind" collected from several other of the hospitals "tend to show the negligence and injustice of the Director General and of *some* of the officers connected with him."

Rush inferentially magnifies his indictment of Shippen by pointing out that his records of the *true* mortality rate reflect only those in four hospitals (Reading, Bethlehem, Lancaster, and Princeton) over the preceding four months, and expresses the belief "from the best general accounts I can collect that the number of deaths in the hospitals from which I have obtained no returns [i.e., statistics] cannot amount to less than seven or eight hundred more." This account, he advises, "will appear to be more distressing when I add that the mortality was *chiefly* artificial and not the consequences of diseases contracted at camp. Eight-tenths of them died with putrid fevers caught in [Shippen's horribly mismanaged and corruptly administered] hospitals."

Pouring oil on the fire, Rush notes that this "extraordinary mortality among our soldiers is not necessarily entailed upon military hospitals." Dr. Potts, whom he cites as an example, lost but 203 men between 1 March and 10 December, "inclusive of all those who died of wounds." The patients under his care wanted for "*nothing*." The putrid fever "never made its appearance in any one of his hospitals."

Rush was "sorry to add" that while "our brave countrymen were languishing and dying from the *total* want or *scanty* allowance of hospital stores" under Shippen's purview, the villain "was employed in a manner wholly unbecoming the dignity of his office and the liberality of his profession in selling large quantities of Madeira wine, brown and loaf sugar, &c., &c., which had been transported through the country in hospital wagons and secured as hospital stores under the name of *private property.*"

Had a letter of this nature come from any other former physician general, Washington would doubtless have replied immediately and ordered a thorough examination of the charges. But this particular former physician general was, in the eyes of the commander in chief, one of those out to replace him with Gates as leader of the Continental army. General Washington passed the letter on to Shippen—who, it need hardly be stated, dismissed Rush as a troublemaker. A month later [21 March], Washington forwarded the letter to Congress with a note implying approval of Shippen's judgment and confidence in his management of the hospital system.

When no reply from Washington was forthcoming, Rush took his indictment of Shippen back to Congress by sending it a copy of his letter to Roberdeau. In a postscript he added, "Since writing the enclosed letter I had the pleasure of seeing the resolutions of the Congress of the 6th of February amending the system of the military hospitals . . . Had I expected such a change would have been made in the system, I should *not* have resigned my commission."

The statement is puzzling, since in his 25 February letter to Washington he had said, "I have only to congratulate your excellency upon the change which the Congress have made in the medical system whereby the business of providing for the sick"—i.e., procuring supplies—had been put into the capable hands of Dr. Potts, while Shippen was to be responsible for the medical management. In other words, the so-called British system Rush had championed had at last been adopted.

Since there was no reason for Rush to distort the facts, it's quite probable that he wrote the letter to which the postscript is appended not on 9 March, as it is dated, but a month earlier. In fact, according to a letter to four members of Congress (*infra*), Rush says that he "transmitted an account of [Shippen's] conduct to the Commander in Chief of the Army before I wrote to a member of Congress [Roberdeau] upon the subject."[20]

Like a preternaturally obsessed avenging angel, Rush traversed the countryside gathering more evidence of Shippen's malfeasance; he visited hospitals he had missed on his earlier tour, and even stopped at Valley Forge, where he found the men still "dirty and ragged" while Washington and the generals lived comfortably in requisitioned houses "out of camp." Though Washington would hardly have welcomed him with open arms, it can be assumed that if they met they behaved civilly—though whether they did in fact meet on this occasion has gone unrecorded.

*   *   *

During the second week of April Rush learned that on the third of that month his letters to Washington and Roberdeau, along with Washington's letter of transmittal of the Rush letter, were put before the Congress. Congress, in turn, referred them to a committee of three with orders "to enquire into the charges contained in Dr. Rush's letters against Dr. Shippen, and into the conduct of Dr. Shippen as director general of the hospitals, and to report specially to Congress."[21] The three—William Henry Drayton of South Carolina, Samuel Huntington of Connecticut, and John Banister of Virginia—were ordered to contact Dr. Rush "to ascertain with precision, and transmit to us [in person, before the delegates in York], the charges, and upon oath the evidence you have, or can procure, against [Shippen]; also the names of the witnesses, and places of their residence."[22]

Upon receipt of the resolution, the invitation, and the requests, Rush replied that he foresaw "many difficulties" in having a committee of Congress "coming at a knowledge of facts" with respect to Shippen's "maladministration of the hospitals." The only way to resolve the issue was by court-martial. His argument: "The army has *written* laws for the government of all its members; Dr. Shippen belongs to the army." Ergo, Dr. Shippen must be subjected to the same laws as any commander with proven charges against him as grave as those against the medical director.

"Besides," Rush reminded the committee, "there is a *positive* resolution of Congress for this purpose in the regulations of the hospital of the 11th of April, 1777. The words are: 'That the *director,* deputy directors, physicians and surgeons general, and all other officers before enumerated shall be tried by a court-martial for any misbehavior or neglect of duty as the Commander in chief shall direct.' " Should Congress "agree to this mode of inquiring into Dr. Shippen's malpractices," Rush was prepared to submit a list of the names of witnesses, with their requested "respective places of residence," and would "esteem myself bound by the duty I owe to my country to appear at the court as his prosecutor."[23]

Rush was not being difficult here, merely pragmatic. As he explained to Dr. Morgan, he had already "experienced the partiality of a large body of [Congress] to the Doctor," what with those two influential brothers-in-law, and "objected to appearing before the committee at Yorktown, but offered to prosecute him before a court-martial agreeably to a resolution of Congress for trying all the delinquent officers of the hospital by the Articles of War."

The offer was declined. Rush's letter to the committee was read to the Congress on 4 June, and carried the endorsement, "Ordered to lie on the table"—a parliamentary way of saying it was to be forgotten—"and the Doctor continued to enjoy as large a share as ever of his republican masters' favor."[24] Rush's letter may have been "ordered to lie on the table," but the Shippen controversy would not, as Congress and Washington hoped, lie at rest.

Dr. Morgan would see to that.

Having abandoned any idea of returning to army service, Rush now entertained serious thoughts of abandoning medicine. He was living with his wife and son in her father's Princeton home. But professionally he felt he was leading "an inactive, and of course, a disagreeable life. The village of Princeton afforded no prospects of business in my profession, and I had no desire by changing my place of residence to enter into country practice." Rush now "resolved to study the law, and to come forward to the bar in New Jersey." Richard Stockton was all for the idea, and promised his not inconsiderable influence to have his son-in-law admitted to the New Jersey bar in a year, two at the most. Rush was now thirty-two years old, but the "labor of acquiring a sound profession did not discourage me from this undertaking."[25]

What did discourage so dramatic a career change, just as he was about to commence his legal studies, was the news that Sir Henry Clinton, the Tory pre-Revolution governor of New York who had defeated Washington in the Battle of Long Island, and only recently succeeded Howe as commander in chief of British forces in North America, had ordered the evacuation of Philadelphia. At the end of May, with the route of the retreating British expected to pass Princeton, Rush took his wife and child back to the relative safety of the Maryland farm where she had already spent much of the war.

On 21 June, he returned with his family to Philadelphia. Dr. Benjamin Rush was now back in business as a civilian physician.

The irony of it all is that Rush was equally if not better qualified as a physician and was certainly a more honest man than Shippen. He would have been the ideal chief of the Continental army's medical service. But it was never in his nature to aspire to high position. In this context it was just as well, given Shippen's connections in the Congress—and Rush's imprudence in alienating Washington's good will.

13

"Leonidas"

By the time Rush returned to Philadelphia the new nation was achieving cohesion and international acceptance. On the previous 15 November Congress had agreed upon perpetual union with the Articles of Confederation and sent them to the states for ratification. Styling the confederacy as *The United States of America*, they would be superseded by the Constitution drawn up in the summer of 1787 and adopted in the following year. Burgoyne's defeat at Saratoga a month earlier had encouraged France, eager to reestablish the prestige in Europe it had lost as a result of the Seven Years' War, to sign (6 February 1778) treaties of commerce and alliance with the United States—to which it had been covertly supplying money and supplies for two years. Marquis Marie Joseph de Lafayette and Baron Johann de Kalb had arrived the summer before to offer their military expertise.[1]

Eleven days after the Franco-American treaties were signed, Lord North proposed to Parliament a plan of conciliation with the Americans that included Britain's renouncing the right to tax what were still considered "the colonials." Commissioners were sent from London to present the peace offer to Congress. On 17 June, Congress rejected it outright. With the French alliance in effect, and France and Britain still at each other's throat on the Continent, "the colonials" felt confident to settle for nothing less than total independence. The war would last another three years. The Continental army would lose more battles. But independence would come. The Loyalists, who were openly aiding the British in the southern states, doubted that indisputability. But, as the Americans would demonstrate, the metaphysical certitude of indisputability is itself subject to dispute.

In a letter to John Adams's wife, who remained home in Braintree, Massachusetts, with their younger children when her husband undertook his diplomatic mission in Europe, Rush "rejoice[d] in the happy changes that have taken place in the appearance of our [nation's] affairs" and fairly gloated that "An alliance has been formed with the first monarchy in Europe [i.e., France]; the haughty Court of Britain has been forced to sue to [*sic*] her once insulted colonies for peace [and] the capital of Pennsylvania, the object of the expenses and blood of a whole campaign, has been evacuated." He also notes, with overconfidence playing handmaiden to wishful thinking, that "the flower of the British army has been defeated."

Unable to suppress his denigration of how Congress was managing the war—"The wisdom of our counsels was often foolishness, and the strength of our arms was too often weakness"—Rush puts his own spin on the end of his military career: He was

> forced to resign my commission of physician general to the army, having no prospect of being supported in doing my duty either by the Congress or principal officers in the army. This prepared the way for my returning to Philadelphia as soon as the enemy left it, where I am now settled with my family in the business of my profession. Our city has undergone some purification. But it still resembles too much the ark which preserved not only the clean, but unclean animals from the deluge which overwhelmed the old world.[2]

Though the city had "undergone some purification," it still had a way to go: "The filth left by the British Army in the streets created a good deal of sickness." Soon after Julia, now in her second pregnancy, and baby John ("Jack") joined Rush in Philadelphia, an outbreak of typhoid ("a malignant bilious fever") prompted him to send her and the baby back to her parents' home at Princeton. With the outbreak, Rush "quickly recovered my business, with a large accession of new patients."[3] In July, he realized £8 in cash from 18 patients; in August, he saw 62 patients, which brought total billings for the month to £500. But with the rapidly rising inflation £10 in paper money equaled just over half that value in gold. Within two months the rate of exchange declined further to ten to one. Like many professionals, Rush was reduced to barter in order to remain solvent.

In a facetious request on 24 August 1778 to Julia indicative of the precarious economic state in the nation's capital, he wishes she "would try to get me a dozen pounds of purging salts of Mr. [Enos] Kelsey [a Princeton merchant who had been Rush's classmate at the college] or Mr. Robt. Stockton [her father]." Rush urges that this request "must not be neglected nor forgotten, as I have discovered by a new species of alchemy the art of converting a pound of that saline matter into 16 square dollars."[4]

In mid-September, Rush "was seized with a most malignant bilious fever (caught from one of my patients) which reduced me to the brink of the grave." His physicians—Redman, Kuhn, and Morgan—"shook their heads as they went out of my room. My friends could do little more than weep at my bedside. I made my will and took my leave of life. But in the extremity of my danger it pleased God (on the 11th day) to break the violence of my disease, and I am now through divine goodness so perfectly recovered as to be able to do business as usual."[5] The only lasting effect from Rush's fever was that, though only thirty-two, his hair had "become a good deal gray." Having "recovered my usual health and activity in business," he "now turned my back for a while upon public pursuits, and devoted myself exclusively to the duties of my professions."[6]

The illness, which seems to have been close to fatal, left Rush in a transient depression, a depression aggravated by the news that Washington had "banished from [his] headquarters" two close friends Rush most respected among the general staff: Lee and Conway. Especially Lee ("I shall always view him as the *first* general in America"). Unable—or perhaps unwilling—to see that the two had brought about their own downfall, as had another close friend, Thomas Mifflin, Rush was convinced that the three had been "sacrificed to the excessive influence and popularity of *one* man. . . . Where," he demanded, "is the republican spirit of our country?" For his part, Rush wished "to see something like the ostracism of the Athenians introduced among us.* Monarchies are illuminated by a *sun*, but republics should be illuminated only by *constellations* of great men."[7]

---

*Any Athenian of prominence, no matter his accomplishments, could be banished, usually for ten years but sometimes for life, if enough citizens wrote approval on a pottery shard, an *ostraca*, hence the term.

But whence, wondered Rush in a long, at times rambling letter to his friend William Gordon (10 December 1778), might such a constellation come? Certainly not Congress: a body of opportunists who had so enthusiastically accepted his resignation, and, worse, confirmed "the unjust sentence that was passed upon General Lee"; a body who spoke only "of *state necessity* and of making justice yield in some cases to policy." To Rush's way of thinking, men of "ambition, avarice, craft, and dissolute manners" had supplanted those who "loved liberty for its own sake." "*Fiat justicia, ruat coelum*" ("Let justice be done, though the heavens fall") was Rush's "maxim during the short time I acted for the public" (as a member of Congress). He had "no political ambition to gratify." His "political race was short. I thank my countrymen for dismissing me from their service. I want no offices nor honors from them." He longed to see "the image of God restored to the human mind . . . to see virtue and religion supported, and vice and irreligion banished from society by wise and equitable governments . . . to see an asylum prepared for the persecuted and oppressed of all countries, and a door opened for the progress of knowledge, literature, the arts, and the gospel of Jesus Christ to the ends of the earth." But "these great blessings" were to be accomplished only by establishing and perpetuating liberty throughout the country. "It is liberty alone that can make us happy. And without it the memorable 4th of July 1776 will be execrated by posterity as the way in which Pandora's box was opened in this country."

Rush's letter reflected the spirit of the year 1778: a wide-ranging cynicism that the Revolution had lost the intent of a great crusade, a noble cause. This was attributable in large measure to war profiteers, whose extravagant coaches created minor traffic jams as they and their ladies, in the best of imported finery, made their way to or from their extravagant mansions, where opulence had pervaded every aspect of home life from dining to décor.

Meanwhile the miserably armed Continental army, clad in what appeared to be not so much uniforms in the conventional sense as outfits improvised from rags that offered no protection against the elements, struggled to survive on half rations, a modicum of supplies, and, more often than not, no pay, let alone contend with a well-clothed, well-fed, well-armed, numerically superior British army. While visiting the city to confer with Congress, Washington vented his disgust that "Speculation, peculation, and an insatiable thirst for riches seem to have got the better of every other consideration and almost every order of men." From Europe, where he was kept abreast of events at Philadelphia by Rush, John Adams was convinced that, to judge by the rampant war profiteering and open, quite shameless display of conspicuous (and often excessively tasteless) consumption, "a civil war in America" seemed to be the only alternative unless there occurred a hasty revival of public morality.[8]

By November, Rush had recovered his health sufficiently to resume his practice full time; on the first of December, he resumed his chemistry lectures at the college, for which twenty-four students had signed up. Just after his first lecture, Rush's father-in-law came from Princeton for consultation regarding a cancerous sore on his lip. Its excision was a success, but while Stockton was recovering, another cancer was discovered in his throat; he died in February 1781 after two years of constant pain. Rush's despondency over the suffering of a man he so admired was alleviated by the joy in the birth, on the first day of 1779, of his second child and first daughter, Anne Emily.

Upon his return to Philadelphia, Rush had intended to isolate himself from politics. In October 1778, while recuperating from his illness, he was visited by Joseph Reed, who sought to persuade him to rejoin the fray. It was Reed, the reader will recall, who, while Washington's military secretary, spoke so pessimistically about the outcome of the war when accompanying Rush to Washington's headquarters just before the Battle of Trenton. At war's end, having served as adjutant general of the Continental army, he became a leader of Pennsylvania's radicals. Reed's initial opposition to the Pennsylvania Constitution, in which Rush joined him, had led him to refuse the position of chief justice of the state when it was offered. But just a few days before visiting Rush, he did a volte-face, took the requisite oath of allegiance that Rush found most offensive about the constitution, and agreed to stand for election as president of the Executive Council.

Along with George Bryan and the Reverend John Ewing, two former friends of Rush's who became his foes when they supported the constitution upon its adoption in 1776, Reed sought to convince him that, having "reprobated the Constitution when it was first made . . . they soon discovered that it might be converted to desirable private purposes." In other words, as Rush phrased it when recalling the events to John Adams retrospectively, "this triumvirate" planned to stage a "premeditated usurpation," in which they invited him to "share." Rush "objected to the proposal" as he had objected to their supporting the constitution, for no matter what ultimate purpose, and told Reed "he would ruin himself by taking part in the establishment or support of so bad" a state charter.[9] Rush may have decided to abstain from personal involvement in the whole constitutional issue. But he did not abstain from continuing to criticize it—at times obsessively so—going so far as to sacrifice friendships.

Rush's opposition to the Pennsylvania Constitution puzzled contemporaries and historians alike, given that much of the reform-minded assembly enacted legislation that found great favor with him, such as "An act to prohibit, for a limited time, the making of whisky and other spirits," "An act for the suppression of vice and immorality," and "An act for the gradual abolition of slavery." But looming ominously, in his considered opinion, was the unalterable conviction that any legislature born out of what he insisted was an appallingly fashioned constitution could never serve the people well. However, it was in Rush's nature to believe that even when faced with the most ostensibly hopeless situation, as he was fond of saying, "all will end well." Reed's election to the Executive Council presidency struck in Rush a cautious note of optimism: "Our new government is demolishing," he wrote David Ramsay in the above-cited letter, "and those furious patriots who have ruined our state are now sinking into obscurity and contempt."

He became even more optimistic when it was announced that the assembly would hold a plebiscite on the constitution in March 1779. The radical Republican Society ("Republicans," of which Rush was a founding member), a recently formed citizens group whose intent was to alter and amend the constitution, propagandized its opposition to the charter, while the conservative Constitutionalists, who favored it, petitioned the assembly with some ten thousand signatures opposing the March poll. On the twenty-seventh of that month the assembly rescinded the plebiscite on the grounds that with the state suffering its worst inflationary spiral, it was felt that the people were incapable of judging the constitution objectively. Said Rush, the "contest about the constitution soon ended, for it was supported by being exclusively in the hands of its friends [i.e., the Constitutionalists], who did not see its defects, or who were too much interested to acknowledge it required any amendment, especially at the time in which it was proposed."[10]

Indicative of the inflationary spiral, by May the streets of Philadelphia were taken over by mobs seeking out the war profiteers to whom they attributed responsibility for the horrific rise in prices, and merchants they believed guilty of contributing to the rise—and thus profiting by it—were being looted. Rush was not immune from the runaway inflation. At the beginning of the year, he had received £430 in paper money from thirty-three patients. By year's end, only thirteen patients had paid their bills, whose aggregate total in paper was £1,060 in Continental currency, though in hard money it amounted to less than £50. (Hence the birth of the new nation's phrase "Not worth a Continental.")

It came as no surprise that Rush deposited total blame for the inflation at Congress's doorstep. Congress's reaction was to announce that it condemned profiteers and conferred responsibility for resolving the problem on the states themselves. On 25 May, arrogating to itself the status of a state, and confident the outer counties would follow their example (though not really caring whether they would), a town meeting chose a committee "to save the money by regulating the prices of goods." Rush insisted that this would "ruin commerce and check agriculture." He equated this approach to administering "a violent puke [purge] to a man in the last stage of consumption." He saw only one solution to the problem: "Nothing but the *immediate* application of a foreign loan can rescue [the nation] from destruction." But, Rush went on to advise his correspondent,

> These detached thoughts are the speculations of a closet, for I now converse with nobody but my patients, my books, an amiable wife, and a healthy boy and girl. I have shook hands (I hope) forever with public life. In my beloved retirement I have recovered the enjoyment of peace, independence, and happiness, none of which in the present distracted and corrupted state of this country are to be found in power or office.[11]

Outraged by the runaway inflation, Rush emerged from his "beloved retirement" after but a month, when he published in the 3 July 1779 edition of the *Pennsylvania Packet* a long letter, framed in the form of a "SPEECH which *ought* to be spoken *to* the Congress" on how that august body should confront the new nation's financial chaos. Its author identified himself pseudonymously as "Leonidas," in itself an intended irony. Here Rush likens himself to the historical king of Sparta slain at Thermopylae: Rush's own brief political career had been "slain" shortly after he signed the Declaration of Independence.

Rush may have termed it a speech, but it was in truth an extensive harangue by "one of the people from whom you derive your authority" who "presume[s] in the name of all the honest Whigs in America to address you as the SERVANTS of the public upon a subject of the utmost importance to the safety and liberties of this country . . . the low value of your money." Demanding to know "why have you delayed so long to complain of this evil to your constituents" and why "the disease [has] been suffered to run on to its last stage before you raised the cry of danger in the ears of your country," he "hasten[ed] to point out those defects in your management of the affairs of this country which have had the principal effect in depreciating" the currency.

Congress had "committed the expenditure" of money "to too many hands," whereas it "might have saved millions to the Continent" by making "the PRINCIPALS" of each of the department staffs responsible for disbursements. Congress had been "too negligent in the choice of the officers to whom you have committed the treasure of your country." How many of these, Rush wondered, had "been called from billiard tables and taverns to execute the most important commissions?" These were men who had reduced the value of the nation's currency, he insisted. How, he wondered rhetorically, could the public be expected to "esteem it when they saw it entrusted to such hands?" Furthermore, Rush charged, Congress's failure to call for an accounting of all expenditures had led to "opportunities for embezzlement and fraud." Equally bad, if not more so, Congress had "injured" the economy by "neglecting too long" to recommend taxation to the states, substituting in its stead "the *palliative* remedy of laws for regulating the prices of goods." Since such laws "may ever be partial and temporary in their operation," they were inherently self-defeating "by relaxing the springs of enterprise and industry." The delegates, Rush hypothesized, might just as well "attempt to prevent the rising of the tide" of the Delaware River by congressional resolution as to prevent the depreciation of the nation's currency by laws for regulating the prices of goods.

"Having pointed out the causes of the depreciation" of the currency, Rush now arrogated to himself the obligation to "mention those things which alone can restore" Congress's credibility and "secure to you the esteem and confidence of your countrymen." First, "do justice to the widow and orphans." He believed "the injustice which has been committed under the sanction of law to the helpless members of our community" was one of the primary reasons why the Lord "has so long kept back from us the blessings of peace." Seeing the quantity of money "in the source of its depreciation," he begged leave to "conjure you immediately to stop your presses." Here Rush was dramatically propounding a theory that has long since become a basic tenet of economics: printing money willy-nilly "proves the falsehood of its denomination" and results in a horrendous inflation that can be analogized to a posse on horseback attempting to halt a runaway train loaded with explosives. After offering a few other suggestions—e.g., opening loan offices in every county and township in every state of the Union and persuading citizens "to deposit their money in your funds," offering interest "as an encouragement"— Rush called for an "instant negotiation" of a foreign loan, and instituting an improved, more equitable taxation.

Having thus presented to the Congress not only the problem but the solution to the nation's fiscal woes, Rush warned, as the prophet Jeremiah had warned—in vain, as it turned out—of the misery that must befall the recidivistic Israelites for not re-embracing the God from whom they had turned away—that not ameliorating the problem would render independence "a misfortune," and peace "a curse" to the country. He also insisted eloquently that liberty, not independence, was the goal of the young nation's struggle. Of this barrage of criticism thrown at it, Congress took greatest umbrage at Rush's perorational "I have fears within me that I am almost afraid to utter." The quality of delegates had declined since the First and Second Continental Congresses, as so many of the original titans, to cite but a few, had either returned to serve in their respective state governments, like Samuel Adams and Patrick Henry, or were on missions abroad to secure loans, military assistance, and recognition of the United States, like John Adams, Franklin, and Jefferson. Rush's "fears": Surely none of the delegates were "unacquainted with the depravity and morals" that preceded the overthrow of the Roman Republic.

> Are you sure we have no Caesars nor Cromwells in this country? Are your new governments equal to all the exigencies of the states? Have not the committees now establishing among us arisen from the mischiefs that have been introduced by the quantity of your money ["stop your presses"]? What is their tendency? Do they not lead to the necessity of more arbitrary governments than by fixed laws and constitutions? But I must quit the subject. Let your own knowledge in history and of human nature supply the rest.

Urging that the delegates "rouse" the Congress to "a sense of the danger of these infant states that are committed to your care," Rush ends on a note of near hysteria based not on a feeling of bitterness for its having forced him out but an empirical reading of the intolerable inflation that he saw as the Congress's priority:

> Your money—your money—demands every thought and every hour. You have more to dread from this quarter than you have from the hosts of Britons, Hessians, New Levies, Refugees, Indians, and Negroes that are now in arms against you. I conjure you, therefore, immediately to bind yourselves to each other by an oath not to eat, drink, or sleep until you have arrested your money in its progress toward destruction and fixed it upon a permanent foundation.[12]

The only thing a furious Congress "bound" themselves to do was launch a counterattack against "Leonidas." A day after the letter appeared, Elbridge Gerry, one of the holdovers from the First Continental Congress, moved that John Dunlap, publisher of the *Packet,* "be directed to attend the bar of this house to answer such questions as shall be proposed"—chief of among them being, Who is this "Leonidas" that has the temerity to attack Congress? The objection of some members that "it would be lowering and degrading the dignity of Congress to take any notice of the printer or author" was followed by an extended, heated debate that ended with the death of the Gerry motion.[13] Ironically, since Rush did not have an ally like John Adams to keep him apprised of the debates in Congress, which were held behind closed doors, he probably never knew that his essay had created a momentary turbulence among his erstwhile colleagues—and Gerry apparently never knew that the cause of the turbulence was his friend dating back to 1774!

Rush's blanket attack on the delegates seems to have upset even nonmembers of Congress, to judge by a piece in the *Pennsylvania Packet* (13 July 1779) by a pseudonymous "Socrates" addressing "Leonidas": "I applaud your zeal, but cannot approve your delicacy in concealing from public view the names of those who are misapplying public money." Rush, again writing as "Leonidas," wrote a feeble response in that newspaper a week later, and there the matter ended.

But not the staggering inflation. When the people of Philadelphia demanded that all prices be brought under control before they would accept a price schedule proposed by the city administration, and Congress refused to act, the Constitutionalists in the Assembly insisted on an imposition of price controls, maintaining that refusal to put a cap on prices was tantamount to an added tax on the most economically challenged citizens. This brought forth from the merchants a collective cry that high prices were not a *cause* of inflation but a *consequence,* and price controls would drive them out of business by forcing them to sell their wares below cost. Furthermore, they argued, enforcing such controls in a state that was loosely knit and suffered a weak government, would not be possible. Besides, they pointed out, only a merchant who was certifiably committable would accept a fixed price for his goods paid with overinflated American currency when the French continued to pay in hard money what the market demanded for their thousands of soldiers and sailors now joined in the revolutionary cause.

A mass meeting was called for 27 July "to determine the mode of choosing a new committee" of 120 members for the purpose of regulating prices. The Constitutionalists, equally determined to halt the daily soaring of prices, sought to dominate the meeting by announcing that "no person who does not produce his certificate of having taken the OATH OF ALLEGIANCE to this [state] or the United States [shall] be admitted into the State House yard," where the meeting was to be held. When the crowd had gathered, the Constitutionalists posted a mob of some hundred men armed with clubs and fife and drum close to the speakers' platform to drown out the speakers. General John Cadwalader tried to convince the crowd that more harm than good would come from price regulation. He was shouted down by "a majority of those present," who then moved the meeting to the yard of the College of Philadelphia. There they accomplished little more than to name a committee, on which Rush was included, to publish an account of the proceedings. With tensions still running high over price controls, a meeting of all the city's merchants was held two mornings later to discuss how to deal with "the present alarming occasion." That evening, the Republican Society met for essentially the same reason.[14]

While little was being accomplished except charges and counter-charges flying from opposing camps, Rush had to focus his attention on his medical practice when another epidemic hit the city. This one he blamed on the British for having chopped down trees throughout the city during their occupation, thus releasing into the atmosphere noxious fumes that were the disease's source. He sent his wife and babies back to the safety of Rush Hill and devoted himself to an ever-growing number of patients. Though the epidemic soon subsided, as much could not be said for Rush's gloom. What elation he derived from the French alliance was more than offset by the epidemic, the inability to resolve the problem of inflation, the fear that the state would suffer complete economic collapse, and, on a more personal note, the absence of his wife ("My loveliest Girl") and children.

Even more dispiriting was Rush's conviction that the ideals of the revolution had been subsumed in the behavior and attitudes of the people, a conviction expressed in responding (12 October 1779) to a letter of John Adams inquiring "after the state of the government." The "best answer" he could give was that he was "afraid to commit my opinion of men and measures in our state to writing." Sharing in retrospect Adams's comment the first time he saw a printed copy of the Pennsylvania Constitution—"Good God! The people of Pennsylvania in two years will be glad to petition the crown of Britain for reconciliation in order to be delivered from the tyranny of their Constitution"—Rush argued that the perfect government "consists in providing restraints against the tyranny of rulers on the one hand and the licentiousness of the people on the other," and bemoans, "By our

Constitution we are exposed to fill the miseries of both with a single remedy for either."

Rush then goes on to describe the "insurrection in our city" on 4 October when a mob of radicals whose intentions were "unknown or confusedly understood . . . enraged chiefly by liquor"—actually, as it eventually came out, they were enraged by the continued depreciation of Continental money—marched on the house of James Wilson, "whose only crime" was having defended legal action against a number of dispossessed and imprisoned Loyalists who had not fled the city in the wake of the British evacuation. "Our streets were for the first time strained with fraternal blood." Seven were killed, nineteen wounded. "Since this melancholy affair we have had a calm in our city. But," he lamented to Adams, "every face wears the marks of fear and dejection. We look over our shoulders and then whisper when we complain to each other in the streets of the times. I feel the slave [of tyranny] sealing upon me every day. O! liberty, liberty, I have worshipped thee as a substance, but—" Here Rush cuts himself off—"A patient calls for me in a hurry"—but manages to add a postscript: "I *perfectly* agree with you in your plan of prosecuting the war. Congratulations upon your new and *most* honorable embassy!" Adams, who had returned from France in August on his own initiative to propose a plan to Congress, was nominated (25 September 1779) to negotiate peace.

Rush sank even further in depression a week later when the assembly election gave the Constitutionalists full control of the Pennsylvania legislature. This was owing in large measure to the continuing inflation, which made it easy for them to blame it on the merchants, most of whom were Republicans and had resisted the Constitutionalists' popular fight for price controls. "Poor Pennsylvania! has become the most miserable spot upon the surface of the globe," Rush lamented to his friend Charles Lee (24 October 1779), repeating words he had written to Adams.

> Our streets have been stained already with fraternal blood—a sad prelude we fear of the future mischiefs our Constitution will bring upon us. They call it a democracy—a mobocracy in my opinion would be more proper. All our laws breathe the spirit of town meetings and porter shops. But I forget I am not safe in committing

my opinion of men and measures to paper. Oh! Liberty—liberty, I have worshipped thee as a substance.

Rush's mood continued on a downward slide, pushed along by the fact that Pennsylvania—the nation's capital and richest, most geographically important state—was in economic and political disarray, and the Continental army's tribulations were compounded by what seemed to be a successful British attempt to overrun the southern states. Moreover, all lectures at the college had been suspended when the Assembly, prompted by its Constitutionalist majority, subsumed it into the newly created University of the State of Pennsylvania. Rush welcomed the conversion, and many of the innovations, most notably the creation of two new professorships, one in astronomy and one in German classics, and the addition of a German School to bring German-speaking youngsters into the mainstream of Pennsylvania affairs. Rush did object, though, to the Assembly's "illegal" transferring of the private college's lands, funds, building, and charter to a semi-state institution; to the control that the state would have over the enlarged institution; and, above all, to the loyalty oath required of all faculty members. But this all was, no pun intended, academic. His future with the university seemed doubtful. He could not have been unaware that, given their opposition to, and detestation of, Rush, the Constitutionalists, notwithstanding his expertise and the admiration he elicited from his students, were hardly expected to welcome his return when the turbulence that surrounded the college's absorption settled.

Rush spoke again of abandoning medicine. This time, though, it would not be to take up the law. Rather, it would be to abandon Philadelphia, with its intolerable inflation, politics, and infighting among the academicians, and retire to Princeton where, in light of his father-in-law's impending death, he could enjoy life with Julia and their children as a gentleman farmer. A quite wealthy gentleman farmer, given the inherited fortune that would come his way through his heiress wife.

14

Civilian Physician Redivivus

Rush was too committed to medicine, both as practitioner and teacher, and too unwilling to forego politics, though as observer and critic rather than active participant, to be a gentleman farmer in a bucolic setting far removed from the arena of the action. It wasn't long before he was back in Philadelphia and a modest practice. Between January and March 1779 he averaged sixty patients a month, few of whom paid their bills. When they did, it was in near-worthless currency. He raised the cost of a house call to £60 in hopes of keeping pace with the rampant inflation, but his total recompense during that period in gold coin was a mere £3.

Rush's spirits soared just after the turn of the year, when he was able to inform his friend James McHenry (19 January 1779), "Dr. Shippen I hear is at last arrested." The public, which could not "expect that justice from the army which they have in vain looked for from the Congress," would soon "see that solecism explained—how the Director General of the hospital of the united [sic] States is enabled with 6 dollars a day to vie with the Minister of France in the magnificence of his equipage." There were, Rush maintained, "two crimes that never yet found pity or favor in our army, viz., *cowardice* in an officer of the line, and *fraud* in an officer of the staff department. The proofs of Dr. Shippen's guilt with respect to the last crime are as clear as the noonday sun."

Six months earlier, after long deliberation, Congress had apologized to Morgan for his summary dismissal as the army's director general,

commending all that he had accomplished in that office. If the delegates thought that that put an end to the affair, they could not have
been farther off the mark. Like his friend Rush, Morgan definitely did
not subscribe to Juvenal's maxim, "Indeed, it's always a paltry, feeble,
tiny mind that takes pleasure in revenge." Morgan immediately took
to the pages of the *Pennsylvania Packet* with a series of *Vindications*
(beginning in the 17 June 1779 issue) in which he solicited the contribution of facts intended to bring Shippen down.

Washington at first refused to order a court-martial, on the grounds
that the charges against Shippen were ambiguous and lacking in foundation. Besides, he insisted, his director general was very much needed
for the upcoming summer campaign. Morgan persevered relentlessly,
turning to Rush for help. Rush promised a scrupulous narrative of
"matters I am willing to testify upon oath" respecting their mutual
enemy. In October 1779, at the insistence of Congress, Washington
agreed to a court-martial after the present campaign. Five charges were
filed with the judge advocate, of which four were essentially those
made by Rush: that Shippen had sold hospital stores as his own property, had speculated in battlefield stores and adulterated hospital wines
("whilst the sick were perishing for want of them"), had kept no records of expenditures by his office, and had neglected his hospital
duties and given false reports to Congress. Morgan provided the fifth
charge: Shippen had been responsible for "scandalous and infamous
practices such as are unbecoming the character of an officer and gentleman." This was rooted in Morgan's assumption that Shippen had
schemed to have him removed as director general.[1]

On hearing of the upcoming court-martial, Rush reported—
indeed, gloated—to John Adams (19 October 1779) that Morgan's
witnesses were "numerous, and his proofs of [Shippen's] peculation so
irrefragable that I have no doubt of his being broken. In any of the
European armies he would be hanged. From the time I accepted my
[army] commission till the time of my resignation, which was not
quite a year, he murdered 4500 of our countrymen by his inhumanity
and injustice. *This* will be proved before the court-martial. He has
amassed a princely fortune by selling wine and other hospital stores
out of the hospital magazines."

There was a long delay between the indictment and commencement
of the trial, a delay owing as much to allow Morgan and Rush to amass

their evidence as to the exigencies of battlefield activity. Moreover, witnesses were difficult to locate, and Shippen, from his official position, had ample time to intimidate some, or have them transferred. But Morgan was unrelenting and resolute. Rush consigned the care of his patients to his apprentices, with the stipulation that Dr. Redman or Dr. Kuhn would be called in should any emergency occur, and hurried off to Washington's headquarters at Morristown, where the trial was to be held. When it opened on 14 March, Shippen "appeared sanguine and indolent," Rush wrote his wife three days later, but when Morgan "opened his evidences" the next day—depositions from officers who had served under Shippen's command—they "produced a *total* change in Dr. S's behavior." He appeared "agitated and distressed. All will end well. The trial will probably last a good while, as S——'s hopes *now* are only from delay and embarrassment."

Rush's suggestion that the trial would probably last "a good while" was prophetic. Having begun on 14 March, it adjourned around the middle of April, was resumed on 15 May, and concluded on 27 June. His certainty that "all will end well" seemed a bit premature: The defendant's objection to the Morgan depositions being read into the record because Shippen had not been present when they were made, or even under arrest at the time, was upheld by the court. At that point, on 20 March, General Edward Hand, the presiding officer, called Rush to the stand.

After testifying for an hour, Rush received an invitation from Washington to dine with him (even "before I had waited upon him"—i.e., paid his official respects). He treated Rush "with a degree of attention which led me to believe he had magnanimously forgotten my letter to Governor [Patrick] Henry." More likely, Washington had not "forgotten" but had forgiven; it was in his nature not to hold grudges. "In consequence of this friendly conduct," Rush "visited him every time he came to Philadelphia and was uniformly treated by him as I had been at Morristown."[2]

Rush testified again for five hours the following day, and gave an additional five and a half hours the day after that (22 March). His eleven and a half hours of testimony added up to little more than a reiteration of what he had already told friends even before Shippen's arrest, with one exception: Under oath, Rush reduced to 1,000 soldiers the total of 4,5000 he claimed to have been "murdered" by Shippen during 1777 and 1778.

Overall, his testimony may not have been "new," but it was quite emotional. Particularly moving was when he described "respectable fathers' sons" dying from the horrible putrid fever in the army hospitals that were "like slaughterhouses" attributable directly to Shippen's negligence and indifference as the army's chief medical officer. On balance, Rush's testimony in the aggregate was less a catalogue of personal observations than a narration of what he had been told from time to time by others. This did not mitigate Rush's belief that it was his testimony that eventually brought Shippen down.

After concluding his role in the trial and dining with his friend General Nathanael Greene, Rush left Morristown to spend the night in nearby Basking Ridge with Julia's uncle by marriage, Elias Boudinot, a successful New Jersey attorney and close friend of Washington's, who was serving at the time as Commissary of Prisoners. A week after leaving Philadelphia, Rush was back (24 March) and devoted his time and energies to his patients and the enjoyment of his family.[3]

Compounding that enjoyment was the memory of Washington's warm welcome at Morristown, where, Rush wrote on 28 April to Adams, now posted to Spain, he found that the Continental Army had "improved greatly since our former correspondence in discipline, economy, and healthiness." However, "The number of our soldiers is small," owing to "the want of money to purchase recruits." Yet he was upbeat: Congress's "new scheme" to confront inflation head-on by calling in the circulating money at a ratio of forty to one would, he believed, "restore to our counsels and arms the vigor of 1775."

Still another antidote to Rush's irritability of the previous year was that Julia, again pregnant, was "one of the ladies employed to solicit benefactions for the army."[4] Here Rush refers to a rather remarkable but little known aspect of the American Revolution—perhaps history's first mobilization of efforts by women to support the fighting troops. But doubtless the most uplifting factor for Rush was his certainty of Shippen's eventual conviction.

To skip ahead chronologically in our narrative: Rush's certainty was sadly misplaced. Though the military court found that "doctor Shippen did speculate in and sell hospital stores, THAT IS, stores proper for hospitals whilst he was purveyor general: which conduct they consider highly improper, and justly reprehensible," it found that the charges had not been clearly established. He was acquitted by a single vote. Washington forwarded the record to Congress on 15 July without approving or disapproving the verdict. On 18 August, after debating the subject for a month, Congress refused approval, and ordered that Shippen "be discharged from arrest."⁵ Thus cleared of all criminal charges against him, Shippen was able to maneuver through adroit politicking to be reappointed director general of the Continental army. Many in Congress opposed the move, but Pennsylvania supported its native son, and the nomination was carried.

This precipitated a letter from Rush to Shippen (18 November, 1780) that, while reading not unlike an acrimonious screed motivated by personal ambition and a thirst for revenge, was essentially a forthright craving to call down chastisement on the party ultimately responsible for the palpable misdemeanors to which he had personally borne witness. Had Shippen, Rush wrote, "been well advised," he would have avoided "a public scrutiny into your conduct by resigning your commission and retiring with your blushing honors thick upon you." Instead, he had allowed himself to be brought to trial—and, in light of its conclusion, had the unmitigated gall to be reappointed through political influence: "The regard I bear your worthy connections obliges me to lament that you have forced me to contribute my mite towards exposing your crimes and awaking against you the resentment of your plundered country."

After airing his disgust that "Congress threw every possible obstruction and delay for two years in the way of your being brought to a trial," only to restore the miscreant to the very position the trial was justly meant to deny him, Rush vented his wrath: "Your injured country, which you have robbed above a thousand of its citizens by your negligence and inhumanity; the parents and children of those brave men whom you suffered to perish without honor or benefit to their country in your hospitals; and the graveyards . . . you have crowded with the bodies of your countrymen, cry aloud for your dismission from office . . . Women bedew the papers that contain the tales of your cruelties to the sick with their tears; and children who hear them read ask if you are made and look like other men. . . . [Y]our reappointment to your present high and important office, after the crimes you have committed, is a new phenomenon in the history of mankind." It would "serve like a high-water mark to show posterity the degrees of corruption that marked the present stage of the American Revolution."

Rush had the letter printed three days later in the *Pennsylvania Packet*, a shrewd move designed to better acquaint the general public with the trial, its outcome, and Shippen's adroit politicking. Within less than two weeks, thanks to the chorus of approbation both within and without Congress to Rush's letter, Shippen resigned his commission. Morgan immediately issued a public statement: "I am happy to inform my fellow-citizens that Dr. Shippen, at length unable to bear further investigation of his conduct [let alone further animadversion from Dr. Rush], has been compelled to quit the station of director general of hospitals by a forced resignation."[6] Washington softened the blow somewhat by giving Shippen, at his solicitation, a good conduct certificate asserting that, insofar as he was capable of judging, "I believe no hospitals could have been better administered"—which encomium Shippen had published in the *Pennsylvania Packet* (14 July 1781).

Rush's elevated spirits upon his return to Philadelphia at the beginning of the year did not extend to the military situation, which had everyone—the Loyalists excepted—in a state of anxiety. As the war entered its fifth year, most of New York was still in British hands, thus cutting off New England from the Middle States (though Washington would soon succeed in securing enough of a toehold to establish a headquarters on the west bank of the Hudson). Adding to the precariousness of the situation, enemy forces under the command of Sir Henry Clinton had laid siege to the major southern port of Charleston. Washington's army had survived the awful winter at Valley Forge, but there was little promise of better things to come as spring approached.

The good news that Count Jean Baptiste de Rochambeau had arrived at Newport with six thousand French troops provided a welcome companion piece, as it were, to the great naval victory the previous September of John Paul Jones and his *Bonhomme Richard* over the British *Serapis* and the *Countess of Scarborough*. But this could not raise American spirits when they sank to an all-time low with the surrender of Charleston in May. Said Thomas Paine, reflecting the consensus, the loss of Charleston "is such a formidable blow that unless some very sudden and spirited exertions be made the distress that will follow will be long and heavy."[7] It would seem that only Rush was unable—or perhaps unwilling—to perceive that the war's darkest hour had come.

Far from being distressed by the fall of Charleston, he wrote Adams, "The reduction (I will not say *loss*) of Charleston has produced a new era in the politics of America, such as you and I saw and felt and admired in the years 1775 and 76. Our republics cannot exist long in prosperity. We require adversity and appear to possess most of the republican spirit when most depressed." Rush was confident that the "reduction" would serve to jump-start the Americans into a new, more positive optimism that would—indeed, must—eventuate in the independence that even many of the revolutionary diehards were beginning to fear might be no more than a chimera. "The papers will inform you of the exploits of our [state] governments, of our citizens, of our soldiers, and even of our ladies," he went on. "The women of America have at last become principals in the glorious American controversy. Their opinions alone and their transcendent influence in society and families must lead us on." Rush went so far as to recommend, "If there is a single philosopher in the cabinet of St. James's [that is, the British government], he will advise immediately to make peace with America."[8]

No such philosopher stood up to proffer Rush's advice. But this was, of course, an unrealistic suggestion on his part. More realistic was his belief that the best in the Americans would be brought out by the adversity of the moment. And this proved true. The loss of Charleston, which gave the British what was tantamount to control of the southern states, infused the new nation with a renewed determination to end the war on their terms: irreversible, irrevocable independence.

With Pennsylvania's now empty treasury making it impossible for the state to contribute to Washington's summer campaign by the purchase of stores and recruits, Paine suggested that if Philadelphia's rich had "any spirit, any foresight of their own integrity or danger," they would "promote a subscription either of money or articles, and appoint a committee from among themselves to solicit the same in the several counties." With the largest and richest state "setting the example," Paine was confident, "the rest will follow." The suggestion precipitated a meeting of the city's aristocrats and wealthy merchants at the City Tavern, at which $300,000 was pledged (Rush gave $2,000) "to support the credit of a bank to be established for furnishing a supply of provisions for the armies of the United States."[9]

While supplies began moving from Pennsylvania to Washington's army (the other states failed to "follow," Paine's prediction notwithstanding), they were not enough to put the Continental army into battle. Furthermore, by the time campaigning should have commenced, in mid-July, Washington had only about one thousand troops available that would qualify as able-bodied: "I have almost ceased to hope. The country in general is in such a state of insensibility and indifference to its interests that I dare not flatter myself with any change for the better."[10] And this from a commander who was never known to be unduly pessimistic!

There was worse to come. On 16 August 1780, Gates was defeated by Cornwallis at the Battle of Camden; two days later General Thomas Sumter suffered a defeat at the hands of Sir Banastre Tarleton at Fishing Creek and was forced to retreat into North Carolina. Especially disheartening was the news that on 23 September, Benedict Arnold, having engineered the command of West Point in furtherance of a plot to surrender it and himself to Sir Henry Clinton, with whom he had been negotiating for a year, had made good his escape when the plot was revealed by Major John André, the go-between for Arnold and Clinton. (André was hanged as a spy on Washington's orders.) It was not until October that the Continentals would savor the taste of victory in the Battle of King's Mountain, and not until 17 January of 1781, in what would prove to be the last year of the war, that they would score another victory over the British, at the Battle of Cowpens.

Meanwhile, except for appearing at the Shippen trial in Morristown, Rush was leading what he called "a most unrepublican life," devoting himself to his patients and his family. In April, an epidemic of "catarrh appeared" among children between the ages of one and seven. Rush thought it heralded a smallpox epidemic, but it disappeared as spontaneously as it had broken out. The patients had barely recovered when an intermittent fever swept through the adult community in May, raising Rush's patient load that month to 100. It decreased to 91 in the following month, then rose in July to 122 and spiked to 181 in August (the month Julia delivered their third child and second son, Richard, who would go on to become the most famous and distinguished of the Rush children). When Rush notified the authorities that "Many have died from drinking cold water," an essay he had written years earlier on the dangers of cold water was printed as handbills and posted on water pumps throughout the city.

It was during this period, consonant with his never-ending attempt to enlighten people in the areas of health and hygiene, that Rush joined with others in founding the Philadelphia Humane Society. The organization, the first of its kind in America, existed essentially on paper until the postwar years, when it was replicated throughout the new nation. Thus did Rush break new ground in an aspect of no small consequence that the world today accepts as crucial in health care: preventive medicine. One of his favorite "lines" to his students was that it "required as much skill to *prevent* diseases as to cure them."[11]

Unlike the almost annual epidemics of a various nature that arrived at Philadelphia with the warm weather in the spring and summer and departed when the weather turned cool in the autumn, the fever that first appeared during the uncommonly warm July and August of 1780 followed a different course. On 20 August, the day after the weather suddenly turned cool, upward of a half thousand people complained of varying degrees of indisposition and a sense of lassitude ascribed to a fever of the unremitting type. Rush's patient load rose to 255 patients in September; on one day alone in that month he visited upward of sixty patients, all in different—and some in very remote—parts of the town. Never before had he seen more than half that number of people sick at one time in the city in the twenty years he had been practicing medicine.

Rush had begun a journal in which he recorded a comprehensive account of the seasonal diseases, which were for the most part unremitting and bilious fevers, together with a history of the weather. He observed that the epidemics increased proportionately as the surrounding areas of the city had been cleared of woods. Consequently, his conviction that the reason Philadelphia became unusually susceptible to such fevers was attributable to the British having cut down the trees for firewood, which led in turn to a flooding of the surrounding meadows. The winds that passed over mill dams and marshes in August and September, Rush further observed, generally carried with them the seeds of the fevers. Therefore, he posited, it was unsafe to sleep with open windows during this period. When the banks of the meadows were repaired to hold back the tides, and marshy grounds formerly capped with stagnant water and filth were cultivated, the city's health improved, as it did with regular street cleaning and enclosure of a large and offensive dock area that divided the two principal thoroughfares near the town's center. The result of his findings prompted Rush to articulate two important hypotheses for dealing with sanitation: clearing the land makes for sickness, cultivating the land makes for good health.

Rush himself came down with this year's disease, which he was the first to describe clinically and to call by its popular name: breakbone fever. It was also known as dengue fever.[12] Not for another century would it became known that insects are carriers of disease and the cause of such epidemics as dengue and the more life threatening malaria and yellow fever. In fact, the mosquito (known as the *Aedes stegomyia* or *Aedes aegypti*) is the same carrier of yellow fever and dengue, and was first reported in Egypt the year before Rush fell victim to it. Today, as then, it is endemic worldwide, especially in the tropics, sometimes reaching epidemic proportions that can afflict every inhabitant of a given community.

The disease is transmitted by mosquitoes, and so does not travel far unless they are borne by the winds. While Rush was ignorant of this (though he did note in passing that "the moschetoes were uncommonly numerous during the autumn, a certain sign of a unwholesome atmosphere"), his description of it, and his prognosis—it was rarely fatal—published in 1789 in the first volume of his *Medical Inquiries and Observations*, remains to this day a medical classic. Though a strong proponent of bleeding in the treatment of any number of diseases or ailments, with dengue fever in its first stages, Rush did not, like most other physicians, resort to bloodletting, However, if the pulse was not weak when the fever continued past the fourth day, he did so by cupping on the neck or behind the ears. Opium he prescribed in moderation unless the patient pleaded "for something to give them relief from their insupportable pain, particularly when they were seated in the eyeballs and head . . . and always with the happiest results." He depended on purges to empty the stomach and bowels, diaphoretics "to excite perspiration," and ordered complete bed rest when the patient's pain could tolerate it, and, at signs of improvement, light exercise in the fresh air. For the ailment's depression-phase he prescribed much ripe fruit and light meals, usually of oysters accompanied by liberal imbibing of porter, a dark sweet beer similar to light stout.[13] All in all, Rush's was an innovative treatment, invariably with better results than anticipated. Such innovations did not endear him to his conservative elder fellow physicians, but they did win him the approbation and admiration of the rising generation of physicians.

While confined to bed during the recuperative stage of his illness, Rush had a strange dream that left him more disposed to attend the poor: "My business from this time was extensive, but less profitable than it should have been, from being obliged to receive the payment of my bills in paper money which frequently depreciated 200 and 300 per cent below their value at the time they were delivered to my patients."[14] Following his return from military service, Rush had more or less confined his patient load to those able to pay either in precious gold notes or, if in popular currency, appreciably higher fees, especially now that he had only recently purchased a new house for his increasingly growing family. As he recalled the dream, "a poor woman came to me . . . and begged me to visit her husband. I told her hastily that I was worn out in attending poor people, and requested her to apply to another Doctor. 'O! Sir (said she, lifting up her hands) you don't know how much you owe to your poor patients. It was decreed that you should die by the fever which lately attacked you, but the prayers of your poor patients ascended to heaven in your behalf, and your life is prolonged only upon this account.' The dream . . . increased my disposition to attend the poor, and never, when I could not serve them, to treat them in an uncivil manner."

Rush now took into partnership his former pupil Dr. James Hall: "This connection was the more necessary, as frequent attacks of a pulmonary affection rendered it unsafe for me to go out in the night and bad weather." It all had a downside, though. The partnership, in which Hall attended mainly the indigent patients, was "represented by some of my medical brethren as a preparatory measure to my declining business and devoting myself exclusively to public pursuits [presumably devoting more and more time to attacking with his facile quill and ink the Pennsylvania Constitution and the assembly]. This partnership [which was dissolved seven years later by Hall's marrying and moving away from Philadelphia], instead of increasing, lessened my business."[15] The allusion here is to the well-to-do Tories, who used their influence to cause many of the city's aristocrats, with whom Rush had reestablished himself in practice following his return to Philadelphia, to put other physicians in charge of their medical management.

There was money coming in from Rush's lectures, though this represented not so much the realization of any appreciable income as it did of prestige and self-satisfaction. After the college's incorporation into the university, all former medical professors were invited to resume their chairs when the school reopened in July. But when Shippen accepted, Rush and Morgan declined the invitation. Only after Shippen had maneuvered himself back into the army's medical directorship, which would preclude his giving his course in anatomy, did Rush relent, giving his introductory lecture in chemistry on 20 November. His enthusiasm about doing so was in marked contrast to the negative feelings he aroused in many of his colleagues. But these feelings were rooted in matters of political difference. His effectiveness as a teacher was undeniable.

But Rush did not deign to concern himself with how he was viewed by people he detested either for their opinions or for themselves. Besides, he was riding out the year on a high note. In October, the Republicans had taken control of the Pennsylvania Assembly from their nemeses, the Constitutionalists, albeit by a slender margin. He was back lecturing. It seemed only a matter of time before pressure would be brought on Shippen to resign his army commission. On 2 January, it appeared that after four years of consideration and debate in the various states, the Articles of Confederation would at last achieve the requisite ratification (which in fact it did on 1 March 1781, remaining in force until the present Constitution went into effect).

On the first day of the new year 1781 there occurred an event which might well have plunged Rush into a trough of dejection. Fifteen hundred men of the Pennsylvania Line, encamped at Morristown, practically the entire force, mutinied. Under their commander, Anthony Wayne, they had gone into the Continental army well fed, well clothed, and well supplied. But for almost a year they had been on short rations, their lack of adequate clothing beggared all description, there were gross deficiencies in their pay, and the terms of their enlistment had been overextended. Having decamped Morristown and headed for Philadelphia, they got no farther than Princeton and Trenton when both Congress and the Pennsylvania government recognized the justness of their complaints and took immediate steps to allay them.

Rather than being disturbed by the mutiny, Rush treated the entire business with equanimity, assuring John Adams (21 January 1781), by now representing the new nation at the Dutch court, that the mutiny "has had no effect upon the minds of Whigs or to Tories. It appears upon examination that most of them were entitled to their discharge above a year ago. They are still devoted to our cause, and such as them as do not reenlist will add to the strength and defense of our country by entering on board privateers or other vessels of war."

General optimism increased with each passing day. In February, when paper money became all but worthless, it was forced out of circulation by bringing back into the marketplace what gold and silver existed. The new nation had at last, in the Articles of Confederation, what would suffice as a viable constitution. Rush wrote Elias Boudinot (30 January 1781), "This our ministers and commissioners abroad tell us was all that was necessary to obtain *loans, alliances,* and even *peace.*" Washington had succeeded in securing new enlistments. A new force of army and naval personnel had arrived from France. Congress had created the departments of foreign affairs, finance, and war out of the ongoing chaos.

And, of greatest significance over time, Robert Morris had been given a mandate to reorganize and superintend the new nation's chaotic finances. Morris, whose glorious career as a financial wizard would end in his spending three years in debtor's prison and dying in near-poverty a quarter of a century later, encouraged confidence both at home and abroad in the new government by establishing at Philadelphia, with Congress's concurrence, the Bank of North America (the oldest financial institution in the United States, in which Rush purchased a share of stock) and confidence in the Continental army by initiating the movement of much-needed food supplies, clothing, and ammunition to Washington's beleaguered forces. "Mr. Morris has become a new star in our American hemisphere," Rush wrote General Gates (5 September 1781), the same letter in which he promised, "Before this reaches you, the fate of Great Britain and the repose of Europe will probably be determined in Chesapeake Bay."[16] It was a promise that would be fulfilled.

Washington's initial strategy had been to concentrate on retaking New York. But that summer Lord Cornwallis moved a force of 7,200 men into Virginia. There they engaged in what was facetiously termed "a country dance" with 1,700 Americans commanded by the Marquis de Lafayette, who dexterously kept his numerically inferior force just out of British artillery range. Lafayette explained that he was willing "to skirmish but not to engage too far . . . I am not strong enough even to be beaten."[17] Altering his battle plan, Washington dispatched reinforcements to Lafayette. This forced Cornwallis back toward the coast where he remained behind a fortified position on the York peninsula, there to await a British fleet to evacuate his troops. Washington now concentrated his attention on the area, where his 5,000 Continentals were joined by a like number of French troops under command of the Comte de Rochambeau.

On 19 August, five days after learning that the Comte de Grasse was en route to America with a thirty-ship armada and an additional 3,000 French marines, Washington took the greatest gamble of his entire career by moving the combined armies from New York to Virginia. The gamble was predicated on the hope that he might entrap Cornwallis's force before a British fleet could arrive to evacuate them. Moving his army across New Jersey toward Virginia, Washington detoured to Philadelphia to plead, successfully as it turned out, that the city accumulate sorely needed food, clothing, and equipment for his troops. Also, under pressure from Washington, Robert Morris somehow—many, including historians, considered it a true miracle—arranged that the troops be given a month's pay in gold. It was a few days after Washington left Philadelphia—it took his army a full day to pass through the city—that Rush wrote his remark to Gates that the fate of the war's outcome would be "determined in Chesapeake Bay."

While Washington, Lafayette, and Rochambeau closed in on Corn-wallis at Yorktown, Admiral De Grasse and his forces, having arrived from France, entered Chesapeake Bay. On the very day Rush wrote the letter to Gates, a naval battle between De Grasse and British admiral Graves forced the latter's fleet to return to New York for resupplying before Cornwallis could embark his army, thereby sealing his fate. Besieged at Yorktown as of 30 September with no chance of escape, by 19 October Cornwallis accepted that he had no choice but to surrender with his remaining 7,000 men. King George's government accepted the loss of its North American colonies (Canada excepted). The revolt by the former American colonies was ended.

(Negotiations for a definite peace consumed two years, mainly because the French government was eager to please both of its allies, Spain and the United States. Impatient at the delay, and not giving a damn about the promises France had made to Spain at the expense of the British, the American commissioners disregarded their instructions not to negotiate a separate peace with Great Britain. Eager to win American friendship and trade, and thus defeat French aspirations vis-à-vis the new nation, the mother country readily gave in to the American demand for the Mississippi as their western boundary and full rights in the rich fisheries off the Canadian coast. The unqualified recognition of the United States of America by Britain became fact with the signing of the Treaty of Paris on 3 September 1783.)

When official word of the victory at Yorktown arrived in Philadelphia five days later, the booming of guns from every ship in the harbor was music to the ears of the citizenry as they attended divine services in the afternoon and celebrated wildly in the streets that night.[18] "How is the mighty fallen!" Rush fairly chortled in a letter to Nathanael Greene (30 October 1781). "Cornwallis, the ravager (for he never compromised) of the South, the pride of Britain, and the pillar of all her hopes in America, is fallen, fallen, fallen! How honorable is this glorious event to the combined arms of France and America!"

Propagandist

Rush's medical practice reached its highest point to date in the year the new nation won its independence. But his professional life was again dominated by the old quarrel with Shippen.

When, in the previous autumn, the college's medical faculty were invited to resume their lectures, the students, ignoring both the Shippen versus Rush and Morgan feud and the revelations of his behavior as director general of the Continental Army's medical department, petitioned the trustees to have Shippen resume his famed lectures on anatomy. On 4 January 1781, the day after resigning from the army, Shippen did just that. In the following month, after completing their own courses, Rush and Morgan submitted their resignations, informing the trustees they could not, "consistent with their own characters, and the interest of science and virtue, consent to accept their appointments in the university with Doctor Shippen."[1] The trustees decided to accept the resignations and, hopefully, resolve the conflict in June, when they sought to restructure the medical faculty to everyone's satisfaction.

Their resolve degenerated into a personality-driven mêlée. Shippen's father, himself a highly respected physician and lecturer, proposed that the chair in chemistry vacated by Rush be given to Dr. James Hutchinson, a Constitutionalist and ipso facto a dedicated Rush antagonist. But Hutchinson put aside political feelings in the interest of the college, and realizing Rush was far and away better qualified, nominated him for the position. Against the protests of trustee Timothy Matlack, another adversary, who insisted that Rush's resignation be allowed to stand, two board members—Rev. William White, a respected divine, and Francis Hopkinson, essayist and a signer of the Declaration of Independence—made it known that Rush had quietly rescinded his resignation (though not to the trustees) and wished to recoup his chemistry chair.

Deciding that the feud among the three men must be resolved for the sake of collegial harmony, the board voted to name Shippen professor of anatomy and Rush professor of medical history. Morgan, who had not rescinded his resignation, was denied the professorship he had held since 1765 and for which he was so well qualified, namely the practice and theory of medicine. Shortly thereafter, Morgan agreed to withdraw his resignation, and was reappointed by the trustees.

No sooner was the settlement agreed upon than it fell apart when the vengeance-ridden Morgan went after Shippen in the public press. In late September Morgan and Rush published their original letters of resignation, in effect rescinding their earlier rescission, announcing they simply could not be members of any faculty that included Shippen. By way of justification, they accused Joseph Reed, president of the Pennsylvania Assembly's Executive Council, who had contrived to bring Rush back into politics and was now pro-Shippen, of conniving to have Shippen recover his professorship in anatomy "to shelter him from merited disgrace." Furthermore, Rush and Morgan charged, Shippen's accounts while on active duty had been audited, "and we have authority to say, *they have not*, and *cannot be passed*, although millions of dollars have been withdrawn from the public treasury."[2]

This prompted Shippen to make public Washington's letter of commendation, along with a series of letters from the army's commissioner of accounts that questioned the authenticity of the Rush-Morgan sources "in the auditor's office," as Shippen's records had not yet been examined. Morgan, considering the commissioner's question "ungentlemanly," refused to respond. Rush responded, but took the low road. Practically calling Shippen a traitor to his country, he wrote, "As well might General [Benedict] Arnold publish the polite letter" Washington wrote to him after his commendable role in the 1777 campaign "to acquit himself of . . . treachery and defection at the post of West Point." Furthermore, Rush told the commissioner that the accounts revealed nothing that bore upon the case, because he was convinced they were fraudulent.[3]

Shippen wisely chose to ignore Rush's thinly veiled insinuation of treason. Conversely, the commissioner, outraged by the attack upon his veracity, publicly dismissed Morgan as a "quibbling son of Aesculapius" and Rush's remarks as a *"jargon of diction,* which if it means anything at all it will only amount to *this,* that should the accounts be approved honest, and *pass muster,* the commissioners must be held out to the world as corrupted, and that Doctor Shippen (after having been charged with the plunder of millions) is actually so poor as not to be able to bribe them." The rejoinder was justified, and Rush, obviously realizing he had gone too far, opted not to respond.

But not Morgan. He continued to attack Shippen. The commissioners demanded that Morgan either produce definitive proof of the charges or drop altogether what Philadelphians now considered, in the words of one of their number, "this *truly hackneyed subject."* Worse for Morgan, he was accused by one correspondent of having engaged in "treasonable flirtation" with the British during their occupation of the city—a charge Morgan dismissed as bizarre before quickly abandoning his epistolary crusade against Shippen and dropping out of sight.[4]

Sadly, Shippen triumphed over Morgan. In failing to destroy his longtime nemesis, Morgan succeeded only in destroying himself. His interest in the medical college (he never taught at the university) declined, as did his once thriving medical practice. Ten years after Congress officially vindicated him, he died devastated, despondent, and deserted. In his *Commonplace Book,* Rush writes under the date 15 October 1789: "This afternoon I was called to visit Dr. Morgan, but found him dead in a small hovel, surrounded with books and papers, and on a light dirty bed. He was attended only by a washerwoman, one of his tenants.... What a change from his former rank and prospects in Life! The man who once filled half the world with his name, had now scarcely friends enough left to bury him."[5]

Though also, in a manner of speaking, trumped by Shippen, Rush, unlike Morgan, chose not to obsess over it. Besides, he had too full a plate to pay any heed to a single defeat. He had his family (a second daughter, Susanna, or Susan, was born on 7 January but lived only five months), his teaching (the lectures were commenced on 19 November), his medical practice, his writing, and his ongoing interest in political affairs.

In part because of his professional talents, in part as a form of compensation for his role in bringing Pennsylvania into the revolutionary movement, Rush now found himself among Philadelphia's highest social stratum (though there were quite a few Constitutionalists who would have preferred he be confined to the lowest). Attesting to his social standing was the invitation Rush and Julia received to join the rest of the city's upper crust at the mammoth celebration given by the French ambassador, La Luzerne, to celebrate the birth of the Dauphin to Louis XVI and Marie Antoinette.[6] La Luzerne's party, a grand exercise in conspicuous consumption, was an excuse to cement Franco-American relations, now that the British had begun preliminary peace negotiations in Paris, with Benjamin Franklin representing the United States.

In March 1782 David Ramsay arrived in the city to serve as one of South Carolina's delegates in Congress, and accepted an invitation to take lodgings in the Rush home. Rush now had a direct line to the heated debates and other business taking place behind the closed doors of the national legislature, which until adoption of the Constitution comprised all three branches of government as we know them today.

The basic obligations and projected course of purpose between the First Continental and subsequent wartime Congresses were diametrically opposite to the first post-Yorktown Congress. The earlier Congresses had been preoccupied all but exclusively for six years with directing the efforts of thirteen autonomous colonies in a war for joint independence. As a consequence, questions of how the states and the central government were to divide power had been dealt with only as a side issue. As a member, however briefly, of the first Congress, the strongly nationalistic Benjamin Rush had urged that the bonds of union be strengthened; more often than not, the various states seemed to be as much at war with each other as with the British. Rush, in a Cassandra-like mode, was able to foresee the danger inherent in deferring consideration of a problem demanding resolution until the problem had presented itself.

Here was an extension of his belief in preventive medicine. And like the handful of men who shared his views, Rush's concerns went unheeded. Perhaps Congress is not to be condemned unequivocally. After all, the first six years of its existence had been precarious ones, resonating in large measure with a lack of certainty how they would come up with the wherewithal to avert total disintegration of an army—one might say an ad hoc agglomeration of provincial militias—opposed by an army superior in every respect: manpower, organization, and supply. Now the Congress was dominated by men who insisted, and rightly so, that the sine qua non for survival of the union of thirteen states they represented required a strong central government.

Forced to suspend payment of interest on war loan certificates, and moving toward a hoped-for increase in powers denied them by the Articles of Confederation—a charter whose weaknesses far outweighed its strengths—Congress had sought permission of the states to levy a permanent 5 percent duty on all imports. Use of the money thus collected would be left to the Congress's discretion. Robert Morris, who insisted that such a measure was vital to winning the war, had suggested the measure. Now, following the victory at Yorktown, Morris insisted the money was needed to retire the accumulated war debt, for which, he argued, the Congress and not the states was responsible; to apportion the debt among the states would be "ruinous" to a strong union. Such a levy required the unanimous consent of the states. In the summer of 1782, tiny Rhode Island's refractory legislature rejected the proposal, thus condemning it to defeat.

This was but one of many conflicts that were to take the nation as long to write a constitution as it took to wage the war. The Founding Fathers had their work cut out for them. So, too, the so-called Second Generation, whose Herculean task it was to create a viable union of thirteen states while allowing each to retain its sovereignty—but within the overall context of one sovereign entity. With his houseguest and now close friend Ramsay providing daily intelligence briefings of what was going on behind those locked doors, Rush was persuaded to take up his quill (not that he needed much persuasion) and, without ignoring his professional responsibilities, compose a series of nine essays dealing with continental affairs.

The essays appeared in the *Pennsylvania Journal* between May and August of 1782; three under the pseudonym "Retaliation," the others signed, yet again, "Leonidas." The concluding four essays were also run in the *Pennsylvania Gazette* that same summer. The early pieces were little more than a reworking of old material, including public credit, the French alliance, and other topics. It was with the fourth article that he hit his stride—the new nation's urgent need, first expounded by John Adams when they sat side by side in the First Continental Congress, was for a strong navy.

By the time France entered the war, the American navy had been allowed by Congress to decline from thirty-four ships in 1777 to seven four years later, on the assumption that the war against Britain on the seas would be capably handled by the French. On 12 April 1782, only six months after Yorktown—and it must be borne in mind that the definitive conclusion of the Revolutionary War lay a year away with the signing of the Peace of Paris—the British fleet under Admiral George Rodney, consonant with England's "plan of a naval war" against America, defeated a French fleet under De Grasse in the West Indies. This Rush referred to when continuing the theme in his fifth letter: "[Given] the insular situation of Great Britain, from the extent of her foreign territory, and above all from the commerce and resources of her American dominions, she necessarily became a great naval power. . . . The ascendancy which Britain has acquired on the ocean has been in exact proportion to the great commerce and populousness of her American colonies."

With Britain "still so powerful and insolent upon the ocean" as ever, Rush argued that if "the resources of America alone gave Britain her present naval advantage, what will not America be capable of doing for herself when she opens her eyes to behold her native strength on the water?" The answer, of course, was to make sure America could meet the world's greatest naval power at least to the extent that she not be at that power's mercy, not only in terms of warfare but in protecting her interests as an international trading nation.

Asking the reader to consider "the composition of the most formidable British navy that has spread desolation and tyranny over the world," he notes that it "consists of nothing but oak and pine, kept together by hemp and iron. And what do we see on yonder shore? Why, forests abounding with oaks and pines, mountains abounding with iron ore, and a soil capable of producing all the raw materials of sails and ropes. Then let not the oaks and pines and iron of America be afraid of the oaks and pines and iron of Britain."[7]

In the eighth of the nine essays, also dealing with the need for a navy, Rush posits that commerce, which he could not advocate strongly enough, "forms the only barrier that can be contrived to check the aristocratic tendency of a monopoly of land. It opens the door to power, rank and influence to everybody. It is the magnet of talents and cherishes of virtue. It is calculated to restore men to their original equality, and to expel tyranny from the world." The great fleet he called upon America to build would be for commercial maritime as distinct from bellicose purposes. Now that America had severed irrevocably the restraints imposed by England's exclusive commercial system, it was bound to all nations as all nations are bound together, by ties of trade, which made all mankind "children of the same father, and members of one great family."[8]

In the most curious of his nine essays (published in the *Pennsylvania Gazette,* 17 July 1782, also pseudonymously as "Leonidas") Rush breaks off from calling for an American navy to sing the praises of "the present Congress," which he believed to be "composed of men of as much integrity and abilities as ever met together for the government of this, or perhaps of any other, country. I insist upon it, that the difficulties which our rulers have surmounted within these two last years, are proofs of a *stronger* and purer virtue than any that were exhibited at the beginning of the war." This led to a remarkable acknowledgment: "So far am I from admitting that the patriots of 1775 or 1776 monopolized all public spirit or wisdom that I believe most of the evils in government, with which we are now contending, have been bequeathed to us by the disaffection of some of them, by the timidity of others, and by the ignorance of them all."

Here was a man who all his life wore proudly the cloak of participation in the events of those two years now appearing to censure himself along with his compeers, whom he compared to an army's light infantry: After sounding the tocsin heralding the enemy's approach, they "fell back when the battle thickened, and made way for the heavy troops [who by] their strength and steadiness have turned the battle from our gates."

Rush's purpose was not to degrade those early fellow patriots—he would never reproach them as individuals or take issue with their collective accomplishments—but, rather, to venerate "those men who have distinguished themselves in *every* stage of the controversy." Their sense of purpose brought independence: "[T]hey deserve encomiums beyond the conceptions of my heart or the expression of my pen." Then begging his reader's indulgence for this digression from his call for a navy, Rush concluded with the statement, "We have sinned beyond repentance or forgiveness," and adds: "It was necessary. It is of consequence for us to know ourselves."

Historians see in this Rush revealing, perhaps unintentionally, a feeling of unease over what amounted to an already committed withdrawal from political life. Never again would he fault the original patriots nor allow himself to be disconcerted by the politics that were the inevitable consequence of a war giving birth to a new—and in vital respects original—nation. He would, though, reserve the right to have his say on, and play a role, usually tangential, in many controversies to come. Rush took solace in Pope's phrase from *An Essay on Man,* "whatever is, is right." He employs the phrase in a letter to Nathanael Greene (16 September 1782), along with his expectation, which he now sees as unattainable, "to have bequeathed at least a naval war to my children." The British, the Dutch, "nay more, all Europe say we *must have peace*," he goes on. But he is "afraid we are not ripe for it." He fears not the threat of "parties and factions without number rising up among the great after a peace." He does fear, though, that unless the power of "our States can be limited," the chance that "we may continue our republican forms of government for centuries to come" is uncertain.

Rush came next to a cause long high on his agenda; he asks that Greene use his "great influence" in South Carolina, where the general planned to settle after the war,

> to obtain a law to prohibit the future of slavery in your country. For God's sake, do not exhibit a new spectacle to the world, of men just emerging from a war in favor of liberty, with their clothes not yet washed from the blood which was shed in copious and willing streams in its defense, fitting out vessels to import their fellow creatures from Africa to reduce them afterwards to slavery. Let it not be said that your soil can only be worked by Negroes. This is to make war upon nature.

He does not, however, "urge the emancipation." The slaves

> are rendered unfit by their habits of vice (the offspring of slavery) for freedom. To make them free therefore would be both to injure them and society. Make their situation comfortable by good treatment. Time may unfold a method hereafter of repairing to their

posterity the injustice that has been done to the present generation. Let Great Britain stand alone as the author of the American trade to Africa. Let not our united republics be stained with the importation of a single African slave into America.[9]

This reiteration of his abhorrence of slavery, reflected in the Greene letter, marked the start of Rush's involvement in the extended series of social reforms he would conceive and promulgate over the next decade.

The first of these, appearing in the 26 June issue of *Pennsylvania Journal*, amounted to a temperance lecture on the evils of hard liquors. The political commentator was now speaking as the medical practitioner. Though the consumption of spirits had risen heavily among all classes, Rush focused on the custom in Pennsylvania of serving them to the harvest workers:

> At a time when public spirit and philosophy are uniting their efforts to *destroy* human life by suggesting improvements in the art of war, I beg leave to lay before my countrymen a few thoughts upon the means of *preserving* life. The approach of harvest reminds me of the custom of consuming large quantities of spirituous liquors at that season. My design in the following essay is to show, first, That spirituous liquors are unnecessary; and, second, That they are mischievous and often produce the diseases they are intended to obviate during the time of harvest.

Noting that they are "injurious inasmuch as they add an internal fire to the external heat of the sun," he cautioned that they "relax the stomach, quicken the circulation of the blood, and thus dispose it to putrefaction." He has even heard of instances of workers suddenly dropping dead in the midst of a harvest, allegedly "from excess of heat or labor," but which subsequent inquiry reveals to "have been occasioned by the excessive use of spirituous liquors."

But that, as the saying goes, is only the half of it. There are the "many quarrels" and "indecent language" that are "extorted from men of the most peaceable dispositions and decent conversations at ordinary times by the prevailing use of spirits in the time of harvest!" And then there is the economic factor. Many farmers were now paying "a fourth part of the whole profits of his crop to a storekeeper for rum or whiskey to be expended at harvest." Not only does the money spent for liquor serve "no purpose," it does "real mischief. It produces fatigue, it destroys health, and in some instances produces sudden death."

Rush urges, instead, that the harvesters "allay the thirst and support the profuse sweats that exerted by his labor" by resorting to "simple, healthy, and frugal drinks." Among these are buttermilk, sour milk, or plain milk and water; cider or table beer with water; plain water "suffered to stand for some time upon parched Indian corn" (recommended by Rush as "a very agreeable and strengthening drink [which] may be improved by the addition of a little vinegar"); and vinegar and water sweetened with molasses or brown sugar ("This drink is pleasant and in some respects is preferable to any that have been mentioned"). All these recommended substitutions for hard liquor, Rush assures his readers, "are cooling and grateful to the stomach. They invigorate the appetite and obviate the disposition for putrefaction in the humors to which excessive heat and labor naturally dispose them." Summing up, Rush advises that to "obviate any ill effects that may arise from receiving these drinks into the stomach in a cold state," he

> would recommend it to reapers never to drink while they are warm without first wetting their hands or feet in cold water or grasping the cup they drink from (provided it is made of earth, glass, or metal) for about a minute with both their hands. The extraordinary heat of the body is conveyed off in both these ways with nearly the same certainty as an accumulated quantity of electric matters is conveyed from any body by means of a rod or any other conductor of electric fire.[10]

No records have come down as to how many people—if any—followed Rush's advice. Rush refused to be discouraged, any more than he would be discouraged if any other cause in which he believed strongly were universally dismissed as no more than words cast upon the waters or tossed to the winds. In fact, temperance was one of the few causes he continued to promote anew into his senior years. His writings on the subject, notably "An Inquiry into the Effects of Ardent Spirits upon the Human Body and Mind, with an Account of

the Means of Preventing, and of the Remedies for Curing Them,"
which Rush included in the second edition of his Medical Inquiries
and Observations (1805), was widely reproduced over the ensuing
years, and is universally credited with influencing the founding of the
first temperance society, at Port Moreau, N.Y., in 1808.[11]

That summer of 1782, while heavily involved in his medical practice, teaching, writings, formulating plans for a new college at Carlisle
in the backcountry, and keeping an eye cocked for what he deemed to
be dangerous shoals as the newly independent states negotiated dangerous waters for the safe harbor of eventual unification, Rush under-
went yet another religious change.

Having been inculcated, while attending his uncle Samuel Finley's
school, in the Westminster Confession, which emphasized the Calvinistic principle of predestination and a wrathful God, he "retained them
but without any affection for them 'till about the year 1780," as he
recalled in his memoirs.[12] That was the year in which the Reverend
Elhanan Winchester, having been ordained a Baptist minister in his
native New England but forced out of his church after becoming convinced of the decidedly un-Calvinistic doctrine of universal salvation,
arrived in Philadelphia after six years in North Carolina. When his
congregation, unable to accept his liberal views on salvation, eased
him out of his pulpit, Winchester was invited by the more tolerant
University of Pennsylvania to hold services in the school's hall.

It was from Winchester that Rush first heard of the Reverend John
William Fletcher, Swiss-born member of the Anglican Church and
one of the founders of Methodism, from whose pen had flowed over
the years a stream of writings that rejected Calvinistic predestination
for the doctrine of universal salvation. After reading Fletcher's chef
d'oeuvre, *An Appeal to Matter of Fact and Common Sense,* Rush
enthusiastically embraced its tenets—the salvation of all men, as distinct from those only prenatally predestined—and promoted the
book's publication at Philadelphia. He may even have written the
advertisement that appeared in the *Freeman's Journal* (31 July 1782),
which promised interested prospective buyers that it had "little or
nothing to do with the controverted points of doctrine, but treats the
essentials of religion (wherein all Christians agree) in a close, ener-
getic, and masterly manner."

To Rush, like so many others who around this time were moving away from orthodox Presbyterianism, the doctrine of predestination hardly seemed fitting for a republic based on the incontrovertible thesis that all men are created equal. Or put another way: Now that the Revolution was approaching the successful goal for which it had waged a six year war against seemingly insuperable odds, it appeared to be as self-evident as the truths mandated by the Declaration of Independence that men were not so evil and the Deity not so wrathful as postulated by Calvin to be irrefutable received wisdom.

In October 1782, Rush's good spirits continued to rise when the state election for the Assembly saw the Republicans increase their control (the deputies now included his brother Jacob) and, in the following month, manage the installation as president of the Executive Council of his friend Dickinson (in whose honor Rush decided to name the college he was planning at Carlisle). With the Constitutionalists now the minority party, Rush wrote his friend John Montgomery ("It will be impossible for them ever to deceive the state again"), the time had come for "rescuing the state from the hands of tyrants, fools, and traitors. Heaven has committed a great and important trust to our care— no less than the liberties of the first state in the Union. We are already a little nation. Our posterity expect that we will do for them what our ancestors did for us. I have pledged myself to my friends that I will never relinquish the great object of a good constitution."[13]

Marring Rush's joy in the election's outcome was the defeat of Montgomery, who represented Carlisle and with whom Rush was planning the establishment of Dickinson College. By way of compensation, Rush wrote him (15 October 1782), "Your friends, I believe will if possible show your country the sense they entertain of their treatment of you by putting you into Congress next month." Rush's belief was fulfilled when, later that month, the Assembly chose Montgomery, along with four other of Rush's friends, to represent the state in Congress.

Rush's renewed involvement in politics rose along with his revivified spirits when in November he was one of nine men to sign a petition (which he may well have written) seeking "the speedy adoption" by the Assembly to pay the interest on loan certificates purchased by the public and to create a sinking fund to pay off the principal.[14] The petition wound up going nowhere. The Assembly passed the plan on to Congress, where it was debated without much enthusiasm, which then further diminished when in March of the following year news arrived that the preliminary articles of peace had been signed in Paris on 30 November 1782.

When Congress ratified the treaty on 19 April 1783, exactly eight years after the war had begun at Lexington, Thomas Paine published his thirteenth and last *Crisis* essay. The first had opened with those immortal words, "These are the times that try man's souls." Now he wrote, " 'The times that tried men's souls' are over—the greatest and completest revolution the world ever knew gloriously and happily accomplished."

16

Educator

On Saturday, 21 June 1783, some three hundred soldiers picketed the Assembly's Executive Council at its office in the State House demanding their back pay before being demobilized. They purposely selected a Saturday out of a desire not to embarrass Congress, which normally did not sit on that day. But Congress happened to convene that particularly Saturday in another room of the State House. Believing that the demonstrators had offended "the dignity and authority of the United States," Congress asked Pennsylvania president Dickinson to arrest them. Dickinson refused, realizing that the soldiers had public sympathy on their side. When the state militia was ordered to halt the demonstration, all but thirteen members refused. Three days later, Congress fled the city and reconvened at Princeton.

Rush addressed his opinion to the delegates through a letter to his friend John Montgomery (27 June 1783): "Every friend to the federal union laments your hasty flight from our city. . . . Our papers already teem with scandal against you. The sooner you return, the sooner the controversy between you and our state will be terminated." Setting aside the grief brought on by the sudden death of his four-and-a-half-month-old daughter, Elizabeth, Rush worked behind the scenes to promote a quick settlement of the protesters' demand, serving as an intermediary between them and Dickinson. Meanwhile Washington, at the request of Congress president Elias Boudinot, had ordered a detachment of 1,500 soldiers to Philadelphia to put down what was now perceived as a popular uprising. Rush was enraged, for the order came at a time when the Assembly was on the verge of considering whether or not it should grant Congress the right to levy a tax on foreign imports. "For God's sake!" he told Montgomery (4 July 1783), "consider what you are doing. . . . The flame of resentment against you is catching fast through the state." If Congress remained one week longer at Princeton," Rush warned, "feeding one another with ideas of insulted and wounded dignity (all *stuff* in a republic), you may lose Pennsylvania forever from your wise plans of Continental revenue." Congress by having fled had not a single advocate in the nation's capital. "For heaven's sake! Forget and forgive."

Anxious to avoid confrontation and probable bloodshed, Washington ordered that his troops be halted at Germantown, in hopes that their imminent arrival in the city would suffice to end the uprising. The protesters did indeed disband. But Congress peevishly refused to return from Princeton. This prompted Rush to express his apprehension directly to Congress through a letter (2 August 1783) to Boudinot, who was not only its president but a friend and kinsman by marriage with whom he need not measure his words.

All of Pennsylvania had turned against Congress, Rush reported. He had "no doubt" but that when the Assembly met, some measures would be adopted "that will separate us [from the other twelve states] forever. Madness you know begets madness." The first measure "will probably be to put a stop to our taxes being paid into the federal treasury. . . . For God's sake," he pleaded, "be wise, and let not those words *dignity of Congress* produce the same fatal effects upon our Union that *Supremacy of Parliament* had produced upon the British empire." (In the proclamation of 24 June announcing Congress's flight to Princeton Boudinot had repeatedly used the phrase "Dignity and authority of the United States.") His tone now almost manic, Rush viewed their "sullen, pettish, puerile absence from our city in so alarming a light to our Union and future consequence as a nation" that "no defeat or catastrophe that happened to us during the war distressed me half so much as your present conduct." Rush reminded Boudinot that while "I honor your authority," he was "zealous above all things for our Union, and I place all my hopes of the safety, perpetuity, and happiness of our government in the success of the late wise and benevolent resolutions of Congress upon the subject of finance." (Congress's plan for establishing a permanent federal revenue had been passed in April and sent to the states, with an eloquent endorsement written by James Madison.)

Rush's words fell on deaf ears. Congress remained at Princeton an additional four months. Still, the cataclysm he foresaw as a result of Congress's flight failed to materialize, and he shortly put out of his mind fears about the future of the United States. He now dedicated his concerns to the affairs of his home state. He asked John Penn, Jr., the state's last colonial governor and lineal descendant of William Penn, to whom Great Britain had given Pennsylvania as a proprietary province, to donate a tract of land to the proposed college in Carlisle (which will be dealt with in detail further along in this narrative).

Montgomery, with whom he shared the idea, lauded the request but deprecated the timing. In October, the people would be voting not only for a new Assembly but also for the first Council of Censors. Montgomery was seeking election to this council, which was empowered to propose any needed amendments to the state constitution and call for a convention to deal with them. The Penn family had been in a long-standing contentious relationship with the Pennsylvanians. Any candidate for the council associated, however indirectly, with a Penn— which would be the case, given Montgomery's known support for the Carlisle college—would almost certainly be defeated, especially now that the Constitutionalists had had it bruited about that the Republicans planned to let the Penn family restore its lands in unsettled regions throughout the state. As anticipated, Montgomery lost election to the council by fifty votes, and Rush's brother Jacob, deemed "guilty by association," was defeated for the Assembly. President Dickinson named Jacob to the state supreme court. The Republicans, having retained their control of the Assembly and won control of the Council of Censors (though not by the two-thirds majority requisite to calling a constitutional convention) rewarded Montgomery by renaming him to Congress.[1]

The year 1783 saw Rush riding a "high." With the Republicans again dominating state politics, he was confident a convention would be called to rectify the evils of the old constitution. If the Council of Censors refused to do so, he was confident, as he wrote Montgomery (15 November, 1783), "it may easily be brought about by an appeal from the Assembly to the state." More good news: Massachusetts had adopted Congress's import tax, and Rush was confident that this would encourage the smaller states to follow suit. Such was his mood that not even Congress's insistence on remaining at Princeton could bring it down: "Their enmity to Pennsylvania and their attempts to check her progress in wealth and power is as absurd as if a man should refuse to receive food by his mouth least his head grow too big for his body and should consent to be nourished only by [enemas]. They are the ridicule of our whole city.... Poor creatures. Don't be angry at them. They are only proper subjects for pity—and bleeding."

Rush's mantra, "All will end well," reflected not only his hope for the nation's future following the Treaty of Paris (3 September 1783). Hope became the mother of success as he commenced a series of innovations in the field of education that resonate to this day. Since some of these were brought to life only after a gestation not of weeks or months but of years, I have decided to treat with them thematically instead of chronologically. Dates will be given where deemed necessary for purposes of clarity and overall continuity.

In addition to enjoying a thriving practice, Rush was honored by the Pennsylvania Hospital with a staff membership in 1783. The position offered no emolument but inestimable prestige; he and his fellow staff members were held to be among the most illustrious members of their profession. The honor was owing to John Morgan, whom the trustees preferred for the position, as he was less controversial politically. But Morgan, on the brink of his descent into oblivion, refused to devote his time and talents without recompense. Some trustees opposed the contentious Rush. But their opposition was more than counterbalanced by the reputation the thirty-seven-year-old Rush had achieved as one of the foremost physicians in the United States. When the vacant post was offered, Rush quickly accepted.

Shortly thereafter came an even greater mark of Rush's reputation when, on 22 November, Rush was reelected by the university trustees to his former post as lecturer in chemistry. To obviate opposition by his Constitutionalist detractors, the invitation was issued at a prearranged rump meeting of the trustees, at which fewer than half the twenty-four members, Rush supporters all, showed up. One change initiated by the university was to have the professors lecture daily, "to lessen the expense to young gentlemen who may come from other states" by thus shortening their obligatory stay in the city. Though carrying on a full practice, Rush met with his class six days a week from the end of November until mid-January, except only for Thanksgiving and Christmas.[2]

Rush resumed his teaching as an epidemic of scarlatina anginosa (as scarlet fever was then called), which first appeared in midsummer, had by September become epidemic among adults. It abated somewhat through October and November, but by December and January the disease "revived with great violence." As panic gripped the city, anyone with a sore throat but lacking any other of the classic symptoms was convinced he had fallen victim. Rush made known his complete lack of faith in the disposition of those physicians who recommended wearing a bag of camphor around the neck as a preventative: "I have reason to entertain a more favorable opinion of the benefits of washing the hands and face with vinegar, and of rinsing the mouth and throat with vinegar and water every morning, as a means of preventing the disorder."

His treatment, which followed generally that recommended by his old teacher and mentor, Cullen—emetics not only to empty the stomach but to "cleanse the throat in its passage downward"; "detergent gargles" to keep the throat clean; and a "steam of warm water mixed with a little vinegar, through a funnel into the throat" for patients who had trouble breathing—"never failed of completely checking the disorder, or of so far mitigating its violence, as to dispose it to a favorable issue in a few days." If Rush's treatment failed to yield proper results by the third day, he "applied a blister [for bleeding] behind each ear, or one to the neck, and I think always with good effects." Only on rare occasions was he able to leave a patient's bedside without expressing his confidence, "All will end well."[3]

Four years earlier, political controversy in the state had led to the Assembly's suspending the charter of the College of Philadelphia and establishing in its stead the University of the State of Pennsylvania. As has been noted, Rush's ire over his nemesis Shippen being offered a position had led to Rush's declining an invitation to resume his lectures. By November 1781 that ire had subsided, and he agreed to resume his lectures in chemistry. Eight years later, as the new United States Constitution was going into effect, the Pennsylvania legislature returned to the old College of Philadelphia its original property and authority. Three days later, on 6 March 1789, the first of several reorganization meetings was held at the home of Benjamin Franklin, and by the summer the College of Philadelphia had again resumed functioning. On 28 October, following the death of Morgan, Rush was elected to the chair his old mentor had held in the theory and practice of medicine, and was succeeded as professor of medicine by Dr. Caspar Wistar.

When it became apparent that the College of Philadelphia and the University of the State of Pennsylvania could not move forward as separate entities, the two were merged, in the fall of 1791, as the University of Pennsylvania. In the following January Rush was elected professor of the institutes of medicine and clinical medicine in the new university, and four years later was given the additional appointment of professor of the practice of physic. Until his death seventeen years later, Rush lectured in the institutes and supervised the medical clinics, acquitting himself admirably in all responsibilities. In the words of his first biographer, Nathan Goodman,

> As a teacher, Rush exerted more influence on the medical professional in America than any other one person during the quarter century following the War for Independence. His students practiced throughout the country from Massachusetts to Georgia [the northern- and southernmost states] and kept in touch with his medical ideas through correspondence and through his published writings. As a physician, he outranked the members of the profession in Philadelphia, the largest and most important city in the new nation, and was used as a consultant by physicians in all parts of the country. For a time he was easily one of the most prominent physicians in America and certainly the busiest in his native city. Boasting the first medical school in America, Philadelphia remained the medical center of the nation for over a century.

Between 1779 and 1812, there were 2,872 students registered in Rush's medical classes. Additionally, he had numerous private apprentices, many of whom went on to establish reputations as illustrious as that of their mentor. In South Carolina alone, sixty members of the South

Carolina Medical Society—more than half the total membership—had been his students.[4]

Besides being exacting in his methods of instruction, Rush had strong ideas on ancillary factors that he insisted should be a part of medical school curricula. One of these, however, failed to take hold among the succeeding generations of physicians: penmanship. A single mistake in a prescription due to the doctor's illegible hand, Rush insisted, could well prove fatal to the health and even the life of a patient. "A fair and legible hand should be considered as part, not only of learning, but of the morality of a physician." As usual ahead of his time, he also urged including the study of Indian medicine (which he found to be based on ideas from which Americans could benefit), climate, weather conditions, soils, and the foods, manners, and medicines of different countries, along with history and literature, the latter two because they enlarge the students' "sphere of social intercourse."

Rush set down three ways of acquiring medical knowledge: reading textbooks, attending lectures, and observing diseases as they occur. ("Diseases [are] much more instructing than books: as well might a man attempt to swim by reading, as practice medicine from books.") The texts, though, should not be read until the student has had an opportunity to observe clinical practice. The best method is to read as cases occur. ("Ears are sometimes more retentive than eyes.") Attendance at lectures should be punctual, notes should be copied not during lectures but afterward, and not many courses should be taken in one season. Great attention must be paid to nature—more so in the United States where "our diseases differ much from those of Europe." Of vital importance to any student was economy of time: "As a means of retaining the strength and activity of the intellectual faculties, no portion of them should be wasted upon unprofitable studies."[5]

In November 1807 Benjamin Rush became the father of American veterinary medicine, although, to belabor the metaphor, he would not live to see his child's acceptance as a medical discipline. Veterinary science had not yet been taught as a formal course anywhere in the country when he advised its inclusion in the curriculum of every medical school. His primary concern was not so much the treatment of diseases in animals as it was the knowledge that such treatment could bring to dealing with human diseases: It would "add greatly to the certainty and usefulness of the profession of medicine as far as it relates to the human species. The organization of their bodies, the principles of animal life, and the manner in which the remote and proximate causes of diseases produce their morbid effects, are the same as in the human body; and most of the medicines produce in them, and in us, nearly a similar operation. Their acute diseases are the same as ours."[6] Not until more than a decade later was the first veterinary school founded, in Boston. It would take another forty-seven years before the first such school was opened in the University of Pennsylvania.

Two years after his appeal for the teaching of veterinary medicine, Rush proposed yet another innovation in the formal curriculum of America's medical schools: a course in natural philosophy. He drew up a list of "Duties of a Physician" that ran the gamut of advice from the young physician going out into rural areas to convince the farmers that he entertained "no superiority over them" because of his education, and promoting scientific improvements in agriculture that would redound to the farmer's healthy body and healthy frame of mind, to not believing his education had ended the day he received his diploma. He must continue to learn both by practical application and keeping up with the latest advances in methodology both in America and in Europe, and to cultivate a calming and solicitous bedside manner, which Rush considered an imperative to gaining the patient's confidence and furthering his chances for recovery. (Rush himself was celebrated for his bedside manner, which he bestowed with impartiality upon his most destitute patients as well as his most affluent.)

In short, Rush was proposing a set of ethics for medical practitioners. A year later, he proposed a corollary, "On the Duties of Patients to Their Physicians." Here he urged that patients seek treatment only from trained physicians (preferably one "whose habits of life are perfectly regular"); that the patient describe, in full detail, only what is ailing him, and not go into extraneous factors such as concerns of a business or familial nature; that the patient take, faithfully, only those medications prescribed, never seek a second opinion without first consulting with his primary doctor, nor dismiss his physician without giving reason; and bear in mind that "the last duty which a patient owes to his physician is to remunerate him for his services."[7]

Throughout these years Rush became involved with two institutions for which he retained a lifelong personal favoritism. The first was the College of Physicians of Philadelphia, which came into existence in 1787 under the aegis of Rush's revered mentor, Dr. John Redman, its first president. The "college," of which Rush was one of twelve senior fellows, was in fact a forum that met monthly for an exchange of ideas on matters medical. One of its principal actions was to endorse Rush's call for temperance, praying that laws would be passed to diminish consumption of hard liquors, whose pernicious effects upon the human body could not be overrated. It is of some sartorial interest— which says something for Rush—that the dress at these meetings ranged from the simplicity of its Quaker members to the more fashionable knee breeches, silk stockings, and low-buckled shoes, complemented by many carrying gold-headed canes and snuffboxes into which they dipped with habitual regularity; powdered wigs were beginning to go out of fashion among the younger generation, but many of them still wore their hair in queues. Though he wore the knee breeches, Rush believed that when it came to dress, "The formal and pompous manner, whether accompanied by a wig, a cane, or a ring should be all avoided as incompatible with the simplicity of science and the real dignity of physic."

A year after the college's founding, Rush, ever the social and medical radical, promoted the inauguration of the Philadelphia Dispensary. This institution for the medical relief of the indigent was the first of its kind in the United States. Patients too ill to come to the dispensary could leave their names with the assurance that one of the staff physicians would make a house call. Rush continued to offer his services gratis, to the extent that it reduced the number of his private patients by one fourth; during its first five years alone, the Dispensary treated close to 8,000 patients who doubtless would otherwise have gone without needed medical attention. In a sense, Rush, who "fathered" many innovations and reforms, can be considered the father of the nation's free clinics.[8]

Let us turn back now to the post-Yorktown period. Just as Rush pressed implacably for revisions in a flawed state constitution despite powerful opposition, so did he press implacably against powerful opposition for a cause he passionately believed in: establishing a college in Pennsylvania's backcountry.

Rush believed that for a state to confine its venues of higher education to its capital city was tantamount to saying that young people worthy of a college education were to be found only in the capital. Admittedly, distance posed no problem for students from the outer counties—indeed, from the remotest backwoods—whose families could afford the expense of sending them to and maintaining them in Philadelphia. But must those indigent youngsters who might carry within them the seeds of, say, a physician or a lawyer, be condemned to have those seeds blossom into no more than farmers or laborers? Not that Rush looked down on such means of livelihood. But he did look down on the idea of not permitting anyone to achieve his full potential. In what may be termed a variant on the old adage, If you can't bring Mohammad to the mountain, then bring the mountain to Mohammad, Rush accepted as a moral obligation as well as a future contribution to the state's—and by extension the nation's—intellectual and professional well-being that the opportunity for a college education must be brought to those who would otherwise be denied higher learning.

As earlier indicated, Rush selected as the site Carlisle, some 125 miles west of Philadelphia, just beyond the Susquehanna River in the beautiful Cumberland Valley. Deep in country predominantly Scotch-Irish, it lay beyond the range of the orbit of Princeton, the nation's leading (Presbyterian) school of higher learning, and close enough to the Great Wagon Road, which led southward to the Carolinas, to attract a student body from the predominantly Presbyterian backcountry. Altruistic as Rush's motives were, there was yet another one—equally motivating—that was political in general, religion-oriented in particular. Here can be seen a revival—or was it not merely a continuation?—of the conflict dating back to Rush's childhood between Old Light and New Light Presbyterians.

Rush had long been at odds over matters of education and religion with the Reverend Dr. John Ewing, provost of the University of Pennsylvania and pastor of the First Presbyterian Church (from which Rush had resigned). How better to retaliate for slights, whether real or imagined, against his enemies within the Presbyterian Church, symbolized by Ewing, who wielded great political control in Philadelphia to the exclusion of all other sects, including their own fellow Presbyterians in the backcounty, than to found his own college on the frontier to which would be drawn Presbyterians prepared to combine against the "city Presbyterians" and thereby secure adequate representation in the state's power structure. "Every religious society should endeavor to preserve a representation of itself in government," Rush wrote in a pamphlet he drafted, "Hints for Establishing a College at Carlisle in Cumberland County." To combat the power of the Philadelphia Presbyterians, he argued that the rural Presbyterians increase their strength and influence in the state by opening schools, "the true nurseries of power and influence." Now that the church had managed to take control of the state legislature from the Quakers, the time was opportune to seek a charter from the Assembly for his proposed college. While the student population was to be nonsectarian, the twenty-four man board of trustees he proposed, as well as all officers and faculty members, were to be members of the Presbyterian Church. Only in this way could a direct relationship be maintained between religion and education.

A campaign was launched to fund the obligatory buildings—classroom building, laboratory, library, church, and chapel—and to purchase houses for the principal faculty members. There were to be no dormitories; students were either to live at home or, if from out of the area, to board with local families: "The custom of crowding boys together under one roof is the remains of monkish ignorance. It expressed them to many vices and unfits them for future commerce and connections in the world. Men are made to live in families. They cannot therefore be too early and too constantly preserved in a close connection with them."[9] Rush sought the support of influential Pennsylvanians, mostly "enlightened" Presbyterian ministers, and in the fall of 1782 circularized a petition to the Assembly for a charter. His arguments were rooted in logic, as if hoping that the two mutually antipathetic sects would in no way enter into the equation. Stressed was the distance of Princeton from the homes of many of its Pennsylvania students, and the resultant high cost of transportation and room and board for their families. Also to be considered was the disadvantage of the college in Philadelphia given its location in a city that was not only prohibitively expensive for potential students from indigenous rural families but, being a metropolis, with all the unwholesome distractions to be found in such a venue, could well suffuse the more susceptible student with a discreditable moral tone.

The idea's reception was hardly what Rush wanted, but he was not so naïve as to expect otherwise, given Ewing's hostility—a hostility shared by Rush's quondam friend-turned-foe, the politically powerful Philadelphian, Joseph Reed. Taking the lead, Ewing sought to convince the Cumberland County ministers that a new college would divide the Presbyterians and that it was doomed to failure from the outset because it lacked funding. Supporting Ewing was the equally influential John Armstrong, who, though a close friend of Rush's, feared it would not only split the state's Presbyterians, it would weaken the Presbyterian College of New Jersey (Princeton), with which he was closely associated.

In a long, impassioned letter to Armstrong (19 March 1783) "to explain more fully to you the advantages to be derived to the state at large and the Presbyterian society in particular from a nursery of religion and learning on the west side of the river Susquehanna," Rush played what would be in today's parlance "the religion card"—specifically, the Presbyterian religion card. He pointed out that less than half of the present university trustees were Presbyterians (eleven of twenty-four), and Ewing, who had been elected by a single vote, would "probably be the last Presbyterian clergyman that ever will be placed at the board of that institution, should it even continue upon its present footing." Rush was "sorry to say that" since no one religion prevailed at the school, "so no religious principles are inculcated in it." (The fault, however, lay "only in the charter," for he believed all the teachers to be "friends of Christianity and men of pious and moral characters.")

Religion, he contended, was "best supported under the patronage of particular societies. Instead of encouraging bigotry, I believe it prevents it by removing young men from those opportunities of controversy which a variety of sects mixed together are apt to create and which are the certain fuel of bigotry. Religion," he went on, "is necessary to correct the effects of learning. Without religion I believe learning does real mischief to the morals and principles of mankind; a mode of worship is necessary to support religion; and education is the surest way of producing a preference and constant attachment to a mode of worship." Religion "could not long be maintained in the world without forms and the distinctions of sects [that the] "weaknesses of human nature require them." Such distinction was "as necessary in the Christian Church towards the perfection and government of the whole as regiments and brigades are in the army. Some people talk loudly of the increase of liberality and sentiment upon religious subjects since the war, but I suspect that this boasted catholicism [*sic*] arises chiefly from an indifference acquired since the war to religion itself. We only change the names of our vices and follies in different periods of time. Religious bigotry has yielded to political intolerance."

Rush capped his thesis that "colleges are the best schools for divinity," witness New Jersey's Princeton. What with the emigration of many Pennsylvania Presbyterians, in particular the Scotch-Irish in the western counties, to other states and the great influx of other sects, most notably the Lutheran Germans who not only proliferated in Philadelphia but in the outer counties, e.g., York and Lancaster (where their descendants constitute a strong force both politically and economically to this day), Rush was "pretty certain" that the Presbyterians "do not now compose more than one fourth or fifth part of the inhabitants of the state." Therefore, his proposed new Presbyterian college at Carlisle would "by diffusing the light of science and religion more generally through our society . . . check this spirit of emigration among them [and] teach them to prefer civil, social, and religious advantages, with a small farm and old land to the loss of them all with extensive tracts of woods and a more fertile soil."

To bolster his argument, Rush noted that Carlisle had the support of the Quaker John Dickinson, president of the state, for whom the school was to be named, and the wealthy and politically prominent Philadelphia Episcopalian William Bingham. Moreover, on a more mundane level, property values were sure to increase at Carlisle with the coming of a new college, a point which should not have been lost on Armstrong, a big property owner in the area. Though interested, Armstrong was not prepared to support the school, lest it prove competitive with his beloved Princeton. Rush invited Armstrong to become one of the trustees. With a now enthusiastic Armstrong aboard, the Carlisle presbytery formally approved the plan for the college, chose a twenty-four-man board of trustees, and arranged to petition the Assembly for a charter at its fall session.

However, the state synod, meeting in Philadelphia, opposed the project. Not about to give up, Rush suggested that the board of trustees be increased to thirty, to include several Germans, in light of the state's large German population, which would be a good source of funding. In its petition to the assembly, sixty-four signatories stressed the importance of education and the advantageousness of locating the new college at Carlisle, giving its proximity to the new and growing settlements in the northern and western parts of the state.

"The ice is at last broken and leave has been obtained to bring in a bill to found a college at Carlisle," Rush wrote Montgomery (11 September 1783). As anticipated, the Ewing-Reed clique exploited their influence in the assembly to stop the project dead in its tracks. Rush urged the influential Montgomery, "Do come to town [Philadelphia] *immediately*. We suffer daily from the want of your advice and *passionate honesty....* Everything hangs upon the next *two weeks....* Do set off the same day after you get this letter. We have not a moment to lose."

Both Ewing's efforts and Rush's fears went for naught. On 9 September 1783, the state legislature passed An Act for the Establishment of a College at the Borough of Carlisle, in the County of Cumberland, in the State of Pennsylvania, to be named in honor of President Dickinson, "for the education of youth in the learned and foreign languages, the useful arts, sciences and literature." The school's management was to be by a board of trustees not to exceed forty in number (one was, of course, Rush) of whom more than a third of the original trustees were clergymen, with the stipulation that "persons of every religious denomination among Christians shall be capable of being elected trustees." The most pressing problems—raising of funds and the academic organization and appointments—consumed more of Rush's time than his medical practice through the rest of 1783.

Though the war had created a small class of newly rich that seemed a logical source to tap, this was more than offset by inflation and worthless paper currency, in tandem with high prices, all of which posed a formidable if not impossible obstacle. In the words of historian Nathan Goodman, "The task Rush and his fellow trustees took up was, on the face of it, a hopeless one.... There seems to have been no high-powered executive director for this campaign, but Rush was easily its life and spirit." Without neglecting his private practice, his family, his sizable correspondence, and writings for publication, and his ongoing concerns about Pennsylvania's constitution and its position on the forthcoming convention to write a federal constitution, Rush worked diligently—one could say obsessively—to raise funds for launching the new college "He buttonholed his wealthy friends in Philadelphia, wrote to prospects throughout the state, and lost no opportunity to land a chance pledge."[10]

It was the archetypical uphill battle, exacerbated by the Pennsylvania Assembly's unwillingness, inhibited by a depressed state treasury, to vote much needed financial support that would be effective not only in and of itself, but would quite possibly catalyze pledges in the private sector. But uphill battles were the kind that brought out the best in Rush. His pleas to the Assembly through individual members at last paid off when on 7 April 1786 it appropriated £500 and ten thousand acres of land. "I have great pleasure in informing you," wrote an exultant Rush to Dickinson (5 April 1787), "that your College is in a very flourishing condition. Pupils are coming and expected in great numbers from Maryland, Virginia, and even North Carolina. Twenty young men will graduate there in May.... Thus, sir, after all our difficulties and disappointments, heaven has crowned our labors and wishes with success." In fact, the college was a long way from being "in a very flourishing condition."

What with money being as tight as the Assembly's purse strings—which were loosened, but only occasionally and only to a degree over the ensuing years—the college met with a multitude of vicissitudes that included a forced five-year closure in 1816. Reorganization was made possible with a substantial appropriation from the Assembly. After prospering for another decade, troubles over administration—a chronic issue—rose anew. But though by then in his grave, the labor in which Rush never ceased proved ultimately to have endowed Carlisle with a capability for survival that obtains to this day as a highly respected small college of twenty-two hundred students offering courses in the liberal arts and sciences.

Getting Dickinson College off the ground was hardly the alpha and omega of Rush's promotion of education. With the independence of America guaranteed, he believed in training the nation's leaders, instead of leaving their selection to the people basing their choice on any one of a number of slapdash factors, or combinations thereof, that is the custom to this day—party affiliation, personal prejudices, willingness to be seduced by false promises, and the like. Toward that end, he urged that Congress found a "federal university," in which "let every thing connected with government, such as history—the law of nature and nations—the civil law—the municipal laws of our country—and the principles of commerce, be taught by competent professors." To here should come young men, upon completion of their "academical studies in the colleges of their respective states." Not only would these young men be further schooled in political science, the law, and commerce, but also in "everything connected with defensive and offensive war," along with "the principles and practice of agriculture and manufactures of all kinds." Moreover, "The honors and offices of the United States should, after a while, be confined to persons who had imbibed federal and republican ideas in this university."

Benjamin Rush "conceived of republican education as a process of social evolution. His importance as a political thinker lies in the fact that he was the first to spell out this idea."[11] Ancillary to this thinking was his view of education as more than a means of fostering a literate nation, in particular one that, like his own, was still in its metaphorical swaddling cloths. Only through a proliferation of colleges and universities, Rush believed, could a nation comprised of disparate national and ethnic groups achieve the cohesion necessary to ensure not only America's stability but its growth and endurance.

Rush was hardly a man free of prejudices, in particular when it came to his attitudes toward religious education: "It has been found by experience that harmony and Christian friendship between the different religious societies is best promoted by their educating their youth in separate schools. Besides, this practice is more favorable to the religious instruction of youth, as catechisms and forms of worship are more readily introduced into schools where all the children are of one sect than where they are of different religious denominations."[12]

Out of his belief in schools of higher learning as a medium for unifying the nation came the campaign Rush began in 1785 to establish a college for the educating of German youth. It was not a case of rushing about trying to get colleges started to accommodate every American ethnic group (though it's not unreasonable to assume he might well have entertained such an idea, were it even remotely practicable). Though Rush found the Pennsylvanian Germans a bit too materialistic for his taste, there was much about them he found admirable, notably their predilection for eschewing infighting and discord, their obses-

sion with cleanliness both personally and in their homes, their punc-
tuality and sense of responsibility in conducting business, their love of
music, their custom of training their children from an early age in the
habits of hard work, and, something which sat particularly well with
Rush, their avoiding hard liquors in favor of beer, wine, and cider.

But advocating that this particular group be given its own college
was rooted in a commingling of social fairness and political practical-
ity. As he pointed out when presenting the idea to the public in an
essay published in the 31 August 1785 issue of the *Pennsylvania
Gazette*, the Germans, who made up nearly a third of the state's population, "fill the treasury with their taxes, and their blood was shed
liberally" in the recent war for independence, yet few of their sons
were in "the learned professions, or possess office in the state."
Instead, they were "at the mercy of the lawyers of other societies, and
of the quacks" of their own community, often losing their estates
"from the ignorance of the laws of their country, in making their wills
and in buying and selling property."

Did they not, Rush asked rhetorically, "often sacrifice their lives by
trusting in men who pretend to inspiration in physic but who are
without principle or education?" Had they, predominantly Lutherans.
"not often been misled by demagogues of other nations" such as the
Scotch-Irish majority, and religious "societies," e.g., Roman Catholicism and the other major Protestant groups such as Presbyterians and
Episcopalians? "All this is entirely owing to their want of learning,
which would defend them from mistakes, deceptions, and abuses in
law, physic, and in government."

Rush knocked down the arguments he anticipated from the Scotch-
Irish majority against such a scheme: Having a college of their own
"will be the means of keeping up their [German] *language* in our
country," and therefore their sons should be sent to the English colleges in Philadelphia and Carlisle; a German college would "tend to
render the Germans a distinct people from the other citizens of the
state"; and it would "lessen the cultivation of the state by converting
some of our best farmers into scholars."

Argued Rush: by teaching and learning in their own language, they
would sooner acquire a knowledge of the English language. A thirst
for learning excited by German books would naturally lead them to
study the English language for the sake of becoming acquainted with

English authors "who abound with knowledge in all arts and sciences." Besides, when the students realize that a command of English is a sine qua non for advancement in the professions, they would eagerly learn "to speak and write it with force and elegance." (Here Rush takes it "for granted" that one of the first faculty appointments would be "a professor of the English language.") As for the argument that a German college would "tend to render the Germans a distinct people from the other citizens of the state," he said it was "*ignorance and prejudice* only" that separated men of different countries and religions, and that a German college, "by removing *these*, will prepare the way for the Germans to unite more intimately with their British and Irish fellow citizens and thus to form with them one homogeneous mass of people." As for the fear that a German college would lessen the state's capacity for cultivation "by converting some of our best farmers into scholars," Rush argued that the state's agriculture "will always keep pace with our improvements in arts and sciences."

Convinced, in a burst of lyrical anticipation, that, with his proposed college, "the different religious sects, like the different strings in a musical instrument, shall compose a harmony delightful in the ears of Heaven itself!" thanks to the "churches, courts of justice, and seminaries of learning" being "filled with men who have been educated in the principles of religion and liberty in our American colleges!" the author eagerly anticipates the day when descendants of the original British and Irish colonials would "come from the east and from the west and meet their German fellow citizens on the *same footing* in the councils of the state! And when religion without superstition, learning without pedantry, and liberty without licentiousness shall blend their rays together and enlighten every corner of the land!" Rush signed the essay "A Friend to Equal Liberty and Learning in Pennsylvania." Two years later, thanks in great measure to Rush's initiative and the kind of effort he put into starting Dickinson College, Franklin College (today Franklin and Marshall), of which Rush was a charter trustee, was established at Lancaster.

Rush's educational innovations extended beyond founding colleges. He came out in favor of free tax-supported schools for indigent children. Here, however, he revealed what could easily be interpreted today as a narrow-mindedness bordering on bigotry, but in fact was no more than a reflection of his strongly held religiosity. Believing that one's morals are more consequential than one's health or even one's life, and that the paramount prerequisite for achieving untainted morality is religion, he went one step beyond insisting that to ignore religion in education was an abomination. He recommended most strongly sectarian supervision of public schools, and recommended further that the religion be that of the New Testament, on the grounds that "A Christian cannot fail of being a republican"—that is, an upright citizen of the American republic. In Rush's defense, it must be admitted that he was free of bias and intolerance when it came to people whose origins were alien to his own. Though an ardent Christian, he held to the highest values of Judaeo-Christian ethics. As revealed in various of his correspondence and writings, he was sympathetic to and respectful of the Indians, and he came away from the few occasions in which he was exposed to observers of Orthodox Judaism with not only an interest in their ways but an admiration as well.[13]

Though there were already a number of free, nonsectarian schools in New England—Connecticut alone had six hundred—the parochial view of education, dating back to prewar colonial days, prevailed throughout Pennsylvania as well the rest of the country. Rush's strong sectarianism in this regard can be seen as no more than his conforming to the philosophy of his times. On other suggestions, he was rather progressive. He advocated that less emphasis be put on the study of Greek and Latin and that the study of English could not be overly stressed. He called for the inclusion of athletics in the curriculum, on the grounds that it would not only relieve the tedium of academic study but would be most advantageous to the health and strength of the human body. He favored the inclusion of music and dancing. But he favored the exclusion of the then established practice of corporal punishment (primarily by use of the rod) for recalcitrant students. To Rush, this represented a form of tyranny—though he considered this was acceptable when it came to preschool children below the age of four or five. Like religion, he believed that a child whose proper deportment was inculcated would carry over his conditioning into adulthood.

Rush was among the earliest and most outspoken of what today we refer to as "feminists." Eager to see the removal of "the present immense disparity which subsists between the sexes, in the degrees of their education and knowledge," he insisted that it was no more than "the prejudice of little minds" that the idea of improving the female mind by giving them parity with male minds was "considered by some men as unfriendly to the domestic character of a woman." He was "confident that the cultivation of reason in women would contribute both to the private and to public happiness. In fact, he believed that education alone, for all citizens, could save mankind."[14]

Perhaps nowhere was Rush more zealous when educating his future doctors (as well as his medical colleagues!) than in calling for "An inquiry into the influence of physical causes upon the moral faculty."[15] Moral faculty Rush defined as "a capacity in the human mind of distinguishing and choosing good and evil, or, in other words, virtue and vice. It is a native [i.e., innate] principle, and though it be capable of improvement by experience and reflection, it is not derived from either of them." Considering "virtue and vice to consist in *action*, and not in opinion, and as this action has its seat in the *will*, and not in the conscience," he hypothesized that this moral faculty, and therefore man's behavior, being dependent upon the integrity of memory, imagination, and judgment ("The state of the moral faculty is visible in actions, which affect the well-being of society"), can be affected by various mental and physical conditions, such as climate and diet. Not only madness, he concludes, but also hysteria and hypochondriasis can dispose one to vice. However, "it is in vain to attack these vices with lectures upon morality. They are only to be cured by medicine."

Here we see Rush, ever the man in advance of his time, moving toward the postulates that made him the recognized Father of American Psychiatry. As will be dealt with further along in this narrative, he insisted on treating a *mental* illness as one would treat a *physical* illness, instead of confining the patient as one would lock away a sociopathic menace to society. Rush's concern with man's moral faculty informed his hostility toward excessive punishment in the belief that public chastisement, especially for what we today call noncapital crimes, only increased the miscreant's inclination to commit more crimes: "A man who has lost his character at a whipping post, has nothing valuable to lose in society."

Moving toward earning yet another title, Father of Penological Reform, "Rush opposed all jails, proposing instead "houses of repentance," where moderate punishment ("just and private") and useful work under hygienic conditions might well turn the prisoner around. Of all Rush's theories relating to the "moral faculty," on one he would brook no argument: his inalterable opposition to the death penalty no matter how heinous the crime.

Before leaving this admittedly superficial survey of the writings by which he established himself as much a philosopher as a prophet whose writings command to this day (or, at any rate, *should*) the attention of serious thinkers, let us note that Rush also considered true for nations what he considered true for individuals, as in the following remarkably astute assertion: "Should the same industry and ingenuity, which have produced these triumphs of medicine over diseases and death, be applied to the moral science, it is highly probable that most of those baneful vices, which deform the human breast, and convulse the nations of the earth, might be banished from the world."

The assertion—one dare hardly call it a prediction—has yet to be proved. The best that can be said is that, as Dr. Carl Binger so fittingly put it, man is still laboring for fulfillment of "this sovereign remedy for man's cosmic ills, as Rush did, with hope and perseverance."[16]

17

Back in the Political Arena

Rush's interest in public affairs, which had lain largely quiescent in the post-Yorktown period, was stimulated anew in the spring of 1786 by the forthcoming Annapolis Convention. The Virginia legislature sent out a call for the thirteen states to meet in Annapolis, Maryland, "for the sole purpose of agreeing upon certain commercial regulations and of suggesting such alterations in the [Articles of] Confederation as will give more extensive and coercive powers to Congress." Rush wrote to his London friend and resolute American sympathizer, Richard Price (25 May 1786), "We entertain the most flattering hopes from this Convention, especially as an opinion seems to have pervaded all classes of people that an increase of power in Congress is absolutely necessary for our safety and independence."

Rush contributed his considerable journalistic aptitude to publicizing the convention with *An Address to the People of the United States* in which he deplored the defects of the Confederation. The Annapolis Convention did not meet until 14 September due to a number of factors. These included the demand by northern merchants who indeed wanted national regulation of commerce but felt that the convention leaders were aristocrats more interested in politics than commerce; and the insistence by some state legislatures that Congress, and not the Annapolis Convention, was the proper body to propose measures for strengthening the Confederation. (In fact, Congress was at the time preparing sweeping amendments to the Articles.)

The essay, which Rush probably wrote in the preceding May while recovering from "a fever," opens with what is considered his most famous statement on the Revolution:

There is nothing more common than to confound the terms of American Revolution with those of the late American war. The American war is over; but this is far from being the case with the American revolution. On the contrary, nothing but the first act of the great drama is closed. It remains yet to establish and perfect our new forms of government, and to prepare the principles, morals, and manners of our citizens for these forms of government after they are established and brought to perfection.

Rush wanted the convention to concern itself with more than Congress's authority over trade.. Heading his list was a recommendation that each state cede to Congress its power to create "a uniform currency [that] will facilitate trade and help bind the states together," instead of continuing the practice of each state printing its own money; an end to annual elections, a practice he had supported at the beginning of the war but now dismissed as irrational as it would be "to dismiss a general, a physician, or even a domestic [servant] as soon as they have acquired knowledge sufficient to be useful to us"; and, a particular concern, the substitution, for a single national legislature, then currently existing, of a bicameral one. There then followed a laundry list of other ways to mitigate the defects of the Articles, including one that the president be chosen annually by the proposed both houses (one, the Council of States, comprised of one representative from each state, the other, the Assembly of States, comprised of several delegates from each state). The president would "possess certain powers, in conjunction with a Privy Council, especially the power of appointing most of the officers of the United States."

Next, Rush turned from recommending remedies for the Articles to establishing the character of the American people along republican lines.

We have changed our forms of government but it remains yet to effect a revolution in our principles, opinions, and manners so as to accommodate them to the forms of government we have adopted. This is the most difficult part of the business of the patriots and legislatures of our country. It requires more wisdom and fortitude than to expel or to reduce armies into captivity.

Toward that end ("Call upon the rulers of our country to lay the foundations of their empire in *knowledge* as well as virtue") Rush urged that we "have colleges in each of the states, and one federal university under the patronage of Congress, where the youth of all the states may be melted [*sic*] (as it were) together into one mass of citizens after they have acquired the first principles of knowledge in the colleges of their respective states." In this federal university "the law of nature and nations, the common law of our country, the different systems of government, history, and everything else connected with the advancement of republican knowledge and principles, should be taught by able professors." Rush felt that this "plan of general education alone [would] render the American Revolution a blessing to mankind."

Rush concluded with a reproof for those who believed that Americans "are not proper materials for republican governments." The new nation was "traveling peaceable into order and good government," he wrote, unaware that Shays's Rebellion—an uprising of mostly poor Massachusetts farmers threatened with loss of their property and imprisonment for debt—was a few months in the offing.[1] "They know no strife but [that which] arises from the collision of opinion; and in three years they have advanced farther in the road to stability and happiness than most of the nations in Europe have done in as many centuries." To those Americans who since the war had abandoned politics he pleaded that they once more become involved: "Your country demands your services! . . . Hear her proclaiming, in sighs and groans, in her governments, in her finances, in her trade, in her manufactures, in her morals, and in her manners, 'The Revolution is not over!' "

Only five of the thirteen states—Virginia, New York, Pennsylvania, New Jersey, and Delaware—sent delegations to Annapolis. After three days, they managed to agree on one point: A second convention to address a general change in the Articles of Confederation was called for May of 1787 at Philadelphia. This was the convention that would replace the Articles with what was to become the Constitution of the United States.

In publishing his "Address to the People" Rush failed to update it to include Shays's Rebellion, which had yet to run its course. Whatever his reaction to the rebellion, he told Price (27 October 1786) that the "commotions in New England have happily subsided without the loss of a life or the effusion of one drop of kindred blood." In fact, the rebellion would not be put down without bloodshed. He admitted to having heard proposals to break up the Confederation ("secretly proposed") into three confederacies—Eastern, Middle, and Southern—"to be united by nature, by interest, and by manners, and consequently they will be safe, agreeable and durable." This was all, of course, "at present a mere speculation. Perhaps necessity, or rather divine providence, may drive us to it."

But whatever "form of political existence" lay ahead for the new nation, Rush was "fully satisfied that our independence rests upon a firm basis and that Great Britain will never recover from any of our changes in opinion or government her former dominion or influence in this country." He hoped that Price would spread the word, lest some of his more influential fellow countrymen conveniently overlook the problems Parliament was having, such as "the present distractions in Ireland"—distractions that remain to this day—and to "convince them that stability, contentment, and perfect order are no more the off-springs of monarchical than of republican forms of government."

Let it never be forgotten, he urged Price—and, by extension, all who believed the American Revolution would result not in the rise of America but in its inevitable fall—in what would go down inarguably as Benjamin Rush's most famous remark: "The kingdoms of Europe have traveled into their present state of boasted tranquility through seas of blood. The republics [sic] of America are traveling into order and wise government only through a sea of blunders."

While waiting for the delegates to gather for the Constitutional Convention, Rush devoted much of his energies—and writing—to matters other than continental politics. In an essay "To the Citizens of Philadelphia: A Plan for Free Schools," published in the 28 March 1787 edition of the Philadelphia *Independent Gazette*, he insisted that public schools be open to all children, regardless of social or religious background, subject to the following conditions. Funding was to be achieved through a legal property assessment for the rent of schoolhouses, payment of schoolmasters, "and other expenses connected with this undertaking," and a tax on products to support the schools in perpetuity. The children to be taught to read and write English "and (when required by their parents) the German language." The girls to be instructed in needlework, knitting, and spinning, as well as in the academic subjects along with the boys. Above all, both sexes were to be "carefully instructed in the principles and obligations of the Christian religion."

This was to Rush "the most essential part of education" as it would "make them dutiful children, teachable scholars, and, afterwards, good apprentices, good husbands, good wives, honest mechanics, industrious farmers, peaceable sailors, and, in everything that relates to this country, good citizens." To effect this "important purpose" it would be necessary "that the children of parents of the same religious denomination should be educated together in order that they may be instructed with the more ease in the principles and forms of their respective churches. By these means the schools will come more immediately under the inspection of the ministers of the city, and thereby religion and learning be more intimately connected."

Rush's plan, which was doomed to modification with ratification of the as-yet-to-be-written Constitution with its mandated separation of church and state, was, in its overall purpose, laudable. "Citizens of Philadelphia," he concluded the essay in what was nothing less than a clarion call,

> awaken at last to check the vice which taints the atmosphere of our city. The profane and indecent language which assaults our ears in every street can only be restrained by extending education to the children of poor people. The present is an era of public spirit—the Dispensary and the Humane Society [for both of which, it should be remembered, Rush was the primary mover] will be lasting monuments of the humanity of the *present* citizens of Philadelphia. But let not the health and lives of the poor exhaust the whole stock of our benevolence. Their morals are of more consequence to society than their health or lives, and their minds must exist forever. "Blessed is he that considereth the poor, the Lord will deliver him in time of trouble. The Lord will preserve him, and keep him alive upon the earth—he will not deliver him into the will of his enemies."[2]

On 9 March, in the home of Benjamin Franklin, who had returned from his years as colonial agent in Europe and was now the elected president of Pennsylvania, Rush read before a meeting of the Society for Promoting Political Enquiries his essay that would mark his emergence as the father of penal reform, "An Enquiry into the Effects of Public Punishment upon Criminals, and upon Society."[3]

In the following month, Rush, whose views on slavery had won him a good name among those, not only in Pennsylvania but throughout New England, who favored manumission, again became news when, largely through his efforts, the Pennsylvania Society for Promoting the Abolition of Slavery and the Relief of Free Negroes Unlawfully Held in Bondage, organized in 1774, was reconstituted and enlarged. Rush was one of the secretaries of the new society (1787–1789) and served as a delegate to the early national conventions of abolition societies (1791–1798), of which he became president in 1803. In forwarding a copy of the essay to his London friend and fellow laborer in the field of penal and other reforms, John Coakley Lettsom (18 May 1787), Rush added, with misplaced confidence, "We expect to petition our Convention next week to make the suppression of the African trade in the United States an essential article of the new Confederation." But abolition became one of those issues that the framers of the Constitution, unable to achieve an acceptable consensus, decided to defer, in hopes that the problem would be resolved in due time. That due time became, of course, the Thirteenth Amendment, for which a Civil War had to be fought seventy-five years later.

Rush now directed his attention back to national politics with the opening of the Constitutional Convention (May to September 1787). Though he had quite a lot to say about it, in public letters and private correspondence with interested friends in London, he played no part in the deliberations, the purpose of which was originally intended to amend the Articles of Confederation, but which quickly became transmogrified into the writing of a new charter. Rush would, though, play a major role in Pennsylvania's ratifying convention, to which he was named a delegate. (After the delegates present signed the Constitution, it was sent to the states for ratification, with the provision that it become operative upon acceptance by nine states; this was achieved in June 1788 when New Hampshire became the ninth state.)

Rush was eminently pleased, by and large, with Pennsylvania's eight-man delegation, of which the first among equals was his idol, Benjamin Franklin. It contained in addition two good friends—

George Clymer and Thomas Fitzsimons—and two politicians for whom he had the highest regard and respect—James Wilson and Robert Morris. Fleshing out the delegation were two Constitutionalists Rush had befriended despite their politics, Thomas Mifflin (destined to be the state's first governor) and James Ingersoll—and Gouverneur Morris, a New Yorker temporarily living in Philadelphia, who turned Rush off with his cynicism, womanizing (Morris was a bachelor), and reputation as a man of suspected loose morals. The important thing is that six of the eight—a comfortable majority—were determined nationalists whom Rush was confident would work for what he wanted most to come out of the convention: a strong central government.

Among the arriving delegates were friends from the days of the First and Second Continental Congresses, notably John Dickinson (representing Delaware, where he now resided). Elbridge Gerry again representing Massachusetts, and Roger Sherman again representing Connecticut. Absent, to Rush's disappointment, were such of his old allies as John Adams and Thomas Jefferson, now serving as American ministers to, respectively, England and France; Samuel Adams and John Hancock, and Virginia's Richard Henry Lee and Patrick Henry, all four of whom decided to stay home for various reasons. (Henry's refusal to attend was based on the contention that he "smelt a rat").4

Rush socialized with the delegates to the extent of entertaining many of them in his home during those epic five months, when he could tear himself away from his responsibilities as physician and educator. He got to know some of the younger ones like James Madison (Jefferson's brilliant disciple, who was to emerge as one of the major constructors of the Constitution) and Alexander Hamilton (Washington's brilliant disciple, who was to emerge as Jefferson's foremost bête noire).

As the delegates were gathering, Rush helped a group of like-minded friends that petitioned them to "make the suppression of the African slave trade in the United States an essential article of the new confederation" (the fate of which petition has been described above). At his instigation, John Adams's intricate, rather verbose yet persuasive three-volume justification for bicameralism and a strong chief executive—*Defense of the Constitution of Government of the United States of America*—was published at Philadelphia so that the delegates could hear Adams's views on what would prove to be one of the most contentious issues of the convention: "Mr. Adams has diffused such excellent principles among us that there is little doubt of our adopting a vigorous and compounded legislature"—which in fact proved to be the case. "Our illustrious [envoy to the mother country] in this gift to his country has done us more service than if he had obtained alliances for us with all the nations in Europe."[5]

Even before the necessary quorum was effected and the delegates could get to work, Rush published a few articles in the press praising them for the task they were about to undertake and promoting Washington and Adams for president and vice president respectively: "I *first* pointed the public attention to him as the future President of the United States in several of our newspapers while the Convention was sitting which framed the Constitution, at the same time that I mentioned your name as Vice-President," he wrote Adams years later. Their differences long since forgotten, Rush entertained Washington a few times in his home during that convention summer, and the future president agreed to study several of his host's pamphlets on education.[6]

Once the convention got under way, Rush was kept abreast of the secret proceedings, and was quite encouraged. He reported to Richard Price (2 June 1787) that Benjamin Franklin considered it "the most august and respectable assembly he ever was in his life, and adds that he thinks they will soon finish their business, as there are no prejudices to oppose nor errors to refute in any of the body." Dickinson had informed him "that they are all *united* in their objects, and he expects they will be equally united in the means of attaining them."

Rush left the city to attend a convocation at Franklin College, encouraged by the way events were progressing in the State House, quite unaware that all was not as well as reported, and, furthermore, that he was in a sense being "used" by his two friends. Their glowing confidence notwithstanding, the convention, now only in its second week, was in fact rampant with disagreement, and some members actually feared its collapse. Happy in his ignorance of the facts, Rush told Price in his 2 June letter that should word get around London "of our new system of government meeting with some opposition" and of "little characters" who "will excite factions among us," they would "be of a temporary duration," they would be brought down by "time, necessity, and the gradual operation of reason." Should these factors fail, "*force* will not be wanting to carry [the organization of a new and viable government] into execution, for not only all the wealth but all the military men of our country . . . are in favor of a wise and efficient government." Hypothesizing philosophically that "The order of nature is the same in the political as it is in the natural world—good is derived chiefly from evil," Rush wanted it known that

> We are traveling fast into order and national happiness. The same enthusiasm *now* pervades all classes in favor of *government* that actuated us in favor of *liberty* in the years 1774 and 1775, with this difference, that we are more *united* in the former than we were in the latter pursuit. When our enemies triumph in our mistakes and follies, tell them that we are *men,* that we walk upon two legs, that we possess reason, passions, and senses, and that under these circumstances it is as absurd to expect the ordinary times of the rising and the setting of the sun will be altered as to suppose we shall not *finally* compose and *adopt* a suitable form of government and be happy in the blessings which are usually connected with it.

An overly confident Rush spent the month of August visiting with Julia and the children at Morven, where they spent the summers, tending to his medical practice, and refining his ideas on prison reform, abolition, compulsory education, and the numerous other advances with which his name and labors are known only to historians of the period.

Meanwhile, the supporters of Pennsylvania's constitution were working to destabilize, if not destroy entirely, the efforts of the convention delegates. The efforts of these "little characters," which Rush described with such contempt in his letter to Price, to "excite factions among us," soon brought Rush back into the center of the political action, where he secretly longed to be. John Dickinson, seeing in him the ideal candidate, asked Rush to "come forward in support of the proposed Constitution of the United States"—which is to say, to lead what amounted to a public relations campaign to promote public opinion in favor of the convention's work. "I had heard enough of its forms and principles to be satisfied with it, and readily obeyed the call of my friend by recommending and defending it in a number of addresses to the citizens of the United States."[7]

The "addresses," a slew of which began appearing in the press, were all written pseudonymously and have never been collected or definitely identified. Not so the letters to his friends, all of which dealt with the new national government, a few of which he used to knock the Reverend Ewing and the Pennsylvania state constitution, both of which took pride of place on Rush's hit list, e.g.,

> Keep a *good heart,* and put a *bold face* upon things. *All will end well.* The new federal government like a new continental wagon will overset our state dung cart with all its dirty contents (reverend [Ewing] and irreverent) and thereby restore order and happiness to Pennsylvania. From the conversation of the members of the Convention, there is reason to believe the federal Constitution will be wise, vigorous, safe, free, and full of dignity. General Washington, it is said, will be placed at the head of the new government, or in the style of my simile, will drive our new wagon.[8]

On 28 September, eleven days after the Federal Convention completed its work and prepared to submit the new constitution to the states for ratification, Rush reported to one of his favorite London correspondents, John Coakley Lettsom, of his pleasure on the progress of some of his major reforms. Influenced by the prison society he had helped organize and that had put him in the vanguard of penal reform, "a reformation has lately taken place in the jail of this city in favor not only of humanity but of virtue in general." While it was "impossible as yet to tell the extent of that *good* which may be effected by such societies," of one thing he was certain: "men grow *good* by attempting it. A prison sometimes supplies the place of a church and out-preaches the preacher in conveying useful instruction to the heart."

Rush also lauded Lettsom's efforts in uniting, in England, with his in America, efforts to abolish slavery, going so far as to predict—prematurely, as events would play out—that by 1808 there would be an end of "the African trade" in America. To the "influence of Pennsylvania chiefly is to be ascribed the prevalence of sentiments favorable to African liberty in every part of the United States," Rush boasted, an influence owing in large measure to the Quakers and Methodists. (Rush somewhat naïvely explains away the Constitutional Convention's failure to tackle the slavery issue head-on: "No mention was made of *Negroes* or *slaves* in [the] Constitution only because it was thought the very words would contaminate the glorious fabric of American liberty and government." Translation: Since manumission was soon to "descend in plentiful dews and at last [cover] every part of the land," or so he believed, making it a constitutional issue would be unnecessary.)

Next, Rush went on to advise Lettsom of his latest writings, which would be forwarded, on a number of topics: observations on the cause and cure of tetanus, "Free Thoughts on Pulmonary Consumptions, " "An Account of the Effects of the Late American Revolution upon the Human Body, "a small tract upon female education" ("I shall have no objections, if you approve of it, to its being reprinted in one of your magazines"); his ongoing work in the field of mental health ("I have lately obtained the exclusive care of the [thirty-four] maniacal patients in the hospital"); and his expectations that the punitive treatment of criminals in Pennsylvania would "probably be repealed" and would, he hoped, "pave the way for the adoption of *solitude* and *labor* as the means of not only punishing but of reforming criminals."

Having thus updated Lettsom on matters of mutual concern, Rush concluded exuberantly with news he knew the pro-American Lettsom would appreciate:

> Our new federal government is very acceptable to a great majority of our citizens and will certainly be adopted immediately by [the mandatory] *nine* and in the course of a year or 18 months by *all* the States. When this shall happen, *then* to be a citizen of the United States *with all its consequences* will be to be a citizen of the freest, purest, and happiest government upon the face of the earth. It contains all the theoretical and practical advantages of the British Constitution without any of its defects or corruptions. While the nations of Europe have waded into order through seas of *blood,* you see we have traveled peaceably into order only through seas of *blunders.*[9]

Nineteen delegates to the Pennsylvania Assembly sought to throw a roadblock in the path of ratifying the new constitution by preventing a quorum necessary to attend a legislative session called to decide when the process would commence. The Republicans, beginning to call themselves Federalists, resolved the dilemma by going directly to the people.* On the afternoon of 29 September a mob forcibly carried two of the recalcitrant truants into the chamber, thus establishing a quorum, and the Assembly voted to open the ratifying convention on 21 November.

Now began the war of words in the press, a war in which Rush joined James Wilson, one of the framers of the Constitution and like Rush a master orator, especially when it came to attacking the Antifederalists (or as they soon became known, the Antifeds). To both sides the struggle was seen as decisive in determining the success or failure of the Constitution nationwide, given Pennsylvania's size, wealth, and the political cachet of being the nation's capital. To paraphrase a modern cliché of politics, it was seen as a sort of "As Pennsylvania goes, so goes the nation." (In fact, much to Rush's disappointment, Pennsylvania would not be the first state to ratify—that honor would go to tiny Delaware—but was third, after New Jersey.)

It began in the first week of October, when Wilson and Rush addressed a large gathering of citizens who came to the State House "to fix on a ticket of representation" for the upcoming legislative election. The outcome would decide whether the state was going to even consider ratification of the Constitution or allow it to expire by default. Of course, as even both sides realized, ratification could be achieved by only nine of the thirteen states, and perhaps Pennsylvania's influence on the outcome was being overplayed. Still, Pennsylvania's failure to support the charter could redound nationwide disadvantageously.

The Federalists were taking no chances. Speaking in favor of the failure of the framers to include a bill of rights, on the grounds that the proposed rights involved were already inherently guaranteed by the charter, Wilson next defended the proviso, attacked by the Antifederalists, to maintain a standing army, knocked down the argument that the Senate would become the seat of a "baneful aristocracy" since it was restrained on one side by the House of Representatives, on the other by the president; and reduced to ridicule those who opposed

---

*The Federalists were the nation's only political party until the advent of Jefferson and his founding of the two-party system with the Democratic Republicans, which under Andrew Jackson evolved into the Democratic Party as we know it today, and thus the Democrats' cognomen "The Party of Jackson and Jefferson."

granting the new government the power of direct taxation (men he described as "alarmed with visionary evils"). Indeed, he promised, as events would prove, thanks to the fiscal brilliance of Alexander Hamilton, "The state of Pennsylvania particularly, which has encumbered itself with the assumption of a large proportion of the public debt, will derive considerable relief and advantage." As borne out by Hamilton's so-called assumption program, Wilson prophesied correctly that the state would be "discharged from an extraordinary burden, and the national creditor will find it to be his interest to return to his original security."

Warning that those who opposed the Constitution were doing so from self-interest—the new government would "necessarily turn the stream of influence and emolument into a new channel," and those who gained power from the current state governments "will object to the proposed innovation; not, in truth, because it is injurious to the liberties of his country, but because it affects his schemes of wealth and consequence"—Wilson concluded with an admission. He was not "a blind admirer of the Constitution." There were parts of it that "if my wish had prevailed, would certainly have been altered." But in light of the differences prevalent among the Americans, not the least of which were state and sectional interests, he was "satisfied that anything nearer to perfection could not have been accomplished."

Wilson's speech was thoughtful and analytical. Rush resorted to blatant emotional rhetoric. In the belief that logic must be complemented by passion, Rush, in the words of one observer, spoke "in an elegant and pathetic style" as he described the state's "present calamitous [fiscal] situation, and enumerating the advantages which would flow from the adoption of the new system of federal government." The Constitution, he insisted, would advance the growth of commerce, agriculture, manufacturing, the arts and sciences, and encourage immigration, precipitate the abolition of paper money (a ruination it would take the nation a century to obviate), eradicate party divisions (an evil to Rush which would, even in his own lifetime, prove to be one of the nation's surest guarantees against a dictatorship), and prevent war. Rush's dramatic conclusion: "Were this the last moment of my existence, my dying request and injunction to my fellow citizens would be to accept and support the offered Constitution."[10]

Despite a low voter turnout for the 3 November election of delegates to the ratifying convention, the Federalists led the field. Rush, with 1,200 votes, placed second on the winning ticket. Five days after his return to political life, brief though it would be, Julia brought him even more joy with the birth of their fourth son, William. On 21 November 1787 the sixty-nine delegates convened in Philadelphia. The opening day saw Rush take to the floor with a motion considered trivial by many of the delegates: "[T]hat a committee be appointed to request the attendance of some minister of gospel tomorrow morning in order to open the business of the convention with prayer." When an objection was made on the grounds that it would be "impossible to fix upon a clergyman to suit every man's tenets," and besides, no precedent existed for such action, and even the convention that drew up the Pennsylvania Constitution had managed without an opening prayer, Rush shot back that that was "probably the reason that the state has ever since been distracted by their proceedings."[11]

The first business of the convention was given over to a long oration by James Wilson on "the general principles that have produced the national Constitution," and in a sense it was a sign of things to come: Wilson dominating every discussion until the convention adjourned three weeks later (15 December 1787), and Rush, who spoke often, playing second fiddle to his friend. His first clash came when a backcountry opponent of the Constitution, one William Findley, opined it was the convention's obligation to scrutinize the new "house" that had been erected for the United States, to determine if its parts were "fitting and combining . . . with each other" and reject "everything that is useless and rotten." Rush picked up on his opponent's metaphor:

> That is not our situation. We are not, at this time, called upon to raise the structure. The house is already built for us, and we are only asked whether we choose to occupy it. If we find its apartments commodious, and upon the whole that it is well calculated to shelter us from the inclemencies of the storm that threatens, we shall act prudently by entering it; if otherwise, all that is required of us is to return the key to those who have built and offered it for our use.

Rush was more than answering Findley in kind. The Antifeds had made clear from the outset that they would fight adoption of the charter, by resorting to amendment after amendment. Rush and the Federalists were determined to block any such effort.[12]

He continued the block-amendments strategy on 30 November when he took the floor to respond to his friend Thomas Hartley of York on the absence of a bill of rights. Beginning his argument with the thesis that a balanced government rather than a list of rights was the most efficacious way to preserve one's liberties, Rush continued:

> While the honorable convention who framed this system were employed in their work, there are many gentlemen who can bear testimony that my only anxiety was upon the subject of representation. And when I beheld a legislature constructed of three branches, and in so excellent a manner, either directly or indirectly, elected by the people and amenable to them, I confess, sir, that here I cheerfully posed all my hopes and confidence of safety.

Going on to argue that "our rights are not yet all known," and there should be no attempt to enumerate them, Rush became so carried away by his own rhetoric, he blurted out that he "considered it an honor to the late convention that this system has not been disgraced with a bill of rights. Would it not be absurd to frame a formal declaration that our natural rights are acquired from ourselves?" It was a remark he would never be allowed to forget. In conclusion, he reminded Hartley that the new government was not going to be administered by "strangers to our habits and opinions and unconnected with our interests and prosperity," but by men who shared his eagerness to protect the rights of all Americans.[13]

On 3 December, in response to "an eloquent and powerful speech" by Findley "to prove that the proposed plan of government amounted to a consolidation, and not a confederation, of the states," Rush, speaking with equal eloquence and power, expressed to the delegates his joy in seeing the annihilation of state sovereignty: "This passion for state sovereignty despoiled the union of Greece. A plurality of sovereigns is political idolatry." Expressing delight that with the new constitution Pennsylvania's sovereignty (along with that of all the other states) was ceded to the federal government, he proclaimed: "I have now a vote for members of Congress. I am a citizen of every state." He was now assured "more security for my property" under a strong central government, which he was confident would do much more for all Americans.

He promised, moreover, that the new government would abolish paper money (which had caused such horrendous inflation) and religious tests like the hated Test Oath he so opposed under the Pennsylvania constitution (it was repealed by the Assembly). Commerce would "hold up her declining head under the influence of general, vigorous, uniform regulations [and the] communication of the Mississippi with the Atlantic will be opened under the new Constitution." Moreover, Congress would assume the public debt. And, the crowning glory of it all, there would be "an increase of freedom, knowledge, and religion" throughout the land. Many of the delegates were apprehensive of Rush's seemingly excessive claims for the government that was to be brought into being by the Constitution, an apprehension summed up by one opponent: "I never heard anything so ridiculous."[14]

On Wednesday 12 December, after closing arguments by the two leading opponents of the Constitution, a vote on ratification was called for. Whereupon, in a move that left delegates of both factions convinced that Rush had suddenly fallen victim to terminal logorrhea, and Wilson apoplectic with rage, Rush rose to "solicit the indulgence of the delegates for a few moments"—and held it for close to an hour. There was a collective sigh of relief when he declaimed in peroration, "Nothing short of an unanimous vote can indeed complete my satisfaction. And, permit me to add, were that event to take place, I could not preserve the strict bounds of decorum, but, flying to the other side of the room, cordially embrace every member who has hitherto been in opposition as a brother and a patriot. Let us then, sir, this night bury the hatchet and smoke the calumet of peace!"[15]

Rush may have been eager to fly to the other side of the room to bury the hatchet and smoke the peace pipe with the Antifeds, but all he succeeded in doing was to reopen the debate, thus playing into the hands of those who hoped to forestall ratification in the unrealistic hope that success in that direction might well forestall acceptance of the Constitution. Thus the fury of even his closest brothers in Federalism. Denying vigorously Rush's claim, one of the opposition delegates "regretted that so imperfect a work should have been ascribed to God," and then proceeded to offer a number of petitions calling for a catalog of changes in the document, most notably a bill of rights. As the evening passed into the morning hours, the Federalists managed to have the petitions tabled and a vote on ratification again called for. The convention at last ratified the Constitution on 12 December by a vote of two to one (46 to 23).[16]

The opposition did not accept defeat with grace. Two weeks later, at a celebratory bonfire and much oratory to celebrate the Constitution, a mob of Antifeds armed with clubs attacked James Wilson, knocking him down and beating him mercilessly. An old soldier who threw himself on Wilson's body and took the blows till the attackers could be chased off saved him from death.[17]

Rush's labors were not yet ended. With Wilson and a few others, he formed the core of a committee to urge, through letters and pamphleteering, ratification by the other states, many of which had not yet even convened for that purpose. (Massachusetts scheduled hers for 9 January 1788, Virginia put hers off until May, New York until July, and Rhode Island would not even hold a convention until the other twelve states had made their decision.) During this period Rush suffered personal tragedy—the death of his infant son William from pleurisy during January—and his own near death: "On the 2nd of March I was seized with the same disorder and lay for nine days in such a situation that my recovery is thought the next thing to a miracle. For my own part, I had taken leave of life. I not only settled all my worldly affairs but gave the most minute directions with respect to everything that related to my funeral."[18] In his Commonplace Book for the year 1799 noting the death of William Gruber, "a native African whom I bought [as a slave] and liberated after he had served me 10 years," Rush recalls that the reformed drunkard who "swore frequently" and after a year or two "was reformed from both these vices" and became "a sober, moral man and faithful and affectionate Servant," remained constantly at his side during Rush's brush with death. "William refused to go to bed on the night in which he expected that event would take place," saying, "If massaw die, put me in de grave with him. He be the only friend I got in dis world."[19]

Though the effects of his illness plagued Rush for months, he refused to despair over his weakened constitution and continuing opposition of the Antifeds as the state geared up to draft a new constitution consonant with the federal charter. "The new government," he promised John Montgomery in all confidence (9 April 1788), "*will* be established, nor will its establishment be followed with a civil war anywhere. Then will its enemies become like the enemies and opposers of independence—infamous and contemptible."

With the Constitution now the law of the land, Rush saw the new nation's past as a decade of misery now compensated. Confident that the new charter would "demolish" what he referred to contemptuously as Pennsylvania's "*Balloon Constitution*," he wrote Adams (2 July 1788),

> If it had no other merit, this would be enough with me. But it has a thousand other things to recommend it. It makes us a nation. It rescues us from anarchy and slavery. It revives agriculture and commerce. It checks moral and political iniquity. In a word, it makes man both willing to *live* and to *die*. To *live*, because it opens to him fair prospects of great public and private happiness. To *die*, because it ensures peace, order, safety and prosperity to his children.[20]

Rush did have one reservation, though, as he subsequently wrote Adams (15 June 1789): the wish that "the name of the Supreme Being had been introduced somewhere in the new Constitution. Perhaps an acknowledgement may be made of his goodness or of his providence in the proposed amendments. In all enterprises and parties I believe the *praying* are better allies than the *fighting* past of communities." Doubtless it was well that the framers allowed themselves to be guided less by religion than by reason.

On the Fourth of July, Philadelphia staged America's greatest parade, to celebrate both Independence Day and official acceptance of the Constitution. In a long letter to Elias Boudinot, now living in New Jersey, Rush describes the glorious event in all its detail, concluding with an exultant

> 'Tis done! We have become a nation. America has ceased to be the only power in the world that has derived no benefits from her declaration of independence. We are more than repaid for the distresses

of the war and the disappointments of the peace. The torpid resources of our country already discover sins of life and motion. We are no longer the scoff of our enemies. The reign of violence is over. Justice has descended from heaven to dwell in our land, and ample restitution has at last been made to human nature by our new Constitution for all the injuries she has sustained in the old world from arbitrary government, false religions, and unlawful commerce.[21]

Rush now had two more courses on his political plate: campaigning vigorously for Federalist candidates for the first national Congress, for which he wrote a series of newspaper pieces and personal letters; and campaigning, in the face of obdurate hostility by the Antifeds, for a state constitution modeled along the lines of the federal charter.

From the day the 1776 Pennsylvania Constitution was framed, as required of all states by the Continental Congress, Rush had opposed it primarily because it provided for a unicameral legislature. On 15 September 1789, in response to a demand prompted by a number of circular letters and petitions in the preparation of which he played a paramount role, the Assembly passed a resolution calling for a convention to alter the state constitution. On 24 November, the convention met and, following a series of prolonged meetings and debates, agreed on a two-house legislature and a single executive with veto power, consonant with the federal Constitution. On 2 September 1790, the new Pennsylvania Constitution was proclaimed.

Rush had in the meantime labored with quill in hand for the election of Federalists to the first Congress under the Constitution. He was successful to the extent that the party won not only the Senate races (senators were chosen by the state legislatures until ratification of the Seventeenth Amendment, on 31 May 1913, which provided for direct popular election to the Senate), but, and to Rush even more gratifying, won all eight of Pennsylvania's allotted seats in the House of Representatives.

If there was one disappointing note, it was that his old friend, John Adams, whose candidacy he had advocated and labored for, lost out to Washington as the nation's first president. But even Rush recognized that, regardless of his past feelings about Washington, his election—in fact, selection—was inevitable, as if divinely ordained, and took comfort in Adams attaining the second-highest office in the land. He assumed Adams would succeed Washington. (So, too, did Adams.)

Having, over the previous twenty years, given freely of his time and energy, in addition to sacrificing income, to the fight for American independence and then for her cohesion, Rush could take both satisfaction and pride that, to paraphrase his personal mantra, all *was* well. The United States of America was at long last functioning under a constitution that is inarguably the single greatest governmental charter ever written. Admittedly, it had its flaws, as witness the failure to come to terms with the slavery issue. But the beauty of it all is that the document is organic, and not fixed in concrete, demonstrated by Madison's Bill of Rights and subsequent amendments and the fact that it will always be subject to amendment where necessary.

18

Retirement from Politics

While the Continental Congress was sitting out its last days in New York City awaiting ratification of the Constitution, Rush instigated the drive to make Philadelphia the nation's capital. On 21 February 1789 he wrote John Adams, whose extreme popularity among the Pennsylvania Federalists would play a major role in bringing about his election to the vice presidency, "There is an expectation here . . . that your influence will be exerted immediately in favor of a notion" to center the federal government where the entire process of confederation was started thirteen years previously, "for two reasons *principally:* To silence the clamors, which begin to circulate in some of the southern states, of the interested and local views of the eastern states, and 2ndly to prevent a *few years* hence a removal of the seat of government to a more southern, a less healthy, and less republican state."

A month later, in what was tantamount to an essay, Rush pursued the idea, playing on his fears regarding the safety of the government being centered in New York, where only one-third of the citizens were "honest Federalists," while one-third were Antifederalists, and one-third "American citizens with *British hearts.*" This two-thirds, hence the majority, he warned Adams on 27 March 1789, would "be the principal companions of the new Congress. From the first they will learn to speak of the necessity of amendments in the new government in order to 'quiet the minds of the people,' and from the last they will learn to be very complaisant to all the vices of monarchy and to the corrupt manners of the city of London." Apparently forgetting that he had once called Philadelphia "a seat of corruption," Rush now touted the city as "wholly and *highly* federal," where the new government was not only framed "but received from our citizens the impetus or *offing* [a nautical phrase for being well clear of land] that finally carried it into every port in the United States." Moreover, he added a discerning caveat which, had it been heeded, might have precluded the nation's ultimate capital becoming a southern city: "By *delaying* the removal of Congress to Philadelphia, you will probably be dragged in a few years to the banks of the Potomac, where Negro slaves will be your servants by day, mosquitoes your sentinels by night, and bilious fevers your companions every summer and fall, and pleurisies every spring." Had he been blessed with the prescience of a Jeremiah or a Cassandra, Rush could have added, "and, in effect, a captive of the South for the next seven decades."

When George Washington took the oath of office in New York City on 30 April 1789, Rush neither attended nor had anything to say about it to any of his epistolary correspondents.[1] He did, though, have quite a bit to say to Vice President Adams five weeks later (4 June 1789), continuing to harp on the selection of New York City ("the *sink* of British manners and politics") as the federal capital. His "principal objection" was "the influence which a city contaminated by having been for seven years a garrison town to a corrupted British army must have upon the manners and morals of those men who are to form the character of our country." He feared that already there was a "progress of our government towards monarchy"; and he warned that "The citizens of Pennsylvania are truly republican, and will not readily concur in a government which has begun so soon to ape the corruption of the British court, conveyed to it through the impure channel of the city of New York."

William Maclay, the U.S. Senator from Pennsylvania who was resolute in his antagonism to Federalists in general, and to Adams, the arch-Federalist, in particular, nourished these fears in Rush. Visiting on 14 August to brief him on how the new government was faring, Maclay "observed that half the Senate were lawyers; that he never knew one of them to retract or alter an opinion after the fullest discussion of it, which he ascribed to their habits of contending for victory instead of truth at the Bar. He added further that he had heard [John] Adams say, in private company, 'The more ignorant people are, the more easily they will be governed.'"[2]

Maclay was not the first, and hardly the last, to charge that Adams might not be totally averse to some form of monarchical cast to the new government (as president the pudgy Adams was often referred to derogatorily as His Rotundity). Anxious lest there be a breach in their close friendship on ideological grounds, yet determined to stake out his position, Rush had already told Adams on 4 June 1789, "I find you and I must agree not to disagree, or we must cease to discuss political questions." Then hoping Adams would "never mistake any of my opinions or principles in my future letters," Rush wanted it remembered that he was

> as much a republican as I was in 1775 and 6, that I consider *hereditary* monarchy and aristocracy as rebellion against nature, that I abhor titles and everything that belongs to the *pageantry* of government, that I love the people but would sooner be banished to Iceland . . . than gain their favor by accommodating to one of their unjust popular prejudices, that I feel a respect for my *rulers* bordering upon homage . . . and that I have applied for no office and shall apply for none.

Rush's claim that he had "applied for no office and shall apply for none" was a somewhat pathetic attempt to deal with the failure of the new government to reward him with a government position, more so since so many friends with whom he had worked to hasten the Constitution's ratification now held offices that ranged from the U.S. Senate (Morris and Maclay) to the Supreme Court (Wilson). "There was a time," he admitted to Adams on 24 February 1789, "when I would have accepted an appointment abroad." His "knowledge of several European languages" and acquaintance with many eminent literary figures "would have added frequent opportunities to my disposition to serve my country." He admitted to having "meditated with great pleasure upon the pains I should have taken in such a situation to employ my leisure hours in collecting discoveries in agriculture, manufactures, and in all the useful arts and sciences, and in transmitting them to my American fellow citizens. But the time is past for my accepting of that or any other appointment in the government of the United States."

To hope for a foreign assignment was unrealistic, given the debt-ridden federal government's ability to send abroad no more than a handful of envoys, who perforce had to be men who knew something about diplomacy. Besides, even if Adams had been willing out of friendship to give Rush what he obviously wanted, Washington would have vetoed the idea. Given their past differences, there could be no place for Rush in any government of which George Washington was the chief magistrate.

What Rush saw, with justification, as the insult of being ignored by Washington's government played a part in reducing his commitment to it, and was one of the reasons he began to move away from the Federalists. Committed to republicanism, fearing corruption at the highest levels, and opposing the concept of aristocracy that seemed to permeate the new government, he feared that under Washington "the principles of the Revolution were being plowed under, that out of the battle for a strong central government had come a behemoth controlled by an aggrandizing elite determined to manage the great beast for their own interests."[3] The "behemoth" was not yet a year old, and Rush told Adams he could "already see a system of influence bordering upon corruption established in our country which seems to proclaim to innocence and patriotism to keep their distance." So disgusted with, and indifferent to, national politics had Rush become by news reaching Philadelphia from New York, he doubted he would "give a vote at our next election."

In light of the imminent break in the Adams-Jefferson friendship, mention should be made here that in Rush's letter to Adams cited above, he told Adams of "a conversation that passed between Mr. Jefferson and myself on the 17th of March, of which you were the principle subject.* We both deplored your attachment to monarchy and both agreed that you had changed your principles since the year 1776." Though he didn't mention it to Adams, it was as a result of this meeting that Rush, who had first met Jefferson in 1775 and saw him whenever the latter visited Philadelphia over the intervening years, became a confirmed philosophical Jeffersonian.[4] Despite the rift between Rush and Adams in their respective philosophical approaches to governance—what Rush saw as Adams's defection from what would become known as Jeffersonian republicanism—that rift did not extend to their friendship, which remained immutable.

---

*Jefferson, having returned from France, where he had been U.S. minister, in October, was on his way to New York City to assume the office of Secretary of State.

There now emerged in Rush's letters—to Adams and to others—a tone bordering on self-pity. Where once he had been hailed as "one of the firebrands of independence," he now believed himself put upon by enemies both in the medical and political arenas. Being "put upon" was not a new sensation, but one that stretched over the years. This was especially true when it came to his urging opposition to, and constantly disparaging, the 1776 Pennsylvania Constitution—which, it should be noted, reflected the philosophy of his idol Benjamin Franklin, a strong proponent of what was to Rush the hateful unicameral legislature:

> The perfect knowledge I had of these gentlemen's characters enabled me to detest and expose their schemes in every period of their administration [he wrote—indeed, complained—to Adams]. They knew this well, and hence my destruction was a favorite object with each of them. From my taking the part of the persecuted Quakers and Episcopalians I was represented as the enemy of the Presbyterians in our state, and so far did this calumny succeed that it obliged me to retreat from their society to the church of my ancestors and in which I was born, viz., the [Episcopalian] Church of England. Such was the industry of Dr. Ewing in circulating the above calumny that he reduced my business by it *among the Presbyterians* in the course of two years from near an 100 to only ten families. For these sacrifices to my principles I did not receive the support I should have done from the friends of order and justice. Some of them avoided me at the time I was most persecuted as if I had been bitten by a mad dog. Others of them joined the hue and cry against me in order to recommend themselves to the tyrants of the day. Nor is this all. One of the Republican party [never identified] who had long seen with pain the seal and success of my services, I have reason to believe employed his talents for evil and ridicule against me in the public service.

Rush felt "no difficulty in exercising the Christian virtue of forgiveness" toward his enemies.

> They are open and sincere in their enmity against me. They moreover did me the honor of considering me as the principal in all the

measures that were taken to oppose and defeat them. But my friends were unkind, ungrateful, and even treacherous, and while most of them wanted a subordinate part in schemes planned by myself, they considered me only as an instrument in their hands to effect the purposes of their ambitions in revenge. I wish I could love them as I ought. In reviewing their conduct and my own in the disputes in our state, I am led to conclude this narrative with the famous Spanish prayer: "God deliver me from myself and my friends."[5]

Rush was overstating the case. He was still very much respected, and could count on a legion of friends both at home and abroad. But nothing hurt Rush more than his not being called upon to play a role in framing the new Pennsylvania constitution. His was a legitimate grievance; nay, the omission was an egregious insult. Here was a goal for which no man in the state had fought with more tenacity. Even those who most opposed him on the issue conceded he "bore away the palm and shone conspicuous beyond all the imps of the *well-born*" for the thirteen years he had attacked the still operational 1776 state constitution.[6] "I could as soon embrace the most absurd dogmas in the most absurd of all the pagan religions as prostitute my understanding by approving of our state Constitution," he wrote Adams on 22 January 1779. "It is below a democracy. It is a mobocracy, if you will allow me to coin a word."

Ironically, it was Rush who played a major role in bringing to fruition the idea of revising the 1776 charter. Girding for what he foresaw as a divinely ordained foray back into the political arena, he convened a group of like-minded friends, including Maclay and Wilson, around his fireside to formulate battle plans: "My parlor will therefore be the *Bingham's porch* of the new constitution," he wrote to John Montgomery on 27 March 1789, alluding to the porch where the two had initiated their Dickinson College plan. Three days earlier, following a rump meeting of the Assembly at the City Tavern, the legislature had voted to poll the people on whether or not to call a constitutional convention. The "triumphs of reason in Pennsylvania" showed every promise of being achieved, Rush promised Montgomery. But to make that a certainty, he instigated a campaign to gather "subscriptions to petitions to the next session of the Assembly calling for a constitutional convention," and urged that Montgomery become equally "active" in the Carlisle area: "The sooner you set about this business the better. Otherwise the Antis will be beforehand with you. We shall have the best government in the Union."

By early September, having received more than ten thousand signatures, the Assembly called for a convention, and several weeks later a statewide election for delegates was held. Though a number of caucuses were necessary before an acceptable slate to represent Philadelphia could be agreed upon, Rush's name did not appear on a single one. Not even the one finalized at a town meeting held in the State House yard when a final slate was winnowed down from twenty-seven candidates. It was as if he had suddenly become a political pariah. His only conclusion was that the times had passed him by:

"Your remarks upon the conduct of the tories and the 'young fry' who are now crowding into the councils of our country," he wrote Adams (12 February 1790), "perfectly accord with my own observations. The present Convention and Assembly of Pennsylvanians and the present Corporation of Philadelphia are all filled chiefly with men who were either unknown in 1776 or known only for timidity or disaffection. [Our] old friends have mingled with the [worthless] Continental money of that memorable year and are as much forgotten as if they had paid the last debt of nature."

Such was his "apathy *now* to public affairs," Rush often passed "whole weeks without reading our newspapers." Not even news of the explosive events of the French Revolution, which were available in the Philadelphia newspapers, let alone news from the seat of government at New York or events in his own state, could reverse the course of his total uninterest in politics, an uninterest perhaps genuine, perhaps feigned out of pique: "I have never once been within the doors of our Convention, nor have I broken bread with a single member of the body who compose it." He saw—and was doubtless rubbed the wrong way by—"many men high in power or affluent in office who in the year 1776 considered me as one of the firebrands of independence." He could "feel the effects in a debilitated constitution of the midnight studies which I devoted for 16 years to my country." He foresaw "nothing before me during the remainder of my life but labor and self-denial in my profession—and yet I am happy. I envy no man—and blame no man. O! Virtue, Virtue, who would not follow thee blind-fold! I want nothing but a heart sufficiently grateful to heaven for the happiness of my family and my country."

Rush had to have been extremely gratified with the outcome of the convention, which saw Pennsylvania wind up with a new constitution that embodied two factors he had long fought for: a strong executive and a bicameral legislature. Still, despite the contentment he found in his family, his teaching, his medical practice, and the further pursuit of reform in so many areas, from abolition to mental health, he must have felt pain, albeit residual, from no longer being in the political arena:

"That man will be egregiously disappointed who expects the rewards of his patriotism or successful enterprises on this side the grave," he told—indeed, warned—Noah Webster on 29 December 1789. "Having lived to see my last political wish accomplished in the change of the Constitution of Pennsylvania, I have taken leave of pub-lic life and public pursuits. Hereafter I expect to live only for the ben-efits of my family and my patients." In fact, Rush could never bring himself to admit, for whatever reason—if indeed he knew for himself that reason—that he had not so much "taken leave of public life" as he had been forced out of it.

Rush may have retired from politics, whether willingly or otherwise, but he still maintained a life that to describe it with the adjectival "full" comes hazardously close to understatement. There was his large private practice, training a full cadre of apprentices, his medical lec-tures at the University of Pennsylvania, clinics at the Pennsylvania Hospital and Philadelphia Dispensary, his ever voluminous corre-spondence, and his equally voluminous writings for public consump-tion. These embraced everything from ongoing "causes" (abolition, penal reform, and humane treatment of the mentally ill, to cite but three among many) to theories on medical disorders including con-sumption and cancer (the logic of which would be proved over time) to the role of the physician general in an army to tracts condemning capital punishment to—a particular favorite—stressing the study in schools of history and geography over what was then an emphasis on the teaching of Latin and Greek: "Let [a boy] read an account of the rise, progress, and fall of the Greek and Roman nations, and examine upon maps the countries they inhabited and conquered, and their languages will soon become interesting to them." Otherwise, save for the rare student who would go on to read the great classics of antiquity, such as the *Aenid* of Virgil or the *Iliad* and *Odyssey* of Homer, having to learn these "dead languages" without being taught their historical context would be a waste of time, if only because the student would lack any reason to remember their syntax and grammar, let alone their pronunciation.[7]

His correspondents now began to include, in addition to historian Jeremy Belknap, political figures James Madison and Thomas Jefferson, to whom he was drawing particularly close and by whom he was kept abreast of, and with whom he commented on, what was transpiring in the federal government. In this correspondence can be traced Rush's evolution into what can be termed a charter member of what would culminate in Jefferson's formation of the Democratic Republican Party. Though Rush and Adams were now moving toward opposing philosophical polarities, Adams the paradigmatic Federalist, Rush the paradigmatic Republican, the two never allowed these differences to compromise their friendship. It is a mark of Adams's character that he accepted gracefully Rush's supporting Jefferson for the presidency, which denied Adams the second term to which he felt entitled.

On a personal level, Rush began to experience what everyone negotiating the passage into and through middle age must come to terms with: the loss of old friends. Gone now were his early mentor, Dr. Morgan, and his revered Edinburgh teacher and inspiration, Dr. Cullen. There would be others. One passing that particularly pained him was that of his lifelong hero Benjamin Franklin. At Franklin's funeral on 21 April 1790 ("The concourse of spectators and followers were supposed to amount to 20,000 people") Rush, at a viewing of the body, obtained a promise from Franklin's son-in law of a lock of his hair, "which I afterward procured, and sent some of it to Dr. [Richard] Price and some of it to the Marquis [de La] Fayette."[8]

Rush found his greatest pleasure within the family circle, despite the infant mortality that could almost be anticipated by any parent in those days. On 3 July 1789 Julia gave birth to another son, Benjamin, who lived only a short time, thus becoming the fourth Rush child (along with Susanna, Elizabeth, and William) not to survive childhood. The five who remained among the living were James, three,

Mary, five, Richard, eight, Anne Emily, ten, and the firstborn, twelve-year-old John, his parents' favorite and, ironically, the one who would bring them the most grief. Rush's wife would bear him four more children: a second Benjamin (1791), Julia (1792), Samuel (1795), and a second William, her thirteenth and last child, in 1801, when she was forty-two and Rush was forty-six.

In 1789 Rush left the Episcopal Church, for which he had, it will be recalled, earlier left the Presbyterian faith in which his widowed mother had raised him, "in consequence of an alteration made in the forms of baptism and the communion." (The allusion here is to the revised Prayer Book adopted by the Protestant Episcopal Church of America in that year, on which Rush had much to say, none of it very complimentary.) Though he had his children "baptized by Presbyterian ministers," Rush "still attended public worship in the Episcopal church and occasionally in the Presbyterian churches, but alas! with coldness and formality." But he never again belonged to either as a confirmed communicant. "I was under the influence of an unholy temper, and often wounded the peace of my mind by yielding to it." Still, he was, and would remain for the rest of his life, "strongly impressed with a sense of divine things" and was "animated by a hope in God's mercy."[9]

From this point onward, in the words of his biographer David Freeman Hawke,

> Medicine would cease to be simply a way to earn a living. It would supplant politics and humanitarian projects and become the core of his new life. Out of his college lectures on the theory and practice of medicine came a new theory of disease that he hoped would . . . win the fame for him in medicine that Newton had achieved in physics. That honor never came, but from his work at the Pennsylvania Hospital, where he supervised the treatment of the mentally ill, he gathered material for his most famous medical work, a book on the diseases of the mind. Each year the size of his classes at the college and the number of those who read his books increased. For good or ill, the most influential physician in the history of American medicine down to the Civil War became Benjamin Rush.[10]

19

"Dr. Vampire"

Philadelphia was riding the crest of postwar prosperity when it was suddenly devastated by the great yellow fever epidemic of 1793. The subject of entire books, the epidemic was one of the major events of Dr. Benjamin Rush's entire career, both for the major role he played in it and the cloud it cast upon his good name and reputation. For that reason, no biography of the man would be complete without more than a cursory examination of it.

Almost since the founding of Philadelphia, epidemics, in varying degrees of intensity, of diverse diseases struck the city periodically. But none was as horrendous as the yellow fever that struck in the summer of 1793. The Old Quakers saw it as divine vengeance for their sons having forsaken the sect's drab traditional garb for the lace and ruffles and bejeweled shoe buckles favored by the fashion-conscious dandies of the day, as well as forsaking traditional values, opting instead to gather in taverns or merely perambulate the streets, often in a somewhat raucous manner, to idle away an hour or two to gossip or carouse.

With a building boom and an influx of new dwellers, more than forty thousand people lived, depending upon the social stratum they inhabited, either in crowded hovels or in a high density of red brick houses two or two and a half stories high, many of them along the Delaware. The city's docks were the scene of round-the-clock frenzy. Wagons heavy with merchandise for the backcountry had to negotiate the narrow streets in competition with private and public coaches and sedan chairs whose occupants were spending money as if the boom would go on in perpetuity. The tumult of the day increased, weather permitting, as the men hurried off boisterously to their favorite taverns while their ladies sat chattering and laughing on their doorsteps in the dusk created by the street lamps that were but another of Benjamin Franklin's highly utilitarian inventions.

From unpaved streets clouds of dust rose in dry weather and gave way to thick mire in wet. Within the city proper hygiene ranked low on the list of municipal priorities. Except for street-corner pumps there was no water supply, and no sewage system. Dead animals were left where they fell until eaten by the hogs and chickens that rooted and strutted everywhere.

On 21 August of that fateful year, Rush wrote to his wife at Morven, that "a malignant fever has broken out in Water Street between Arch and Race Streets, which has already carried off twelve persons. . . . It is supposed to have been produced by some damaged coffee which had putrefied on one of the wharves near the middle of the above district." The coffee had come in toward the end of July and the beginning of August with some two thousand French-speaking blacks and whites from Santo Domingo (today the Dominican Republic and Haiti) fleeing the chaos and desolation of three years of war and a slave insurrection. They had brought with them what was initially believed to be this "malignant fever" which though "violent [is] of short duration. . . . in no case has it lasted more than four days." Rush went on to assure Julia, "As yet it has not spread through any parts of the city which are beyond the reach of the putrid exhalation which first produced it." Meanwhile, she and the children were to "remain where you are till you receive further advice and information from me."

Life continued at its normal pace in the as yet unaffected areas. Even Rush, in support of his abolitionist activities, attended a dinner to celebrate the raising of the roof of the African Church.

> They forced me to take the head of the table much against my inclinations. The dinner was plentiful. . . . We were waited upon by nearly an equal number of black people. I gave them the two following toasts: "Peace on earth and good will to men," and "May African churches everywhere soon succeed to African bondage. After which we rose, and the black people (men and women) took our seats. Six of the most respectable of the whole company waited upon them. . . . Never did I witness such a sense of innocent—nay more—such virtuous and philanthropic joy.[1]

Rush had by then treated a number of patients, a few of whom had died, from what was quickly concluded to be a "bilious fever," most likely influenza. Among his patients were printer Thomas Bradford's wife, the former Polly Fisher, whom Rush had loved during his student days, and a couple of his own apprentices. On 19 August, in consultation with two other physicians, Rush was called in to examine a Mrs. Peter LeMaigre, wife of a merchant from the West Indies, who lived in the same district where most of the other patients lived—close to Ball's wharf, where the putrefying coffee had been dumped. Mrs. LaMaigre was found to be in the last stages of a severe bilious fever—vomiting constantly and complaining of great heat and burning in the stomach. She died the next day.

As the three physicians were leaving the LeMaigre residence, Rush remarked, as if something had clicked in his mind, that he had within the preceding weeks attended an unusual number of bilious fevers, all accompanied with uncommonly malignant symptoms. He suspected the possibility of an unusually severe epidemic in the making. The other two remarked that the preponderance of patients they had treated lived in the same general area. Having experienced a similar epidemic in 1762, Rush concluded that highly contagious and mortal "Bilious remitting Yellow Fever" had not only struck again but, based on the symptoms among the number of cases to date, threatened to reach massive proportions. Because the epidemic was confined thus far to the waterfront area, his conclusion was greeted with ridicule and contempt by his fellow physicians and ordinary citizens, including municipal officials.

They insisted it was at most just another outbreak of influenza or scarlatina—perhaps both—that would, as did such outbreaks in the past, run its course, leaving in its wake but a comparatively few victims unfortunate enough not to recover. Rush insisted otherwise. He began to air his fears within the medical community—only to be branded an alarmist. Except during an epidemic, and given that immunological tests were unknown in those days, clinical diagnosis of yellow fever was highly problematic. Yellowing of the skin was not always associated with the disease; moreover, jaundice was often found among victims of such common febrile diseases as dengue and malaria. Convinced as he was of the true nature of the current epidemic despite his condemnation as the proverbial boy who cried wolf, all that Rush could do was attend to his increasing patient population, and await proof—by the disease's spread and the resultant death rate.

On orders of Governor Mifflin, who had become concerned enough to have it determined whether or not a deadly contagious disease was prevalent in the city, Dr. James Hutchinson, the port physician, asked Rush for his opinion. Rush's opinion: "A malignant fever has lately appeared in our city, originating I believe from some damaged coffee, which putrefied on a wharf near Arch-street. This fever was confined for a while to Water-street between Race and Arch-streets; but I have lately met with it in Second-street, and in Kensington; but whether propagated by contagion, or by the original exhalation, I cannot tell." He added that he had "not seen a fever of such malignity, so general, since the year 1762."[2]

Though most of Rush's colleagues tried to play down his obvious fears, the general public became concerned as the death toll mounted daily. Most, however, preferred to believe the cause to be influenza, mild bilious remittent fever, and scarlatina, which had the city in its grip before the yellow fever was recognized. And it was the general consensus that yellow fever rarely if ever struck concurrent with any other of the comparatively mild epidemics. When these epidemics disappeared almost entirely by early September, yellow fever was recognized as the sole epidemic.

Rush and his colleagues blamed it on "noxious miasma," an "evil air" caused by decaying matter, stagnant swamps, or the breath of infected patients. Citizens took to lighting fires on every street corner to burn the miasma away. A committee of physicians headed by Rush announced that the fires were probably ineffectual and potentially dangerous, and suggesting burning gunpowder instead. Whereupon the citizens took to spending their evenings firing their muskets out their windows at the miasma. So many people were wounded that this was soon stopped by the mayor. The miasma remained.

People stayed in their houses behind locked doors. Because tobacco was believed to counteract miasma, women and children joined their husbands and fathers in chain-smoking cigars from the time they arose in the morning until they retired for the night. Many preferred to put their faith in garlic and chewed it continually or kept it in their shoes. Homemakers spent their every waking hour white-washing their rooms, starting all over the moment they finished, while their children followed in their wake sprinkling vinegar and lighting gunpowder.

Wealthier citizens tried to flee, but communities both contiguous and distant hastily enacted ordinances barring entry to all Philadelphians. Baltimore, for one, blocked the road from Philadelphia with a company of militia. The New York council ordered the patrolling of every ward by at least ten men when word got out that refugees from Philadelphia had managed to make it across the Hudson in rowboats with muffled oars. Were a Philadelphian to show the least sign of illness on a stagecoach, the coach was stopped and the unfortunate individual was evicted, even if it be on a lonely road in the dark of night. Farmhouses in the backcountry refused to admit any suspected travelers, so that some who were not the least bit ill died of exposure in the woods. At Milford, Delaware, a woman driving a wagon of goods from Philadelphia was tarred and feathered by a group of locals as the torch was put to her wagon. "Yet, the refugees were made so agile by fear that a third of the population managed to find lodging elsewhere," writes historian James Thomas Flexner.

> In the terrorized city husbands abandoned sick wives, mothers their children. Ailing rich men, their wills forgotten, were deserted by their heirs, and could procure no attendants at the end of their luxurious lives except dissolute Negro laborers who drank up the wine in their cellars; Negroes were supposed to be immune. Many persons died alone in empty houses, their screams going on and on through the silent night while hundreds of anguished listeners stopped their ears. Sometimes a sufferer would use his last strength to stagger out into the deserted street, and pound unavailingly at the bolted doors of his neighbors. The next morning his corpse would be found lying face downward in the gutter.[3]

At the request of Mayor Clarkson, who feared that efforts to prevent the spread of the disease might get out of control, the College of Physicians drew up a list of recommendations: Unnecessary contact with infected persons should be avoided. The strictest personal hygiene should be observed. Signs were to be posted on the doors of any house in which an infected person resided. The sick should be placed in large, clean, airy rooms. A building was set aside for hospitalizing the poor. Burials were be private. All streets and wharves were to be kept as clean as possible. And not only intemperance but mental and bodily fatigue were to be avoided. The college insisted that if these measures were followed scrupulously "to prevent the contagion being excited into action in the body," the disease could exit and enter and exit the body without producing the fever and its ultimate consequences. Listed among the causes were exposure to the sun or currents of air—and intemperance. The college believed fires were both ineffectual and dangerous, and urged continued reliance on the burning of gunpowder and the use of vinegar and camphor in infected rooms.[4]

On 29 August, Rush published in the *American Daily Advertiser* an address to his fellow Philadelphians giving his own explanation of the rapidly spreading epidemic, in which, while supporting its domestic origin, he exposed himself to much abuse by listing among the secondary causes what he termed "*indirect debility.*" These included not only fatigue, heat, cold, and intemperance, but also fear and grief. Indeed, he maintained the disease could be brought on in many people, he posited, by a paroxysm of grief and in many others by an abandonment of hope. He also arrived at a number of supplementary epidemiological assumptions; for example, he ascribed the high mortality rate in wooden houses to their small size and want of cleanliness—which proved to be logical—and he thought the contagion adhered to the wood—which it didn't. Since contagion— "morbid exhalations"—was predominantly rampant in the city's more crowded quarters, it could easily migrate across narrow streets and alleys. While this was true, it was also true, though Rush seems not to have considered it, that such exhalations could navigate a distance of two or three miles in flat open country unless obstructed by habitations, woods, or hills. Another Rush assertion later disproved was that reinfection was very common. Yet another false assertion, which he himself would shortly abandon, was that Negroes were immune.

Rush—along with all his contemporary physicians, whether they agreed with his conclusions or condemned them—had no way of knowing that yellow fever was spread by infected mosquitoes, a discovery that would come only with the passage of time, a long time, which would extend well beyond the century in which these physicians, and many who would follow them, played out their lives.

＊　　＊　　＊

It was of little assurance to the public that the doctors could not agree among themselves as to the best course of treatment to follow, let alone the true cause of the disease. Rush at first prescribed general purges, but soon decided they were ineffectual, and experimented with bark in its diverse forms to be administered with wine, brandy, and aromatics. He also applied blisters to the limbs, neck, and head. When this treatment proved unsuccessful, he tried wrapping the body in blankets dipped in warm vinegar and rubbing the patient's sides with a mercurial ointment in order to stimulate the system through the liver. When this, too, proved ineffectual, and he was advised by a doctor who happened to be visiting from St. Croix that cold baths and the administration of bark were beneficial, he ordered that buckets of cold water be thrown on his patients. Of those subjected to this treatment, three out of four died.[5]

Through letters Rush wrote to Julia almost daily, sometimes twice in the same day, we can follow the course of the epidemic, including the deaths of many, which affected Rush deeply (including his own sister Rebecca the first week in October), and the almost unbearable patient load he attended to, a load that grew daily. As Rush made his rounds, frightened people kept their distance. They held handkerchiefs soaked with vinegar to their noses, carried pieces of tarred rope, or hung bags of camphor round their necks, so fearful were they of contagion from the houses where his patients had died.

By now many of the city's physicians had themselves become infected by their patients, and many, fearing a like fate, also fled the city. Rush was one of the very few physicians who remained loyal to the Hippocratic Oath, even as their patient load grew exponentially. Between 8 and 15 September, when the epidemic was at its height, he attended and prescribed for between 100 and 120 patients a day, while his apprentices saw between 20 and 30 more each. Realizing that he could reach the greatest number of sufferers through the newspapers, Rush, in the 13 September edition of the *American Daily Advertiser,* offered directions for the prevention and cure of the fever. To avoid the fever a temperate diet—chiefly vegetables—and moderate exercise of the mind as well as the body, along with warm clothing, personal hygiene, and normal bowel movements. Should sickness occur, calomel and jalap were prescribed to cleanse the bowels (which "should be kept constantly open, whether by another powder, or by small doses of cream of tartar, or cooling salts"), the diet to consist of "gruel, sago, tapioca, tea, coffee, weak chocolate, wine whey, chicken broth, and the white meats, according to the weak or active state of the system. The fruits of the season may be eaten with advantage at all times." He also advised that after the bowels were "thoroughly cleansed, if the pulse be full or tense, eight or ten ounces of blood should be taken from the arm, and more, if the tension or fullness of the pulse should continue."

A day after his piece in the *American Daily Observer,* Rush himself became symptomatic. Yet he continued to see patients.

> It is computed that 100 persons upon an average have been buried every day for the last eight or ten days [Rush wrote on 25 September to Elias Boudinot]. The sick suffer from the want not only of physicians, bleeders, nurses, and friends, but from the want of the common necessities of life. . . . [T]he mortality falls chiefly upon the poor, who by working in the sun excite the contagion into action. Whole families have been swept away by it. . . . By the help of a banister I contrive to climb up about a dozen pairs of stairs every day. My milk and vegetable diet (for I loathe most meat and fermented liquors), an obstinate wakefulness for nearly a week before my late indisposition, profuse night sweats, my disease, my remedies, and above all my constant labors, have reduced me to the weakness of an old man of 80. Nothing scarcely is left of what I was two months ago but my voice and my usual spirits. . . . In my parlor, on my couch, and even in my bed I prescribe for 50 to 100 people, chiefly the poor, every day.

By now accepting that purges were not achieving the desired response, Rush was sitting one night in his study depressed by the sounds of creaking wagons in the street carrying away their still living cargo when he suddenly recalled reading a paper submitted by one Dr. John Mitchell, a Virginia practitioner, to the American Philosophical Society a half century earlier. Seeking out the paper and studying it, he was impressed by Mitchell's argument that physicians should not be fooled by seeming weakness in a patient; yellow fever was in fact caused by "over-excitement of the body." Even were the pulse so thin as to be hardly discernible, the most violent purges should be described. Rush reacted as if struck by divine revelation: Under all circumstances the only acceptable treatment was depletion. Increasing the strongest purges then common—ten grains of calomel and ten grains of jalap—he added a 50 percent increase in the dosage of jalap, to be administered three times a day.

Moreover, he would draw blood proportionately.

On 4 October, Rush collapsed while visiting a patient, and on being carried home insisted on bleeding himself excessively—as he had been doing his patients. Many physicians who condemned Rush's excessive purging and bloodletting at first, now agreed they were the proper remedies. A number of influential ones, though, condemned him—as have historians to this day.

While the epidemic raged, so did the battle—in the press—between Rush and his many colleagues who insisted his purging and bleeding and concomitant administering of heavy dosages of mercury was doing more harm than good. Rush refused to believe their opposition had any scientific basis: "The envy and hatred of my brethren has lately risen to a rage. They blush at their mistakes, they feel for their murders, and instead of asking forgiveness of the public for them, vent all their guilty shame and madness upon the man who convinced them of both."[6]

His colleagues were not the only ones demeaning Rush. "A new clamor has been excited against me in which many citizens take a part," he wrote his wife (28 October 1793).

> I have asserted that the yellow fever was generated in our city. This assertion they say will destroy the character of Philadelphia for healthiness. . . . Truth in science as in morals never did any harm. If I prove my assertion (which I can most easily do), I shall at the same time point out the means of preventing its ever being generated among us again. I am urged to bring forward my proof immediately. To this I have objected—until I am able to call upon a number of persons for the privilege of using their names. To a gentleman who pressed the matter upon me this day, I said that the good opinion of the citizens of Philadelphia was now of little consequence to me, for that I thought it probable from present appear-

ances that I should begin to seek a retreat and subsistence in some other part of the United States.

This marked the beginning of a controversy that extended beyond Rush's death; indeed, it must be admitted that his erroneous insistence that yellow fever was entirely local in origin was almost as objectionable in the business community as his purging and bleeding therapy was in the medical community.

In the last week of October, a cold snap killed off the true but still unrecognized culprits—mosquitoes. Suddenly the epidemic was over, an epidemic that had killed 4,044 people, upward of 10 percent of the population. Rush believed that had he not practiced his regimen of extreme purging and bleeding, an additional six thousand would have succumbed.

From our perspective, it is not difficult to denounce Rush for his excessive bloodletting. And here in his defense it should be noted that the way of measuring the amount of blood in humans had not yet been discovered. Rush, as did his contemporaries, believed that the body of a man of average size contains twelve quarts of blood, and not six, which is the norm. By present-day standards, despite the great advances of men such as Cullen and Boerhaave and Sydenham, the origin of many diseases, let alone their most efficacious treatment, remained in its Dark Ages. And if we are to dismiss Rush as Dr. Vampire, as do some otherwise responsible historians to this day, many of his colleagues deserve equal scorn. Rush doubtless championed purging and bloodletting to an extent that present-day medical practitioners would consider as constituting malpractice. But so did other leading physicians of the time. Whether his treatment killed patients who might otherwise have lived, or, for that matter, saved patients who might otherwise have died, can never be determined, and for that reason alone does not merit further mention.

Also not to be overlooked are the many advances attributable to Rush in the area of nosology (the branch of medicine dealing with the classification and description of known diseases) and medical case management, along with his educating of future physicians, which proved over time to have been as definitive as they were revolutionary.

We must look at what Rush accomplished overall, not only as a physician and educator but also as a social reformer and, and for that matter, as one of the Founding Fathers. Simply stated, it would not be an exaggeration to define Benjamin Rush's catalog of positive accomplishments with a paraphrase of Lord Byron's words in *Childe Harold's Pilgrimage:* "But his are deeds which should not pass away, / And a name that must not wither."

Philadelphia had been so thoroughly infected by the 1793 epidemic that yellow fever returned yearly, albeit in milder form. Rush blamed it on a "noxious miasma" generated by the marshes and foul gutters in and surrounding the city, and he recommended that the marshes and gutters be drained. And herein lies an irony. Though he was ignorant of the part played by mosquitoes in the disease, the disease could have been eradicated had his recommendation been adopted. But the business and real estate operators, in collusion with money-minded doctors, fearing that the federal government, having relocated there from New York City while waiting to take up permanent residence in Washington, D.C., would decamp for a healthier place and thus end Philadelphia's leadership among the nation's cities—all insisted that Rush was a fool, and a dangerous one at that. In the following year, they maintained that the disease could not have originated locally, but must have been imported by cargo ships from the West Indies. Many physicians even went so far as to assert that the current yellow fever victims were not in fact suffering from that disease and denounced Rush as a traitor when he proclaimed the disease's true nature. "Such has been the clamor against me," he wrote a friend, "that a proposal has been made in a company of citizens to 'drum me out of the city.' I am not moved by insults or threats, but persist in asserting and defending all my opinions respecting the disease. The only revenge I seek of my fellow citizens is to save their lives, and the only notice I take of the slanders of my medical brethren is to refuse to consult with them."[7]

There were less severe epidemics in 1794, 1796, and 1797. By then Rush had lost his mother and remaining sister, Rachel. While he took comfort in his strong religion, he found little comfort in that fact. Though over the preceding four years his "business was stationary," now "it sensibly declined." No new families "except foreigners" sought out his services, and "many of my old patients deserted me." The bulk of his patients had always been the indigent, from whom he could expect little payment beyond perhaps a chicken, and he would not desert them now. Even the cures he achieved—due to, if not in spite of, his excessive bleeding and purging—"added to the distraction that had taken place against my character," a "distraction" orchestrated by prominent colleagues who would have liked nothing better than to ship Rush out of town on the wave of blood he insisted could cure 99 percent of those who still came to him. "No ties of ancient School fellowship, no obligation of gratitude, no sympathy in religious or philosophical opinions, were able to resist the tide of public clamor that was excited by my practice." His name "was mentioned with horror in some companies, and to some of the weakest and most insignificant of my brethren false tales of me became a recommendation to popular favor."[8]

Julia encouraged her husband to abandon the city that seemed to have abandoned him, not only for his medical views but his republican ones. These latter hardly went down well with the aristocratic former Constitutionalists, now the dominant force, with their Federalist champion John Adams having succeeded to the presidency upon the retirement of George Washington. Rush wrote to his old friend John R. R. Rodgers, now on the medical faculty of New York's Columbia University that, having "lived in Philadelphia as in a foreign country," and "were I not employed by strangers I could not maintain my family by my Philadelphia patients," he "contemplated leaving this city and settling in New York." Might not Rodgers consider recommending him for a professor's chair at Columbia, which, with his "estate in Philadelphia would be sufficient" to maintain his family?[9]

Fortunately, Rush had made some shrewd real estate investments in central and northern Philadelphia, and Julia had inherited valuable land from her father near Princeton. But this was of little help were he to remain in Philadelphia. His practice had all but vanished, except for the indigent, and there were living at home eight of his children, ranging in age from two-month-old Samuel to the twenty-year-old John (at the time his father's medical apprentice, and fated to become within a few years his father's patient).

Rodgers and his Columbia colleagues, anxious to have Rush, recommended him unanimously for the chair of the practice of medicine. However, the appointment was blocked by the board of trustees through the influence of its most illustrious member, Alexander Hamilton, who hated Rush's republican political beliefs as he hated all who shared them, most notably their ideological leader, Thomas Jefferson. In reporting this to Rush the next day, Rodgers assured him that his friends intended to try again to ascertain "whether the old leaven of Bigotry & political resentment shall triumph or not."[10]

Replying to Rodgers on 6 November, Rush requested that he not pursue the matter "and assure the trustees of the University that I shall not accept of the appointment should it be offered to me after the obstacles that have been thrown in the way of it by Mr. Hamilton." Rush added facetiously that he found it "particularly gratifying" to learn that "the opposition to my appointment has come from that gentleman." (Rush found it most gratifying to be hated by a Federalist, especially one of Alexander's caliber.) He then informed Rodgers "that prospects of independence and usefulness have lately been opened to me in my native state far more respectable, though much less agreeable, than the one I wished for in your University." Those "prospects of independence and usefulness" was Rush's appointment as treasurer of the mint. The dating of his and Rodgers's correspondence more than suggests that the appointment was already in the works when Rush sought the Columbia appointment. The position was little more than a glorified bookkeeper, his main responsibilities being to sign receipts of bullion and coin (most of which receipts were signed by an assistant) and made little demand on Rush's time.

Two years previously, according to Rush's *Commonplace Book* for 9 April 1795, he had been approached by his friend Tench Coxe.[11] Would Rush accept overall directorship of the mint in place of David Rittenhouse, who was about to resign? Rush "declined the offer on the steps of my door without deliberating one moment upon it" for a number of reasons, among them being that it would "expose" him to "the calumnies" of his colleagues, "who would say it interfered with my business," and because he had "devoted myself to the establishment of a new System of Physic." His old friend and uncle by marriage, Elias Boudinot, received the appointment.

Two years later, Rush's situation had changed. He believed, erroneously, the reappearance of the yellow fever to be in a more virulent form, and his subsequently applying his bloodletting therapy more rigorously than ever before had subjected him to relentless criticism and a further dramatic loss of business. When the office of Treasurer of the Mint fell vacant due to the death of the incumbent, Boudinot made it known to President Adams that Rush would like the position (and could use the $1200 salary that went with it). Whether Boudinot acted on his own, or was asked to do so by Rush is not clear. In all probability, Boudinot acted on his own, or perhaps at the request of Rush's wife. Rush's account in his memoirs is ambiguous on this point. Boudinot's petition was vetted by Secretary of State Thomas Pickering, a neighbor of Rush's.

Though there were some forty applicants for the post, and considering how far apart Adams and Rush had drawn politically, it might have been expected that the president—who had fled Philadelphia to his home in Quincy on the outbreak of the epidemic—would recuse himself and leave the selection to his secretary of the treasury. Adams was one of those people who never found it difficult to bear grudges. And there was certainly much now for him to begrudge in Rush, a confirmed Jeffersonian Republican. Worse, the two parties were opposed in their attitudes vis-à-vis European affairs, with the Republicans sympathetic to the French Revolution, and the Federalists supporting Britain's opposition to French democracy. But to Adams's credit, and despite heavy opposition led by, among others, Alexander Hamilton and Adams's outspoken wife, Abigail, the president put long-standing and cherished friendship ahead of politics and sanctioned Rush's lifetime appointment.

This in no way prompted Rush to consider abandoning his Antifederalist beliefs, and it is, again, to Adams's credit that their close friendship continued until the day Rush died—again, to the dismay of Adams's political confreres and Abigail. Years later, in thanking Adams for congratulating Rush on the revival of his "business" (Rush's word), a revival that was the result of the international reputation he now enjoyed as a great and innovative medical practitioner, educator, and social reformer, he told the long-retired former president, with whom he continued to carry on a voluminous correspondence,

In an examination I have lately made of my books, I find that the diminution, and of course the loss from it, amounted between the years 1797 and 1807 to upwards of 30,000 dollars. . . . Had it not been for the emoluments of the office you gave me (for which I hope gratitude will descend to further generations in my family), I must have retired from the city and ended my days upon a farm upon the little capital I had saved from the labors of former years. I say *little*, for my sacrifices and losses during the war (which amounted to at least the same sum I have mentioned) had prevented my accumulating more than was sufficient to settle myself [away from Philadelphia as a farmer]. Even with the addition of the income from the Mint which you gave me, I spent for several years from 12 to 15 hundred dollars a year more than the income from my business. In no period of my depression did I regret the conduct that occasioned it. My opinions and practice I was sure were correct, and I believed they would prevail. I acted uprightly and consulted the health of my fellow citizens and the benefit of society more than I did my own interest or fame. Most of my fellow citizens (the physicians excepted) have forgiven me, and *they* dare not openly, as they once did, assail my character.

Expressing pride that his "business now through divine goodness is more profitable than ever it was," Rush recalls, in a commingling of vestigial resentment and ongoing satisfaction, how those "physicians excepted" united against him and were later shown to have backed the wrong horse in what has come down as the first great case of journalistic libel since the American Revolution, and one of the greatest down to modern times: the Cobbett-Rush Feud.

The idea that Rush would have abandoned his medical practice and teaching for the life of a country farmer should be taken as no more than the "threat" of a once-hailed, now-assailed patriot rapidly succumbing to a self-pity that while somewhat exaggerated was nonetheless justified. The more so since his position at the mint provided added income, and, of greater consequence, the idea of actually abandoning his indigent patients and his students was beyond consideration. As for what his enemies thought of him—and Lord knows he had more than his fair share of them by now—Rush could manage to live with that, thanks to his faith in God and his resolute conviction that his good name would in time be redeemed. He could accept being criticized, even reviled. But he could not accept being libeled. On 2 October 1797 Rush announced publicly that he had initiated suits for libel against John Ward Fenno and William Cobbett, publishers of, respectively, the *Gazette of the United States* and *Porcupine's Gazette*, two virulent pro-Federalist newspapers.[12]

Hurling broadsides at Rush's "lunatic system" of medicine in the form of letters to the editor, Fenno sought to "arouse" the public against Rush's reliance on heavy bloodletting, much as the citizens in Mary Wollstonecraft Godwin's masterpiece were incited to march up the hill to Dr. Frankenstein's castle and do something about that damn monster he'd created. Fenno pounded away at the man he practically accused of being an out-of-control vampire who was daily sending to their graves seven out of eight of his patients and, in the bargain, causing the streets of Philadelphia to run with blood. When Rush brought suit, an enraged Fenno called it an "Assault on the Liberty of the Press." He claimed he had attacked Rush's doctrines because he was convinced they were dangerous to society: "The plain fact is that the Dr. still retains the same principle of ambition and that same thirst for popularity, which has ever distinguished him through life. His great aim seems to have been to retire from the practice of medicine, with the fame of an Esculapius, and to carry to his grave the credit of some wonderful discovery," et cetera, et cetera, et cetera.

Rush soon dropped the action against Fenno, assuming he would lose, since libel suits against Americans were rarely decided in favor of the plaintiff. But the main reason for doing so was that he wanted to concentrate his legal attack on Cobbett, partly because he was foreign-born and would thus be easier to prevail against, but mainly because Cobbett's attacks were even more vicious. For here was a man who remains to this day the true master of journalistic vitriol. In Rush's words, "his genius for savage journalistic satire remains perhaps without a rival in any era."[13]

An accomplished English agriculturalist, politician, journalist, and pamphleteer whose satirical writings, in today's parlance, went for the jugular, Cobbett arrived at Philadelphia in 1792 at the age of twenty-six after being driven from his beloved homeland for his attacks on corruption in the army. Though he detested the United States for having revolted against England, he saw an opportunity to make his fortune here by serving as the mouthpiece for the Federalists. (They did not particularly care for his style, but they weren't about to throw away a new adherent to the cause.) Shortly after his appearance in Philadelphia, Cobbett opened a bookshop on Second Street, opposite Christ Church. He also wrote letters to the newspapers and essays, some pseudonymously, against republicanism, which he hated even more than he hated the American people, whom he considered lazy and dishonest.

In 1797, he began to publish *Porcupine's Gazette,* and set out to devote his not inconsiderable talents to blasting the targets of his wrath. With the Federalists now divided midway through Adams's administration and the country moving toward Jeffersonianism, Cobbett cast about for an unpopular target. The most logical was Dr. Benjamin Rush. His resumption of heavy bleeding and purging in this epidemic year had elicited in the city's newspapers and taverns the kind of animadversion that not only cut into Rush's income and sullied his reputation but conveniently overlooked all the good he had accomplished not only in practicing and teaching medicine over two decades but also in the run-up to and playing out of the Revolutionary War. Cobbett saw in Rush a perfect twofold cause for denunciation: his democratic principles and his medical practices. That Rush had brought upon himself so much condemnation was a major factor in the equation. Journalistic werewolves much prefer going after unpopular figures than run the risk of bringing down opprobrium upon themselves for attacking popular ones.

On 17 December 1796, three months before Cobbett ("Peter Porcupine") started his rag, Rush delivered a eulogy before the American Philosophical Society in memory of his friend the aforementioned David Rittenhouse, the distinguished astronomer, mathematician, and patriot who had succeeded Benjamin Franklin as president of the society. In the audience were the elite of the federal government and the city of Philadelphia: President Washington, Secretary of State Jefferson, U.S. senators and congressmen, federal and state judges, the city's leading officials, clergymen, physicians, and men of influence. (Adams was back in Massachusetts, where he spent much of his vice presidency— and his presidency as well.) Rush eschewed politics in the hour-long eulogy, making only passing reference to Rittenhouse's republicanism and urging the nation's leaders and the state's movers and shakers to follow in Rittenhouse's path: "Be just, and loose the bonds of the African slave. Be wise, and render war odious to our country. Be free, by assuming a national character and name, and be greatly happy, by erecting a barrier against the corruptions in morals, government, and religion, which now pervade all the nations of Europe."[14]

Cobbett was quick to detect political propaganda in the address. So far as he was concerned, Rush had spouted hyperbolic bombast and a litany of untruths. Rittenhouse, averred Cobbett, had never done good for anyone, except possibly himself. "The remorseless Dr. Rush," he vowed, "shall bleed me till I am white as this paper before I'll allow that this was doing good to mankind."[15] Others in the city joined in the sentiments. But none could match Cobbett for invective.

With the first issue of *Porcupine's Gazette*, its founder was off and running, proving, if nothing else, that no man was his equal as a vicious adversary, slanderous, cunning, ruthless, a master of derision and the toxic art of character assassination. In an article "Rush and His Patients," Cobbett inserted: "Wanted, by a physician, an entire new set of patients, his old ones having given him the slip; also a slower method of dispatching them than that of phlebotomy [opening a vein], the celerity of which does not give time for *making out a bill.*" When it appeared that Rush might be moving to New York City, a newspaper there concluded the notice of his possible appointment at Columbia University: "He is a man born to be useful to society." Cobbett reprinted the paragraph, to which he added: "And so is a *musquito* [sic], a *horse-leech, ferret*, a *pole cat*, a *weasel*: for these are all *bleeders,* and understand their business full as well as Doctor Rush does his."[16]

As the attacks mounted so, too, did Rush's ire. In the 19 September issue of his *Gazette*, Peter Porcupine published a libelous article, "Medical Puffing." Starting out with a couplet,

> *The times are ominous indeed*
> *When quack to quack cries purge and bleed*

he called to the reader's attention the arts that Rush, the "remorseless Bleeder is making use of to puff his preposterous practice." Quoting from one of the letters commending Rush, which he had allegedly prevailed upon friends to write to the various newspapers in his support, Cobbett commented: "Dr. Rush, in that emphatical stile [sic] which is peculiar to himself, calls mercury 'the Samson of Medicine.' In his hands and those of his partizans [*sic*] it may indeed be justly compared to Samson; for I really believe they have slain more Americans with it, than ever Samson slew of the Philistines. The Israelite slew his thousands, but the Rushites have slain their thousands."[17] On the seventh of the following month, Cobbett, relying not on fact but vivid imagination, ran a narrative in his *Gazette* purporting to be a true account of Rush's conduct during the 1793 epidemic:

So much was the Doctor about this period possessed with the notion that he was the only man of common sense existing, that he not only refused to consult with any but his former pupils who submitted to obey his dictates, and rudely intruded his advice upon other people's patients. He also appointed two illiterate negro men, and sent them into all the alleys and by places in the city, with orders to bleed, and give his sweating purges, as he empirically called them, to all they could find sick, without regard to age, sex, or constitution; and bloody and dirty work they made among the poor miserable creatures that fell in their way. That his mind was elevated to a state of enthusiasm bordering on frenzy, I had frequent opportunity of observing; and I have heard from popular report, that in passing through Kensington one day, with his black man on the seat of his chaise along-side of him, he cried out with vociferation, "Bleed and purge all Kensington! Drive on, boy!"[18]

In Rush's failing to follow through with his suit against Fenno, Cobbett assumed that he too was to be spared the threat of legal action. In fact, Rush was advised by some friends to ignore Porcupine on the presumption that he, like the epidemic, would run its course. But Rush had had enough. Moreover, he feared his entire medical practice, not just his teaching career and his own sanity, would run its course first. Rush persisted and the suit came before the state supreme court in December 1797. For a number of reasons, the trial was delayed for two years—and came before a judge and jury, claimed Cobbett, "packed" in Rush's favor. After deliberating two hours, the jury found for the plaintiff in the amount of $5,000.

Including the cost of defending the suit, Cobbett's attacks on Rush had cost him $8,000—a truly considerable sum for the times. Ruined in Philadelphia, his property falling under the sheriff's hammer, Cobbett fled to New York in a state of determination: not to pay the damages, and to continue his assault on Rush's reputation: "Nothing provokes me but the thought of such a whining republican rascal putting the 5,000 dollars in his pocket. . . . I would sooner beg my bread from door to door. The villain shall not enjoy his prize in peace. I shall find the means of reaching him be wherever I may."[19] The damages were paid, after a fashion, in the summer of 1801, when his attorney reached a settlement of $4,000, which Rush donated to charity.[20]

The threat of "reaching" Rush was another matter. In a farewell issue of *Porcupine's Gazette* printed in New York on 13 January 1800, Cobbett declared that his sole motive in going after Rush from the very beginning was to expose the menace to the lives of all Philadelphians that lay beneath the doctor's "sleek-headed, saint-looking" appearance. He also noted that on the very day Peter Porcupine was found guilty, the nation's first president had died at his Mount Vernon estate "in precise conformity to the *practice of Rush*. . . . On that day the victory of RUSH and of DEATH was complete." In fact, as Rush was later to prove and have well aired, of the three physicians who attended and overly bled Washington (now believed to have died of a septic sore throat) Dr. Elisha Dick, the only one of the three who opposed the excessive venesections, had been a pupil of Rush's.[21]

That didn't stop Cobbett from seeking revenge on Rush, less for his bleeding and his politics than for having won the libel suit. In mid-February 1800 he published the first issue of a small periodical, *The Rush Light*, in order "to assist the publick view, in the inspecting of various tenebrious objects," of the villainous head of the "Bleeders" who was "remarkable for insinuating manners, and for that smoothness and softness of tongue, which the mock-quality call politeness, but which the profane vulgar call blarney. To see and hear him, you would think he was all friendship and humanity." Among the various murky "objects" Cobbett set forth for "the publick view," these ranged from Rush joining different churches over the years to his accepting "that lucrative sinecure the treasurership of the mint" to his engaging the services of corrupt lawyers to the belief that Rush "had constantly endeavored to place himself at the head of something or other [and] had ever been upon the search for some discovery, some captivating novelty, to which he might prefix his name, and thus reach, at a single leap, the goal at which men seldom strive but by slow cautious and painful approaches."[22]

Rush, preoccupied with yet another yellow fever outbreak, heeded the advice of friends to ignore Cobbett in the expectation that the enraged pamphleteer was running out of steam. That came to pass in the 15 March issue, wherein Cobbett strenuously defended the charges he had previously made against Rush, whom he now defined as a "vainboaster" who continually boasted in print of his superiority as a man of medicine (a charge that could be argued in Cobbett's favor), and went on to state categorically that Rush by his excessive bloodletting "slew his patients" (a charge which might be argued in Cobbett's favor, though certainly not conclusively). When a fourth number of *The Rush Light*—a screed subtitled "A Peep into a Pennsylvanian Court of Justice"—was published, Cobbett heeded the advice of his friends that to remain in America would surely leave him vulnerable to yet another lawsuit instigated by others he had lampooned libelously. He fled back to England on the first day of June 1800.

Rush could now look forward to the new century finally free from the thorn that had been in his side for three years, content that, irritating—indeed, painful—as the ordeal had been, no permanent damage had been inflicted. Restorative to his spirit were a number of pleasant factors: the annual yellow fever attacks had declined; Thomas Jefferson was in the White House (and Adams was back home in Massachusetts sulking that he had been denied the second term he felt he so richly deserved, an opinion not endorsed by most historians); and he could now, with pleasure, write as a testament for his children his autobiographical "Travels through Life." But, as Butterfield notes in his collection of Rush's correspondence, "The self-justifying tone sometimes apparent" in the *Autobiography*,

as well as in many of his letters in the following years, must be partly attributed to the wounds inflicted by the barbed quills of Peter Porcupine. The protracted feud with Cobbett hastened Rush's retreat from public life and humanitarian causes toward the sequestration of his later years. He was more tranquil, but he was also more disillusioned. His unbounded optimism had given way to resignation tinged with embitterment. Full knowledge of the Rush-Cobbett feud is necessary to understand that embitterment.[23]

20

The Last Years

On 4 November 1812 Dr. Benjamin Rush sent John Adams a copy of his just published *Medical Inquiries and Observations upon the Diseases of the Mind.* It marked the culmination of his attempts, dating back decades, to convince the world that mental disease was to be equated with organic disease. Rush said he would "wait with solicitude" to receive Adams's opinion of the inquiries and observations, which were "in general accommodated to the 'common sense' of gentlemen of all professions as well as medicine."

The subjects, Rush went on, "have hitherto been enveloped in mystery." He had "endeavored to bring them down to that level of all the other diseases of the human body, and to show that the mind and body are moved by the same causes and subject to the same laws." For this attempt to simplify medical thinking, he expected "no quarter from my learned brethren." But he hoped that time would "do my opinions justice. I believe them to be true and calculated to lessen some of the greatest evils of human life. If they are not, I shall console myself with having aimed well and erred honest." Though Rush would not live long enough to see it, he had indeed aimed well—and erred honest. Time would indeed do his opinions justice.

But before we deal with what is universally conceded to be both Rush's greatest gift to medical science and greatest claim to immortality, let us go back to pick up his story following the Cobbett Feud. Remarkably, it was Cobbett himself who inadvertently—and certainly unintentionally—led to the restoration of Rush's good name and reputation, and reminded those who needed reminding that he was America's greatest medical practitioner and educator as the nation entered the nineteenth century. To quote historian James Flexner, "Cobbett's hysterical attacks had helped him in the end, for they reduced what should have remained a medical dispute to terms of personal abuse and Federalist politics. After Jefferson's election in 1800, it was almost a patriotic duty to believe in the discoveries of a good Republican like Rush."[1]

Rush's self-pity notwithstanding—a self-pity that complemented his at times somewhat immutable conviction in the correctness and provability of his ideas—he had his defenders. Militating in his favor was the belief that with the Revolution having brought independence from Europe, the solutions to all problems must be built upon seeds planted on America's shores. Who better, in their collective opinion, than a scientist of Rush's caliber to lead in the planting and harvesting? They accepted Rush's rather questionable belief that American patients differed from their European counterparts and must therefore be treated differently. American patients, they reasoned, were more virile, and therefore needed stronger purges and more heroic bloodletting to restore their health. By the time of his death, Rush had lectured to more than 2,800 students, many of whom in turn became professors themselves and taught his more acceptable theories of case management to young men throughout the growing nation. It is said that every outstanding physician up to and including the Civil War period, whether Union or Confederate, was either a Rush pupil or a pupil of a Rush pupil.

Rush was not a progressive scientist. In fact, his life's record is devoid of any effective experiment. He was typical of his times when it came to employing logic in the evolution of theoretical cures. Contemporaries, especially in Europe, envisioned science moving into uncharted waters. But these, in Flexner's felicitous words, "realized that you can build a house only by putting one small brick on another"; they were "content to spend their lives discovering seemingly unrelated facts about the body. Such careful technique was too slow for Rush, who solved all problems by an act of will."[2]

While there have been more advances in medicine in this century than in all the centuries since Hippocrates and Galen flourished, as recently as the mid-nineteenth century too few facts were scientifically recognized to ensure a basis for the practice of medicine that is now taken for granted. Rather like the many ideas of Da Vinci that had to wait centuries before technological advances could bring them to fulfillment, intelligent medical treatment had to wait on the natural advancement of knowledge. Still, sickness was an inevitable consequence of having been born, and sufferers could not wait for answers to evolve. Physicians were wanted to cure them; in particular, physicians who were sure of themselves and of what they prescribed.

An essential prerequisite for a great practitioner was a great self-assurance, and Rush was imbued with more than his share. Granted, many of his remedies failed, remedies that were resorted to out of ignorance that devolved, for the most part, upon the concepts we now take for granted. But, as Flexner notes, "a Svengali who could hypnotize himself, his patients, and above all his colleagues into believing he was right was certain to be regarded as a great scientist. Rush was such a man."[3]

Given Rush's obvious command of the medical literature of the day, and the almost mesmerizing manner in which he lectured; his celebrated piety (though he moved back and forth no less than four times between the Episcopalian, Presbyterian, and Unitarian faiths, Rush set the record among Philadelphia physicians for attending worship, even keeping pews in several churches simultaneously so that he might visit the nearest one should he desire communion with his Maker during rounds); his simplicity of dress; his commanding demeanor both on the lecture platform and even off the platform while passing through the halls of the medical school, pausing to wish a passing student "I hope you are well, sir"—one doubts there were few who could not but bask in the pride of being a Rush pupil.

And then there was the library of works he wrote as an advocate on so many nonmedical subjects in which he believed unqualifiedly and further enhanced his influence among the overwhelming majority: prison reform, opposition to capital punishment, occupational therapy, and the outrageousness of public punishment for felons as a first step toward their rehabilitation; better education for women; the evils of slavery, liquor, and tobacco. There were his essays on the need to abolish loyalty oaths and on the Indians (for whom he had, as he did for the Jews, a respect for their religious beliefs and high regard for their medical theories and social customs), on the cultivation of sugar, the obligation to extend charity to the less fortunate, journalism, famous men of his period, philosophy, and the evils of paper currency not backed up by precious metal.

Often Rush would commit to paper observations and opinions which, while based on meticulous notes he had recorded, might have benefited from some quiet reflection. But such was his habit—one could call it a compulsion—to make known his views on a given subject, he would literally fling into print ideas that were both first-rate and flawed, brilliant and bizarre. For example, the man who was in the vanguard of the observation of focal infections, demonstrating the relation of decayed teeth to chronic diseases, was the same man who argued that Negroes were black because they suffered a kind of leprosy and insisted that he could cure just about every malady of an organic nature with heavy doses of mercury and bloodletting.

In writing his autobiography, which he commenced with the beginning of the new century, Rush reveals himself as a man so imbued with self-righteousness that to accuse him of being at times quite disingenuous when writing about himself is to commit understatement. For instance, he likens himself to some modern Jeremiah (his favorite Old Testament personage) for having sacrificed his medical practice upon the altar of his many virtuous crusades—yet assures us that during those two decades in Philadelphia he pulled down more fees than any other doctor. And each time Rush particularizes with unconcealed acrimony against an enemy, he assures us he is doing so only that he can forgive him. And just as he was circumspect in recalling his life, since he was writing not for posterity but for his children—why, for instance, did he omit the name of, let alone his romantic attachment to, Sarah Eve?—so did Rush destroy hundreds of pages dealing with the men and events of the Revolutionary War, as an act of patriotism, he insisted, lest any future reader beyond the bounds of his family know that his fellow Founding Fathers he had attacked were less than perfect. (But only some of the men. Those with whom he shared a mutual detestation, such as Dr. Shippen and Alexander Hamilton, were fair game for his quill and ink.)

The point here is not to attack Benjamin Rush. Even the greatest men down through history had their share of failings. But with all his faults, Rush earned the right to be honored for all that he accomplished, in so many areas.

*   *   *

The intense aggravation to which the Cobbett affair had subjected him was soon forgotten, as Rush, while discharging his professional duties, now turned inward and homeward, finding great joy in his family and in his correspondence. To his friend John Montgomery he wrote on 5 August 1801, "I now cultivate about twelve acres of ground two miles from our city, to which I retire two or three times a week in an afternoon to take tea with my family, and where I forget for a few hours the bustle, the sickness, and selfishness, and scandal of Philadelphia." Two months previously, Julia had given birth to their ninth living child, named William for his dead brother. His eldest daughter was married, his elder sons were well along in pursuit of careers. Rush's joy in his beloved Julia and their children was marred only by the fate of John, the firstborn, whose career as a naval surgeon was showing great promise when he was forced to return home, and was now incarcerated as clinically insane. Always a staunch Christian, Rush had by now retreated from politics into religion: "Thrones and kings and secular priests and usurpers must fall and perish. Their doom is fixed in the Scriptures of truth. The Messiah alone shall reign as King of Saints and Lord of the whole earth. *All will end,* not only *well,* but gloriously for those who believe and trust in his name."

Though no longer involved politically, Rush remained very much concerned with the state of the nation. He was not above offering advice gratuitously, especially to his friend Thomas Jefferson, as when he suggested that while in the Constitution titles "are wisely forbidden," there was "a mode of honoring distinguished worth which is cheap and which, if directed properly, would stimulate to greater exploits of patriotism than all the high-sounding titles of a German." This consisted "in calling *states, counties, towns, forts,* and *ships of war* by the names of men who have deserved well of their country." He did stipulate, though, that such a reward should not be conferred until after the honoree had died. It is a practice that is observed to this day.[4]

In his response, dated seventeen days later, from his home at Monticello where he was waiting out the last weeks of his vice presidency before returning to what was then referred to as Federal City as the nation's third president, Thomas Jefferson vetted Rush's proposal and then went on to continue what had become an epistolary exchange of ideas on religion. Rush, a firm believer in the inclusion of the Bible in school curricula (it "contains more knowledge necessary to man in his present state than any other book in the world"), insisted "Christianity is the only true and perfect religion; and that in proportion as mankind adopt its principles and obey its precepts they will be wise and happy."⁵ Jefferson, on the other hand, was a confirmed deist, whose belief in God (which, interestingly, he wrote with a lower case "g") was based on reason rather than revelation, embracing the view that the Deity did indeed set the universe in motion but does not interfere with how it runs.

Jefferson had promised Rush "a letter on Christianity," which the latter had earlier requested, and had "not forgotten. On the contrary, it is because I have reflected on it, that I find much more time necessary for it than I can at present dispose of." For the moment, however, Jefferson could offer "a view on the subject which ought to displease neither the rational Christian nor Deists, and would reconcile many to a character they have too hastily rejected." However, he did "not know that it would reconcile [those] who are all in arms against me." There was one moment, Jefferson recalls, when the constitutionally mandated freedom of religion "had given to the clergy a very favorite hope of obtaining an establishment of a particular form of Christianity thro' the U.S.; and as every seed believes its own form the true one, every one perhaps hoped for his own, but especially the Episcopalians & Congregationalists." Fortunately,

> The returning good sense of our country threatens abortion to their hopes, & they believe that any portion of power confided to me, will be exerted in opposition to their schemes. And they believe rightly; for *I have sworn upon the altar of god, eternal hostility against every form of tyranny over the mind of man.* [Author's italics.] But this is all they have to fear from me; & enough too in their opinion, & this is the cause of their printing lying pamphlets against me, forging conversations for me with [some of the leading ecclesiastics of the time] & which are absolute falsehoods without a circumstance of truth to rest on; falsehoods, too, of which I acquit [the mentioned ecclesiastics], for they are men of truth.⁶

Whatever concerns Rush may have had for Jefferson's rigid views on religion have not been recorded, doubtless because he realized that Jefferson was in his own way as pious as was Rush in his. Rush expressed concerns for Jefferson's health, soliciting a history of his ailments, and sending along (12 March 1803) a detailed program of the proper diet and exercise to follow in alleviating any and all ailments, in particular the chronic diarrhea with which Jefferson, now in the third year of his first presidency, was afflicted.

Such was his affection for Jefferson, an affection reciprocated in kind, Rush accepted with good grace Jefferson's denying his request of 29 April 1805 for appointment to replace Elias Boudinot, who was moving to New Jersey, as director of the mint at Philadelphia. Interestingly, in denying the request Jefferson does not mention that he had already decided upon a replacement for Boudinot. Rather, he cites the need for a "man of mathematical talents" for the position. Why Rush even wanted the directorship in the first place—he already held the treasurership for life—is questionable. He was not hard-pressed financially, and his plate was full, what with his practice, his teaching, his ongoing involvement with any number of social causes and reforms, and in particular his work in the area of mental health.

Rush had by now resumed his correspondence with John Adams, with whom Jefferson had once enjoyed a friendship that had long become an animosity. That Rush was able to maintain close friendships with the two attests not so much to his talent for balancing relationships as for the fact that the two presidents held Rush in the highest esteem.

After Adams left the White House, bitter that the electorate had decided that four years under his presidential headship was quite enough, he returned to his home in Braintree and the life of a semi-recluse. Though no longer active in seeking public office, his name, his deeds, and his opinions occasionally appeared in the newspapers; in particular, his fears of what might befall the nation under Jeffersonian republicanism. Adams not only indicted Jefferson on charges of weakening the Federalist policies of his own administration, he indicted him for the change he saw in the character and direction of the nation, for the dangers to America's peace and security he saw springing up everywhere like the Myrmidons before the gates of Ilium, and for how Jefferson the Francophile was (or was not) preparing for the nation's possible involvement in Europe, now that the continent was again caught up in war.

Though Adams and Rush kept au courant of each other through newspaper references and publications, the two had lost contact since Adams left the White House. Jefferson had recently been elected to a second term, which not only irritated Adams, but exacerbated his fears about what lay ahead for the American people: "I read the public papers and documents, and I cannot and will not be indifferent to the condition and prospect of my country. I love the people of America and believe them to be incapable of ingratitude. They have been ... deceived."[7] It was in this mood that Adams wrote to Rush, as if from out of the blue, on 6 February 1805: "It seemeth to me that you and I ought not to die without saying goodbye or bidding each other adieu." After inquiring solicitously after "that excellent lady, Mrs. Rush" and the Rush children, Adams likened "Democracy" to "a distemper" analogous to "yellow fever and all other epidemic diseases [which] once set in motion and obtains a majority, it converts everything, good, bad, and indifferent into the dominant epidemic." He then begged leave to

> put a few questions to your conscience, for I know you have one. Is the present state of the nation republican [here used in the sense of "democratic"] enough? Is virtue the principle of our government? Is honor? Or is ambition and avarice, adulation, baseness, covetousness, the thirst of riches, indifference concerning the means of rising and enriching, the contempt of principle, the spirit of party and of faction, the motive and the principle that governs? These are serious and dangerous questions, but serious men ought not to flinch from dangerous questions. ...

In his reply, dated 19 February, after bringing Adams up to date on his family, Rush addressed "the second part" of Adams's letter parabolically:

> I am reminded of the answer of Sancho [Panza] in [Cervantes'] *Don Quixote* when he was asked how he liked his government. "Give me," said he, "my shoes and stockings." In like manner I feel disposed to reply to your questions relative to the present state of the

United States, "Give me my lancet and gallipots [small pots used as containers for medications]."

In other words, such was his disillusionment with how the new nation was faring, a disillusionment this confirmed Republican shared with his confirmed Federalist friend in Massachusetts, Rush preferred to concentrate on his medicine to concerning himself with matters over which he had either no control or on which whatever solutions he might be called upon to offer would undoubtedly be ignored.

Thus was begun an expansive and illuminating correspondence that would be ended only by Rush's death eight years later. It was as far-ranging topically as it was extended in quantity: comings-and-goings of their respective children, condemnation of political enemies both present and past, the political situation both at home and abroad, advances in medicine and science, shared disillusionment with the fruits of the Revolution, recollections of the past both pleasant and painful, evaluation of such disparate characters as Napoleon Bonaparte and Aaron Burr, Rush's defense of his methodology in the 1793 yellow fever epidemic—which earned him gold medals from the King of Prussia in 1805, Queen Marie Louise of the short-lived Kingdom of Etruria (the region on Italy's northwest coast where the Etruscan civilization flourished in the first millennium B.C.E.) in 1807, and a diamond ring from Russia's Czar Alexander I in 1811—and exchanges on biblical prophecies and human depravity, the futility of political efforts to improve men, Rush's pleas that Adams write his memoirs or, barring that, a memoir on his role in the Revolution, veterinary medicine, insanity, ad finitum. The subject matter included just about everything but the irony that two men of such disparate political beliefs could agree on so much regarding the direction the nation had embarked on since the election of its first president, for whom both had a less than elevated regard, without once engaging in a sort of Federalist vs. Republican debate. It was as if the two tacitly agreed that their friendship must transcend even the hint of philosophical differences.

Four years after the friendship was resumed, Rush decided that the time had come to heal the breech between Adams and Jefferson—a breech of which Adams wrote on 25 October 1809,

There has never been the smallest interruption of the personal friendship between me and Mr. Jefferson that I know of. You should remember that Jefferson was but a boy to me. I was at least ten years older than him in age, and more than twenty years older than him in politics. [Adams was forty-one, Jefferson thirty-three when the First Continental Congress convened.] I am bold to say I was his preceptor in politics and taught him everything that has been good and solid in his whole political conduct. I served with him on many committees in Congress, in which we established some of the most important regulations of the army &c., &c., &c.

Adams's remarks were a response to a letter of 17 October 1809 in which Rush describes a dream in which he has read in a history of the United States, "Among the most extraordinary events of this year [1809] was the renewal of the friendship and intercourse between Mr. John Adams and Mr. Jefferson, the two ex-Presidents of the United States." Adams's initial reaction, which preceded the above quoted paragraph: The dream "is not history. It may be prophecy."

Why Adams denied a breach had indeed occurred between the two, when it was a matter of historical record, is difficult to understand, unless, perhaps, this was Adams's attempt to justify, if only in his own mind, that the breach had been one-sided, on Jefferson's part. Adams being Adams, he could not have taken responsibility for any action in which he considered himself, rightly or wrongly, the injured innocent party. In fact, he was as responsible as Jefferson for the breach, which developed in 1800 during their contest for the presidency.

Basically, the 1800 contest was the culmination of a chasm that had divided the two men during the years when both represented the emerging United States in Europe. The antimonarchical Anglophobic Francophile Jefferson standing in fierce opposition to the Francophobe Adams, whose favoring of Britain over France, especially during the Napoleonic Wars, led the Republican Jefferson to wonder just how committed the Federalists, and in particular their avatar in the White House, Adams, were to a uniquely democratic government as distinct from one imbued with monarchist inclinations, if not some modified inclination. The friendship was broken, seemingly beyond the most exiguous chance of repair, when Jefferson—whose republicanism symbolized the future that had already arrived—took the White House from Adams, whose Federalism was like a corpse awaiting official burial, and who felt almost as if a second term were owed him by divine right, a second term that in fact became Jefferson's first of two by voters' right.[8]

With both ex-presidents now living in retirement and getting along in years, Rush was more determined than ever to effect a reconciliation. On the second day of the year 1811 he wrote Jefferson,

> When I consider your early attachment to Mr. Adams, and his to you; when I consider how much the liberties and independence of the United States owe to the concert of [both] your principles and labors; and when I reflect upon the sameness of your opinions at present upon most of the subjects of government and all the subjects of legislation, I have ardently wished a friendly and epistolary intercourse might be revived between you before you take a final leave of the common object of your affections. Such an intercourse will be honorable to your talents and patriotism and highly useful to the course of republicanism not only in the United States but all over the world. Posterity will revere the friendship of two ex-Presidents that were once opposed to each other. Human nature will be a gainer by it. I am sure an advance on your side will be a cordial to the heart of Mr. Adams. Tottering over the grave, he now leans wholly upon the shoulders of his old Revolutionary friends.

Rush knew that the stubborn Adams would not make the first move. What he did not know until his letter of response two weeks later was that Jefferson had in fact made an overture toward reconciliation seven years earlier. While still in the White House, he had received from Abigail a letter of condolence on the death of his daughter, Mary Jefferson Eppes. Several exchanges of letters between the two followed, unbeknownst to Adams, in the course of which Jefferson hoped to heal the breach. But Abigail, who had been quite fond of Jefferson during the years both he and her husband represented the United States concurrently at various European courts, could never forgive any man who had fallen out with her husband. Jefferson soon felt obliged to give up.

He forwarded a copy of this correspondence in his 16 January response to Rush, who nevertheless persevered. On 16 December

1811, he included in a letter to Adams part of a letter from Jefferson in which the latter had been told by mutual acquaintances that Adams had told them,

> "*I always loved Jefferson and still love him.* This is enough for me, I only needed this knowledge to revive towards him all the affections of the most cordial moments of our lives. It is known . . . that I have ever done him justice myself and defended him when assailed by others with the single exception as to his political opinions, but with a man possessing so many estimable qualities, why should we be separated by mere differences of opinion in politics, religion, philosophy, or anything else? His opinions are as honestly formed as my own."9

Next day, Rush wrote to Jefferson that he had forwarded to Adams some kind words Jefferson had sent along in a letter of 5 December, and advised that he had written to Adams, "Were I near to you, I would put a pen into your hand and guide it while it wrote the following note to Mr. Jefferson: 'My dear old friend and fellow laborer in the cause of the liberties and independence of our common country, I salute you with the most cordial goods wishes for your health and happiness. John Adams.'" Rush next added an outright appeal that this "second effort to revive a friendly intercourse between [the two former friends] will be successful. Patriotism, liberty, science, and religion will gain a triumph by it."

On 11 February 1812, Rush wrote Jefferson of his pleasure in learning that Adams had kindly acknowledged Jefferson's expression of concern for Adams's daughter, Nabby, who had undergone a serious operation: "It will give me pleasure to hear of a frequent exchange of letters between you and Mr. Adams. I associate the idea of your early friendship for each other, founded upon a sympathy of just opinions and feelings, with every retrospect I take of the great political, moral, and intellectual achievements of the Congresses of 1775 and 1776."

On 17 February, Rush wrote Adams even more fulsomely,

> I rejoice in the correspondence which has taken place between you and your old friend Mr. Jefferson. I consider you and him as the North and South Poles of the American Revolution. Some talked, some wrote, and some fought to promote and establish it,

but you and Mr. Jefferson *thought* for us all. I never take a retrospect [*sic*] of the years 1775 and 1776 without associating your opinions and speeches and conversations with all the great political, moral, and intellectual achievements of the Congresses of those memorable years.

On the last day of February Rush wrote to Jefferson of his great pleasure in learning from Adams "that four letters had passed between you and him," and that in speaking of Jefferson's letters, Adams said, "They are written with all the elegance, purity, and sweetness of style of his youth and middle age, and with (what I envy more) a firmness of finger and steadiness of chirography [calligraphy] that to me are lost forever." Thrilled that he had healed the breach between the two men, Rush added, "It will give me pleasure so long as I live to reflect that I have been in any degree instrumental in effecting this reunion of two souls destined to be dear to each other and animated with the same dispositions to serve their country (though in different ways). . . ." Unfortunately, he had but a year of life left in which to enjoy that pleasure.

Now as we conclude this account of the many accomplishments of Dr. Benjamin Rush, let us return to the work that culminated in his magnum opus, *Medical Inquiries and Observations upon the Diseases of the Mind.* It is a work that can be seen as the valedictory to an extraordinarily productive life for which mankind must remain forever in his debt; it is the work that would earn him the posthumous appellation Father of American Psychiatry.

Prior to Rush's time, information on psychiatry and the treatment of the insane was practically nonexistent, as was any book either written or published in America. With few exceptions, there were no facilities for the insane, whose affliction was often linked in the eighteenth-century popular mind with the devil, and accordingly earned them horrific abuse. Since ignorance of the disease extended not only to laymen but to physicians as well, "treatment" encompassed incarceration with ordinary criminals, confining the insane in almshouses along with paupers, or allowing them to roam about at large. In 1752, when the Pennsylvania Hospital was opened, a section was set aside for the insane—not to care for them so much as to keep them separated from other patients.

The first state hospital in the colonies exclusively for the insane was the Public Hospital for Persons of Insane and Disordered Minds, opened in the colonial capital at Williamsburg, Virginia, in 1763—again, as a place of confinement as distinct from a center for diagnosis and treatment. Not until about eighty years later, by which time Rush's pioneering work in the field had taken hold, was the movement launched for building state hospitals for the insane.

When Rush joined the medical staff at the Pennsylvania Hospital in 1783, its patient population included twenty-four designated "lunatics"—a number that was doubled by 1804. For the thirty years he served with the hospital until his death, Rush maintained a particular interest in the mentally ill, carefully recording observations. Almost from the day he went on staff at the Pennsylvania Hospital he railed against their pitiless and reprehensible treatment, all the while protesting that they should be treated as humanely as were the clinically ill patients, and not as criminals and maniacs beyond the pale of redemption and possible cure. For the rest of his life, Rush would complement his demands for alleviating the subhuman miseries inflicted upon the insane with a close study of the nature and pathology of insanity, identifying its various causes, be they psychological, moral, or organic in origin.

In time, the directors of the Philadelphia Hospital heeded Rush's demand that the "patients afflicted by madness" be provided with accommodations ("cells"). As the city's most distinguished physician Rush could not be ignored when, on 11 November 1789, he rebuked the hospital's board of managers. The "apartments" were damp in winter and too warm in summer and "moreover so constituted, as not to admit readily of a change of air; hence the smell of them is both offensive and unwholesome." Most of the patients were deleteriously affected "by a cold in two or three weeks after their confinement, and several have died of consumption in consequence of this cold," a condition "dishonorable both to the science and humanity of the city of Philadelphia."[10]

Rush then carried his fight to the people, publishing a series of articles in the city newspapers, and petitioning—actually, haranguing—personally members of the state legislature. On 28 February 1792 the assembly appropriated $15,000 for construction of what Rush called "the mad-house"—a new wing of the Pennsylvania Hospital, completed in November 1796, containing improved quarters. At Rush's insistence, a two-room facility—one with cold water, the other hot, for bathing the patients—was subsequently added. Concurrent with this demand came another suggestion from Rush that was yet another milestone on the road to reform in the treatment of the insane: occupational therapy.

The "deranged people" capable of doing so should be given such chores as spinning, sewing, churning butter, and so on, for the women, and for the men, grinding Indian corn to feed the hospital's horses and cows, cutting straw, gardening, and simple carpentry. (An ancillary benefit: the proceeds from such labor might "afford a small addition to the funds of the hospital.") A few years later came another suggestion: the employment of a well-qualified person "as a friend and companion to the lunatics, whose business it shall be to attend them and when the physicians direct their enlargement, to set them safe in their apartments."[11] Thanks to Rush's perseverance, they were beginning to be treated as unfortunately afflicted human beings after centuries of misapprehension and ignorance. But Rush was still not satisfied that enough had been done.

In 1810 he made a series of further recommendations to the board, which were received favorably although action had to be deferred on some due to lack of adequate funding. Among the recommendations: constructing "small and solitary buildings at a convenient distance from the west wing of the hospital" for those patients "in the high and distracted state of madness, in order to prevent the injuries done by the noises to persons in the recent or convalescent state of that disease, and to patients in other diseases, by depriving them of sleep, or by inducing distress from sympathy with their sufferings." Male and female patients should be confined to separate floors. Additionally, "an intelligent man and woman" should be hired to attend the different sexes, "whose business shall be to direct and share in their amusements and to divert their minds by conversation, reading, and obliging them to read and write upon subjects from time to time by the attending physicians."[12] Also, after observing that more deaths, not only of the mentally ill but of all patients, occurred during the night, when by custom the "fires in the hospital were covered at twilight," thus exposing the patients "in a debilitated state to a reduced temperature in the air," Rush demanded that the hospital rooms be kept as warm during the night as during the day, and suggested the appointment of an officer "to renew the fires in all the wards as often as it shall be necessary.[13]

Perhaps nowhere in his work with the mentally ill was Rush more enlightened and advanced in his thinking than in claiming that madness—believed by the medical profession to be uniquely an arterial disease, an inflammation of the brain—was a disease of the entire body; which is to say, it could be both organic in origin as well as psychological. He classified more than a score of causes in several groups. In the first he included those causes that act directly upon the brain, such as injuries; certain local disorders induced by abscesses and tumors; certain diseases such as apoplexy, palsy, epilepsy, and vertigo; overexposure to the sun; even certain odors. (He noted that in Scotland insanity was sometimes induced by lead fumes, causing the addicted patients to bite their hands or tear the flesh on other parts of the body.) The second group of causes for inducing insanity included such factors affecting both the brain and the body as gout, dropsy, tuberculosis, pregnancy, and fevers, along with exhaustion from lack of nourishment, excessive intake of alcoholic beverages, "inordinate sexual desires and gratification," excessive labor or exercise, and exposure to extremes in environmental temperatures. Comprising the third group were corporeal causes, "which act sympathetically upon the brain," such as narcotics, suppression of any usual evacuation of bodily fluids (menses and milk in women, semen or blood from the hemorrhoidal vessels in both genders), even worms in the alimentary canal and irritation from retained foreign matters in the more irritable parts of the body. ("I once knew some small [gun]shot which were lodged in the foot of a small boy, induce madness several years after he became a man.")[14]

Rush also observed that derangement could be caused by factors that act upon the body through the medium of the mind, among them intense and valueless study, for example, "the means of discovering perpetual motion; of converting the base metals into gold; or prolonging life to the antediluvian age; or producing perfect order and happiness in morals and government, by the operations of human reason; and, lastly, researches into the meaning of certain prophecies in the Old and New Testaments." Also an indirect cause of madness was the part played by one's imagination, and "impressions that act primarily on the heart" such as joy, love, terror, fear, grief, distress, defamation, ridicule, loss of liberty, property, or beauty, even an inordinate thirst for love or esteem. Terror was known to have induced insanity in persons who had escaped from fires, earthquakes, and shipwrecks.

He told of how King Charles VI of France went mad following a paroxysm of rage, and of how in 1803 a Philadelphia actor committed suicide after being hissed off the stage. Loss of one's savings and wealth, he found, could lead to insanity; here Rush made the interesting observation that insanity "occurs oftener among the rich who lose only a part of their property, than among persons in moderate circumstances, who lose their all." He told of an American Indian who became unhinged and consequently took his own life when he saw his face in a mirror for the first time after having survived a particularly virulent form of smallpox. One of his patients went insane after losing an eye in a tavern brawl; and "a clergyman in Maryland became insane in consequence of having permitted some typographical errors to escape [notice] in a sermon which he published upon the death of General Washington." Yet another cause for derangement was "occasionally through the medium of the moral faculties," a frequent one being a guilty conscience, whether real or imagined. Rush knew of one woman "of the most exemplary character" who lost her mind "from a belief that she had been unfaithful to the marriage bed," though it was discovered that "the supposed criminal connection was with a man whose very person was unknown to her."[15]

Only after years of study and clinical observation did Rush conclude that insanity occurs more commonly from mental than from corporeal causes, its origin usually psychic rather than physical. Many and varied causes lay at the root of circumstances and condition which predisposed the patient to madness, among them hereditry. Remarkably, he found a great disposition to insanity between the ages of twenty and fifty than in any other age group. Women he found to be more predisposed to insanity than men, presumably because of menstruation, pregnancy (an inordinately high rate among married women of the times, to compensate for the inordinately high rate of death in infancy and early childhood), and "by living so much alone in their families." Moreover, "the distressing impressions made upon the minds of women frequently vent themselves in tears, or in hysterical commotions in the nervous system and bowels, while the same impressions upon the minds of men pass by their more compact nervous and muscular fibers, and descend into the brain, and thus more frequently bring on hypochondriac insanity."

Among other conclusions: Single persons were more predisposed to insanity than married persons. The rich were more predisposed to madness than the poor. Climate definitely influenced the mind (insanity was uncommon in uniformly warm climates, more common in alternately warm and cold climates, most common in climates usually moist, cloudy, and cold). The body was predisposed to derangement depending upon societal environment and ways of life: It was a rare disease among savages, common in commercial countries where fortunes can be made and lost overnight, and most prevalent "at those times when speculation is substituted for regular business."[16] As Nathan Goodman has observed, "All these causes, remote and exciting, direct and indirect, cover in one way or another the etiology of insanity as we know it today, even if current medical terms assigned to the various phases of mental diseases have been changed. Although future findings have completely outmoded Rush's classification of causes, the general conception was remarkable."[17]

Outmoded, almost immediately after his death, was Rush's penchant for bloodletting in treating certain forms of madness, though—to mention but a few among many courses of treatment, depending on the specific manifestation of madness—purgatives and emetics, diet, counterirritants (e.g., application of mustard to the patient's feet sufficiently strong to trigger pain, itself a remedy), warm and cold baths, and activities ranging from such outdoor activities as shooting and hunting to indoor games such as chess and checkers, to "interest the mind or exercise the body," were deemed beneficial even if not restorative to normality.[18]

In some extreme cases, electricity was used to supplement opium, iron, strong tea and green coffee, garlic, and valerian—a form of treatment that would not find general favor among the medical profession until many decades later. In the most extreme cases, the patient was strapped in a chair of Rush's own design called a "tranquilizer," his head fixed rigidly by the lowering of a hinged block fastened to the back. By thus lessening muscular action or reducing motor activity, the tranquilizer was supposed to control the rush of blood toward the brain and presumably reduce the force and frequency of the pulse, thereby inducing a calming effect. The chair was soon dispensed with, due to the resultant bruises and fractures. It did, though, point the way to the future straitjacket.[19] Yet another Rush-devised contraption—a gyrator—was a turntable on which the patient was so placed that the flow of the brain was increased by centrifugal force, the theory being that some forms of mania depended upon the amount and force of blood entering the brain. This, too, was abandoned when Rush decided that bloodletting was the preferred treatment—which, as has been indicated, went the way of the tranquilizer chair and gyrator following Rush's death.

One remarkable insight was in advocating that physicians encourage the patients to, where possible, verbalize their subconscious thoughts. In addition to hearing the patient out sympathetically and in all seriousness—which further encouraged such verbalizing—Rush frequently had his patients articulate on paper as best they could a comprehensive account of their symptoms. Not only did the patient feel better for having been encouraged to do so, but, and of greater consequence, the physician often learned more than he might by simple observation. In advocating what Freud would term mental catharsis, it can be said that Rush anticipated by a century the theory of psychoanalysis, just as his recognizing deviant behavior as a manifestation of unpremeditated illness rather than an act of deliberate transgression laid the groundwork for what we now recognize as personality disorder.

Its flaws notwithstanding, Rush's epochal *Medical Inquiries and Observations upon the Diseases of the Mind* was so complete and so unique a study of mental diseases that it remained the only comprehensive American study on the subject for seventy years, and was the foundation upon which superseding studies incorporating scientific advances were based. We can attribute to Rush's efforts more innovation in the hospitalizing and treatment—above all, the understanding— of the mentally afflicted than to any other physician of his time. His pioneering work in the field brands him as truly a benefactor—indeed, a godsend—of humanity's distressed. Or as Carl Binger put it,

> Although his psychological insights were often astute, the therapeutic measures he employed by no means kept pace with them, because he was bound by the mechanistic attitudes [explaining human behavior or other natural processes in terms of physical causes and processes] that prevailed in his time and that he had brought back with him from Edinburgh. Nevertheless, as the harbinger of American psychiatry he needs no further apology.[20]

Farewell

Over the last two years of his life, Rush had been suffering episodic attacks of a cough that impaired his strength somewhat but did not interfere with his work. With March of 1813 came rainy, damp days, which had a severely adverse effect on the cough, though this did not inhibit his seeing patients. On Wednesday, 14 April, after making his usual rounds, Rush complained of a chill. Barely getting through dinner, he retired at nine o'clock after combating the chill by drinking some brandy and soaking his feet in hot water. During the night a fever developed; this, concomitant with the onset of severe pains in his side, made further sleep almost impossible. Early next morning, with his breathing having become labored, he had his attending physician, Dr. John Dorsey, summon a bleeder, who drew ten ounces from his arm.

This gave him some relief, and he was able to sleep fitfully. At midmorning, Dr. Dorsey found his patient's pulse normal, though the pain continued. Next morning the severely weakened Rush was approaching total exhaustion. He was given some wine-whey, and this seemed to brace him; but as his pulse gradually became weaker, Dr. Dorsey made a diagnosis of typhus. Stimulants were administered, but did not produce the desired effect.

When Rush awakened Saturday morning with severe pains, he asked that a bleeder be called in again. He believed that his *tussis senilis* was in fact advanced pulmonary tuberculosis (probably a more correct diagnosis than Dr. Dorsey's typhus), and had now reached an acute stage. After consulting with another of Rush's colleagues who had been called in, Dr. Dorsey drew an additional three ounces of blood. This gave Rush some relief, and when he awakened on Sunday morning, his spirits had improved to the degree that he was able to discuss his case with the two physicians.

But around four that afternoon his temperature began to spike, and by nine o'clock his condition had become critical. When he awakened the following morning, he realized the end was near. At five o'clock that afternoon, Monday 19 April, surrounded by his beloved Julia (who would survive him by thirty-five years) and those of his children not away at school or raising their own families in other states or confined elsewhere, as was John in the Pennsylvania Hospital lunatic ward, Dr. Benjamin Rush died. To the very end, he was rational, composed, and lucid.

His last words were to his son Richard: "Be indulgent to the poor."[1]

Encomiums and eulogies filled the newspapers, typified by the editorial that appeared next morning in one local journal lamenting the passing of "the great and good Doctor Benjamin Rush":

> The columns of a newspaper are not the place, nor our feeble pen the instrument, for commemorating the transcendent virtues, talents and usefulness of such a man. Biography and history will no doubt hereafter do them the justice they deserve. In the meanwhile it is the painful duty of every press to contribute its transient notice of an event, which has deprived the country of a patriot, society of a most superior and fascinating a member, and science of an illustrious ornament. . . . Few men, if any, in this or any other country, have so eminently combined public with professional services as Dr. Rush. From the time of his signing the Declaration of Independence to the last moment of his career, he has always displayed the first requisites for a great statesman; while his multiform works in medical science have been almost annual productions of his knowledge in this department. . . . As a father, a husband, a brother, a friend, a companion, a citizen, in every sphere of existence, his attributes were of the highest character, his loss leaves a chasm which time alone can fill.[2]

On 22 April, in the presence of a large crowd that ranged from ordinary citizens to patients, students, and colleagues, to deputations of the American Philosophical Society, Pennsylvania Society for the

Abolition of Slavery, and the Pennsylvania Hospital, Rush was laid to rest in the Christ Church Burial Ground at Fifth and Arch Streets, fifty yards east of the grave of the one man he revered above all others, Benjamin Franklin. The inscription on the gravestone reads:

IN MEMORY OF

BENJAMIN RUSH M.D.

WHO DIED ON THE 19TH OF APRIL

IN THE YEAR OF OUR LORD 1813

AGED 68

Well done good and faithful servant
Enter thou into the joy of the Lord.
MATT. 25C 23V[3]

That Benjamin Rush died recognized as America's leading physician and social reformer, and fondly recalled as one of the Founding Fathers, is probably best summed up in the letter of condolence John Adams wrote to Richard on 5 May 1813:

In what terms can I address you? There are none that can express my sympathy with you and your family, or my own personal feelings on the loss of your excellent father. There is not another person out of my own family, who can die, in whom my personal happiness can be so deeply affected. The world would pronounce me extravagant and no man would apologize for me if I should say that in the estimation of unprejudiced philosophy, he has done more good in this world than Franklin or Washington.

Rush could not, of course, have known that such would be the appreciation beyond the bounds of Philadelphia of his many accomplishments that in addition to the Benjamin Rush State Park in the northeast city that was his lifelong home, there would arise such disparate memorials bearing his name as an elementary school in Washington State, a county in Indiana (organized 1821), Rush Street and Rush Medical College (now Rush-Presbyterian Medical Center) in Chicago, the Benjamin Rush Society for Healing Arts and Professionals at Franklin and Marshall College, and, unveiled in 1904, a statue on the grounds of the Washington, D.C., Bureau of Medicine and Surgery, across from the entrance to the old Observatory Building.

There were eulogies from throughout the country that seemed almost bent on topping each other in praising the man. As late as 1887, the eminent physician and litterateur S. Weir Mitchell pronounced this arguably most outstanding medical practitioner in eighteenth-century America, this man who had raised his profession to a higher level than it had ever attained previously, "the greatest physician this country has produced . . . a sanitarian far in advance of his day."[4]

While the knowledge of being so honored and eulogized would surely have pleased Rush no end, one tends to suspect that perhaps his greatest posthumous satisfaction would have been Thomas Jefferson's letter of 27 May 1813 to John Adams upon learning of the passing of their mutual friend:

Another of our friends of seventy-six is gone, my dear Sir, another of the co-signers of the Independence of our country. And a better man than Rush could not have left us, more benevolent, more learned, of finer genius, or more honest.[5]

NOTES

ABBREVIATIONS: USED IN THE NOTES

Auto. The Autobiography of Benjamin Rush.
BR Benjamin Rush, when cited in letters.
BR-MSS Rush manuscripts in University of Pennsylvania Archives and
    Pennsylvania Historical Society
PHS Pennsylvania Historical Society.

PROLOGUE

1. Paine, *The Crisis*, Introduction.
2. C.F. Adams, vol. 2, 512.
3. *Auto.*, 110; Butterfield, *John Adams*, vol. 1, 182.
4. Morrison, 277.
5. *Auto.*, 139.

CHAPTER I

1. Cromwell quote in Goodman, 3; Rush, 24.
2. BR to John Adams, 8 August 1812.
3. *Auto.*, 168.
4. Ibid., 26; see also BR to Adams, 8 August 1812.
5. "made my first": BR to Adams, 8 August 1812; "mortal rage": quoted in
    Hawke, 8.
6. *Auto.*, 27–28, 166–167.
7. Goodman, 4.
8. Johnson, 109–110. Remarkably, the term is never used at all in George
    Bancroft's *History of the United States* (1834–74), the first major history
    of America; a few modern historians argue that the phrase, and to a
    degree the concept behind it, was actually invented as late as 1842 by

Joseph Tracey in his *Great Awakening: A History of the Revival of Religion in the Times of Edwards and Wakefield.*

9. Hawke, 13–14.
10. BR to John Adams, 26 December 1811.
11. *Auto.*, 31.
12. Ibid., 32.
13. See also D'Elia, 13.
14. "Lives of the same species": BR, "Oration . . . on the Moral Faculty," *Modern Inquiries and Observations* (1789), 46; "For I consider": BR to Walter Minto, 24 March, 1792.
15. *Auto.*, 35.
16. D'Elia, 15.
17. Jordan, 188.
18. Davies quoted in BR, "A Dream Containing a Dialogue . . . ," in "Letters and Thoughts," BR-MSS, 70.
19. *Auto.*, 36.
20. D'Elia, 16–17.
21. Quotes from Davies's "Religion and Public Spirit. A Valedictory Address . . ." from a copy printed in Portsmouth, N.H., 1762, now in the Rare Book Room of Dartmouth College Library.
22. BR to Enoch Green, [?] 1761.
23. *Auto.*, 36.
24. Ibid., 36–37.

CHAPTER 2

1. Binger, 16.
2. *Auto.*, 38.
3. Binger, 28–30.
4. Hawke, 27–29.
5. *Auto.*, 39.
6. Ibid.
7. Rush, Benjamin, *Medical Inquiries and Observations* (Philadelphia, 1815 edition, published originally 1805), vol. 3, 125.
8. *Auto.*, 38.
9. Hazard went on to become a New York bookseller, postmaster general, founder of the Insurance Company of North America, and a pioneer in editing the archives of the new nation. For some unknown reason, the early friendship between the two broke off suddenly in 1770. Hazard later wrote to Jeremy Belknap, "Take care how you commit yourself to your new correspondent [i.e., BR]. Neither his stability nor prudence are to be depended upon." Butterfield, *Letters*, vol. 1:6, n. 1.
10. BR to Ebenezer Hazard, 2 August 1764.
11. BR to Ebenezer Hazard, 8 November 1765.

12. Hawke, 40–41. The undated letter to Hazard, from which Hawke quotes, is not in the collection of published letters. A copy is in the BR-MSS.

13. Hawke, 33.

14. BR to Vine Utley, 25 June 1812.

15. Sanderson, 19; Biddle, 223.

CHAPTER 3

1. Potts married her, her health having returned miraculously upon his own return, took his medical degree at the College of Physicians, established a successful practice in Redding, and, like Rush, served during the Revolutionary War in the Continental Army's medical department. Potts's distinction was complemented by a dedication that so undermined his health he died in 1777 at the age of thirty-six. Butterfield, *Letters*, vol. 1, 28, n. 2.

2. *Auto.*, 40.

3. Ibid., 40–41.

4. Quoted in Goodman, 14.

5. Butterfield, *Letters*, 27–28, n. 1.

6. *Auto.*, 43.

7. The Pepys quote is in Ackroyd, Peter, *London, the Biography* (New York, 2001), 333. Rush's quotes are from a letter dated 29 December 1766 to an unidentified party.

8. *Auto.*, 51–52.

9. D'Elia, 22.

10. Ibid., 24. The Rush quotes are from his *Scottish Journal.*

11. David Ramsay, *Eulogium*, 29–30, quoted in D'Elia, ibid.

12. *Auto.*, 87–88.

13. Thompson, *William Cullen*, 1:620–621.

14. "An Eulogium in Honor of the late Dr. William Cullen." "I consider Dr. Cullen as the Columbus of Medicine," Rush, "Introductory Lecture to a Course of Lectures on the History and Practice of Physic," quoted in D'Elia, 25.

15. BR to Morgan, 20 January 1768.

16. D'Elia, 28.

17. Rush, "Three Lectures upon Animal Life," *Medical Inquiries and Observations,* 1–54.

18. BR to Smith, 30 April 1767. Smith subsequently became prominent in Pennsylvania politics during and after the Revolution, a member of Continental Congress, and a trustee of both the University of Pennsylvania and Princeton University.

19. BR to John Adams, 21 July 1789.

20. *Auto.*, 46.

21. Ibid., 47.
22. BR to Jonathan Bayard Smith, 30 April 1767.
23. *Auto.*, 51.
24. D'Elia, 31.
25. *Auto.*, 43; "Scottish Journal."
26. BR to Morgan, 20 January, 1768; Redman to BR, 21 December 1767 and 12 May 1768; "Redman ended": Hawke, 59.

CHAPTER 4

1. Interestingly, as a Pennsylvania delegate to the Continental Congress, Dickinson opposed rebellion against Great Britain in favor of conciliation and refused to sign the Declaration of Independence. However, he fought in the Revolution, wrote the first draft of the Articles of Confederation, went on to represent Delaware in the 1787 Constitutional Convention, and effectively urged adoption of the Constitution, which he played a leading role in framing, in a series of letters signed "Fabius."
2. BR to John Morgan, 27 July 1768.
3. Binger, 49.
4. *Auto.*, 52–53.
5. Ibid., 54.
6. Hawke, 69–70.
7. Binger, 54–55.
8. Ibid., 57.
9. *Auto.*, 55.
10. BR to James Abercrombie, 22 April 1793; *Auto.*, 59.
11. *Auto.*, 61–62.
12. BR to Jacob Rush, 19 January and 26 January 1769.
13. *Auto.*, 61.
14. Ibid.
15. The request to his Paris bankers, dated 13 February 1769, for a credit line of £200, among the Franklin papers in the Library of the American Philosophical Society, is Franklin's only mention of the incident, and is probably the basis of the apocryphal story that he paid for Rush's education abroad.
16. D'Elia, 46.
17. Butterfield, *Letters*, 77, n. 1.
18. *Auto.*, 68; see also Butterfield, *Letters*, 77, n. 82.
19. The thirty-two-page handwritten document (not in Rush's hand), presumably a copy of the original, which is lost, is now in the Pierpont Morgan Library in New York City.
20. *Auto.*, 71–72.
21. Ibid., 73–74.
22. Ibid.

23. Ibid., 75.
24. D'Elia, 49.
25. *Auto.*, 77–78.

CHAPTER 5

1. *Auto.*, 78–79.
2. Morison, 185.
3. Ibid., 180.
4. *Pennsylvania Chronicle*, 19 March 1770.
5. *Auto.*, 83–84.
6. Ibid., 84–85.
7. Watson, vol. 1, 294.
8. Binger, 71–72.
9. *Auto.*, 82–83.
10. *Pennsylvania Chronicle and Universal Advertiser*, 14 August 1769.
11. Toner, 99.
12. *Auto.*, 81.
13. Rush, *Medical Inquiries and Observations* (1805 ed.), vol. 4, 366–380.
14. *Auto.*, 82.
15. Ibid.
16. Binger, 84–85; Herbert S. Klickstein, "A Short History of the Professorship of Chemistry of the University of Pennsylvania School of Medicine, 1766–1847," *Bulletin of the History of Medicine* 27 (1953), 53.
17. Hawke, 93.
18. Rush, "An Account of the Effects of the Strammonium or Thorn Apple," in *American Philosophical Society Transactions I* (1771), 318–322.
19. *Auto.*, 82.
20. BR to Barbeu-Dubourg, 29 April 1773.

CHAPTER 6

1. In *Pennsylvania Magazine of History and Biography*, vol. 5, 19–36, 191–205 (Philadelphia, 1881).
2. For the Rush-Sarah Eve romance, see Flexner, 66–70.
3. *Auto.*, 116.
4. Ibid.
5. Ibid., 168.
6. BR to Mrs. Rush, 27 May 1776.
7. *Auto.*, 109, 149; 155, 190.
8. Ibid., 110.
9. Riedman and Green, 116.
10. Morison, 274.
11. *Auto.*, 110, n. 9.

12. Ibid., 111.
13. Ibid., 112.

CHAPTER 7

1. "A Speech delivered in Carpenter's Hall, March 16th before the Subscribers toward a Fund for Establishing Manufactures of Woolen, Cotton, and Linen, in the City of Philadelphia. Published at the Request of
   the Company." It was published in two sections in the *Pennsylvania Evening Post*, 11 and 13 April 1775.
2. Hawke, 129.
3. *Auto.*, 113–114.
4. BR to James Cheetham, 17 June 1809. Cheetham, an English radical who
   immigrated to the United States in 1798 at the age of twenty-six, had
   been an admirer of Paine. Like Rush—like so many others—he would
   turn against Paine in later years, in Rush's case because he found the
   antireligious attitudes in his *Age of Reason* personally offensive.
5. Ford, vol. 1, 75 ff.
6. Keane, 106.
7. Burnett, 126, 177.
8. Keane, op. cit., 106.
9. BR to James Cheetham, 17 June 1809; *Auto.*, 114–15.
10. Known as Hartley the Younger, to distinguish him from his father the
    noted philosopher, Hartley would with Benjamin Franklin draft the
    1783 Treaty of Paris that ended the American War for Independence.
    Hailed in his day as one of Burke's leading collaborators in opposition to
    Lord North, who served as prime minister from 1770 to 1782, Hartley's
    claim to historical fame was his invention of a system of fireproofing
    homes.
11. Montross, 64–65.
12. Morison, 285–286.
13. *Auto.*, 113, 151; BR to Thomas Jefferson, 6 October 1800.
14. BR to John Adams, 12 February 1812, in Schutz and Adair.
15. Morison, 289–290.
16. Hawke, 127.
17. *Pennsylvania Packet*, 24 November 1774; *Pennsylvania Journal*, 25 Janu-
    ary 1775.
18. *Auto.*, 91–92.

CHAPTER 8

1. Hawke, 143–144.
2. Joseph Shippen to Edward Shippen, 29 February 1776, Shippen Papers,
   vol. 12, PHS.
3. Joseph Shippen, 12 March 1776, ibid.

4. Hawke, 145.
5. Letter dated 7 May, 1776, in Franklin Papers, American Philosophical Society.
6. BR to John Adams, 11 July 1806.
7. Quoted in Lincoln, 249.
8. Charles Francis Adams, vol. 2, 159–160.
9. BR to Julia Rush, 29 May 1776. The pronominal "me" was in the original but BR lined it out. McKean, a delegate and signer from Delaware, was equally active in Pennsylvania politics.
10. BR to Julia Rush, 29 May, 1 June 1776.
11. *Pennsylvania Gazette,* 22 May 1776.
12. Ibid., 29 May 1776.
13. Ford, *Journals of the Continental Congress.*, vol. 5, 603–604.
14. Hawke, 160.
15. The so-called Financier of the American Revolution, Morris would organize the finance for the Continental Army, found the Bank of North America in 1782, and die bankrupt twenty-four years later at the age of seventy-two.
16. BR to John Adams, 20 July 1811.

CHAPTER 9

1. Flexner, *Washington in the Revolution,* 116–117.
2. *Auto.,* 140.
3. Ibid., 120.
4. Ibid., 123–124.
5. Ibid.
6. Hawke, 175.
7. BR letters to Richard Henry Lee, 21 December, 25 December, 30 December, 1776, 6 January (2 letters), 7 January, 14 January (2 letters), 15 January 1777.
8. Butterfield, *Further Letters,* 124.
9. Ibid., 125.
10. *Auto.,* 125–127.
11. Ibid., 127–128.
12. Ibid., 128.
13. Ibid.
14. BR to Richard Henry Lee, 7 January 1777.
15. *Auto.,* 129.
16. BR to Lady Jane Wishart Belsches, 21 April 1784. Rush's letter was in response from one from Lady Jane, now lost, inquiring about him; from the text it is obvious that she was not even aware that he had married and started a family. For the background of the Rush letter, see *Princeton Univ. Libr. Chron.,* 9 (1947–1948), 1–12.
17. Mitchell, 129–150.

18. Ibid.; *Auto.*, 142.
19. BR to John Adams, 24 February 1790.
20. Mitchell, 136.
21. *Auto.*, 141.
22. Hawke, 185.
23. BR to Robert Morris, 22 February 1777; "This resolution": cited in Hawke, 286.

CHAPTER 10

1. *Auto.*, 189. As soon as he got to Philadelphia Rush submitted his accounts for service in Congress (£143 for the first period, £34 for the second, and an additional £10 for traveling expenses to and from Baltimore).
2. Flexner, 73. The quotations are from a letter of 12 February 1812 to John Adams, in which Rush's reminiscences were prompted by his eagerness to support Adams's retrospective dislike of Washington, by then thirteen years in his grave.
3. Hawke, 191.
4. BR to Nathanael Greene, 1 February 1778; see *Letters*, 145–146, n.1.
5. *Auto.*, 131–132.
6. Hawke, 204.
7. *Auto.*, 132.
8. Goodman, 129.
9. BR to Horatio Gates, 27 July 1803.

CHAPTER 11

1. Flexner, 25.
2. Binger, 112.
3. Wainwright, 420–421, 425.
4. Rush's testimony at Shippen's court-martial, *Pennsylvania Packet*, 7 October 1780; it was during the court-martial that Shippen published Rush's commendatory letter of 28 November 1776 in the 18 November 1780 issue of the *Pennsylvania Packet*.
5. Flexner, 43.
6. *Auto.*, 131.
7. *Pennsylvania Packet*, 7 October 1780; this formed part of the testimony in Shippen's trial.
8. BR to Adams, 21 and 31 October 1777; BR's proposed affidavit and threat to resign: Gibson, 225.
9. Adams's reaction is only surmisal. His letters to Rush now in print (Schutz and Adair, *The Spur of Fame*) that comprise their voluminous two-way correspondence cover only the years 1805 to 1813.
10. BR to Adams, 31 October 1777, op. cit.

11. BR to James Searle, 19 November 1777. Searle, a leading Philadelphia merchant and fervent patriot, was a member of the Continental Congress and later a commercial agent for Pennsylvania in Europe.

12. BR to Elizabeth Graeme Ferguson, 24 December 1777. Ferguson, a prominent member of the pre-Revolution Philadelphia aristocracy, was a close friend to both the Rush and Stockton families; she came to ultimate grief as the result of a disastrous secret marriage while visiting England to a Scot who appeared two years later in Philadelphia with Howe's army; through unscrupulous involvement in an unsuccessful scheme to effect a quick peace, he was attainted and his share in his wife's inherited estate was confiscated, and his wife's remaining property was forfeited. Through the assistance of friends, including Rush, the property was restored to her after the war, but she never saw her husband again, and she died in comparative property. (Butterfield, *Letters*, 179, n. 1)

13. Duer, second only to Robert Morris in knowledge of matters financial, served afterward as Alexander Hamilton's assistant secretary of the treasury.

14. *Auto.*, 134–136.

15. Butterfield, *Letters*, 182, n. 2; see also Fitzpatrick, ed., *Writings*, vol. 10, 297.

CHAPTER 12

1. BR to John Adams, February 12, 1813. See also Butterfield, *Letters*, vol. 2, 1124, n.1.

2. BR to Julia Rush, 15 January 1778.

3. Butterfield, *Letters*, 162, n. 4.

4. BR to Julia Rush, 15 January 1778.

5. Rush's regret in this matter can be measured in his somewhat frantic letter (5 September 1804) to then Chief Justice of the United States John Marshall. (See reference note 2, Chapter 14, *infra*.)

6. Hawke, 216.

7. Fitzpatrick, vol. 6, 453.

8. For a complete record of the Rush-Washington controversy, the details of which need not detain us, see Butterfield, *Letters*, Appendix 1, vol. 2, 1197–1208.

9. Binger, 137.

10. BR to John Adams, 22 January 1778; BR to James Searle, 21 January 21, 1778.

11. BR to [Dr.] John Morgan, n.d., June 1779.

12. Ibid.

13. Ibid.

14. Ibid.

15. BR to Henry Laurens, 30 January 1778.

16. BR to John Adams, 8 February 1778.

17. Adams's letter is dated 8 February, 1778, five days before he sailed for Europe.
18. Shippen's letter of 18 January 1778, from which Rush quotes, is printed in Gibson, 213.
19. BR to Nathanael Greene, 1 February 1778.
20. See Butterfield, *Letters*, vol. 1, 208, n. 7. The letter to the three—William Henry Drayton, Samuel Huntington, and John Bannister—is dated 20 April 1778.
21. Ford, *Journals of the Continental Congress*, vol. 10, 303, cited in Butterfield, *Letters*, vol. 1, 208, n.10.
22. Butterfield, *Letters*, vol. 1, 211, n.1.
23. BR to William Henry Drayton, Samuel Huntington, and John Banister, 20 April 1778.
24. BR to John Morgan, June 1779; "Ordered to lie": Butterfield, *Letters*, vol. 1, 211, n. 2.
25. *Auto.*, 137–138.

CHAPTER 13

1. In June of the following year, Spain would come to the aid of the Americans, albeit tangentially, by entering the war against Britain, conditional to France's promise to assist Spain in recovering Gibraltar and Florida.
2. BR to Abigail Smith Adams, 3 September 1778.
3. *Auto.*, 138.
4. In the letter, Rush laments: "Poor General Lee has been found guilty of all the charges brought against him" following his court-martial for his behavior at the Battle of Monmouth Court House, "viz., disobedience of orders, an unsoldierly retreat, and insolence to the Commander in Chief. . . ." Lee's suspension from army duty for twelve months had "not diminished my veneration nor lessened my attachment to my honored friend. I shall always view him as the *first* general in America." That Lee deserved the court-martial and punishment mattered not a whit to Rush, whose loyalty to friends took precedence over personal behavior.
5. BR to David Ramsay, 5 November 1778. Ramsay, a graduate of Princeton and the College of Philadelphia, was at the time a member of the South Carolina legislature, and would later represent that state in Congress. He wrote a number of important works in medical and political history, including *A History of the American Revolution* (Philadelphia, 1789), which Rush aided him in writing and getting published.
6. It is here that the autobiographical part of Rush's *Autobiography* ends. See 138, notes 16 and 17.
7. BR to David Ramsay, 5 November 1778.
8. Hawke, 227.
9. BR to John Adams, 24 February 1790.
10. *Auto.*, 158.

11. BR to James McHenry, 2 June 1779.
12. Butterfield, *Letters,* vol. 1, 229–235.
13. Ibid., 236.
14. Full coverage was run in the *Pennsylvania Packet,* 22 and 29 July 1779, and *Pennsylvania Gazette,* 28 July 1779.

CHAPTER 14

1. Gibson, 267.
2. BR to John Marshall, September 5, 1804. At the time the chief justice of the United States had just published the first two volumes of his *Life of George Washington* (Philadelphia, 1804–1807) and Rush's recounting of his cordial visit with Washington at Morristown was intended to support his request that Marshall not include the letter to Patrick Henry and Washington's resultant reproof of Rush in the third volume, which was then being printed. "I declare I neither conversed with nor corresponded with the gentlemen who were publicly said to be hostile to General Washington. The fears and apprehensions I expressed in my letter to Governor Henry were founded upon the fatal tendency of the disorders I saw in the department of the army in which I acted, and upon some private anecdotes that had been communicated directly not indirectly to me by officers of high rank and respectability.... The private anecdotes alluded to, with the names of the persons who related them, I have always intended should descend to the grave with me. They were not suspected of entertaining them. You will be surprised when I add that *Governor Henry was one of them.*" (See Appendix I, "Rush and Washington," in *Auto.*)
3. See Rush, "Notes on Congress," Notebook No. 2, and "Substance of information and evidence against Dr. Shippen, June 29," BR-MSS. Morgan quoted Rush's testimony in the 7 October 1780 edition of the *Pennsylvania Packet.* Later a delegate to Congress, Boudinot served as its president, 1782–1783, and was a member of the first three Congresses under the Constitution.
4. BR to John Adams, 13 July 1780.
5. *Pennsylvania Packet,* 25 November, 1780; Ford, *Journals of the Continental Congress,* vol. 17, 744–746.
6. Binger, 144.
7. Hawke, 239.
8. BR to John Adams, 13 July 1780. Word of the loss of Charleston had not arrived at Philadelphia until June.
9. *Pennsylvania Packet,* 27 June 1780.
10. Hawke, 241.
11. The quote is in a letter to Rush from his former apprentice James Hall, dated 27 April 1780, in BR-MSS. Hall would be taken on by Rush to relieve the pressure of his patient load, in which capacity he would serve

for seven years before relocating to Yorktown to establish his own practice.

12. The term, derived from corruption among Caribbean Negroes of the word "dandy," described the high-stepping gait of its victims, much in the way of the dandified step of the popular American "cakewalk" dance among American Negroes, because their leg pains, a side effect of the disease, caused them to walk or "strut" in that manner.

13. "An Account of the Bilious Remitting Fever, as It Appeared in Philadelphia in the Summer and Autumn of the Year 1780," reprinted in *American Journal of Medicine II* (1951). In a letter of 25 August to John Adams, Rush wrote, "The heat of the weather in the shade has been for several days 93 up to 95° of Fahrenheit's thermometer, within these three weeks. Many have died from drinking cold water, and a few have expired suddenly without labor or exercise from the excessive heat.

14. *Auto.*, 85.

15. Ibid, 85–86.

16. Also in this letter Rush passed on the rumor that if the Republicans were victorious in the upcoming assembly election, John Dickinson would doubtless become president. But the vote was split almost evenly between Republicans and Constitutionalists, and the presidency went not to Dickinson but to William Moore, a relatively unknown compromise candidate, which did not go down well with Rush.

17. Hawke, 248.

18. *Pennsylvania Packet,* 23 October and 2 November 1781.

CHAPTER 15

1. Hawke, 250.

2. *Freeman's Journal,* 26 September 1781.

3. Ibid., 3 and 10 October 1781.

4. Ibid., 17 October and 7, 14, and 21 November.

5. *Auto.*, 180.

6. Born 22 October, 1781, Louis-Joseph died eight years later, and was succeeded as heir by his equally ill-fated brother, Charles, titular king of France as Louis XVII, who died in the Temple prison in Paris at the age of ten, two years after the regicide of his parents.

7. To the Editor of *The Pennsylvania Journal,* "On the United States Navy," 4 July 1782.

8. *Pennsylvania Gazette,* 31 July 1782, "The Subject of an American Navy Continued," by "Leonidas."

9. Rush concludes the letter by revealing himself as the "Leonidas" over whose name he "endeavored to serve my country lately by publishing some essays upon a navy." He adds that they "were attacked with virulence by Dr. Arthur Lee under the signature of Virginius" (in the *Freeman's Journal* on 7 and 21 August 1782). "This Dr. Lee," Rush adds, "is

the brother-in-law of Dr. Shippen"—as if that alone would account for "Virginius's" objurgation.

10. The essay is reproduced in Butterfield, *Letters,* vol. 1, 270–272.

11. The only problem facing Rush's followers as they crusaded toward what would eventuate as the Eighteenth (Prohibition) Amendment was what they saw, in his subsequent writings on the subject following the 1782 essay, as his insidiously recommending wine and beer as substitutes for hard liquor. In fact, he prescribed both, but especially wine, for medicinal purposes.

12. *Auto.,* 163.

13. BR to John Montgomery, 5 November 1782. The *Autobiography,* 314, contains Rush's moving eulogy following the death of the Ireland-born Montgomery, who achieved so much despite a lack of formal education and being barely literate. He was, with Rush, one of the two men most responsible for building Dickinson College.

14. Dated 31 October 1782, the petition was published in the *Pennsylvania Journal* on 13 November 1782.

CHAPTER 16

1. The Republicans are not be confused with the present-day Republican Party, which did not come into existence until the eve of the Civil War, when its members broke away from the Whigs because they felt the Whigs had not taken a strong enough stand against slavery.

2. Hawke, 268.

3. Ibid., 269.

4. Goodman, 128–129, 132–133.

5. These and other exercises in didacticism, under the umbrella title *Sixteen Introductory Lectures,* are now preserved, in manuscript form, in the University of Pennsylvania Library.

6. Ibid., "On the Duty and Advantages of Studying the Diseases of Domestic Animals, and the Remedies Proper to Remove Them."

7. *Sixteen Introductory Lectures.* See also Goldman, 136–141.

8. Binger, 173–174.

9. Goodman, 321–322. The Rush quotations are from various letters.

10. Goodman, 325–326.

11. Binger, 169.

12. "To the Citizens of Pennsylvania of German Birth and Extraction: Proposal of a German College," *Pennsylvania Gazette,* 31 August 1785. Reproduced in Butterfield, *Letters,* vol. 1, 364.

13. Binger, 170.

14. Ibid, 171.

15. The title of an annual oration, his second, which Rush gave at the invitation of the Philosophical Society in 1786, the address, which attracted much attention, was subsequently printed as a pamphlet and later in-

cluded in the second volume of his *Medical Inquiries and Observations.* It forms part of the section "On Natural and Medical Sciences" in the *Selected Writings of Benjamin Rush,* edited by Dagobert D. Runes, upon which collection the material I have used in this section is based.

16. Binger, 173.

CHAPTER 17

1. The rebellion, led by one Daniel Shays, was precipitated by excessive land taxation, high legal costs, and economic depression following the war. It was only one of many such protests during this period. The insurgents demanded protective legislation, the abolition of the court of common pleas, and a radical reduction of taxes. After preventing the sitting of the courts at Northampton, Worcester, Great Barrington, and Concord, Shays and his followers broke up a session of the state supreme court in Springfield, and on 25 January 1787 tried to seize the federal arsenal at Springfield but were repulsed by a force of militia, and the rebellion was thus ended. Most of the men were pardoned later in the year. Shays was condemned to death but escaped to Vermont and was pardoned a year later. Shays's and similar rebellions forced the nation's leaders and politicians to accept that the Articles of Confederation, while providing for the basic laws of the nation, did not suffice as an effective means of governing. The protests thus helped push the nation's leaders closer to drawing up and ratifying the Constitution of the United States.

2. The essay is represented in Butterfield, *Letters.* The quotation is from Psalms 41:1.

3. The essay was published in London that same year, thereby "internationalizing" Rush's reputation as a pioneer in prison reform.

4. Hawke, 345.

5. BR to Richard Price, 14 February 1787.

6. BR to John Adams, 12 February 1812.

7. *Auto.,* 160.

8. BR to Timothy Pickering, 30 August 1787. See also Butterfield, *Letters,* vol. 1, 440, n. 1.

9. BR to John Coakley Lettsom, 28 September 1787. Note that the last line is a paraphrase of his remark to Richard Price, *supra,* prior to the meeting of the Constitutional Convention.

10. The mass meeting was covered in its entirety in the 10 October 1787 edition of the *Pennsylvania Packet.*

11. McMaster and Stone, *Philadelphia and the Federal Constitution,* 214.

12. Ibid., 218–231 and 234–235 for, respectively, Wilson's and BR's speeches.

13. Ibid., 294–295.

14. Ibid., 300, 771.

15. Ibid., 419–425.

16. Ibid., 424, 425.

17. Bowen, 277.
18. BR to John Montgomery, 9 April 1788.
19. *Auto.*, 246. Rush adds: "He obtained some of my hair secretly, and had it put into a ring in London, which ring he gave to one of the maids to keep for him, with an injunction 'not to tell me of it.' William lived with Rush "occasionally afterwards" following his manumission, "and after returning from sea [apparently as a deckhand] always made my home his home." Apparently one of those returns from sea coincided with Rush's illness.
20. Adams had just arrived back in Boston from Europe and was immediately elected to Congress, but because the old Congress was dissolved he never took his seat.
21. BR to Elias Boudinot, "Observations on the Federal Procession in Philadelphia," 9 July 1788. The letter was printed that month in *The American Museum*, 4, 75–78.

CHAPTER 18

1. BR to John Adams, 4 June 1789.
2. *Auto.*, 176.
3. Hawke, 386.
4. In the 17 March entry referred to in the letter, Rush wrote: "Visited Mr. Jefferson on his way to New York, It was the first time I saw him since his return from France. He was plain in his dress and unchanged in his manners. He still professed himself attached to republican forms of government, and deplored the change of opinion upon this subject in John Adams, of whom he spoke with respect and affection as a great and upright man. He said Mr. [James] Madison 'was the greatest man in the world' . . ." (*Auto.*, 181).
5. BR to John Adams, 24 February 1790.
6. "Centinel," 13 November 1788, quoted in Hawke, 386.
7. BR to James Muir, 24 August 24 1791.
8. *Auto.*, 182–183. John Adams, who from the earliest days of the Revolution cultivated grudges against Franklin and Washington and nurtured them as would a lepidopterist nurture a prize species of butterfly, wrote Rush: "The history of our Revolution will be one continued lie from one end to the other. The essence of the whole will be *that Dr. Franklin's electrical rod smote the Earth and out sprung General Washington. That Franklin electrified him with his rod, and thence forward these two conducted all the policy, negotiations, legislatures and war.*" (Cited in Brands, 548.) In sending the lock to Price (24 April 1790) Rush is more eulogizing. In a letter six days previously to Congressman Elias Boudinot, he suggests "an idea of Congress's showing by some public act their sympathy in his death and their respect and gratitude for his eminent abilities and services to his country." Four days later James Madison introduced a

resolution in the House of Representatives that members wear mourning for a month. Though the motion was carried, the Senate rejected it. A suggestion, presumably by Secretary of State Jefferson, that the cabinet go into mourning, was vetoed by President Washington, since "he should not know where to draw the line, if he once began that ceremony." (Butterfield, *Letters*, vol. 1, 563, n.1.)

9. *Auto.*, 165.
10. Hawke, 391–392.

CHAPTER 19

1. BR to Julia Rush, 22 August 1793. In the account in his *Commonplace Book* dated August 22, Rush wrote, "About 100 white persons, chiefly carpenters, dined at one table, who were waited upon by Africans. Afterward about 50 black people sat down at the same table, who were waited upon by white people. Never did I see people more happy." (*Auto.*, 228.)
2. Rush's recollection of the epidemic appears in "An Account of the Bilious Remitting Yellow Fever as It Appeared in the City of Philadelphia in the Year 1793," on which this account is based, augmented by J. H. Powell's *Bring Out Your Dead*.
3. Flexner, 95.
4. *American Daily Advertiser*, 27 August 1793.
5. Goodman, 175–176.
6. Flexner, 105.
7. BR to John Redman Coxe, 19 September 1794.
8. *Auto.*, 102.
9. BR to John R. B. Rodgers, [16?] October 1797. The date is conjecturable, for which see Butterfield, *Letters*, vol. 1, 794, n.1.
10. Ibid., n. 4.
11. A member of the Pennsylvania militia when the war began, he resigned to become a Loyalist, and was later arrested, whereupon he reaffirmed his allegiance to the Americans, who forgave him. He is considered the "Father of the American Cotton Industry."
12. For a detailed account of the feud, see Goodman, 214–221, and Butterfield, *Letters*, Appendix 3, vol. 2, 1213–1218, on which this account, limited by the constraints of space, is based.
13. Butterfield, *Letters*, vol. 2, 1213.
14. "An Eulogium, Intended to Perpetuate the Memory of David Rittenhouse, Late President of the American Philosophical Society, Delivered before the Society in the First Presbyterian Church, in High Street, Philadelphia, on the 17th Dec. 1796." (Reprinted in *Essays Literary, Moral and Philosophical* [Philadelphia, 1798]).
15. Binger, 241.
16. Butterfield, *Letters*, vol. 2, 1215.
17. Goldman, 217.

18. Butterfield, *Letters,* 1214–1215.
19. Cole, 25.
20. Goodman, 220.
21. *Auto.,* 248–249, n.11
22. *The Rush Light,* 2, 28 February 1800 (in Mitchell, S. Weir).
23. Butterfield, *Letters,* vol. 2, 1218.

CHAPTER 20

1. Flexner, 109.
2. Ibid.
3. Ibid., 110.
4. BR to Thomas Jefferson, 22 August 1800.
5. "A Defense of the Bible in Schools," from an early collection of Rush tracts published by the American Tract Society around 1830.
6. Thomas Jefferson to BR, 23 September 1800, in Peterson.
7. Schutz and Adair, 10, 20.
8. This is, of course, a rather simplified overview of the Adams-Jefferson break. For a detailed discussion, the interested reader might wish to consult chapter 1 of the Schutz-Adair anthology of the Adams-Rush letters, *The Spur of Fame.*
9. Butterfield, *Letters,* vol. 2, 1111, n.1.
10. Morton, 143–144.
11. Ibid., 144.
12. Ibid., 149, 150.
13. BR, "To the Managers of the Pennsylvania Hospital," 26 December 1812.
14. Rush, *Medical Inquiries and Observations,* 17–36.
15. Ibid., 36–47.
16. Ibid., 47–71.
17. Goodman, 263.
18. Rush, *Medical Inquiries and Observations,* 98–105.
19. For an extended discussion of Rush's work in the field, including a line drawing of the contraption, see Goodman, chapter 11, "First American Psychiatrist," 254–271.
20. Binger, 280.

FAREWELL

1. William Staughton, *An Eulogium in Memory of the Late Dr. Benjamin Rush,* delivered by this longtime intimate acquaintance of Rush on 8 July 1813 in Philadelphia's Second Presbyterian Church.
2. Quoted in Goodman, 347.
3. Due to centuries of exposure to the elements, general deterioration, and, lately, acid rain, the cemetery, which contains, in addition to Franklin and Rush, the remains of three other signers of the Declaration of Inde-

pendence, was closed after the 1976 bicentennial celebration except for special events and occasional National Park Service tours. In the past few years workers cleared the weeds and reassembled broken monuments, and new markers were made to accompany the gravestones with inscriptions, worn smooth over time, that a church member thought to copy in 1864. The cemetery was reopened in April 2003.

4. Goodman, 351.

SELECT BIBLIOGRAPHY

Ackroyd, Peter. *London, the Biography*. New York, 2001.

Adams, Charles Francis, ed. *Life and Works of John Adams,* 10 vols. Boston, 1850–1856.

Andrews, Charles M. *The Colonial Background of the American Revolution*. New Haven, 1931.

Bancroft, George. *History of the United States*. Boston, 1858.

Beach, Steward. *Samuel Adams*. New York, 1964.

Bennett, William J., ed., *Our Sacred Honor: Words of Advice from the Founders in Stories, Letters, Poems, and Speeches*. New York, 1997.

Biddle, Lewis Alexander. *A Memorial Containing Travels Through Life or Sunday Incidents in the Life of Dr. Benjamin Rush*. Philadelphia, 1800.

Billias, George A., ed. *Washington's Generals*. New York, 1964.

Binger, Carl. *Revolutionary Doctor: Benjamin Rush (1746–1813),* New York, 1966.

Bowen, Catherine Drinker. *Miracle at Philadelphia: The Story of the Constitutional Convention May to September 1787*. Boston, 1986.

Brands, H. W. *The First American: The Life and Times of Benjamin Franklin*. New York, 2000.

Burnett, Edmund C. *Letters of the Members of the Continental Congress,* 3 vols. Washington, D.C., 1921.

Butterfield, L. H., ed. *Letters of Benjamin Rush,* 2 vols. Princeton, N.J., 1951.

————, ed. *Further Letters of Benjamin Rush*. Princeton, 1956.

————, ed. *Diary and Autobiography of John Adams,* vol. 1. Cambridge, Mass., 1961.

Christman, Margaret C. S. *The First Federal Congress, 1789–1791*. Washington, D.C., 1989.

Clark, Mary E. *Peter Porcupine in America: The Career of William Cobbett, 1792–1800.* Philadelphia, 1939.

Cole, G. D. H., ed. *Letters from William Cobbett to Edward Thornton, 1797–1800*. London, 1937.

D'Elia, Donald. *Benjamin Rush: Philosopher of the American Revolution.* Philadelphia, 1974.

Duane, William, ed. *Excerpts from the Diary of Christopher Marshall Kept in Philadelphia and Lancaster during the American Revolution, 1774–1781.* Albany, N.Y., 1877.

Elkins, Stanley, and Eric McKitrick. *The Age of Federalism.* New York, 1993.

Ellis, Joseph J. *Founding Brothers: The Revolutionary Generations.* New York, 2000.

Fitzpatrick, John C., ed. *The Diaries of George Washington,* 4 vols. Boston, 1925.

Flexner, James Thomas. *Doctors on Horseback: Pioneers of American Medicine.* Garden City, N.Y., 1939.

Ford, Washington Chauncey, ed. *Journals of the Continental Congress, 1774–1779.* Washington, D.C., 1904.

Gianta, Mary A. *The Emerging Nation: A Documentary History of the United States under the Articles of Confederation.* Washington, D.C., 1996.

Gibson, James E. *Dr. Bodo Otto and the Medical Background of the American Revolution.* Philadelphia, 1937.

Goodman, Nathan G. *Benjamin Rush, Physician and Citizen, 1746–1813.* Philadelphia, 1934.

Gummere, Richard M. *Seven Wise Men of Colonial America.* Cambridge, Mass., 1967.

Hawke, David Freeman. *Benjamin Rush, Revolutionary Gadfly.* Indianapolis, 1971.

Higginbotham, Don. *The War of American Independence.* New York, 1971.

Johnson, Paul. *A History of the American People.* New York, 1997.

Jordan, Winthrop D. *White over Black: American Attitudes toward the Negro, 1550–1812.* Chapel Hill, N.C., 1967.

Keane, John. *Tom Paine: A Political Life.* Boston, 1995.

Knollenberg, Bernard. *Washington and the Revolution.* New York, 1940.

Langguth, A. J. *Patriots: The Men Who Started the American Revolution.* New York, 1988.

Lincoln, Charles H. *The Revolutionary Movement in Pennsylvania, 1760–1776.* Reprint, Philadelphia, 1901.

Lipscomb, Andrew E., ed. *The Writings of Thomas Jefferson* 20 vols. Washington, D.C., 1903.

McCullough, David. *John Adams.* New York, 2001.

McGee, Dorothy Horton. *Famous Signers of the Declaration.* New York, 1959.

McMaster, John Bach, and Frederick D. Stone. *Pennsylvania and the Federal Constitution, 1787–1788.* Philadelphia, 1888.

Mapp, Alf J., Jr. *Thomas Jefferson, Passionate Pilgrim.* Lanham, Md., 1991.

Meigs, Cornelia. *The Violent Men: A Study of Human Relations in the First American Congress.* New York, 1949.

Mitchell, S. Weir. *Historical Notes of Benjamin Rush*. Pennsylvania, 1903.

Montross, Lynn. *The Reluctant Rebels: The Story of the Continental Congress, 1774–1779*. New York, 1950.

Morison, Samuel Eliot. *The Oxford History of the American People*, vol. 1: *Prehistory to 1789*. New York, 1961.

Morton, Thomas G. *History of the Pennsylvania Hospital, 1751–1895*, rev. ed. Philadelphia, 1897.

Mumby, Frank Arthur. *George III and the American Revolution*. Boston, 1923.

Paine, Thomas. *Common Sense, Rights of Man, and Other Essential Writings* (reprint). New York, 2003.

Peterson, Merrill D., ed. *Jefferson: Writings*. New York, 1984.

Powell, John Harvey. *Bring Out Your Dead: The Great Plague of Yellow Fever in Philadelphia in 1793*. Philadelphia, 1949.

Reidman, Sarah R., and Clarence C. Green. *Benjamin Rush: Physician, Patriot, Founding Father*. New York, 1964.

Runes, Dagobert D., ed. *The Selected Writings of Benjamin Rush*. New York, 1947.

Rush, Benjamin. *The Autobiography of Benjamin Rush: His "Travels Through Life" Together with His Commonplace Book for 1789–1813*, edited by George W. Corner. Princeton, N.J., 1948.

Rush, Benjamin. *Dr. Rush's Eulogium upon Dr. [William] Cullen*. Philadelphia, 1827.

Rush, Benjamin, *A Bibliographic Guide*, compiled by C. G. Fox, G. L. Miller, and J. C. Miller. Westport, Conn. 1996.

Sanderson, John. *Biography of the Signers of the Declaration of Independence*, 5 vols. Philadelphia, 1828.

Schutz, John A., and Douglass Adair, eds. *The Spur of Fame: Dialogues of John Adams and Benjamin Rush, 1805–1813*. San Marino, Calif., 1966.

Stille, Charles O. *The Life and Times of John Dickinson*. Philadelphia, 1891.

Thacher, James. *American Medical Biography, or Memoirs of Eminent Physicians Who Have Flourished in America*, 2 vols. Philadelphia, 1867 (reprint of 1828 edition).

Thompson, John. *An Account of the Life, Lectures, and Writings of William Cullen, M.D.* Edinburgh, 1859.

Toner, Joseph. *Contributions to the Annals of American Progress and Medical Evaluation in the United States before and during the War of Independence*. Washington. D.C., 1874.

Van Tyne, Claude Halstead. *The Loyalists in the American Revolution*. New York, 1922.

Watson, John F. *Annals of Philadelphia and Pennsylvania in the Olden Times*, 2 vols. Philadelphia, 1857.

INDEX